Harlem Renaissance
and Beyond

Harlem Renaissance and Beyond

Literary Biographies
of 100 Black Women Writers
1900–1945

❧

Lorraine Elena Roses

Ruth Elizabeth Randolph

With a Foreword by Mae Gwendolyn Henderson

Harvard University Press
Cambridge, Massachusetts
London, England

This Harvard University Press paperback edition is published by arrangement
with G.K. Hall New York/Macmillan Library Reference, A Division of Simon &
Schuster, Inc.

All photographs courtesy of Moorland-Springarn Research Center,
Howard University, except the following:
Photograph of Sarah Collins Fernandis courtesy of Hampton University Archives
Photograph of May Miller courtesy of May Miller
Photograph of Brenda Ray Moryck Francke by Bachrach, courtesy of
Wellesley College Archives
Photograph of Charlotte Hawkins Brown courtesy of Wellesley College Archives
Photograph of Clarissa Scott Delany - Wellesley College Class of 1923
Photograph of Ann Spencer courtesy of Chauncey Spencer
Photograph of Ellen Tarry courtesy of Ellen Tarry
Photograph of Bessie Woodson Yancey courtesy of Belva Clark

Library of Congress Cataloging-in-Publication Data

Roses, Lorraine Elena, 1943—
The Harlem renaissance and beyond: literary biographies
of 100 black women writers, 1900–1945 / Lorraine Elena Roses,
Ruth Elizabeth Randolph.
p. cm.
Includes bibliographical references.
ISBN 0-674-37255-7
1. American literature—Afro-American authors—Dictionaries.
2. Authors, American—20th century—Biography—Dictionaries.
3. Afro-American women authors—Biography—Dictionaries.
4. Women and literature—United States—Dictionaries.
5. American literature—Women authors—Dictionaries.
6. American literature—20th century—Dictionaries.
7. Afro-Americans in literature—Dictionaries.
8. Harlem Renaissance—Dictionaries.
I. Randolph, Ruth Elizabeth.   II. Title
PS153.N5R65   1989
810.9′9287′03—dc20   89-38731
CIP

For Jonathan, Wilhelmina and Rayfield

CONTENTS

Contents

Contents

Contents

FOREWORD

When I first met with Ruth Randolph and Lorraine Roses in spring 1985 to offer suggestions on how they might pursue a project on black women writing during the Harlem Renaissance, little did I imagine the scope and magnitude of their endeavor or the rich ore that their painstaking research would mine. It is my pleasure to have been a part of the incipient stages of this important project, which has taken on a historical, literary, and cultural significance that none of us would have predicted when it was begun.

The prominence of black women in contemporary literature has led to a search for "precursors" or "foremothers" among late nineteenth- and early twentieth-century black women writers. It is perhaps this need to account for the considerable critical and popular success of contemporary black women writers that has led to the current project of recovery. The rediscovery of black women's texts by what I call "literary archaeologists" may have far-reaching consequences for revising and reconstructing what we categorize as schools, movements, and periods – indeed, for the very ways in which we read and configure literary history. As critic Sydney Janet Kaplan argues, "studying groups of women writers within a particular time-frame and social class [read black women writers before 1945] may actually lead to a redefinition of periods [schools, movements] in literary history. The traditional parameters of a period may be shifted through the perspective of women writers." The Harlem Renaissance, traditionally defined by the works of male writers such as Jean Toomer, Alain Locke, Countee Cullen, Langston Hughes, Claude McKay, and Wallace Thurman, is a primary example. Zora Neale Hurston's magnificent novel, *Their Eyes Were Watching God*, along with the works of writers such as Alice Dunbar-Nelson, Georgia Douglas Johnson, Angelina Weld Grimké, Anne Spencer, Helene Johnson, May Miller, Nella Larsen, and Jessie Redmon Fauset, have only recently been recognized as contributions to this watershed in Afro-American letters. Drawing on the poetry, fiction, drama, and chronicles of these women, black feminist critics Gloria Hull, Deborah McDowell, Cheryl Wall, Nellie McKay, Claudia Tate, Mary Helen Washington, and others have compelled us to shift the geographical and gender-exclusive parameters traditionally defining this period.

The discovery of such works makes possible an enlargement of what Annette Kolodny calls "that vast storehouse of our literary inheritance," which is "a resource for remodelling our literary history, past, present, and future." It broadens the fields of scholarly inquiry while opening up the possibility of a revised history and tradition in black, women's, and American literature. If, as Alice Walker suggests, literature is one grand story in which individual writers contribute different perspectives or single chapters, then we can only imagine in what ways the "master" narrative of literature – as well as literary history – can be reshaped by the revival of "repressed" stories.

The reconsideration of black women writers from earlier generations also has enormous implications for how we reconstruct the literature, experience, and culture of black women. Just as the black movement of the 1960s and 1970s spawned the reissue of a number of out-of-print texts by predominantly black male authors, so the reemergence of the women's movement in the 1970s and 1980s resulted in the reprinting of many "lost classics" by white women. The exclusion of black women's texts from the canons of black, women's, and American literature raises significant questions among literary scholars concerning the reasons for what they have variously called the "suppression" or "burial" of women's writing in general. The neglect of women writers, according to Kaplan, raises questions concerning "the crucial connection between the politics and economics of publishing and the course of women writers' careers – which of their books get printed, how long those books are allowed to remain in print, and why many of them disappear as if they had never been written." Black feminist critics have additional concerns, which involve the articulation of a black female aesthetic and the acknowledgment that an authentic tradition of black women's writing exists.

As early as 1977, Barbara Smith outlined the tasks of the black feminist critic in her landmark essay, "Towards a Black Feminist Criticism," presupposing the existence of an "identifiable" and "verifiable" tradition of black women's writing:

> Beginning with a primary commitment to exploring how both sexual and racial politics and a Black and female identity are inextricable elements in Black women's writings, she [the black feminist critic] would also work from the assumption that Black women writers constitute an identifiable literary tradition. The breadth of her familiarity with these writers would have shown her that not only is there a verifiable historical tradition that parallels in time the tradition of Black men and white women in this country, but that thematically, stylistically, aesthetically, and conceptually Black women writers manifest common approaches to the act of creating literature as a direct result of the specific political, social, and economic experience they have been obliged to share.

Responding to Smith in the essay "New Directions for Black Feminist Criticism," Deborah McDowell challenged the basis of a black feminist aesthetic and the validity of a "separatist position," but nevertheless suggested imagistic, thematic, and particularly linguistic commonalities in the works of black women writers. On the other hand, Erlene Stetson argues that a tradition of black women writers is configured less in language and rhetorical structures and more in a common experience that gives unity and cohesion to their literary expression. In the introduction to *Black Sister,* her collection of poetry by black women, Stetson rejected current theories of "influence" and "style," stating that the "themes and subjects [of black women writers] have developed over generations out of common historical experiences." Whichever of these positions is espoused by the student or scholar of black women's writing, the examination of these resurrected texts surely provides an opportunity to define common concerns and connections as well as individual differences and ruptures in the tradition.

Like a host of other dedicated black and feminist scholars, Ruth Randolph and Lorraine Roses are committed to recovering and reclaiming a body of writing and, in the process, to addressing either directly or indirectly a number of the issues surrounding contemporary black feminist thought. A work that distinguishes itself as a fusion of bio-bibliography and literary biography, *Harlem Renaissance and Beyond: Literary Biographies of One Hundred Black Women Writers, 1900-1945* extends and complements the collections and bibliographies by scholars such as Ora Williams, Ann Allen Shockley, and Dorothy Chapman. With its publication, Randolph and Roses contribute to the ongoing process of literary excavation–the uncovering of the authors, titles, and locations of works largely forgotten. This volume brings to light works by black women whose writing constitutes a largely unknown legacy.

Numerous works by nineteenth- and early twentieth-century black women have been published in the past several years. Beginning with the republication of such works as Zora Neale Hurston's *Their Eyes Were Watching God* (reprinted 1965 and 1987), Harriet Jacob's *Incidents in the Life of a Slave Girl* (reprinted 1973 and 1987), Paule Marshall's *Brown Girl, Brownstones* (reprinted 1981), Harriet Wilson's *Our Nig* (reprinted 1983), Ann Petry's *The Street* (reprinted 1985), and Nella Larsen's *Passing* and *Quicksand* (reprinted 1971 and 1986), both commercial and university presses have continued to reissue lost and neglected works by black women. In 1988 Oxford University Press reprinted the multivolume *Schomburg Library of Nineteenth-Century Black Women Writers,* edited by Henry Louis Gates. Along with Hazel Carby and Marilyn Richardson's work on nineteenth- and early twentieth-century black women writers there has appeared a number of anthologies and collections of slave narratives, fiction, essays, and poems, including Gerda Lerner's *Black Women in White America* (1973), James Loewenberg and Ruth Bogin's *Black Women in Nineteenth-Century American Life* (1976), Erlene Stetson's *Black Sister* (1981), Dorothy Sterling's *We Are Your Sisters* (1984), William Andrews's *Sisters of the Spirit* (1986), and Mary Helen Washington's *Invented Lives* (1987).

Harlem Renaissance and Beyond includes an occasional extended treatment of a major figure as well as a considerable number of "minor" writers – minor insofar as they have published, to the authors' best knowledge, relatively little, sometimes (although this is exceptional) as few as two or three poems in a local newspaper or journal. What, one might well ask, is the value of these inclusions? How might they have an impact on the present configuration of literary history or even our understanding of black women's literature and culture? Although critics accord to major writers a synecdochic relationship to their contemporaries, that is, allowing the part to represent the complex whole, this is done only at a certain risk.

First, if we accept that literary history, like other forms of history – social, political, intellectual – is in large part a fictional configuration, which we may both construct and "read," then we can begin to imagine the possibilities of revision as we learn to reread the major works in the context of marginal works. What appear to be the "discontinuities" that Hortense Spillers described as characterizing the "tradition" of black women's writing may well arise from the uncharted spaces between "major" works, spaces occupied by "lost" texts. The reemergence of these texts may fill in some of the gaps in what I believe to be a tradition of black women writers. As the so-called major writers are located on a continuum with lesser-known writers, patterns of identity and difference defining that tradition become more clear and reliable.

Second, unless we place major writers in relation to their contemporaries, we are likely to read their concerns as exceptional, rather than representative of the issues preoccupying other writers of the period. Commenting on the importance of both the rediscovery processs and the significance of minor women writers, Elaine Showalter wrote,

> While the process of rediscovery is primary, minor women writers need to be treated historically as well as critically, to be placed in a theoretical framework which treats them as more than the flotsam of popular culture, and to be connected to each other and to a female literary tradition. A feminist literary history would describe the continuity and coherence of women's writing and provide the hypothesis against which individual writers could be assessed.

In other words, a viable approach to literary and cultural studies must neither neglect minor writers nor isolate major writers – especially in the case of black women's writing, where the work is likely to represent not only an individual statement but a cultural one, reflecting its racial, sexual, and, frequently, class matrix.

Third, with the uncovering of additional material, the so-called minor writer may well become a noteworthy figure in the reconstruction of black women's literary and cultural history. Wilson's *Our Nig* is a case in point; the works of Hurston provide a more dramatic example. Much of the achievement of the present volume lies in the authors' description of the archaeological process by which these works have been and will continue to be uncovered. Even as I write this foreword for the "completed" volume, I am informed by Randolph and Roses that additional information has arrived concerning one of the writers whose birth and death dates had been unknown. Undoubtedly, much more information will be culled by scholars and students of history, culture, and literature as they respond to the call of these newly found precursors and foremothers. As I conclude, I am struck by the unique opportunity afforded those of us engaged in the study of black women's literature at this critical juncture. We stand at a moment when both new and earlier authors are being discovered, when we can witness both the prospective and retrospective development of a tradition.

Mae Gwendolyn Henderson
University of Iowa

PREFACE

It is the purpose of this book to focus attention on black women writers whose work belongs primarily to the early half of the twentieth century and whose achievements or very existence has been little recognized, even within specialized circles. Although the book is not intended to provide a comprehensive account of the black women writers of five decades, we provide new factual information and critical comment on a large number of neglected writers, placing them in a context of *their* history as women and persons of African descent. Included, too, are more prominent figures who have enjoyed considerable attention but who also belong to a group that, in the larger context of American literature, deserves much wider recognition.

During its four-year duration, our research took several turns. At first, we focused on those women who, like Zora Neale Hurston, Jessie Fauset, and Nella Larsen, could be viewed as participants in the Harlem or New Negro Renaissance, according to the following criteria: (1) they were born before 1915; (2) their writing was introduced to the public in such period publications as *Opportunity, Crisis, Black Opals, Saturday Evening Quill, Messenger,* and *Palms,* or in significant period anthologies such as Countee Cullen's *Caroling Dusk* or Charles S. Johnson's *Ebony and Topaz*; (3) their work appeared between 1917 and 1935; and (4) they were associated with central figures of Harlem literary circles.

These criteria allowed us to identify writers who have rarely been mentioned in the critical literature and to search for new information to add to existing texts. Examples: Ottie Beatrice Graham, Hazel Vivian Campbell, Marion Vera Cuthbert, Mae V. Cowdery, May Miller, Mercedes Gilbert, and Eulalie Spence.

When many other figures emerged whose birth dates were much earlier or who worked in locations far from Harlem, yet they had published in the target time period and their themes and styles overlapped with those of the other women, we decided that we did not wish to ignore them. Thus we changed course in order to include writers located at the chronological and geographical fringes of our original field. In this manner, our list grew, stretching back to birth dates of 1860 and forward to 1918; most were born between 1880 and 1910, yet they were contemporaries in terms of publishing dates. No longer a book solely on Harlem Renaissance women, our work became a more expansive undertaking centering on writers active between the two world wars. By moving beyond the notion of Harlem/New Negro Renaissance, we also avoided adhering to a critical construct that itself must be reexamined.

It should be noted that the number "one hundred" was selected for convenience and because of space considerations; there are other writers who belong in the same company and might have been included.

For each writer we provide a brief literary biography and a bibliography of selected primary and secondary sources, in some cases including a list of anthologies where some of the author's work can be found. We have on occasion omitted mention of the later works of writers who continued to publish after the period covered by this book. We are also aware that more information on the writers' lives and their works may come to light in the future, since ongoing research is constantly uncovering fresh documentation to add to our knowledge of this important group of twentieth-century writers.

Those who published the bulk of their work after 1945 lie beyond the scope of this book. In that year Gwendolyn Brooks published *A Street in Bronzeville* and went on to become the first black woman to win a Pulitzer Prize – an event that marked the beginning of a new era for black women writers.

ACKNOWLEDGMENTS

It is impossible to name all the individuals and institutions that aided us in our pursuits; our sincere thanks to each and every one.

We wish to express our gratitude to the Center for Research on Women at Wellesley College, which through the Anna Wilder Phelps Fund provided two summers of internship assistance; to the National Endowment for the Humanities for a 1987 summer stipend; and to the Wellesley College Faculty Grants Committee for additional support for travel and miscellaneous expenses. We also wish to acknowledge the valuable contributions of the Wellesley College student researchers who assisted us in this project: Aviva Ben-Ur, Deborah Bandanza, Colette Blount, Amy Dillard, Doreen Lutterodt Watson, Jeannie Park, Cheryl Nath, and Mary Angela Valante.

Many archivists, reference librarians, and information specialists across the United States graciously responded to our queries and provided us with dates and documents we could not have otherwise obtained. Among them were Robert Fleming of Emerson College, who located records for Mary Burrill and Grace Vera Postles; Claire Pancero of the Public Library of Cincinnati and Hamilton County, who sent us an obituary for Clara Ann Thompson; Fritz Malval of Hampton University, for information on Sarah Collins Fernandis; Jean Jones of Edward Waters College, who searched for records on Mercedes Gilbert; Betty Gubert of the Schomburg Center for Research in Black Culture, New York Public Library, who sent us information about Regina Andrews and an unpublished autobiographical article by Mercedes Gilbert; John Beauregard of Gordon College, who sent us a short story by Florence Harmon; Lew Herman of the Public Library of Charlotte and Mecklenburg County, who sent an article on Rose Leary Love; Dennis Lawson of the Duke Power Company, Charlotte, North Carolina, who researched the death date of Rose Leary Love; the National Personnel Records Center, National Archives, St. Louis, Missouri, for the death date of Lucia Mae Pitts; Martha C. Slotten of Dickinson College, for records and dates on Esther Popel Shaw; Lester Sullivan, Amistad Research Center, New Orleans, Louisiana, for assistance at the center; Chauncey Spencer and the Friends of Anne S. Spencer Memorial Foundation, Lynchburg, Virginia, for information on Anne Spencer and Lula Lowe Weeden; Ralph Pugh, Chicago Historical Society, who researched Zara Wright; Margie Flood, Oberlin College, for information on Octavia Wynbush; Jeanne D. Mead, research librarian, Jones Memorial Library, Lynchburg, Virginia, for introducing us to Chauncey Spencer; George T. Johnson, library director, Hallie Q. Brown Memorial Library, Central State University, Wilberforce, Ohio, for information on Clara Ann Thompson and the town of Rossmoyne, Ohio; Clifton H. Johnson, executive director, Amistad Research Center, for putting us in touch with a descendant of Florida Ruffin Ridley; Judith Savage, Santa Barbara Public Library, and Michael Redmon, Santa Barbara Historical Society, who researched Elizabeth Laura Adams; Marcia Battle Bracey, Moorland Spingarn Research Center, who reproduced many photographs of black women writers of the early twentieth century; and Carol Larsen, Registrar's Office, University of Nebraska at Omaha, who verified Ida Rowland's college degrees.

The archives and alumnae offices of the following colleges graciously provided us with biographical background on writers who were graduates or were otherwise connected with their institutions: Radcliffe College Alumnae Office (Caroline Bond Day); Smith College Archives (Eunice Hunton Carter); Wilma Slaight, archivist, Wellesley College Archives (Clarissa Scott Delany, Ethel Caution-Davis, Brenda Ray Moryck); Boston University Mugar Memorial Library (Edythe Mae Gordon, Marion Vera Cuthbert); Anthony Cucchiara, archivist, Brooklyn College (Marion Vera Cuthbert); William J. Novak, registrar, Pratt Institute (Mae V. Cowdery); Valeria Millender, Talladega College (Marion Vera Cuthbert); Jacqueline Y. Brown, Rembert E. Stokes Learning Resources Center Library, Wilberforce University (Ruth Gaines-Shelton); Faye T. Carter, acquisitions librarian, Lincoln University (Myrtle Smith Livingston); and Ann Allen Shockley, Fisk University, and Gertrude Jacob, Oberlin College (Lucy Ariels Williams Holloway).

Thanks to David Andrews, Christian Science Church Archives, Boston, Massachusetts, for confirming that Marita Bonner and her husband were church members; to Marshall Wright, Christian Science Church, Boston, for confirming Ruby Berkley Goodwin's church membership and death date; to Christopher Publishing House, Norwell, Massachusetts, for information on Aloise Barbour Epperson and Mercedes Gilbert, whose work it published; to James Hatch and Camille Billops for assistance at the Hatch-Billops Collection, Inc., which provided secondary sources on several playwrights. We also extend our gratitude to Professor Maceo Dailey, Jr., of Boston College, for his response to our inquiry about Emmett J. Scott's daughter; to Edna Aizenberg, Marymount Manhattan College, who searched out the last residence of Mercedes Gilbert in South Jamaica, New York; to Marilyn Silverman for her work on Eslanda Robeson; and to Rufus C. Brooks, principal of the Hungerford Elementary School, Eatonville, Florida, and Mollie B. and Herbert A. Silvershine, of Indialantic, Florida, for information and clippings on Zora Neale Hurston. Other valuable resources were the various Departments of Health and Vital Statistics whose offices we contacted for birth and death dates of "lost" writers: Boston, Los Angeles, and New York City and the Office of Mayor Edward Koch.

We are especially indebted to the writers included in this book who responded to our queries: Anna Mabel Land Butler, May Miller, Ellen Tarry,

Acknowledgments

Ida Rowland, and Ann Petry. We also thank Warwick Gale Occomy, son of Marita Bonner; Ancella Bickley, granddaughter-in-law of Bessie Woodson Yancey; and Dr. Maude Jenkins, great-niece of Florida Ruffin Ridley.

Personal thanks go to the "godmothers" of this book, colleagues Peggy McIntosh, associate director of the Center for Research on Women, Wellesley, Massachusetts; Mae Gwendolyn Henderson, University of Iowa, and Doris Abramson, University of Massachusetts-Amherst (emeritus). From them came the impetus to transform a research project into a book.

Other valuable consultants during the development of our work were Velma Hoover of Boston College, Clara Hicks of the Mason-Rice School, Newton, Massachusetts, and Dorothy Sterling of Wellfleet, Massachusetts. Still other people who read and critiqued early drafts of portions of the manuscript deserve our thanks: Jonathan Leigh Roses, Doris Abramson, Cola Franzen, Eileen D. Hardy, and Carolyn Hasgill.

These librarians at Wellesley College lent their support to our work: Eleanor Gustafson, Sally Linden, Joan Stockard, and Nancy Strong of the Margaret Clapp Library. The technical assistance of Cathy Roberts-Gersch, and Susan Hafer proved invaluable and was greatly appreciated. We wish, too, to acknowledge Dr. Thomas Keighley of the Wellesley College Health Services, who deciphered death certificates and explained causes of death as cited in the 1920s, and Professor Gordon D. Morgan of the University of Arkansas, who provided information on Ida Rowland.

We wish to thank our editors at G. K. Hall: Lee Ripley, Michael Sims, Henriette Campagne, and Borgna Brunner whose support and assistance were essential.

Friends who offered us lodging while we were on the road interviewing and visiting research collections were Cassandra Baines of Washington, D.C., Edith and Steven Rostas of Amherst, Massachusetts, and Millicent Novas of New York City.

Most of all, we relied on the understanding and forbearance of our family members: Jonathan Leigh Roses, constant companion at interviews and trips to library collections and firm believer in our work; Wilhelmina and Rayfield, who have supported our vision and have proud expectations of seeing it fulfilled; Miriam Ben-Ur, Aviva Ben-Ur, David Ben-Ur, Gabriel Roses, and Jonathan B. Roses, who were excited about this book and will write books of their own one day; and Raphael and Matthew Randolph – SPEAK to the mountain.

I think I see her sitting bowed and black

Stricken and seared by slavery's mortal scars

Reft of her children, lonely, anguished, yet

Still looking at the stars.

– Jessie Redmon Fauset

INTRODUCTION

Present-day black women writers like Alice Walker, Toni Morrison, Gwendolyn Brooks, Gloria Naylor, Audre Lorde, and Alice Childress enjoy a success of which their predecessors of earlier generations only dreamed. Constrained by the external realities of segregation, institutionalized discrimination, and exclusion from the suffrage movement, the black women writers of the early 1900s nevertheless were determined to transcend circumstances. Jessie Fauset's verse portrait of an enslaved black woman, separated from her children and alone, yet "still looking at the stars," could serve as a symbol of the black woman writer herself.

It is the purpose of this book to introduce the many talents who have received insufficient or no recognition and to show the abundance of black women's writing surrounding and including the period known as the Harlem Renaissance.[1] Our perspective-gender sensitive and race sensitive, attuned both to historicity and to aesthetic appeal – is shaped by a desire to accommodate the intersecting concerns of literature and history as they relate to black women.

We wish to place these women in a context of their own, regarding their lives and their writing from a perspective that acknowledges their uniqueness. One important category to which black women must be fully restored is that of the Harlem Renaissance. As it has been defined by Nathan Huggins, Margaret Perry, David Levering Lewis, and others, the Harlem Renaissance was a cultural outpouring among black Americans during the 1920s that had its center in New York City. It was a phenomenon that symbolized "the Afro-American's coming of age" (Huggins, 30). A broader term, "New Negro Renaissance," preferred by Alain Locke, perhaps better captures the wide-ranging outpouring of literature that was taking place along the eastern seaboard and, indeed, across the country. But it too has been taken as a male phenomenon with few women participants being recognized. Such women as Hurston, Larsen, and Fauset who were in the thick of the New York scene were only part of a much larger group of over one hundred women writers working in far-flung places. By taking into account this broader picture, we can better understand the era.

In 1971 Alice Walker set out to discover the hometown and burial site of Zora Neale Hurston, a writer whom she admired and whose books had gone out of print long before[2]. Walker's symbolic act of searching for Hurston's grave, erecting a tombstone, and recording her quest can serve as a paradigm for those who engage in the exciting job of rediscovering and reviving the work and reputation of a forgotten group of American women authors. Like Hurston, many other women were born two or three decades after emancipation from slavery and did most of their writing by the end of World War II – women who grew up at a time when hopes for black social advancement and political participation were dampened by the growing prevalence of Jim Crow laws segregating whites from blacks. Though living in inauspicious times, they both opposed Jim Crow and invested their considerable energies in the creative endeavor of writing.

Only a few of these women writers are classified by bibliographers of Hurston's era as "major." Besides Hurston, Margaret Perry (1976) names seven such women: Nella Larsen, Jessie Fauset, Dorothy West, Georgia Douglas Johnson, Gwendolyn Bennett, Anne Spencer, and Helene Johnson. Yet bibliographical sources for the early decades of the twentieth century reveal a surprising reality: well over a hundred black women wrote plays, novels, poetry, short stories, children's books, and essays in the 1920s and the 1930s alone, although very little has been written about their lives or their work. Before we can explore their careers further, we need to construct a more comprehensive picture, bearing in mind that the tradition of black women's writing is discontinuous.[3]

There is no single bibliographical source exclusively on black women writers of the first half of the twentieth century and no scholarship has unearthed extensive material on them. As we began this project, we found bibliographies on women writers, others on black writers (mostly male), but no integrated master work on black women writers from 1900 to 1945. Such books as Mari Evan's *Black Women Writers* covers the period from 1950 to 1980, a time span that is better studied and documented than the one that concerns us here.

The gaps in documentation suggest that an exclusionary process may be at work. In her article, "Archival Materials: The Problem of Literary Reputation," Elizabeth Meese explains that "critics have traditionally adopted a stance of cultural homogeneity and, through unintentional parochialism or willful discrimination," neglected work by people of color, women, working-class people, and other groups because their output debunks "the tidy schematics of traditional literary theory of practice" (37). To this suggestion that exclusion is an attempt to suppress dissent, Erlene Stetson adds another reason black women writers, in particular, have been overlooked: "Descriptions of the massive oppression that [black women] have experienced do not support the white myths of American life" (88). Being both black and female, Afro-American women obviously have been one segment of the nonwhite, nonmale population that Elizabeth Meese concludes has been "generally classified as relatively mediocre and relegated to obscurity" (37).

Even when people of color are studied, the female experience is likely to be overlooked. So it has been with the Harlem Renaissance, a period when black writers achieved an unprecedented degree of recognition. That era has been handed down to us as "womanless history" (McIntosh, 3), with critics for the most part ignoring women's existence and participation. Even the feminist movement, attuned to advancing white middle-class women, has neglected women of color. The tacit assumptions of womanless black literary history are that only negligible numbers of black women were literate and that they were less intellectually and literarily productive. Thus the many women who wrote, edited, and otherwise encouraged the flowering of black letters have escaped serious notice.

The invisibility of these women also may have resulted from the dispersion and fragmentation of their work. Frequently they published short pieces of fiction and nonfiction in journals, magazines, and newspapers, but did not collect them in a volume. What books they did publish came out in limited editions and did not reach a wide readership. Poet Ruby Berkley Goodwin, as if speaking for many contemporaries, wrote: "I am no different – and yet I am different. . . . I have harbored no illusions that my poetry will be judged by the exacting standards of great literature" (11). Recent works by Ann Allen Shockley, Gloria Hull, and Mary Helen Washington suggest that the time is ripe for the rediscovery of an entire generation of forgotten Afro-American women writers and for the reexamination of a canon that has omitted them.

As we made our choices for inclusion in this book, we wondered at the vast discrepancy between the existence of so many black women writers and the recognition accorded them. Who has heard of Mercedes Gilbert, Mae V. Cowdery, Effie Lee Newsome, or Bessie Woodson Yancey, much less read their work? In order to propose that the work of such writers be read, we needed to clear away some of the questions and shadows that surround their names and put in place at least a brief outline of their lives. We pursued this goal by interviewing living writers, traveling to archives, seeking death certificates, and contacting living family members. Wary of copying our predecessors' errors, we endeavored to seek out authoritative information wherever it was accessible. Although the task of verification and expansion, akin to detective work, was facilitated by the generous assistance of many archivists, local librarians, bureaus of vital statistics, and families of deceased writers, we nevertheless arrived at many investigative dead ends. So we leave to other researchers the ongoing task of seeking out missing birth dates, death dates, and other factual information.

Introduction

Following the model of the resurrection of Zora Neale Hurston's literary reputation initiated by Robert Hemenway and Alice Walker, we initially focused on those who published in the 1920s and 1930s. The goal was to identify the other women who had played a role in the expanding artistic creativity of those decades. They were novelists, poets, essayists; they were also critics, historians, editors, and leaders of literary salons. Not only in New York, but in Boston, Philadelphia, Washington, D.C., and as far from the East Coast as California and Texas, black women aspired to authorship, participated in literary enclaves, and, attracted by magazine contests soliciting material from young black talent, submitted their work for publication in the pages of the *Crisis* and *Opportunity*. These magazines contributed most to the flowering that would come to be known as the Harlem Renaissance, with its misleading myth that only the territory above 125th Street in Manhattan was black literary ground in the early twentieth century.

These fledgling women writers were not necessarily as youthful as one might think: Zora Neale Hurston's first story came out when she was thirty or so, Florence Harmon's publications appeared when she was well into her thirties, and Florida Ruffin Ridley was over fifty-five when she wrote for the *Saturday Evening Quill*. Often the competing demands of family, livelihood, profession, religion, and social activism meant that much of these women's time was spent in ways relating to their gender roles, which detracted from their writing. Women born as early as 1863 (Sarah Collins Fernandis, Mary Church Terrell, Anna Julia Cooper) published, lectured, promoted social or cultural enterprises, and wrote memoirs as late as the 1920s, thus overlapping with the next generation. Their complex life patterns merit further scrutiny.

Many of them were educators teaching in or founding black schools (Anna Julia Cooper, Charlotte Hawkins Brown, Anita Scott Coleman, Lucy Ariel Williams Holloway, Grace Vera Postles, and many others). If today teaching is sometimes regarded as a traditionally female-dominated field less than ideal for a woman of ambition, the concept of education in black history was broader and tended to overlap with the religious calling.[4]

Other avenues open to these women of the early twentieth century were social work in black communities (Jane Edna Hunter, Clarissa Scott Delany, Brenda Ray Moryck) and journalism with Afro-American newspapers (Alice Dunbar-Nelson, Ida B. Wells-Barnett, Evelyn Reynolds, Beatrice Murphy). Some were among the first blacks to enter the field of information science (Regina Andrews, Dorothy Porter) or to serve in the armed forces (Lucia Mae Pitts). In addition to being restricted to "female" professions black women were denied access to their profession outside the Afro-American community (one outstanding exception was Eunice Hunton Carter, who was a district attorney in the New York court system). Marita Bonner's short story "One True Love" tells of a domestic's determination to earn a law degree, illustrating poignantly how far beyond the reach of a poor black woman such a profession was.

However much we try to empathize, we still can hardly fathom the struggle of the women who were born at the end of the nineteenth century. We can only imagine the full story of such hardships as are alluded to, for example, in Alice Dunbar-Nelson's diary. The reader discerns that pride often prevented her from divulging how she confronted discrimination and kept together body and soul. Ellen Tarry's autobiography, too, conveys a sense of these silences when she says that there are some incidents that she must pass over in recounting her life and times. Tarry admits to "omissions [as much] because their inclusion might have infringed upon good taste [as] to safeguard the welfare of innocent persons" (viii). Another mystery lies in the silences of the many who were brilliant or prolific and then ceased publication: Mary Burrill, Angelina Weld Grimké, Elizabeth Laura Adams, Marion Vera Cuthbert, and Florence Harmon. As the professional aspirations of black women writers were severely curtailed, outlets for their poems, stories, novels, and essays were likewise quite restricted. Few white publishers would consider their manuscripts (some important exceptions were Christopher Publishing Company of Boston, Macmillan of New York, and J. B. Lippincott of Philadelphia).[5] A very few black women were able to "cross over" to a nonracial audience in their time, but not without cost. Their recognition may have come at the expense of many others who could then be safely excluded. Erlene Stetson has written of this tokenism:

> It is frequently true that a black woman writer who is
> recognized and promoted by the publishing industry and
> literary establishment is a token, the exception they
> condescended to notice. The recent revival of Zora Neale
> Hurston exemplifies this demoralizing practice. Unable for
> most of her life to support herself as a writer, Hurston died
> penniless. Now that interest in her work has no monetary
> and emotional rewards for her, her reputation has soared.
> Moreover, she is portrayed as unique; no mention is made
> of the many black women writers forming the tradition from
> which she wrote. The public is kept in ignorance of black
> women writers – in the plural – and is allowed to think that
> black women are generally incapable of literary creation.
> (89)

With the main avenues to a wide reading public closed, black women had no choice but to bring out their work privately, in chapbooks, or in newspapers. Many of their pieces so published are virtually lost to us. They entered the halls of literature by a different door, one they fashioned themselves. When no one would encourage or publish them, they promoted and published themselves. The ubiquitous imprints "n.d." (no date) and "n.p." (no publisher; no place of publication) on their books stand as emblems of their isolation. It is for this reason that their work, like clandestine literature, has become so hard to obtain. A novel by Lillian Wood called *Let My People Go* has nearly vanished; the same applies to some of the plays of Eloise Bibb Thompson, Doris Price, and Eulalie Spence. Thus our comments on many of the books here represent an effort to give the reader an introduction to the writing itself – its flavor, themes, style, influences, and relationship to dominant literary trends. Since the black woman writer of the early twentieth century had few critics, an open field for commentary lies before us, and we have offered some here. A novel like *Aunt Sara's Wooden God* by Mercedes Gilbert, for example, was scarcely reviewed, despite the quality of its craftsmanship and its thematic parallels to Hurston's *Jonah's Gourd Vine*.

Writers of the so-called minor genres, who all too often have been omitted, are also highlighted here. We agree with Elizabeth Meese's judgment that "literary scholarship is weighted toward poems and novels and, to a lesser degree, plays; it attaches no prestige to short stories, letters, diaries, children's works, travel literature, and educational treatises except insofar as they support the reputations of the writers in 'prestige' genres" (Meese, 38). Accordingly, we have taken care not to omit mention of short stories, a form that was assiduously cultivated by black women writers during the early decades of this century – Ottie B. Graham, Hazel Vivian Campbell, Alvira Hazzard, Octavia Wynbush.

The emergence of black children's literature, generously assisted by such writers as Rose Leary Love, Ann Petry, and Ellen Tarry, permits the black children of America to have a focal point within their own culture instead of having to identify always with an alien society. (Pioneer black children's librarians and writers Augusta Baker [1911] and Charlemae Rollins Rollins [1897-1979], not discussed in this book, should also be acknowledged for their contributions to this field.)

The role these women played within literary circles not exclusively female – the salons, the clubs, the new magazines – is another dimension we have attempted to convey. A'Lelia Walker's "Dark Tower" in Harlem, Dorothy Peterson's modest literary salon in Brooklyn, and Georgia Douglas Johnson's "Round Table" in Washington, D.C., played important parts in the literary life of the 1920s and 1930s.[6]

As a whole, the women chronicled here were highly educated. College was less a place to find one's self than the main avenue by which a black woman sought to arm herself against poverty and oppression. Some earned their degrees at such white institutions as Oberlin College, Wellesley College, Smith College, Radcliffe College, Dickinson College, and Columbia University; others studied at the traditionally black institutions – Howard

University, Wilberforce University, Fisk University, and Tuskegee Institute. Some escaped poverty, but not oppression. In the white schools they confronted blatant racism; in the black colleges, too, there existed exclusionary practices born of classism and colorism.

Education, however, did not always impress white employers and business owners blinded by bigotry. Frequently the women were given piecemeal or odd jobs with trumped-up titles (e.g., Georgia Douglas Johnson's position as "Commissioner of Reconciliation"). Or they might be dismissed once it was known that a fair-skinned woman was indeed Afro-American. Such was the experience of Mary Church Terrell who lost her government clerk position when her superior learned she was "colored." This incident occurred during the depression, when she could ill afford to be without a job. Moreover, employers doubted the intelligence of blacks and questioned the degrees of college-educated black women. America was too accustomed to seeing them only as cooks, cleaning women, and nannies.

It is noteworthy that quite a few women writers discussed in this book did not marry. Perhaps they remained single rather than abandon their studies or give up any measure of their hard-won personal autonomy. Dorothy West's trip to Russia, Katherine Dunham's fieldwork in Jamaica, or Zora Neale Hurston's folklore-collection trips might not have taken place if they had had spouses and children to consider. It is also important to recall that some state laws allowed only single women to teach, requiring them to give up their positions if they married – this was the case in Washington, D.C., for example. Also, having relatives' children and other family to support could militate against marrying. Single, childless women writers from the New England region alone include Ethel Caution-Davis, Angelina Weld Grimké, Florence Marion Harmon, Alvira Hazzard, and Dorothy West. This is yet another topic for further inquiry.

Considering the formidable barriers that confronted these women – they were not supposed to succeed – we find it all the more astounding that their accomplishments were so sizable and that what remains of their work is so abundant. The energy to sustain their journey in life must have come from deep wells of strength and idealism. Only one or two generations removed from slavery, they were determined to transcend and triumph, through public speaking (H. Q. Brown, Ida B. Wells, and Mary Church Terrell were among those who addressed international forums) and writing, which would allow them to present their ideas to a wider audience that would not be blinded by color.

If black women writers shared an awareness of print as power, often their writing emerged as a complementary dimension to their social activism during a historical period of conflict and struggle. For most of our writers, literacy was assumed and taken for granted. Brenda Moryck, an essayist, considered writing a "tradition" in her family: "The Reverend Charles Ray, my great grandfather, was quite a distinguished man of letters. My grandfather was editor of a Boston paper from 1850 to 1860 and my mother writes" (*Opportunity* [June 1926]: 189). Florida Ruffin Ridley, too, followed in the footsteps of her mother and many earlier ancestors who were sophisticated writers. Juanita Harrison's untutored prose is the exception, not the rule.

In their writing these Afro-American women were affirming themselves and advancing their ideas in a way different from their endeavors in the home, the school, the neighborhood, and the church, all bastions of the black communities. Their activity as writers introduced new possibilities of recognition from and communication with ever-widening circles of contemporaries even beyond the Afro-American community. They did not, however, specifically write for recognition; rather, their writing offered an opportunity for self-expression, visibility, and creation of new images of themselves and their futures.

Part of that effort was the possibility of influencing the English language itself. When Delilah Leontium Beasley wrote in the Los Angeles press to urge removal of the words *darky* and *nigger* from common usage, she was becoming an advocate of linguistic change, prefiguring the ongoing efforts in this century to redefine the vocabulary of social relations.

The thematic and stylistic range of black women's writing during the period was extensive. Some wrote of their experiences as Afro-American females struggling to affirm themselves; others created imaginative worlds that omitted questions of race. Dialect was for some a legitimate form of literary expression, but for others a form that could further imprison them in outmoded stereotypes.

These black women, though many united in club movements, organizations, and battles against racism and sexism, did not belong to a single coherent literary movement, nor did they share common regional origins. They did, however, share a historical experience of discrimination and exclusion and a determination to create an expression of their own, a place of their own, in a society that had consistently rejected them.

A thematic dichotomy cuts across their writing, a division between a concern with the immediate cultural surroundings that were so inimical to advancement and an involvement in more aesthetic concerns. Ida B. Wells-Barnett wrote of the fight for equality; Aloise Barbour Epperson created a realm of fantasy and lyrical emotion. These Afro-American women seem to have seen their identity as both separate from the whole of American society and a part of it. Keeping a balance between the sense of separation and the sense of belonging is one of the focal points of their work. The equilibrium is both tenuous and elusive, as we see some writers expressing militant anger (Marion Vera Cuthbert, Dorothy Vena Johnson, Carrie Williams Clifford), others turning to the church for inspiration (J. Pauline Smith, Effie Lee

Newsome), and still others writing as if they were trying to ignore racial oppression (Angelina Weld Grimké, Florence Marion Harmon). Bernice Guillaume has noted the importance of understanding that pressure deriving from institutionalized racism led black writers "to express predominantly religious and patriotic sentiments. It was an effort to display their human commonality with whites" (32).

Sometimes their idiom echoes Victorianism and neoromanticism; other times it is colloquial or in dialect. Of the women who wrote in a mode of evasion, many were using their writing as a sanctuary to which they fled to escape the daily alienation of what Gloria Wade-Gayles calls "the narrow space of race, the dark enclosure of sex." Other times, as we mentioned above, their pride kept them from divulging how they confronted discrimination and supported themselves. The reader needs to be perspicacious, as Gloria Hull has shown in the case of Georgia Douglas Johnson, to detect when such women were actually writing in protest against the stifling of roles and the confinement of women.

Our book should be used as a departure point for the further study of writers who deserve attention. We hope there will follow a wide-ranging effort on the part of scholars, students, and descendants of black women writers to rediscover and reclaim a rich heritage. Since America is a tapestry of varied ethnic fibers, the cultural contributions of black women will ultimately be recognized, their endeavors brought to light as an added reminder that they lived, they created, and they prepared the way for generations to come – all the while looking at the stars.

NOTES

1. Bruce Kellner dates the Harlem Renaissance era from 1917 to 1935.

2. Walker first detailed her quest in *Ms.* magazine and then included her essay "In Search of Zora" in her book *In Search of Our Mothers' Gardens.*

3. Hortense Spillers notes that until the Harlem Renaissance, the black woman's realities were "virtually suppressed" and the resulting tradition of work "is quite recent, its continuities broken and sporadic" (297).

4. Dodson and Gilkes explain that teachers were perceived as leaders and quasi-evangelizers: "If any one ministry could be identified as central to the black sacred cosmos of the twentieth century, it would be education" (84).

5. Mercedes Gilbert was published by Christopher, Jessie Fauset by Lippincott, and Juanita Harrison by Macmillan.

6. The existence of these female-led salons is noted by Kellner.

REFERENCES

Dodson, Jualyne E., and Cheryl Townsend Gilkes. "Something Within: Social Change and Collective Endurance in the Sacred World of Black Christian Women." In *Women and Religion in America*, Vol. 3, *1900-1968*, edited by Rosemary Radford Ruether and Rosemary Skinner Keller. San Francisco: Harper & Row, 1981, 80-91.

Evans, Mari. *Black Women Writers (1950-1980)*. Garden City, N.Y.: Anchor Press/Doubleday, 1984.

Goodwin, Ruby Berkley. *From My Kitchen Window*. New York: Wendell Malliet and Co., 1942.

Guillaume, Bernice F. "Olivia Ward Bush: Factors Shaping the Social and Cultural Outlook of a Nineteenth Century Writer." *Negro History Bulletin* 43 (April/May/June 1980): 32-34.

Hemenway, Robert. *Zora Neale Hurston: A Literary Biography*. Foreword by Alice Walker. Urbana: University of Illinois Press, 1977.

Huggins, Nathan. *Harlem Renaissance*. New York: Oxford University Press, 1971.

Hull, Gloria. *Color, Sex, and Poetry: Three Women Writers of the Harlem Renaissance*. Bloomington: Indiana University Press, 1987.

Kellner, Bruce. *The Harlem Renaissance: Dictionary for the Era*. Westport, Conn.: Greenwood Press, 1984.

McIntosh, Peggy. "Interactive Phases of Curricular Re-Vision: A Feminist Perspective." Wellesley, Mass.: Wellesley College Center for Research on Women, 1983.

Meese, Elizabeth A. "Archival Materials: The Problem of Literary Reputation." In *Women in Print*. Vol. 1, *Opportunities for Women's Studies Research in Language and Literature*, edited by Joan E. Hartman and Ellen Messer-Davidow. New York: Modern Language Association of America, 1982.

Perry, Margaret. *Silence to the Drums: A Survey of the Literature of the Harlem Renaissance*. Westport, Conn.: Greenwood Press, 1976.

Shockley, Ann Allen. *Afro-American Women Writers, 1746-1933: An Anthology and Critical Guide.* Boston: G. K. Hall, 1988.

Spillers, Hortense. "A Hateful Passion, a Lost Love." *Feminist Studies* 9, no. 2 (Summer 1983): 297.

Stetson, Erlene. "Black Women in and out of Print." In *Women in Print.* Vol. 1, *Opportunities for Women's Studies Research in Language and Literature,* edited by Joan E. Hartman and Ellen Messer-Davidow. New York: Modern Language Association of America, 1982.

Tarry, Ellen. *The Third Door: The Autobiography of an American Negro Woman.* New York: D. McKay, 1955.

Wade-Gayles, Gloria Jean. *No Crystal Stair: Visions of Race and Sex in Black Women's Fiction.* New York: Pilgrim Press, 1984.

Walker, Alice. *In Search of Our Mothers' Gardens.* San Diego and New York: Harcourt Brace Jovanovich, 1983.

Washington, Mary Helen. *Invented Lives: Narratives of Black Women, 1860-1960.* Garden City, N.Y.: Doubleday, 1987.

ADAMS, ELIZABETH LAURA (1909-?)

Autobiographer

"My life, as a very small child, was filled with happiness. I saw only the beauty of rose-colored dawns." So wrote Elizabeth Laura Adams in her autobiography (7). Despite an idyllic, artistically rich childhood, Adams suffered disappointments in her ambitions for an education, career, and musical pursuits. Yet in her autobiography she portrays herself as having ultimately overcome her defeats owing to a strength that she attributes to her strict upbringing and religious faith. Adams's use of the autobiographical form joins her with other women who have chronicled their lives in literature as well as to the African-American determination to tell one's own story. Ironically, the only source we found on her life is her autobiography; we found no trace of her in the cities where she lived.

Born in Santa Barbara, California, Adams was the only child of Daniel Henderson and Lula Josephine Holden Adams. Her father, who prided himself on his reputation as "the best qualified head-waiter between the Atlantic and the Pacific," had a deep appreciation for art and music. Her mother was an artist who had given up plans to study in Paris in order to marry; she designed the house they lived in when Elizabeth was born. Growing up in Los Angeles, Santa Barbara, and Santa Monica, Adams was sheltered by her father's love, which she described as being "like that of a curator of a museum." When Elizabeth felt the pain of racial prejudice, her parents encouraged her not to protest but to ignore the derogatory comments. While she was still in grammar school, music provided a positive creative outlet for her, but her dreams of becoming a concert violinist had to be given up because of ill health.

Adams became attracted to Catholicism after a friend invited her to attend mass at the Santa Barbara Mission. Adams told her father of her desire to convert, but her father, a Mason, was adamantly opposed and said, "Never discuss the subject again." She became a Catholic after her father's death, however.

Financial difficulties prevented Adams from attending college. After winning some small prizes from the *Morning Star* for her writing, she tried unsuccessfully to find a position in journalism but failed. She found work as a typist for a Santa Monica author, as a theater maid, and during the depression years, as a domestic servant.

A Catholic magazine, the *Sentinel of the Blessed Sacrament*, accepted a feature article that she had written, and then a prose poem, "Consecrated," won recognition from a literary club. The judges were surprised to learn that the author was a black woman; the poem was not published until six years later when a magazine of verse, *Westward*, accepted it for publication.

Adams's autobiography, *Dark Symphony* (1942), bearing the imprimatur of Francis J. Spellman, archbishop of New York, has as its central motif the search for spiritual peace. Adams describes in vivid terms her charmed childhood, subsequent harsh awakening to prejudice, and the refuge she found in poetry, classical music, and religion.

In *Witnesses for Freedom* Rebecca Chalmers Barton explains that the title *Dark Symphony* alludes to the music of Adams's life as both sorrowful and triumphant. The double burdens of chronic ill health and racism in the church are undertones throughout. Yet her autobiography stresses the joys of spiritual fulfillment and freedom from bitterness. Downplaying the repressive effects of a patriarchal upbringing by a father who directed her every move, Adams explains that "the purpose of my parents' strict training was to prepare me to work purposefully that I might face undismayed the perplexities and disappointments of life." Under such stringent parental pressure to conform, she learned a lesson of stoic individualism, thereby sacrificing awareness of larger social questions. However determinedly Adams centers her narrative on religion, the reader nevertheless senses an unexpressed regret for a literary career that never materialized.

At times the reader also wishes that Adams's tone were less earnest and serious, but she explains why amusing anecdotes are lacking: "As *Dark Symphony* is supposed to deal primarily with my quest for Christ Our Lord, the incidents in a lighter vein would defeat the purpose of this book." Having told the story of her personal and spiritual quest, she considers her goal achieved.

Barton contrasts Adams's accommodation to circumstances and her escapism with the radical attitudes of Zora Neale Hurston* and Juanita Harrison,* the domestic who traveled throughout the world and published her autobiography *My Great Wide Beautiful World* (1936): "Their scorn of conventional morals and religion, their choice of a free-and-easy way of life would seem incredible to this serious-minded woman who finds her answers at last in the Catholic Church."

SELECT BIBLIOGRAPHY

Primary

Nonfiction

Dark Symphony. New York: Sheed & Ward, 1942.

"There Must Be a God Somewhere: A True Story of a Convert's Search for God." *Torch*, serialized from October 1940 to March 1941.

Secondary

Barton, *Witnesses for Freedom*, [1948] 1976.

Campbell, Dorothy, *Index to Black American Writers in Collective Biographies*, 1983.

David, *Growing Up Black*, 1968.

Matthews, *Black American Writers, 1773-1949*, 1975.

Richardson, Marilyn, *Black Women and Religion*, 1980.

Scally, *Negro Catholic Writers, 1900-1943*, 1945.

Spradling, *In Black and White*, 1980.

Williams, *American Black Women in the Arts and Social Sciences*, 1978.

ANDREWS, REGINA M. ANDERSON [Ursula Trelling] (1901-)

Bibliographer

Librarian

Playwright

For forty-four years Regina M. Andrews diligently safeguarded black culture in her dual capacities as professional librarian and dramatist, combining them when possible. She thought that professional librarians could play a crucial role in human relations by stimulating intellectual growth and thereby promoting cultural tolerance. Andrews sought to use her position as a librarian and a playwright to preserve African and Afro-American history and culture. She presented several pictorial and fine arts exhibits at schools and libraries in New York State and instituted "Family Night at the Library," a forum for such renowned speakers as Langston Hughes, Eleanor Roosevelt, A. Philip Randolph, Marcus Garvey, and others.

Regina Anderson was the daughter of William Grant, an attorney, and Margaret Simons Anderson. Born on 21 May 1901 at 4609 Vincennes Avenue, Chicago, she grew up in a middle-class community, attending the Normal Training School and later Hyde Park High School. She received her undergraduate education at Wilberforce University in Ohio and the University of Chicago. She then transferred to City College of New York, where she eventually received her M.L.S. degree from Columbia University Library School. During this time, she was employed by several branches of the New York Public Library: 135th Street branch (now the Schomburg Center for Research in Black Culture), Woodstock, Rivington Street, and 115th Street, where she became the supervising librarian in 1945.

Andrews shared an apartment with two other women at 580 Nichols Avenue in Harlem on Sugar Hill. It became a gathering place for many Harlem residents belonging to the Writers' Guild, amateur dramatic groups and others. Andrews, whom Loften Mitchell describes as having "Class with a capital C," helped organize such events as the Civic Club dinner party given on 21 March 1924 to honor young black writers, a celebration attended by Harlem personalities Gwendolyn Bennett,* Countee Cullen, Langston Hughes, and Jessie Fauset.* Eulalie Spence* and Clarissa Scott Delany* were two other women whom Andrews met at literary gatherings.

Caught up in the momentum of the New Negro Movement, she continued to participate in Harlem cultural activities after her marriage to William T. Andrews in 1926. She expanded her involvement with drama as one of the four organizers (and eventually second executive director) of the Harlem Experimental Theatre, founded in 1927. Still an employee of the

4

New York Public Library and restricted by professional demands, she wrote plays under the pseudonym Ursula Trelling.

Climbing Jacob's Ladder was one of the plays written under her pseudonym. It is a drama about a lynching that takes place while people are praying in church. In Loften Mitchell's *Voices of the Black Theatre*, Andrews says that this work resulted from the influence of Ida B. Wells-Barnett,* an antilynching activist whose activities Andrews had followed as a young woman.

Regina Andrews supported the philosophy of Krigwa (Crisis Guild of Writers and Artists, whose original acronym was CRIGWA): black theater should be exclusively about, by, for, and near Afro-Americans. In her autobiographical sketch in *Voices of the Black Theatre*, Andrews speaks much more about the history of Afro-American drama than about her own work. She credits W. E. B. Du Bois with founding Krigwa, establishing its philosophy, and inspiring her as a playwright. She also recounts how Du Bois demanded that she rewrite *Climbing Jacob's Ladder*, saying she was capable of producing a better script. Du Bois congratulated Andrews after seeing a production of the revised play; he described it as "thrilling."

Andrews herself encouraged the genesis and growth of various Harlem theater groups like the Krigwa Theatre, Harlem Suitcase Theatre, and Harlem Experimental Theatre which was housed in the basement of the 135th Street library where she worked. The groups also worked out of the basement of the 201 West 115th Street branch library, where Andrews was the first Afro-American to be appointed acting supervising librarian in 1936.

In 1947 she became the supervising librarian at the Washington Heights branch. During her twenty years there she served as second vice president of the National Council of Women and representative of the National Urban League to the U.S. Commission for UNESCO. She received both the Musical Arts Group and the Community Heroine awards. She also became involved with the State Commission for Human Rights. Later in her career, as a result of receiving an Asia Foundation Award, Andrews was able to visit some of her guest speakers in their native lands including India, Hong Kong, Japan, Iran, Thailand, and Afghanistan. Andrews, Jessie Fauset,* and Gwendolyn Bennett* were among ten black women recognized at the 1939 New York World's Fair.

Though much of her work remains unpublished, some of her papers are housed at the Schomburg Center for Research in Black Culture in New York City.

SELECT BIBLIOGRAPHY

Primary

Drama

Climbing Jacob's Ladder. 16 pages. Produced by the Harlem Experimental Theatre, New York, 1931.

The Man Who Passed. 8 pages. A one-act play.

Underground. Produced by the Harlem Experimental Theatre and by the Drama Committee of the New York Public Library at the New School, ca. 1933.

Nonfiction

"Black New York, 1619-1970." Presently being considered for publication by the New York Public Library.

"The Community Theatre: A Part of the Life of the People" [radio speech], 14 September 1934, WEVD.

"Intergroup Relations in the United States: A Compilation of Source Materials and Service Organizations." Published by the National Council of Negro Women, 1956.

"The Library's Responsibility for Better Human Relations." *Wilson Library Bulletin* (1949).

"The Rabbit Who Saw the World Outside." An unpublished children's book.

"Top of the News." *American Library Association Magazine* (December 1953).

Secondary

Arata and Rotoli, *Black American Playwrights, 1800 to the Present*, 1976.

Davis, Marianna W., *Contributions of Black Women to America*, 1982.

Ellis, *Opportunity; A Journal of Negro Life*, 1971.

Hatch and Abdullah, *Black Playwrights, 1823-1977*, 1977.

Huggins, *Harlem Renaissance*, 1971.

Kellner, *The Harlem Renaissance*, 1984.

Mitchell, *Voices of the Black Theatre*, 1975.

Rush, Myers, and Arata, *Black American Writers Past and Present*, 1975.

Schomburg Center for Research on Black Culture, New York Public Library, New York City.

Spradling, *In Black and White*, 1980.

Who's Who in America, 1968-1969.

Who's Who of American Women, 1st ed. [1958-59].

BEASLEY, DELILAH LEONTIUM (1871-1934)

Historian

Journalist

Physical therapist

Delilah Leontium Beasley was an aspiring journalist and self-trained historian who, although she had little or no formal education, published one of the first volumes on Afro-Americans in the West.

Beasley was born in Cincinnati, Ohio, and by the age of fifteen, had written for the *Cleveland Gazette* and the *Cincinnati Enquirer*. A career in journalism was thwarted by the death of her parents, however, and she went to work as a maid for a Cincinnati family. She left Ohio to train as a masseuse in Chicago and later returned to the state to practice her profession in Springfield. During this time Beasley took more courses in physical therapy while also beginning research on Afro-Americans of the West, which was to culminate in a book several years later. After completing her courses, she became chief operator in the bathhouse of a family resort in Michigan. Not long afterward Beasley arranged to support herself by working as a nurse to a former therapy patient so that she could move to California to seriously pursue her historical research.

Beasley resumed her interests in journalism while gathering information for her book, *The Negro Trailblazers of California*. As a journalist for the white newspaper *Oakland Tribune*, she compiled a column "Activities among Negroes." Beasley sought to extirpate derogatory terms like *darky* and *nigger* from American newspapers; her efforts were rewarded when many editors in the San Francisco area and elsewhere began to eliminate the use of these words. It was also for the *Oakland Tribune* that the young journalist wrote a series of articles to mitigate the effects of the movie *Birth of a Nation* – an endeavor shared by other black women activists, including Eloise Bibb Thompson* and Carrie Williams Clifford.* Beasley continued to write for the *Tribune* through 1925.

As a delegate and traveler to conferences on women's issues, Delilah Beasley represented the *Oakland Tribune* and the Alameda County League of Colored Women Voters at the National Convention of Women Voters in Richmond, Virginia, in 1925, and in the same year represented the *Tribune* at a conference of the International Council of Women held in Washington, D.C. She was a member of the League of Nations Association for Northern California; she joined others in petitioning for the entry of the United States into the World Court and submitted petitions on behalf of the National League of Women Voters to a disarmament conference in Geneva, Switzerland.

Despite Beasley's lack of formal education, her extensively researched historical account *The Negro Trailblazers of California* (which appeared in 1919), is an impressive collection of poetry, photographs, and excerpts from letters and documents. It consists of three parts: (1) history of Afro-Americans in California from Spanish colonialism to California statehood, (2) biographical sketches of the first black pioneers and miners, and (3) an overview of the situation of black Californians and achievers contemporary with the author.

The history recounts the roles of black women and men in the growth of California. In discussing the origin of the name "California," Beasley gives an interesting quote from *Las Sergas de Esplandián,* a Spanish romance published by García Ordóñez de Montalvo in 1510. Allegedly on "the right hand of the Indies" there was an island called California, populated by Amazon-like black women "of strong and hardy bodies, of ardent courage and great force." Unfortunately Beasley does not develop this thought or connect it to the fabric of her historical work. She does discuss the significance of California's Hispanic origins, however, placing the commonwealth within historical context and quoting from Mexican and Spanish archives.

Negro Trailblazers of California met with mixed reviews. The book is mentioned in Dabney's *Cincinnati's Colored Citizens* (1926): "Miss Delilah Beasley, a girl of this city, who went to California and has written a very creditable history of that state" (20). Carter G. Woodson, not as gracious, wrote an unfavorable review of Beasley's book in the January 1920 issue of the *Journal of Negro History* (128-29). Woodson faults the book for what he calls its unbalanced and incoherent presentation. Little of Beasley's own analysis is integrated into the extensive quotes from other sources, and what she does include suggests little consideration about the relative importance of various documents. As Woodson notes, "the author seemingly wrote all she heard or collected in each case regardless of the worth" (129).

Perhaps Beasley felt she should refrain from making value judgments about little-known episodes. Although the book may indeed be more of a compendium than documented history, it is worthwhile for its intent – to emphasize black contributions to California – and for the sheer volume of new data it presents, a noteworthy accomplishment for the time.

SELECT BIBLIOGRAPHY

Primary

Nonfiction

The Negro Trailblazers of California. A Compilation of Records from the California Archives at Bancroft Library, University of California at Berkeley; also from diaries, old papers, conversations of old pioneers in California. Los Angeles: Times Mirror Printing and Binding House, 1919.

Secondary

Abajian, *Blacks and Their Contributions to the American West*, 1974.

Campbell, Dorothy, *Index to Black American Writers in Collective Biographies*, 1983.

Dabney, *Cincinnati's Colored Citizens*, 1926.

Dannett, *Profiles of Negro Womanhood*, 1964.

Davis, Elizabeth Lindsay, *Lifting as They Climb*, 1933.

Dillon, *Humbugs and Heroes*, 1970.

Logan and Winston, *Dictionary of American Negro Biography*, 1982.

Low and Clift, *Encyclopedia of Black America*, 1981.

Williams, *American Black Women in the Arts and Social Sciences*, 1978.

Woodson, Review of *Negro Trailblazers of California*, by Delilah L. Beasley, 1920.

Work, Monroe N. "California Freedom Papers" [essay]. *Journal of Negro History* (January 1918): 45-54.

BENNETT, GWENDOLYN B. (1902-1981)

Visual artist

Columnist

Essayist

Poet

Short-story writer

From the beginning of her career Gwendolyn B. Bennett was viewed by her peers as one of the most promising authors of the New Negro Renaissance. A talented writer and painter, she wrote the regularly featured column "The Ebony Flute" for *Opportunity* which chronicled and commented upon activities generated by the movement.

Born on 8 July 1902, Bennett was the only child of Joshua and Maime Bennett of Giddings, Texas. As a toddler she moved with her parents to Nevada, where they taught on an Indian reservation. At the age of five Gwendolyn with her family moved to Washington D.C., where Joshua prepared to study law and Maime trained to become a manicurist and beautician at a finishing school. The Bennetts were subsequently divorced, and Maime was awarded custody of the child. But seven-year-old Gwendolyn was kidnapped by her father, and she would not see her mother again until she was employed as a faculty member at Howard University.

Bennett displayed both literary and artistic talent early. She was the first black female to be elected to the Felter Literary Society at Brooklyn's Girls' High School and also received first prize for a poster with the slogan

"Fresh Air Prevents Tuberculosis." In January of 1921 Bennett graduated from Girls' High and then studied at Columbia University for two years. She finished her education at Pratt Institute, where she wrote the class play and performed in its leading role in her final year.

In June of 1924, following her studies at Pratt, Bennett accepted employment as instructor in design, watercolor and crafts at Howard University. In December 1924 she was awarded Delta Sigma Theta's thousand-dollar foreign scholarship, which allowed the young artist the chance to study in Paris at the Julian and Colarossi academies and the École du Panthéon. Her experience in Paris was further enhanced by her association with Frans Maserell, a well-known French modern painter, who invited Bennett to his home occasionally and encouraged her painting. She returned to teaching at Howard in September 1926 and remained active among visual artists. Unfortunately much of her work from these years was destroyed by a fire at her stepmother's home in 1926. The next year, she was one of two Afro-American artists selected to study the Barnes Foundation collection of modern and primitive art.

Bennett wrote several essays about a problem shared by Afro-American artists and writers – namely, how to find a way to express their cultural identity that would be received as an authentic segment of American society. In an essay published in the periodical *Artfront* in 1937, Bennett discussed the importance of the Harlem Artists Guild, initially an organization founded to maintain the cultural, social, and economic integrity of Afro-American artists, but which eventually embraced all artists regardless of color.

While Bennett's art was featured on the covers of *Opportunity* and the *Messenger*, her writing was appearing regularly in *American Mercury*, *Crisis*, *Gypsy*, *Opportunity*, *Fire*, *Howard University Record*, *Palms*, and *Southern Workman* from 1922 to 1934. Some of her work was also included in popular anthologies of the time: Countee Cullen's *Caroling Dusk* (1927), Charles S. Johnson's *Ebony and Topaz: A Collectanea* (1927), and William Stanley Braithwaite's *Anthology of Magazine Verse for 1927*. In the summer of 1926 twenty-four-year-old Bennett became assistant editor of *Opportunity*.

She was well regarded by the artistic luminaries of the time and associated with them often. She attended a dinner given in honor of Jessie Fauset* at the Civic Club in New York on 21 May 1924, and corresponded with several other black women writers of the period – Zora Neale Hurston,* Georgia Douglas Johnson,* Regina Andrews,* Clarissa Scott Delany,* and others – during the time she wrote "The Ebony Flute."

The column effectively places the reader within the cultural atmosphere of the Harlem Renaissance at its liveliest. According to Bennett, its name was inspired by a line from William Rose Benet's poem "Harlem": "I want to sing Harlem on an ebony flute." The purpose of the column was to expound on "literary chit-chat and artistic what-not" and also to relate cultural activities in other cities and towns spawned by the New Negro Movement. Dialogue flourished among all types of artistic groups (musical, literary, visual arts) from the Saturday Evening Quill Club in Boston to the Ink Slingers in Los Angeles. Bennett fairly acknowledged New York's Harlem-centric arrogance when she wrote in one column: "it is ever so refreshing to be brought sharply up against the fact that here and there in other less motley cities are little knots of people writing, reading . . . perhaps hoping and certainly thinking."

Although Bennett never published a volume of her own poetry, she is regarded more often as a poet than a prose writer in spite of her numerous essays and columns. Her poetry like her prose was often influenced by her background as an artist. For example, in "Hatred," sounds and metaphors convey the severity one finds in a painting's contrasting colors or edges. One can hear the "dart of singing steel," the pierce of "swift arrows," and see the pines sober as "they stand etched / Against the sky." The words are infused with a palpable sensory energy.

Her African heritage is another prominent theme in Bennett's poetry, as in "Song," where the soul of Afro-America is looking for a place to rest: "Abandon tells you / That I sing the heart of a race / While sadness whispers / That I am the cry of a soul." "To a Dark Girl" is an ode to black beauty, defying a society that judges physical beauty only by an Anglo-Saxon ideal: "I love you for your brownness / . . . Something of old forgotten queens / Lurks in the lithe abandon of your walk / . . . let your full lips laugh at Fate!"

SELECT BIBLIOGRAPHY

Primary

Fiction

"Wedding Day." *Fire!!* (November 1926): 26-28.

IN ANTHOLOGIES

Johnson, Charles S., *Ebony and Topaz*, [1927] 1971. "Tokens."

Nonfiction

"The American Negro Paints." *Southern Workman* 57 (January 1928): 111-12.

"The Ebony Flute" [column]. *Opportunity* (August 1926-May 1928).

"The Future of the Negro in Art." *Howard University Record* 19 (December 1924): 65-66.

"The Harlem Artists Guild." *Art Front* 3 (May 1937): 20.

"I Go to Camp." *Opportunity* (August 1934): 241-43.

"Negroes: Inherent Craftsmen." *Howard University Record* 19 (February 1925): 172.

"Never the Twain Shall Meet" [review of *Salah and His American*, by Leland Hall]. *Opportunity* (March 1934): 92.

Review of *Banjo*, by Claude McKay. *Opportunity* (August 1929): 254-55.

Review of *The Grand Army Man of Rhode Island*. *Opportunity* (September 1926): 295.

Review of *The Lonesome Road*, by Paul Green. *Opportunity* (September 1926): 294.

Review of *My Spirituals*, by Eva Jessye. *Opportunity* (November 1927): 338-39.

Review of *Plum Bun*, by Jessie Redmon Fauset. *Opportunity* (September 1929): 287.

Review of *Salah and His American*, by Leland Hall. *Opportunity* (March 1934): 92.

Review of *Sorrow in Sunlight*, by Ronald Firbank. *Opportunity* (June 1926): 195-96.

"Rounding the Century: Story of the Colored Orphan Asylum and Association for the Benefit of Colored Children in New York City." *Crisis* 42 (June 1935): 180-81, 188.

Poetry

"Dear Things." *Palms* 4 (October 1926).

"Dirge." *Palms* 4 (October 1926).

"Epitaph." *Opportunity* (March 1934): 76.

"Hatred." *Opportunity* (June 1926): 190.

"Heritage." *Opportunity* (December 1923): 371.

"Lines Written at the Grave of Alexander Dumas." *Opportunity* (July 1926): 225.

"Moon tonight." *Gypsy* (October 1926).

"On a Birthday." *Opportunity* (September 1925): 276.

"Purgation." *Opportunity* (February 1925): 56.

"Song." *Palms* 4 (October 1926): 21-22.

"Song," "Dear Things," and "Dirge." *Palms* 4 (October 1926): 21-22.

"Street Lamps in Early Spring." *Opportunity* (May 1926): 152.

"To Usward." *Crisis* 28 (May 1924): 19; *Opportunity* (May 1924): 143-44.

"Wind." *Opportunity* (November 1924): 335.

IN ANTHOLOGIES

Brewer, *Heralding Dawn*, 1936. "On a Birthday."

Cullen, *Caroling Dusk*, 1927. "Advice"; "Fantasy"; "Hatred"; "Lines Written at the Grave of Alexander Dumas"; "Quatrains"; "Secret"; "Sonnet-1"; "Sonnet-2."

Stetson, *Black Sister*, 1981. "Advice"; "Fantasy"; "Hatred"; "Heritage"; "Secret"; "Song"; "To a Dark Girl"; "To Usward."

Secondary

Campbell, Dorothy, *Index to Black American Writers in Collective Biographies*, 1983.

Chapman, *Index to Poetry by Black American Women*, 1986.

Daniel and Govan, "Gwendolyn Bennett," 1987.

Ellis, *Opportunity; A Journal of Negro Life*, 1971.

Guy, *Women's Poetry Index*, 1985.

Hull, "Black Women Poets from Wheatley to Walker," 1975. Also in Bell, Parker, and Guy-Sheftall, *Sturdy Black Bridges*, 1979.

Kallenbach, *Index to Black American Literary Anthologies*, 1979.

Kellner, *The Harlem Renaissance*, 1984.

Lewis, *When Harlem Was in Vogue*, 1981.

Perry, *The Harlem Renaissance*, 1982.

Rush, Myers, and Arata, *Black American Writers Past and Present*, 1975.

Stetson, *Black Sister*, 1981.

Stetson, "Gwendolyn B. Bennett," 1979.

BIRD, BESSIE CALHOUN (ca. 1906-?)

Poet

Bessie Calhoun Bird, with Mae V. Cowdery,* Ottie Beatrice Graham,* Evelyn Crawford Reynolds,* Nellie Bright,* and other black women writers, were part of the New Negro Movement struggling to surface in Philadelphia. The beginning of Bird's poetic career is marked by her appearance in *Black Opals*, a publication of the Philadelphia clique: her first poem in the journal, "Symbol," in iambic pentameter, appeared in the June 1928 issue. The final issue of *Black Opals* (Christmas, 1928) featured her poem, "A Prayer."

Vincent Jubilee, author of "Philadelphia's Afro-American Literary Circle and the Harlem Renaissance," comments that "publication in *Black Opals* did not, by itself, qualify all contributors as genuine literary aspirants, nor encourage them to continue the pursuit of professional authorship" (36). In other words, not all the authors who published made their literary careers a priority, but simply used *Black Opals* to gratify a desire to see their work or names in print.

Jubilee also observes that the writers' groups were practically ignored by the black press in Philadelphia: "There is no evidence in the black press of the mid-1920s that the city's black affluent class considered literary lectures or forums an essential part of their lives. . . . no announcements appear in the black press of the period indicating the existence of other cultural resources usually generated by a 'renaissance' of interest in black culture" (88). Thus the writers more or less depended upon the support of one another for promotion and visibility. When their literary achievements were noted in the press, they were usually coupled with, and sometimes overshadowed by, society notices. In her column, for example, Evelyn Crawford Reynolds,* who also wrote under the pseudonym of "Eve Lynn," recognized Bessie Calhoun Bird for the poem "A Prayer," but her impressive new "mansion" was mentioned first. (How she amassed her wealth is unclear.)

Bird was a member of both the Philadelphia-based Piranean Club and the Beaux Art Club. These assemblies of Afro-American literary and visual artists were most active from the 1930s to the 1950s. Literary artists convened at Bird's residence at Twenty-second and Bainbridge streets mostly during the 1930s when the Piranean Club gained momentum, coinciding with the publication of her volume of poetry *Airs from the Wood-Winds* in 1935.

Bird, like some other middle-class Afro-American writers, chose not to discuss the condition of blacks or women in society, but opted for more neutral or less poignant themes like nature. *Airs from the Wood-Winds*, with an introduction by Arthur Huff Fauset, a coeditor of *Black Opals*, contains rhyming verse on various themes: emotion, nature, the four seasons. Fauset refers to Bird's poetry as "zephyrs" (meaning "akin to darkness, or the dark side" in Greek) in which "irony is cloaked in wistfulness; humor lies concealed beneath a delicately wrought veil of faith." Seasons and the personification of nature play dominant roles in poems like "October" and "Stripped." The poet is also generous with metaphors, as in "Gypsy Beads:" "MEMORIES / My heart is a harp, / Plucked by memory's fingers – / Thoughts of you, alone, / Make perfect chords," and "SUN / You are the sun, / I am a little summer cloud / Falling in bitter raindrops / Under your burning / Indifference." The poem "Portrait" does incidentally mention race. Perhaps it was written on one of the poet's more optimistic days: "On the wagon's rear / Posed elegantly against / A bale of rose-colored rags / A black boy luxuriates . . . / Freedom . . . bright freedom . . . / He is a king enthroned, / Monarch of all he surveys- / the world belongs to him."

Apparently Bird did not receive recognition on a national level – her works cannot be found in either *Opportunity* or *Crisis*, nor are details of her private life available.

SELECT BIBLIOGRAPHY

Primary

Poetry

Airs from the Wood-Winds. Philadelphia: Alpress, 1935. Limited edition of 300 copies.

"Proof." *Challenge* 2 (Spring 1937).

IN ANTHOLOGIES

Stetson, *Black Sister*, 1981. "Proof."

Secondary

Jubilee, "Philadelphia's Afro-American Literary Circle and the Harlem Renaissance," 1980.

Matthews, *Black American Writers, 1773-1949*, 1975.

BONNER (OCCOMY), MARITA ODETTE
[JOSEPH MAREE ANDREW]
(1898-1971)

Educator

Playwright

Short-story writer

Short-story writer and dramatist Marita Bonner was a sophisticated artist and intellectual who deserves to be placed in the company of the better-known Harlem Renaissance figures like Zora Neale Hurston,* Jessie Fauset,* and Nella Larsen,* and who ought to be recognized as a forerunner of such current-day luminaries as Alice Walker, Toni Morrison, Gloria Naylor, Toni Cade Bambara, and Gayl Jones. Had Bonner published her many stories and other works as a volume during her lifetime, her recognition might not have been so long in coming.

The youngest of three children in a second-generation New England family (a younger brother died in infancy), Marita Odette Bonner was born on 16 June 1898, according to her birth certificate. She grew up in Boston, Massachusetts, and was educated in Brookline primary and secondary schools. During high school she frequently contributed to the *Sagamore*, a student magazine. Discerning Bonner's literary talent, her faculty adviser urged her to study writing at Radcliffe under the well-known Charles Townsend Copeland. Marita recalled, "At the time I was in high school, Copy's class was limited to twenty students each year and admission was on a competitive basis. Students came from all over the world to take his course."

After successfully completing her studies at the Cabot School, Marita prepared to enter Radcliffe College in 1918. She actively participated in college groups including the mandolin, music, German, and English clubs. She wrote her class song and reportedly founded the Radcliffe chapter of the black sorority Delta Sigma Theta.

Though he lauded Marita's ability as a writer, Professor Copeland warned her not to be "bitter." This was "a cliché to colored people who write," as Marita said; in that day blacks who dared to pronounce judgment on a racist society were met with indignation. But her determination to voice protest was only stiffened by this admonition. (That she was a determined woman was evidenced by her ability to change from left-handedness to right-handedness.) Her plays, short stories, and essays were published on the pages of such magazines as *Opportunity; A Journal of Negro Life*; *Black Life*, published in Philadelphia; and *The Crisis: A Record of the Darker Races* from 1924 to 1941. According to Bonner's children, she occasionally wrote under the pseudonym "Joseph Maree Andrew."

Marita Bonner's works penetrated beyond the New York Literary scene: she participated in salon groups in Washington, D.C., where she taught at the Armstrong High School between 1924 and 1930, and she published in *Black Opals*, the magazine produced by black writers in Philadelphia. Bonner later wed William Almy Occomy; the couple raised three children in Chicago, which provided the backdrop for Bonner's later stories.

The writing of Marita Bonner is sensitive to the "double and triple jeopardies" Afro-American women are exposed to in a society that is race-, sex-, and class-conscious. This is a phenomenon Gloria Wade-Gayles describes in her book *No Crystal Stair*; black women, the least paid in the labor force, were constrained by economic factors; within the Afro-American community women met with discrimination on the basis of their sex; and most obvious was the prevailing racism of society. It is Bonner's perception and skill in dealing with these complex issues that link her to the black women authors of today. A work that epitomizes this sensitivity is her prize-winning essay "On Being Young, A Woman and Colored" published in *Crisis* in 1925.

In her stories Bonner constructs situations in which the vulnerability of blacks, especially black women, is delineated in a series of stark black/white dualities: black female versus black male, black female versus white female, and black female versus black female. Out of this kaleidoscope emerges a portrait of human beings perpetually locked in social conflict. Her women particularly are trapped. They seek self-realization, but the odds against them – physically, spiritually, and psychologically – are often insurmountable. This pattern can also be seen in Bonner's play *Exit, An Illusion*. Outwardly silent, her characters' intense desire to triumph is revealed in the feverish outpouring of interior monologue. While Bonner addresses the problems of gender, class, and race, in many stories she also transcends these external factors in order to probe deeper psychological states.

Bonner sets many of her stories in a patchwork Chicago neighborhood where European immigrants live side by side with Afro-Americans, some from the South. Although her portrayal of their lives focuses on their tragedies and her vision tends to be bleak, she also seems to sustain the possibility that men and women can find their voices and achieve wholeness.

A notebook of short stories, unpublished (with the exception of "One True Love") at the time of Bonner's death in 1971, contains six completed works handwritten in fountain pen and dated from 1937 to 1941. The stories include "On the Altar" (29 1/3 pages), "High Stepper" (11 1/2 pages), "One True Love" (almost 13 pages), "Stones for Bread" (slightly over 18 1/2 pages), "Reap It As You Sow It" (17 1/2 pages), and "Light in Dark Places" (11 1/2 pages). Each is dated at the beginning and end, possibly giving the period of composition. On page six is an unfinished draft entitled "White Man's War."

The completed stories were finally published in 1987 in *Frye Street and Environs: The Collected Works of Marita Bonner*. However, it contains no bibliographical listing for the stories as they first appeared in *Crisis* and *Opportunity*, nor is "And I Passed By," a story published under her pseudonym in Johnson's *Ebony and Topaz*, included.

Four of the six notebook stories present situations in which black women and their vulnerability are portrayed. "On the Altar" is the tale of a young black girl's romance thwarted by the manipulations of her socially ambitious grandmother and complicitous mother. Beth, a girl with "curly light brown hair" elopes with high school classmate Jerry Johnson, who is much darker-skinned and of a lower social class. Beth's family rejects Jerry because they fear his offspring are likely to be "tar kettles," thus threatening their tenuous limbo between the "black black" community and their alternative to passing into white society: a fair-skinned, but segregated from whites, bourgeoisie. The grandmother, with her black taffeta garments, "Queen Victoria Style," is the villain who arranges the annulment of Beth's marriage. The stillbirth of Beth's child is but the beginning of her demise, as the grandmother schemes to wed her granddaughter to a wealthier, socially prominent, light-skinned man. Like the novel of manners of the nineteenth century, this piece revolves around marital matchmaking, but Marita Bonner infuses subtle observations of the black experience into her story. Her images of black middle-class matriarchy and intergenerational conflict are dimensions for further exploration.

Bonner's plays are also responsive to social issues complicated by the dynamics of sex and class, and particularly race. *The Purple Flower* is a historical allegory of racial oppression in America, in which the author exposes racism as a political tool to maintain the status quo of the dominant race. Her story "Nowhere" represents the social, political, economic, and educational impoverishments of people of color in the United States, and "Somewhere" represents the privileges and opportunities of white society. In the latter story, discussion takes place among the "Us" concerning theories of uplift (Booker T. Washington, W. E. B. Du Bois), with the final realization being that money, education, and hard work alone will not get them "Somewhere." Finest Blood declares, "White Devil! God speaks to you through me!–Hear Him!–Him! You have taken blood; there can be no other way. You will have to give blood! Blood!"

Curiously, Bonner did not publish after 1941–the year she joined the Church of Christ Scientist. She continued to teach and reside in Chicago until her death (apparently from smoke inhalation) in 1971. Some of Marita Odette Bonner Occomy's papers, including the notebook, are housed at Radcliffe's Schlesinger Library in Cambridge, Massachusetts.

SELECT BIBLIOGRAPHY

Primary

Drama

Exit, an Illusion. Crisis (October 1929): 335-36, 352.

The Pot Maker. Opportunity (February 1927): 43-46.

The Purple Flower. Crisis (January 1928): 9-11, 28, 30.

IN ANTHOLOGIES

Hatch and Shine, *Black Theatre U.S.A.*, 1974. *The Purple Flower.*

Fiction

"Black Fronts." *Opportunity* (July 1938): 210-14.

"Drab Rambles." *Opportunity* (December 1927): 335-36, 354-56.

Frye Street and Environs: The Collected Works of Marita Bonner, ed. Flynn and Strickland, 1987. Includes first publication of "High Stepper," "Light in Dark Places," "On the Altar," "Reap It as You Sow It," and "Stones for Bread."

"The Hands." *Opportunity* (August 1925): 235-37.

"Hongry Fire." *Crisis* (December 1939): 360-62, 377.

"The Makin's." *Opportunity* (January 1939): 18-21.

"Nothing New." *Crisis* (November 1926): 17-20.

"Of Jimmie Harris." *Opportunity* (August 1933): 242-44.

"One Boy's Story." *Crisis* (November 1927): 297-99, 316, 318-20. [Published under pseudonym.]

"One True Love." *Crisis* (February 1941): 46-47, 58-59.

"Patch Quilt." *Crisis* (March 1940): 71-72, 92.

"A Possible Triad on Black Notes." *Opportunity* (July 1933): 205-7.

"The Prison Bound." *Crisis* (September 1926): 225-26.

"Sealed Pod." *Opportunity* (March 1936): 88-91.

"Three Tales of Living." *Opportunity* (September 1933): 269-71.

"Tin Can." *Opportunity* (July 1934): 202-5; (August 1934): 236-40.

"The Whipping." *Crisis* (June 1939): 172-74.

"The Young Blood Hungers." *Crisis* (May 1928): 151, 172.

IN ANTHOLOGIES

Johnson, Charles S., *Ebony and Topaz*, [1927] 1971. "And I Passed By" [under pseudonym].

UNPUBLISHED

"White Man's War" (uncompleted)

Nonfiction

"On Being Young, a Woman, and Colored." *Crisis* (June 1925): 63-65.

Review of *Autumn Love Cycle*, by Georgia Douglas Johnson. *Opportunity* (April 1929): 130.

Review of *Gritny People*, by Robert Emmett Kennedy. *Opportunity* (June 1928): 184.

Secondary

Abramson Doris E., "Angelina Weld Grimké, Mary Burrill, Georgia Douglas Johnson, and Marita O. Bonner: An Analysis of Their Plays," 1985.

Arata and Rotoli, *Black American Playwrights, 1800 to the Present*, 1976.

Campbell, Dorothy, *Index to Black American Writers in Collective Biographies*, 1983.

Crosson, Wilhelmina [Bonner family friend], Interview with authors, Boston and Wellesley, Mass., 1986.

Ellis, *Opportunity; A Journal of Negro Life*, 1971.

Fairbanks and Engeldinger, *Black American Fiction*, 1978.

Flynn, Joyce, "Marita Bonner Occomy," 1987.

French, Fabre, Singh, and Fabre, *Afro-American Poetry and Drama*, 1979.

Hatch and Abdullah, *Black Playwrights, 1823-1977*, 1977.

Kallenbach, *Index to Black American Literary Anthologies*, 1979.

Kellner, *The Harlem Renaissance*, 1984.

Miller, "Black Women Playwrights from Grimké to Shange: Selected Synopses of Their Works," 1982.

Occomy, Warwick Gale, son of Marita Bonner Occomy. Interview.

Richardson, *Black Women and Religion*, 1980.

Rose Bibliography Project, *Analytical Guide and the Indexes to "The Crisis," 1910-1960*, 1975.

Roses and Randolph, "Marita Bonner: In Search of Other Mothers' Gardens," 1987.

Rush, Myers, and Arata, *Black American Writers Past and Present*, 1975.

BRIGHT, NELLIE RATHBORNE (1902-1976)

Editor

Educator

Essayist

Poet

Short-story writer

Nellie Rathborne Bright was a highly respected author and educator in Philadelphia from the 1920s until her death. Although her parents were from the Virgin Islands, and her birthplace was Savannah, Georgia, she was raised in Philadelphia. Bright was the daughter of an Episcopal clergyman and therefore a beneficiary of that Afro-American middle-class privilege – a formal education. She attended the Philadelphia School of Pedagogy and the University of Pennsylvania, where she received a B.A. in 1923 and an M.A. in 1925. Originally painting and music were her chief interests, to which she added writing in 1923. The majority of the short stories, poetry, and essays she wrote on Afro-American history remained unpublished, as she was occupied with her duties as a teacher in the Philadelphia public school system. She spent 1925-26 studying at Oxford University and at the Sorbonne, returning to Philadelphia in 1927.

Although the most acclaimed center of cultural activity among participants in the New Negro Movement was Harlem, Philadelphia also had a large population of Afro-Americans active in pursuit of the New Negro ideals. One of the city's best-known publications was *Black Opals*, which evolved as the efforts of "older New Negroes to encourage younger members" (30). In "Philadelphia's Afro-American Literary Circle and the Harlem Renaissance," Vincent Jubilee describes *Black Opals* as more of a pamphlet (eight-by-five inches) than a journal or magazine. Nevertheless, the list of Renaissance figures that published in *Black Opals* was not insignificant: Gwendolyn Bennett,* Bessie Calhoun Bird,* Marita O. Bonner,* Nellie R. Bright,* Mae V. Cowdery,* Arthur Huff Fauset, Jessie Redmon Fauset,* Ottie B. Graham,* Langston Hughes, Alain Locke, Gertrude P. McBrown,* Evelyn C. Reynolds,* and others.

One of the "older group," Bright was a frequent contributor to *Black Opals* as poet, essayist, and drama critic, as well as its coeditor (with Arthur Huff Fauset). Bright's poem "Longings" appeared in the debut issue and gave the magazine its title: "I want to look deep in a pool at night, and see the / stars / flash flame like fire in black opals." "To One Who Might Have Been My Friend," which hints at the theme of interracial love, also appeared in the

Christmas 1927 issue, and she wrote a review of Leslie Pinkney Hill's *Toussaint L' Ouverture* in the third issue (June 1928).

Bright's arena was not limited to *Black Opals*. She won third prize for a personal experience sketch in *Opportunity*. In November of 1927 her essay "Black" was published in the same magazine. The poet also published in the *Carolina Magazine*, the official literary publication of the University of North Carolina. Unfortunately, according to Jubilee, Philadelphia's black press ignored the literary and intellectual sector of the Afro-American community and its accomplishments. Although clippings of photographs and notices of political leaders, church leaders, society matrons, and debutantes of the period are extant, photographs of Nellie Bright and most of her literary colleagues do not appear. Neglect by local media possibly contributed to the demise of *Black Opals*.

After its cessation, Bright's work was obscure until the appearance of a history book for children which she coauthored with Arthur Huff Fauset in 1969, *America: Red, White, Black, Yellow*. Involved with community service, Bright was not altogether unknown, however. The educator was honored by groups like the Philadelphia Fellowship Commission, concerned with neighborhood development projects dealing with all colors and religions.

In her prize-winning essay "Black" Bright relates her experiences during a trip by steamship from America to Europe. She attempts to buy a third-class tourist ticket, repeatedly being told by "Nordics" that there are no vacancies and that they "don't sell tourist third to Negroes." Five steamship agencies later, she pays for what she thinks is a "tourist third" ticket but finds on sailing day that she is to travel in the bowels of the ship, where winches are "black with shining grease" and steerage passengers must "sit on coils" because there are no chairs.

Bright recalls how her European fellow passengers – Spanish, Welsh, Polish, etc. – are unconscious of her skin color: "They were Nordics, to be sure, but they had seemed kind. ... Perhaps, after all these people were different from Americans in that they did not despise my color." As the "Nordics" chatter about their homelands, the author's throat tightens when an Englishman asks, "Are you going home too?" She can barely reply, "No, America is my home – I'm off on a holiday." Bright is lost in the sting of "black isolation": "How could he know ... that my holidays were honey drained from crystal cups with jagged edges?"

She is further incapacitated by her alienation when she meets Oojoula, a Nigerian who is upset by his experiences in America. A white social worker approaches Bright, asking her to comfort Oojoula since they are both black. It is then that she realizes the abyss of cultural differences cannot be bridged by mere skin color, as is assumed. She cannot claim Oojoula's land as her own; in fact, he has more in common with the "Nordics" because he has a home and a culture to call his own – he has not been deprived of his ethnic and cultural heritage.

As Bright and many Afro-Americans found, travel in Europe and other foreign countries supplied perspective and hope to their experience as people of color. Being treated civilly by white people from foreign countries exposed American racism as a "peculiar beast," not necessarily a global obsession.

SELECT BIBLIOGRAPHY

Primary

Nonfiction

America: Red, White, Black, Yellow. With Arthur Huff Fauset. Philadelphia: Franklin Publishing Co., 1969.

"Black" [essay]. *Opportunity* (November 1927): 331-34.

Review of *Toussaint L'Ouverture*, by Leslie Pinkney Hill. *Black Opals* (June 1928).

Poetry

"Longings." *Black Opals* (Spring 1927).

"Query." *Black Opals* (Christmas 1927).

"To One Who Might Have Been My Friend." *Black Opals* (Christmas 1927).

Secondary

Ellis, *Opportunity; A Journal of Negro Life*, 1971.

Jubilee, "Philadelphia's Afro-American Literary Circle and the Harlem Renaissance," 1980.

Kellner, *The Harlem Renaissance*, 1984.

BROWN, CHARLOTTE HAWKINS (1882-1961)

Educator

Essayist

Short-story writer

Charlotte Hawkins believed gentility and mannerliness to be essential elements if Afro-Americans were to win social respect and acceptance. She also thought interracial contacts an important part of the Negro student's education, and maintained that her campus was one of the first public interracial meeting places in North Carolina. As teacher, president, and financial director of the Alice Freeman Palmer Institute in North Carolina, Hawkins needed more than financial support, especially when the surrounding white community was aroused by the  prospect of the radical ideas – like social equality – a northern-educated woman would instill in her students.

Hawkins-Brown wrote many articles and short stories. Her best-known book, *The Correct Thing to Do, to Say, to Wear*, gave her a reputation as "social dictator," but it nonetheless proved to be influential with young people in both public and private schools across the nation. It incorporated the practices and teachings of the Palmer Institute.

Although Hawkins-Brown was often accused of being a "social dictator" – even "accommodationist" by some – her actions often belied such claims. She frequently spoke to audiences at colleges and universities, including Mount Holyoke, Radcliffe, Smith, and Wellesley, where she would expound not only on the need for progressive race relations but on the complexities of relations between white women and women of color. She openly denounced lynching at a time when it was perilous to do so and publicly declared that black women were humiliated and violated by white men "a thousand times more" than black men offended white women. She was pleased when her rebellion against segregation laws would lead to her expulsion from Pullman berths and seats on southern trains. Hawkins-Brown even won a lawsuit in 1920 when she brought a discrimination case into court. And once, decades before the sit-ins of the civil rights movement, she deliberately entered a coffeeshop in North Carolina and told the waiter, "I am a black American, and I want a cup of coffee." She was served.

Writing was another forum for protest. In one of her better-known works, *"Mammy": An Appeal to the Heart of the South*, she paints the plight of slaves who, even after emancipation, continue to serve the owner of the plantation and his family with blind faithfulness, but without physical, spiritual, or emotional reward for their loyalty. Mammy and Pappy subsist in the rickety shambles of a cabin that Colonel Bretherton, their former master, refuses to fix, dismissing the old couple as likely to die soon. Yet the Colonel, en route to fight in the war that would keep her people in bondage, commands Mammy to "take care of my wife and children, and if I never come back, stay here; if they starve, starve with them; if they die, die with them." Mammy's promise to do so leads to her death.

Charlotte Hawkins was born to former slaves on 11 June 1883 in Henderson, North Carolina. Her parents separated following an unsuccessful marriage. Charlotte, mother Caroline, and brother Mingo were left on the land which had formerly been part of the Hawkins plantation. Taking the name of the land as their own, the family got along decently, living in a five-room moderately furnished house. Hawkins's mother (who took courses at Shaw University shortly after emancipation to learn how to read) was a source of great inspiration to Charlotte, always emphasizing the value of education, courtesy, self-esteem, and faith in God. At the age of six, Charlotte was one of a party of nineteen family members, including her mother (who had remarried), brother, grandmother, aunts, uncles, and cousins, that migrated to Boston, a haven for upwardly mobile Afro-Americans.

From an early age Hawkins exhibited leadership characteristics. At twelve she initiated a small kindergarten Sunday school program at her church. She graduated from the Allston Allison Grammar School in Cambridge with the honor of being graduation speaker. She then attended Cambridge English High and Latin School, also taking private lessons in art, music, and drama. Hawkins described these years as being relatively untainted by racial prejudice and segregation.

Although a normal school diploma was not required to teach in public schools, Hawkins, who wanted as much education as possible, enrolled at the

Massachusetts State Normal School since her mother considered her first choice, Radcliffe, impractical. Before attending the normal school, the high school senior had encountered Alice Freeman Palmer, who not only became Hawkins's most reliable mentor and benefactor but was also a member of the Massachusetts State Board of Education and the second president of Wellesley College. Hawkins, discovering Palmer's association with the board, wrote the philanthropist a letter. Acting upon a favorable recommendation from Maria Baldwin, Boston's first black principal, Palmer gave Hawkins financial aid for her first year of normal school.

Hawkins's first teaching position was offered in 1901 by the Women's Division of the American Missionary Association, a position at the Bethany Institute in McLeansville, North Carolina. In spite of a meager monthly salary of thirty dollars, her mother's encouragement and her own desire to help other Afro-Americans persuaded the young educator to accept the challenge. Thus, she left school almost a year early (with the assurance of administrators that she would be able to complete her normal school training during summer months) to serve as a missionary teacher to black students. When AMA funds for schooling became scarce, the school was forced to close. Charlotte Hawkins returned to Cambridge, inspired to open her own institution, as had Booker T. Washington, Lucy Laney, Fanny Coppin Jackson, and other Afro-American educators. She determined that one of the institution's primary strategies would be to educate young black students socially, as well as academically, to help dismantle segregation.

In 1902, with the support of Alice Palmer, Charlotte Hawkins founded the Alice Freeman Palmer Institute in Sedalia, North Carolina, about ten miles from Greensboro. Mrs. Palmer was responsible for endorsing the institute. She also solicited financial aid from many of her wealthy Boston friends. The institute included elementary, high school, and junior college instruction, with both academic and cultural courses at the junior college level.

After a short-lived marriage in 1911 to Edmund S. Brown, a Harvard graduate, Charlotte Hawkins resumed the presidency of the Palmer Institute until 1952, and served as financial director until 1955. She raised money for her school as a persuasive lecturer, mostly addressing the issue of race relations and the need for integration.

While managing Palmer, Hawkins actively participated in various organizations including the Federation of Women's Clubs of North Carolina, the National Association of Colored Women, and the International Congress of Women. She was one of the founders of the Commission on Interracial Relations and was elected to the Board of Education State of North Carolina Hall of Fame in 1926. In 1928 she became the only black woman to be elected a member of the 20th Century Club in Boston, which honors excellence in art, education, science, and religion.

As one who wanted always to extend her knowledge, she studied further at Simmons College (Boston) and Boston, Harvard, and Temple universities. She also received honorary degrees from Howard, Lincoln, and Wilberforce universities for her accomplishments. In 1944 the educator was elected as an honorary member of the Wellesley College Alumnae Association.

The official location for the papers of Dr. Charlotte Hawkins-Brown is the Elizabeth Schlesinger Library at Radcliffe College, but there are also records at the Greensboro Public Library, the Thomas F. Holgate Library at Bennett College, and the W. C. Jackson Library at the University of North Carolina at Greensboro.

SELECT BIBLIOGRAPHY

Primary

Fiction

"Mammy": An Appeal to the Heart of the South. Boston: Pilgrim Press, 1919.

IN ANTHOLOGIES

Shockley, *Afro-American Women Writers, 1746-1933*, 1988. *"Mammy": An Appeal to the South*.

Nonfiction

"A Biography." Undated. 19 pp. (Schlesinger Library of Women in America, Radcliffe College, Cambridge, Mass.).

"Cooperation between White and Colored Women" [essay]. *Missionary Review of the World* 45 (June 1922): 484-87.

The Correct Thing to Do, to Say, to Wear. Boston: Christopher Publishing House, 1941. Rev. ed. 1965.

"My Theory of Public Speaking" [essay]. (MS, Schlesinger Library.)

Secondary

Campbell, Dorothy, *Index to Black American Writers in Collective Biographies*, 1983.

Daniel, Sadie Iola, *Women Builders*, [1931] 1970.

Dannett, *Profiles of Negro Womanhood*, 1964.

Fairbanks and Engeldinger, *Black American Fiction*, 1978.

Herman, *Women in Particular*, 1984.

Hill, Roy, *Rhetoric of Racial Revolt*, 1964.

Logan and Winston, *Dictionary of American Negro Biography*, 1982.

Low and Clift, *Encyclopedia of Black America*, 1981.

Marteena, *The Lengthening Shadow of a Woman*, 1977.

Matthews, *Black American Writers, 1773-1949*, 1975.

Rush, Myers, and Arata, *Black American Writers Past and Present*, 1975.

Salk, *A Layman's Guide to Negro History*, 1967.

Sims-Wood, *The Progress of Afro-American Women*, 1980.

Spradling, *In Black and White*, 1980.

Stewart, Ruth Ann, "Charlotte Hawkins Brown," 1980.

BROWN, HALLIE QUINN (1845 or 1860?-1949)

Biographer

Although the year of her birth differs widely in various sources, it is possible that Hallie Quinn Brown lived to be at least a hundred years old and perhaps four years beyond that. Like Mary Church Terrell,* Ida B. Wells-Barnett,* and other black female advocates of civil rights and women's suffrage, Brown was an important voice addressing the American white majority on issues of black and female equality. Her career bridged the nineteenth and twentieth centuries.

She was born in Pennsylvania to freed slaves, the fifth of six children of Thomas Arthur and Frances Jane Scroggins Brown. The family moved to a farm in Chatham, Ontario, Canada, when Hallie was still a small child and there she acquired her early education. From this farm she was sent to Wilberforce University, the well-known African Methodist Episcopal Church institution in Wilberforce, Ohio, where she graduated with a B.S. degree in 1873. Later the family moved to Wilberforce and built a home there, Homewood Cottage. She also studied in the Chautauqua Lecture School, graduating in 1886 after several years of summer school.

Brown's first teaching position was on a plantation in South Carolina, where she taught adults, particularly the aged, to read the Bible. Later she took charge of a school on the Sonora plantation in Mississippi and held teaching positions in the public schools of Yazoo, Mississippi, and Columbia, South Carolina. Other positions followed: from 1885 to 1887 Brown served as dean of Allen University in Columbia, headed a night school for adult migrants from the South, and served as lady principal (the title then used for dean of women) of Tuskegee Institute (1892-93) and as professor of elocution at Wilberforce.

While teaching in the public schools of Dayton, Brown had met a Professor Robertson of the Boston School of Oratory and enrolled in one of his courses. She soon launched her career as a speaker and was much in demand in New York, Philadelphia, and other cities. Bishop Daniel A. Payne, whose teachings greatly inspired Brown and with whose family she lived for two years, sponsored a southern speaking tour for her. She appeared in major cities of North Carolina, Georgia, Alabama, Louisiana, Arkansas, and other states.

In 1894 Brown made the first of several European trips. This one extended over six years, during which she lectured and recited in the major cities of Great Britain. In 1895 she spoke at the World's Women's Christian Temperance Union in London. On 7 July 1899, she was entertained by Queen Victoria at tea in Windsor Castle. She spoke at an entertainment of the Princess of Wales, later Queen Alexandra. During Queen Victoria's jubilee year celebration, Brown was the guest of the Lord Mayor of London. The same year she attended the International Conference of Women in London.

Brown returned to Europe in 1910 as a representative of the Women's Parent Missionary Society of the A.M.E. Church at the World Missionary Conference held in Edinburgh, Scotland, 14-23 June. On both of her trips to England Brown raised funds for Wilberforce from an English philanthropist.

After her European travels she spent many years as instructor in the English department and was a member of the Board of Trustees of Wilberforce University. Until a few years before her death Brown taught a Sunday school class of college students.

Women's suffrage became one of Brown's causes when, as a student, she heard Susan B. Anthony speak at Wilberforce. It is likely that she began her later crusade for women's rights in 1900 when she requested the A.M.E. Church to elect her to the office of secretary of education. She did not win the appointment but continued to fight for equal rights for women. She traveled extensively pleading for full citizenship for women, and was an ardent supporter of civil rights for Negroes.

In 1924 she spoke at the Republican National Convention on behalf of Warren Harding's nomination and civil rights, probably the first black woman to make such an appearance.

As early as May 1925, during the All-American Musical Festival of the International Council of Women meeting in Washington Auditorium in Washington, D.C., she delivered a scathing speech protesting the segregated seating of Negroes at the event. Brown declared in her protest that unless the proposed policy of segregation was changed, she would withdraw all performances by Negroes. "This is a gathering of women of the world here and color finds no place in it," said Brown. As a result of this speech, two hundred black entertainers refused to take part in the program and the black members of the audience left the auditorium.

Brown died in Wilberforce on 16 September 1949 of coronary thrombosis and was buried in the family plot in nearby Massie's Creek Cemetery.

Her writings, curiously, are very much in the nineteenth-century Victorian mold – pious descriptions of black and white leaders painted as heroes and heroines on a par with Moses, Paul, Martin Luther, and Abraham Lincoln. *Homespun Heroines* (1926), compiled by Brown, details the accomplishments of some sixty women leaders from colonial times to the early twentieth century. On its dedication page is a stanza of verse by Clara Ann Thompson* praising black women ("Through all the blight of slavery / They kept their womanhood, / And now they march with heads erect, / To fight for all things good"). Throughout, Brown emphasizes the qualities of energy, shrewdness, prudence, devotion, and selflessness in both women and men. Although she views the paramount role of women to be supporters of their husbands and children, she also expects women to be "in touch with things vital and progressive" and praises "that old school of heroines which crossed cudgels with the enemy and battled unceasingly for the full manhood rights of the Negro." Some of the women praised are founders of schools, physicians, and public figures.

Tales My Father Told Me (1925) contains three highly romanticized tales of young women escaping from slavery and finding happiness in the North. Included, too, is a history of black spirituals and a didactic story about the ill effects of drinking, in accordance with her participation in the temperance movement.

Brown's unpublished papers, lectures, correspondence, and other memorabilia are in the Hallie Q. Brown Memorial Library of Central State University (Wilberforce).

SELECT BIBLIOGRAPHY

Primary

Drama

Trouble in Turkeytrot Church. A dramatization of the story by the Reverend P. A. Nichol. Privately printed in 1917.

Fiction

Tales My Father Told Me and Other Stories. Wilberforce, Ohio, 1925.

Nonfiction

Bits and Odds: A Choice Selection of Recitations for School, Lyceum, and Parlor Entertainments. Xenia, Ohio: Chew, 1884.

Our Women: Homespun Heroines and Other Women of Distinction. Xenia, Ohio: Aldine Publishing Co., 1926.

Our Women: Past, Present, and Future. N.p.: N.d.

Pen Pictures of Pioneers at Wilberforce. Xenia, Ohio: Aldine Publishing Co., 1937.

Secondary

Bontemps, *American Negro Poetry*, 1969.

Campbell, *Index to Black American Writers in Collective Biographies*, 1983.

Dunlap, "A Biographical Sketch of Hallie Quinn Brown," 1963.

Herman, *Women in Particular*, 1984.

Kellner, *The Harlem Renaissance*, 1984.

Logan and Winston, *Dictionary of American Negro Biography*, 1982.

Low and Clift, *Encyclopedia of Black America*, 1981.

McFarlin, "Hallie Quinn Brown – Black Woman Elocutionist: 1845-1949," 1975.

Mainiero, *American Women Writers*, vol. 1, 1979.

Matthews, *Black American Writers, 1773-1949*, 1975.

Neely, *Women of Ohio: A Record of Their Achievements in the History of the State*, 1939.

Newsome, "Miss Hallie Q. Brown, Lecturer and Reciter," 1942.

Newsome, "The Significance of Hallie Q. Brown's Closing Days," 1949.

Richardson, *Black Women and Religion*, 1980.

Sherman, *Invisible Poets*, 1974.

Sims-Wood, *The Progress of Afro-American Women*, 1980.

Spradling, *In Black and White*, 1980.

Wesley, "Hallie Quinn Brown," 1971.

BURRILL, MARY ("MAMIE") (ca. 1882-1946)

Playwright

Biographical information on this author of two highly political plays is scanty. Records in the Emerson College archives show that Burrill was admitted to Emerson from a Washington, D.C., high school in 1901, that she was a student there from the fall of 1901 through the spring of 1904, the program at that time being three years, and that she returned for postgraduate work in 1929. Burrill received a B.L.I. (bachelor of literary interpretation) degree in 1930 and published a play in the college yearbook. The play, deemed "the Best Junior Play of the Year," was entitled *Unto the Third and Fourth Generations: A One Act Play of Negro Life*. Between these two periods at Emerson, Burrill taught English and drama at Armstrong Manual and Dunbar high schools in Washington.

Gloria T. Hull has established that Burrill and Angelina Weld Grimké* knew each other well. According to Hull, among the Grimké family papers at the Moorland-Spingarn Collection at Howard University is "a youthful letter" to Angelina dated February 1896. Mixed with apologies, school gossip, and church news are reminders from "Mamie" of secret good times together and shared love: "Could I just come to meet thee once more, in the old sweet way, just coming at your calling, and like an angel bending o'er you breathe into your ear, 'I love you.'" Grimké, who later taught with Burrill in the Washington, D.C., school system, responds in even more ardent terms in a letter written later that year from Carleton Academy in Minnesota. Hull contends that this constitutes documentation of a "clearly Lesbian relationship" between the two writers. It must be taken into account, however, that Grimké was sixteen years old at the time and Burrill perhaps younger (since Grimké calls her "little one") and that Victorian discourse allowed for abstract eroticism in the absence of the physical. More research and analysis is needed in order to comprehend the nature of the bonds that united Grimké and Burrill, and indeed other black women writers of the early twentieth century.

In addition to the play in the Emerson College yearbook, Burrill published at least two more, *Aftermath* and *They That Sit in Darkness*, both of 1919 and both advocating a radical stance on issues of gender and race. *They That Sit in Darkness* deals with an ailing mother and the seven little ones she must struggle to clothe and feed, as her oldest daughter prepares to go off to study at Tuskegee. A visiting nurse regrets that state law forbids her from giving the mother, Mrs. Jasper, the contraceptive information that she has "a right to know." Mrs. Jasper and her family dream of a time when they will be able to put aside a day's work to play family games and tell Bible stories. But the woman's heart has been weakened by repeated childbirth and she dies.

As the play closes, the eldest daughter prepares to renounce her education and take up her mother's burden.

Originally published in Margaret Sanger's *Birth Control Review*, a monthly publication that advocated contraception, the play conveys the message that a woman has an inalienable right to freedom of choice in matters concerning her own body. Like other women activists at the time, Burrill shows a concern for this cardinal point of women's emancipation. James Hatch (*Black Theatre U.S.A.*) notes that some of the characterization in *They That Sit in Darkness* is accomplished through the speech idiom, in a dialect rendering that is much more effective than that attempted by white playwrights of the same period. Burrill's drama does not seem dated even as we read it today and it could probably be very effective on the stage.

The subject of race, not an overt issue in the aforementioned play, is the theme of *Aftermath*. Here Burrill chronicles the plight of the black family realistically, as did most black playwrights of the period, rather than symbolically. A black veteran returning from World War I arrives at his rural home in South Carolina to find that his father has been hanged. The play deals with his measures to seek revenge for the lynching. The play was first published in the *Liberator* in April 1919 and performed by the Krigwa Players on 8 May 1928.

SELECT BIBLIOGRAPHY

Primary

Drama

Aftermath. *Liberator* (April 1919).

They That Sit in Darkness. *Birth Control Review* (September 1919). Also in Hatch and Shine, *Black Theatre U.S.A.*, 1974.

IN ANTHOLOGIES

Hatch and Shine, *Black Theatre U.S.A.*, 1974. *They That Sit in Darkness*.

Secondary

Arata, *More Black American Playwrights*, 1978.

Arata and Rotoli, *Black American Playwrights, 1800 to the Present*, 1976.

Belcher, "The Place of the Negro in the Evolution of the American Theatre," 1945.

French, Fabre, Singh, and Fabre, *Afro-American Poetry and Drama, 1760-1975*, 1979.

Hatch and Abdullah, *Black Playwrights, 1823-1977*, 1977.

Hull, "Under the Days: The Buried Life and Poetry of Angelina Weld Grimké," 1979.

Kallenbach, *Index to Black American Literary Anthologies*, 1979.

BUSH (BANKS), OLIVIA WARD (1869-1944)

Poet

Playwright

Columnist

According to Bernice F. Guillaume, great-granddaughter of Olivia Ward Bush-Banks and author of "Factors Shaping the Social Cultural Network of a Nineteenth Century Writer," the work of her great-grandmother is "a continuum between the black intelligentsia born during Reconstruction and those of the Harlem Renaissance" (32). Within her evolution from New England poet to Harlem Renaissance participant, Bush-Banks's literature reflects the complexity of her Native American/Afro-American heritage.

Bush-Banks stated, "I seemed to have lost my identity regarding the distinctness of race, being of African and Indian descent. Both parents possessed some negro blood, and were also descendants of the Montauk tribe of Indians, which tribe formerly occupied the eastern end of Long Island at Montauk" (32). As a result, she, like Florida Ruffin Ridley,* walked in both the African and Native American traditions; this twofold influence is evidenced by photographs of Bush-Banks in tribal raiment, several poems, and an unpublished play dealing with Indian life. But *Driftwood*, her largest collection of published poetry and prose, has Afro-American themes, among them the atrocities of lynching and discrimination.

Born in Sag Harbor, Long Island, New York, Olivia Ward was the daughter of Abraham and Eliza Draper Ward, whose families had been free since 1810 and 1830, respectively. After the death of her mother, Abraham Ward, a Mormon and polygamist, moved to Rhode Island; Olivia was sent to be raised by her aunt, Maria Draper, who instilled in her niece ethnic pride and Christian values. Bush-Banks completed her education at Providence High School, specializing in nursing. She had to set aside her literary aspirations to provide for her two daughters, Rosamund and Marie, following the departure of her first husband, Frank Bush.

Although Bush-Banks became involved in drama and playwrighting as an assistant dramatic director at the Robert Gould Shaw Community House in Boston, her poetry dominates her literary accomplishments. A preliminary volume, entitled *Original Poems*, was published just prior to the turn of the century, in 1899. It rejected the accommodationist tone that permeated most of the contemporary literature by and about Afro-Americans and, instead, reaffirmed the tradition of black New England writers like Frances Ellen Watkins Harper. *Original Poems* is nonetheless faithful to what Guillaume describes as the three major historical sources of Afro-American literature:

Protestant religion, attachment to the rural South, and uncertainty about the future for black America.

Dedicated to the poet's aunt Maria Draper, her major work, *Driftwood*, contains twenty-four poems and three prose compositions of reflection on Afro-American themes laced with history, pride, and protest. Of this literary accomplishment, Paul Laurence Dunbar wrote, "Your book should be an inspiration to the women of our race." It includes salutations to Afro-Americans (men and women) and white philanthropists alike. Bush-Banks uses the title of *Driftwood* to construct a metaphor that applies to both Native Americans and Afro-Americans: their lives are driftwood; once trees, firm with roots, they are now ravished, uprooted, and tossed about by the tide and tempests of life's oppressors and circumstances. She expands this metaphor in the final stanza of the poem "Evening":

> Ah yes, and thus it is with these our lives,
> Some poor misshapen remnant still survives,
> Of what was once a fair and beauteous form,
> And yet some dwelling may be made more bright,
> Some one afar may catch a gleam of light,
> After the fury of the blighting storm.

In the poem "Heart Throbs" Bush-Banks laments, like Georgia Douglas Johnson* in *The Heart of a Woman* and other black women writers, the anguish of the black mother over the grim realities facing her children:

> The mother of the dusky babe,
>   Surveys with aching heart
> Bright prospects, knowing all the while,
>   Her offspring shares no part.
> The child attains to manhood's years,
>   Still conscious of the same,
> While others boast of Life's success,
>   He knows it but in name.

Bush-Banks clearly drew spiritual strength from her Protestant faith, as many black women writers did. Her only published play, *Memories of Calvary*, is an example. It reiterates the Easter story, celebrating the restoration of all peoples available through belief in the crucifixion and resurrection of Jesus Christ. The main character, Anxious Seeker, an allegorical character representing humankind searching for total fulfillment, is designated to be played by a woman, as is the second most prominent character, Night. There is an invisible male quartet and a choir of mixed voices; each sings only once. Why Bush-Banks sets the characters in roles by gender is unclear. The play itself is eight pages with five poems on remaining pages; the author suggests that the poems may be read at the end of a production of the play. Unfortunately the drama has no publication date, which prevents Bush-Banks from being recognized as one of the first black playwrights.

After World War I Olivia Ward Bush married Anthony Banks. While residing in Chicago for fourteen years, she taught drama in the public schools and opened the Bush-Banks School of Expression. During the depression she lived in New York State and was a cultural arts columnist for the *Westchester Record Courier*. In her column she encouraged participation in the New Negro Renaissance. She was involved in the Federal Writers' Project program, and accepted a position as drama coach at the Abyssinia Community Center in Harlem. She also kept a studio in New York City where individuals of mixed ethnicity could gather to exchange opinions, performances, and exhibitions. Individuals like Countee Cullen, Julia Ward Howe, Paul Robeson, and W. E. B. Du Bois were among her friends.

Although Bush-Banks drew from the aura of primitivism and negritude to expound on the Afro-American experience, she also wanted to reconstruct her Native American past. She wrote *Indian Trails*, a three-act play with eighteen characters, eleven of whom have Indian names. *Indian Trails* mourns the destruction of the Montauk community, but concludes with the idyllic anticipation that one day the "Great White Father" will relinquish the land he has stolen. Its theme is analogous to the efforts of Afro-American history scholars as they reconstruct the rich cultural heritage bestowed on America by peoples of African descent, verifying and reclaiming their role in American history. Bush-Banks's repertoire includes unpublished, recently discovered material known as the "Aunt Viney sketches." They feature a black woman of the depression era who, in dialect, delivers shrewd, insightful, humorous commentaries on a variety of situations and ideas contemporary with the 1930s. Bush-Banks also began an autobiography, entitled "The Lure of the Distance," according to Ann Allen Shockley. In this respect she joins many black women writers whose testament of their lives and visions is an unfinished one.

SELECT BIBLIOGRAPHY

Primary

Drama

Aunt Viney sketches [six sketches].

"Indian Trails" [three-act play].

Memories of Calvary. Philadelphia, Pa.: A.M.E. Book Concern, n.d.

"Shadows" [dramatic monologue].

"A Shantytown Scandal" [one-act play].

Nonfiction

"The Lure of the Distance" [unfinished autobiography].

Poetry

Driftwood. Cranston: Atlantic Printing Co., 1914.

"The Great Adventure." *Messenger* (October 1923).

Original Poems. Providence: Press of Loeis a Baset, 1899.

IN ANTHOLOGIES

Shockley, *Afro-American Women Writers, 1746-1933*, 1988. "Fancies"; "Voices."

Secondary

Ellis, *Opportunity; A Journal of Negro Life*, 1971.

Guillaume, "Olivia Ward Bush: Factors Shaping the Social and Cultural Outlook of a Nineteenth-Century Writer," 1980.

Matthews, *Black American Writers, 1773-1949*, 1975.

Porter, *North American Negro Poets*, 1945.

Richardson, *Black Women and Religion*, 1980.

Rush, Myers and Arata, *Black American Writers Past and Present*, 1975.

Shockley, *Afro-American Women Writers, 1746-1933*, 1988.

BUTLER, ANNA MABEL LAND (1901-1989)

Editor

Journalist

Poet

Anna Land, the author of three volumes of rich and intricate poetry, was born on 7 October 1901 in Philadelphia and has been a resident of Atlantic City, New Jersey, since the age of one. Her father, John Weaver Land, Sr., a doorman at the Hotel Dennis, was also a poet and published *A Few Original Verses* (date unknown). Anna, in fact, excerpted one of his poems for inclusion in her own volume of poetry. Anna Land married and had one son, Maurice Alexander Hayes, who died in 1943.

She attended Trenton State Teachers College from 1920 to 1922 and again in 1936, Temple University in 1953, and the University of Maryland, 1942-45. Her first career was that of an elementary school teacher, 1922-64, and then head teacher-director at the Morris Child Care Center, 1969-72. She published poetry in the *Pittsburgh Courier*, 1936-65, and was an editor-reporter for the *Philadelphia Tribune*, 1965-72. She also edited *Magazine Responsibility*, the official organ of the National Negro Business and Professional Women's Clubs, 1955-59.

Her first volume of poetry was *Album of Love Letters – Unsent*, in 1952, followed by *Touchstone* in 1961. Langston Hughes attended her first book party at the Warwick Hotel in New York. Anna Butler has a treasured picture of herself with Hughes at this event.

Touchstone, her second volume, includes many mysterious and haunting love poems such as "Your Gift," in which an intricate, almost baroque syntax entwines two metaphors: life as book and life as melody. Similar poems are "Request," "Ritual," and "Touchstone." Other poems celebrate nature's seasonal displays ("Lapidary") or describe both sleep and death as transitory states ("Metamorphosis"). Butler shows a vivid consciousness of the importance of seeking equality with courage. The poem "Reward" expresses through analogies that striving must precede fulfillment. "Prince first before king, / The stone found, then the jewel seen; / Seed's sown (not plant or flower), / rain follows after mists that are / a gift without request."

According to David Hudson, poet laureate for the state of Delaware from 1956 to 1960, *Touchstone* manifests "a concern for matter rather than form that makes it a collection superior in accomplishment to the somewhat aimless reaching for effectiveness characteristic of *Album of Love Letters – Unsent*, her first publication in verse" (*Touchstone*, 8). Her work is increasingly lyric in tone, "while acquiring the dramatic overtones instinctive to the woman poet." One of the best poems in his opinion is "Equalities," which speaks of the oneness of human beings notwithstanding class and race.

Butler believes "that God has given each of us at least one talent. . . . Those so endowed have a purpose in life to perpetuate the beauty and wonder of God's creations. Accepting this role we help others grow and experience a realization that God directs the lives of those who pause to listen and do His will. By serving others in love we grow as a person, and help others appreciate God" (Rush et al., 132).

Butler has been an active community figure and the recipient of awards for her teaching and club work.

SELECT BIBLIOGRAPHY

Primary

Poetry

Album of Love Letters – Unsent. Vol. 1, *Morning 'til Noon.* New York: Margent, 1952.

High Noon. Charleston, Ill.: Prairie Press Books, 1971.

Touchstone. Foreword by David Hudson. Provincetown, Mass.: Advocate Press for the Delaware Poetry Center, 1961, 29 pp.

Secondary

Campbell, Dorothy, *Index to Black American Writers in Collective Biographies*, 1983.

Deodene and French, *Black American Poetry since 1944*, 1971.

French, Fabre, Singh, and Fabre, *Afro-American Poetry and Drama*, 1979.

Rush, Myers, and Arata, *Black American Writers Past and Present*, 1975.

Williams, *American Black Women in the Arts and Social Sciences*, 1978.

CAMPBELL, HAZEL VIVIAN (?-?)

Short-story writer

Hazel Vivian Campbell, of New Rochelle, New York, published just two short stories in *Opportunity* in the mid-1930s and left no trace of her life and subsequent career.

The first of these stories is "Part of the Pack," a portrayal of a couple's efforts to survive in Harlem during the depression. Lu, a young Afro-American woman, resorts to stealing food in order to survive, as her husband, Steve, is unable to find work. When a close friend urges the two to join the fighting on the morning of an outbreak of riots (possibly the Harlem race riot of 1935), Steve refuses to go. Inevitably and tragically Steve's ideology of pacifism and Lu's violent desperation clash, illustrating the impossibility of remaining neutral in a climate polarized by racial inequality. The story also raises the issue of those content to be on welfare. The "relief life" makes them parasites and incapable of ever breaking out of the mold that social inequality has created, a reality they do not comprehend. The story's subtitle, "Another View of Night Life in Harlem" is an ironic reference to the glamor attached to Harlem in the Jazz Age.

"The Parasites" also illustrates the life of a young Afro-American couple living on welfare in a run-down city apartment. The two characters and their son live more comfortably now than they did when the husband worked for a salary inadequate to support the family. They prefer welfare and are unconcerned about its stigma. Conflict arises when an investigator from the welfare office arrives one morning to inform them that the husband will be put to work digging ditches. The story illustrates that forced "independence" from the government is a form of economic bondage and puts at risk the very survival of the family unit. The title expresses the situation of being at the mercy of the state and at the same time unable to escape from a stagnant existence.

In both stories, the style is simple and dramatic, with dialogue in black southern dialect. In "Part of the Pack" Campbell also shows skill in incorporating arrestingly ironic dialogue into her story. Her characters and their values are sharply and convincingly drawn, her vision a despairing one.

SELECT BIBLIOGRAPHY

Primary

Fiction

"Part of the Pack: Another View of Night Life in Harlem." *Opportunity* 13, no. 8 (August 1935): 234-37, 251.

Campbell, Hazel Vivian

"The Parasites." *Opportunity* (September 1936): 267-70.

Secondary

Ellis, *Opportunity; A Journal of Negro Life*, 1971.

CARTER, EUNICE ROBERTA HUNTON (1899-1970)

Literary critic
Short-story writer

Even in the pages of *Opportunity*, Eunice Roberta Hunton Carter is credited more for her achievements as scholar and lawyer than as writer. In light of the talent manifest in her book reviews, her short stories are somewhat disappointing, but her efforts to uplift blacks and women found a more effective forum in the occupations that overshadowed her fiction. Her mother, Addie Hunton,* too, is known less for her writing than for her lifelong work with organizations fighting for the same causes.

Born in Atlanta on 16 July 1899, Eunice Hunton was the daughter of William Alpheus Hunton of Canada, a well-known national executive with the YMCA, and Addie Waites Hunton, teacher, author, and activist. Eunice was the third of four children, but only she and her younger brother survived childhood. Both of her parents were committed to public service, a tradition impressed upon Eunice; they worked to establish YMCA services for blacks in Virginia and other southern states. But after the race riots in Atlanta in 1906, her family moved from the South to Brooklyn, New York.

Hunter's education was broad. She attended public schools in Brooklyn and then spent two years in a school in Strassburg, Germany, while her mother studied at Kaiser Wilhelm University. In 1917 she entered Smith College, graduating in 1921 with both an A.B. and an A.M. degree in political science. She wrote her master's thesis on reform in state government, paying particular attention to Massachusetts.

For the next eleven years she attended classes at Columbia University while working with various family service agencies. After marrying Lisle Carter, a Barbados-born dentist, in 1924, she enrolled in night classes in law at Fordham University, receiving her LL.D. degree in October 1932. She was admitted to the New York Bar Association in 1934 and opened a private practice. Like Alice Dunbar-Nelson* and others she participated actively in Republican politics and civic organizations. In 1934 she also made an unsuccessful run for office in the New York State Assembly.

Eunice Hunton Carter gained a foothold in state politics when Mayor Fiorello La Guardia appointed her secretary of the Committee on Conditions in Harlem after the area's race riots in 1935. That August, Special Prosecutor Thomas E. Dewey included her on his ten-member staff for a grand jury investigation into organized crime: she was the only woman and the only Afro-American member of the staff. Because much of the investigation centered around Harlem, Carter was an invaluable staff member, helping to develop crucial evidence. Later in 1935, in recognition of her work on his staff, District Attorney Dewey named her deputy assistant district attorney for New York County. She served in that capacity for the next ten years before returning to private practice. In June 1938, Smith College awarded her an honorary LL.D. degree, an act that *Opportunity* praised as a "reaffirm[ation of] its position of leadership in the education of women in America" (16 [September 1938]: 9).

Carter's association with *Opportunity* extends beyond her notices in its "Who's Who" columns. Apparently, her fiction was published exclusively in the magazine – sources mention no other. Her four known short stories follow the same pattern: meticulous, if cumbersome, description of background leading to a climactic pitch, and then slackening off quickly. In a genre as highly dependent on timing as is the short story, Carter's placement of climax and handling of resolution fail pointedly: a notable flatness results. Her attempts to poetically place the situation are also misdirected as they only further slow the narrative. But the striking, trenchant style that characterizes her nonfiction prose suits the book review form ideally.

Indeed, Carter was featured more often in *Opportunity* as book reviewer (six) than as fiction writer (four). Her reviews explored not only the literary merits of a work but its sociological and societal impact, taking especially into account whether the author was black or white, and qualified to write on race relations, the theme of most of the books she reviewed. Her positions were strongly pronounced if sometimes harsh, ringing with a finality that brooked no argument. In assessing Wallace Thurman's popular novel, *The Blacker the Berry*, for example, Carter savages the "vogue ... for literature by Negroes and about Negroes [that] is so great that there is no apparent incentive or compulsion to conform to any academic standards in the matter of construction." Carter was by no means averse to the use of subverted literary conventions to undermine white social conventions, for she rated Harry Liscomb's singularly absurd parody of Horatio Alger tales rather favorably. As her reviews reflect the respective tones of their subjects, they are uniformly entertaining, certainly more so than her short stories.

Throughout her life, Carter was actively involved in politics, campaigning especially for the rights of women. She was a charter member of the National Council of Negro Women with close friend Mary McLeod Bethune; she served as the organization's legal counsel and as member and chair of its board of trustees. In 1945 she and Bethune, as representatives of the NCNW, attended the founding conference of the United Nations in San Francisco. Carter remained as the official observer for the NCNW until 1952. Throughout her career with the United Nations, she was a consultant for the Economic and Social Council of the United Nations for the International Council of Women in 1947 and chair of the Committee of Laws. In 1955, at the UN conference in Geneva, she was elected to chair the International Conference of Non-Governmental Organizations. Following in the footsteps of her parents, Carter also served the YMCA as member of the National Board and the administrative committee for the foreign division.

Retired from her law practice in 1952, Carter was widowed in 1963. Throughout the final years of her life she remained very active with the NCNW and other organizations on a volunteer basis. She died at the Knickerbocker Hospital in New York City after an illness in January 1970.

SELECT BIBLIOGRAPHY

Primary

Fiction

"The Corner." *Opportunity* (April 1925): 114-15.

"Digression." *Opportunity* (December 1923): 359.

"Replica." *Opportunity* (September 1924): 276.

"Who Gives Himself." *Opportunity* (December 1924): 374.

Nonfiction

Review of *All God's Chillun Got Wings*, by Eugene O'Neill. *Opportunity* (April 1924): 112-13.

Review of *The Blacker the Berry*, by Wallace Berry. *Opportunity* (May 1929): 162.

Review of *Heat*, by Isa Glenn. *Opportunity* (October 1926): 325.

Review of *Holiday*, by Waldo Frank. *Opportunity* (February 1924): 59.

Review of *The Prince of Washington Square*, by Harry F. Lipscomb. *Opportunity* (September 1925): 281.

"A Story about Northern Negroes" [review of *Veiled Aristocrats*, by Gertrude Sanborn]. *Opportunity* (April 1924): 110-11.

Secondary

Ellis, *Opportunity; A Journal of Negro Life*, 1971.

Herman, *Women in Particular*, 1984.

Smith College Archives, Northampton, Mass.

Spradling, *In Black and White*, 1980.

CAUTION-DAVIS, ETHEL (1880-1981)

Educator

Poet

Short-story writer

Ethel Caution-Davis's writings resemble diary entries in their intensely personal nature, a quality possibly explained by the facts that writing for her was an avocation and that she wrote outside of any known literary circles or movements. The years she spent in Boston preceded the formation of the Saturday Quill Club, the Bostonian literary salon active from the mid-1920s to 1930.

She was born in Cleveland, Ohio. Upon the death of her parents, young Ethel was adopted by a Mrs. Davis of Boston and took the Davis name until her foster mother died. Subsequently she was known as Ethel Caution-Davis – and the only black student – to her classmates at Girls Latin School (dates of attendance are unclear) and Wellesley College (1908-12). Ethel worked in her free time and earned several scholarships to pay for her college tuition. She also devoted time to extracurricular activities, becoming a "Wearer of the W" for indoor track and serving as YWCA student secretary for black colleges across the country (some of the happiest years of her life, she told *Wellesley Alumnae* magazine).

After graduating as a Senior Wellesley College Scholar, Class of 1912, Ethel taught in Durham, North Carolina, for two years. She then moved west to Kansas City, where she taught at Summer High School and actively participated in church and civic organizations. Caution-Davis also served on the Executive Committee of the Citizens' Forum of the Kansas branch of the NAACP and continued to work for the YWCA. She was appointed dean of women at Talladega College, a post she held for three years, before spending several years with the public assistance program in New York City.

Her peripheral writing career evidently began in college, as some of her short poems and essays appear in the *Wellesley* magazine and the *News*. After graduation, her works were published in *Crisis*, the *Durham Advocate*, and *The Brownies Book* for children. One source also mentions a play she planned to stage in the winter of 1917, but there is no indication of its title or whether it was ever published.

Her poems are uniformly brief and classical in style. Beneath a formal tone and rhyme scheme lie surprisingly profound themes and deeply private sentiments. Nature also figures greatly in her work, as in "To–," a third-prize winner in *Crisis'* 1927 competition. Its melancholy moodiness stems from the poet's sense of lacking autonomy and freedom. Only nature, in its independence from humanity, seems capable of bringing pure joy. "Longing," a short piece in the *Wellesley* magazine (1911), is heavy with longings for "any and all things that are restless, solitary, inexplicable, for such is my mood today." "Last Night," published in *Crisis* eighteen years later, shifts more abruptly in mood as she dances deliriously "on the rim of the moon," reveling in nature's freedom, before "slip[ping] into my sober self / Just ere the break of day." In "Esthetic Experience," included in Braithwaite's *Anthology of Magazine Verse for 1926,* melancholy turns into acute pain in the last line: "Her more articulate ashes told our blunder."

Although Caution-Davis does not treat race as a theme extensively, in a few early poems she approaches the Afro-American condition uniquely. Often she chooses to explore an individual's personal spiritual nature rather than a group's position in society. "A Man," featured in the Easter 1916 issue of *Crisis*, expresses injustice not in terms of human interaction but in terms of the belief that all humans are created in His image: "For God in black and white is just the same." The next line–"Then, shall my fellowman set me no bounds"–refers to the civil and private liberties she envies in nature in her other works. Can the reader conclude, then, that her other poems are indeed race-related? In another approach, "In '61" broaches race historically in the form of a Civil War vignette. A Massachusetts soldier who is asked by a house slave if he's a "Mas' Yankee" irritatedly replies yes, but softens when he realizes his purpose in Charleston is to free a race, his own. How this simple story neatly addresses multiple issues–black-black relations, North-South divisions–is a good example of her elegantly compact style. In comparison, some of her later poems, like "Shopping," are disappointing in that they trivialize their themes through trite, unoriginal rhyme.

In later years, she was the director of Club Caroline, a residence club for women, before retiring to New Jersey. Life in retirement was rich for Caution-Davis, who though "a few blinks from blindness" tended a garden and kept up with literature through a volunteer reader and Talking Books. She died on 18 December 1981 in New York City.

SELECT BIBLIOGRAPHY

Primary

Fiction

"In '61." *Wellesley College News* (October 1911): 9.

"Longing." *Wellesley* magazine (April 1911): 300.

Poetry

"Being Inland." *Archive* (November 1925).

"Esthetic Experience." *Archive* (January 1926). Also in Braithwaite, *Anthology of Magazine Verse for 1926*, 1927.

"Last Night." *Crisis* (February 1929): 50.

"Long Remembering." *Crisis* (October 1928).

"A Man." *Crisis* (April 1916): 292.

"Shopping." *Crisis* (April 1929).

"Sonnet." *Archive* (April 1926).

"To –." *Crisis* (December 1927): 337.

"Unrest." *Archive* (October 1925).

IN ANTHOLOGIES

Cromwell, Turner, and Dykes, *Readings from Negro Authors*, 1931. "Spring Dawn"; "Sunset."

Secondary

Campbell, Dorothy, *Index to Black American Writers in Collective Biographies*, 1983.

Legenda (Wellesley College Yearbook), 1912.

Nineteen Twelve Five-Year Record (April 1917): 17.

Rose Bibliography Project, *Analytical Guide and Indexes to "The Crisis," 1910-1960*, 1975.

Wellesley Alumnae Magazine (Spring 1977).

Wellesley College Archives, Wellesley College, Wellesley, Mass.

Wellesley College News 20, no. 23 (21 March 1912).

CLARK, MAZIE EARHART (1874-1958)

Poet

Born in Glendale, Hamilton County (near Cincinnati), Ohio, Mazie Earhart was the daughter of David and Fannie Earhart. Left motherless when a child of five, she attended public schools in Glendale and studied chiropody in Cincinnati. Around 1906 she opened a successful establishment in connection with a "shoppe" of beauty culture located in an arcade. A member of the Union Baptist Church, she later married George Clark, a U.S. Army sergeant who passed away in 1919 and was buried in Arlington Cemetery.

Clark wrote songs and poetry as a pastime; her work is occasional, sunny, sentimental, and neutral as to race. She wrote poems of faith, celebrations of personal relationships, and elegies for Americans who died in the First World War.

Her poems appeared in various periodicals and in several collections. Two of them, *Life's Sunshine and Shadows* (dedicated to a sister, Armenia Earhart, who died in 1939), and *Garden of Memories*, differ through the first forty-eight pages, but are identical thereafter. In the foreword to *Garden of Memories*, she states that she has "been moved to publish this book of verse, dedicated to my friends, in the hope and belief that the simple philosophy of the thoughts expressed herein may prove comforting and stimulating to anyone in need of encouragement – just as was I after the death of my husband." One long poem, "The Best," was prepared for commencement exercises at Albion College in Michigan – in it she admonishes her classmates to seek love and beauty rather than gold.

SELECT BIBLIOGRAPHY

Primary

Garden of Memories . . . Dedicated to My Friends in Memory of My Husband Sgt. George J. Clark. Cincinnati, Ohio: Eaton, 1932.

Life's Sunshine and Shadows [published under the pseudonym Fannie B. Steele]. Boston: Christopher Publishing House, 1929. Note: Some bibliographies list a work by this title published in Cincinnati by Eaton, 1940, and called "Book 3." *Lyrics of Love, Loyalty, and Devotion: Poems of Sunshine and Shadow of Sorrow and Cheers: Heartthrobs Revealing What Memory Holds Dear*. Cincinnati: Eaton Publishing, 1935.

Secondary

Dabney, *Cincinnati's Colored Citizens*, 1926.

Porter, *North American Negro Poets*, 1945.

Public Library of Cincinnati and Hamilton County, Ohio.

Reardon and Thorsen, *Poetry by American Women, 1900-1975*, 1979.

Rush, Myers, and Arata, *Black American Writers Past and Present*, 1975.

CLIFFORD, CARRIE WILLIAMS (1862-1934)

Activist

Poet

Carrie Williams Clifford was born and raised in Chillicothe, Ohio. She received her education in Columbus, Ohio, and then founded the Ohio Federation of Colored Women's Clubs, the first organization of its type in the United States. Clifford was the editor of one of the federation's publications, *Sowing for Others to Reap: A Collection of Papers of Vital Importance to the Race*, an effort to promote Afro-American awareness. While in Columbus, she married William H. Clifford, a lawyer and Republican member of the Ohio State Legislature. After the births of her two sons, Clifford and her family left Cleveland for Washington, D.C.

There the young author became more deeply involved in writing and working for the advancement of Afro-Americans. With Howard University nearby, she opened up her home on Sunday evenings to black intellectuals and literary artists such as Mary Church Terrell,* W.E.B. Du Bois, Alain Locke, and Georgia Douglas Johnson* who also hosted a literary guild in her home. A member of the Niagara movement, which eventually evolved into the NAACP, Clifford was also an outspoken advocate for women's rights. Her essay "Votes for Children" was one in a collection featured in a *Crisis* issue (1910) advocating women's suffrage.

Clifford published two volumes of poetry, besides contributing short stories, articles, and poems to periodicals including *Opportunity* and *Crisis*. Her first volume of poetry, *Race Rhymes* (1911), which resurfaced as part of her second volume of poetry entitled *The Widening Light*, forthrightly denounces racial discrimination while encouraging and reminding Afro-Americans of their noble heritage. In lyrical poems like "A Reply to Thomas Dixon," "Atlanta's Shame," "Character or Color–Which?" and "We'll Die for Liberty," Clifford openly expresses the urgency of the race problem with reflection upon specific historical, political, and personal events.

In most of the poems in *The Widening Light*, Clifford still aims at the evils of race hatred, but she also includes themes of nature and global humanity. How fitting that the book is dedicated "To my race"; Clifford's poems, many of them sonnets, are voiced definitively and defiantly–resounding with pride. The sonnets "Silent Protest Parade," "All Hail Ye Colored Graduates," "Howard University," and "Three Sonnets" are, respectively, an appeal, a demand, and finally, a warning that racial equality must exist in practice as well as legislation.

In both volumes the poet identifies women's contributions in general: "Mothers of America" and "To Phyllis Wheatley." Carrie Clifford also comments on the injustices and sufferings peculiar to women of color (such as sexual abuse)–women who were not afforded the courtesies and privileges of white women–as in "Shall We Fight the Jim Crow Car?"

> Mounts the hot blood to the forehead,
> Angry passions leap to life
> At remembered wrongs committed
> 'Gainst a mother, sister, wife.

Despite her outspoken protests, Carrie Williams Clifford did not lose hope that humankind might one day be brought together as one, stating in the preface of her book that she seeks "to call attention to a condition which she considers serious," hoping that her poems "may change some heart, or right some wrong."

SELECT BIBLIOGRAPHY

Primary

Fiction

"Love's Way (A Christmas Story)." *Alexander's Magazine* (January 1906): 55-58.

Nonfiction

"Cleveland and Its Colored People." *Colored American* 8-9 (1908): 365-80.

Sowing for Others to Reap: A Collection of Papers of Vital Importance to the Race. Boston: C. Alexander, n.d. (Ohio Federation of Colored Women's Clubs, Carrie Williams Clifford, editor.)

"Votes for Children." *Crisis* (August 1915): 185.

Poetry

Race Rhymes. Washington, D.C.: Printed by R.L. Pendleton, 1911.

The Widening Light. Boston: Walter Reid Co., 1922. New ed., with an introduction by Rosemary Clifford Wilson. New York: Crowell, 1971.

IN ANTHOLOGIES

Cunard, *Negro Anthology*, [1934] 1969.

Stetson, *Black Sister*, 1981. "The Black Draftee from Dixie."

Secondary

Campbell, Dorothy, *Index to Black American Writers in Collective Biographies*, 1983.

Ellis, *Opportunity; A Journal of Negro Life*, 1971.

Index to Poetry in Periodicals, 1925-1929, 1983.

Kallenbach, *Index to Black American Literary Anthologies*, 1979.

Porter, *North American Negro Poets*, 1945.

Rose Bibliography Project, *Analytical Guide and Indexes to "The Crisis," 1910-1960*, 1975.

Rush, Myers, and Arata, *Black American Writers Past and Present*, 1975.

Sims-Wood, *The Progress of Afro-American Women*, 1980.

Stetson, *Black Sister*, 1981.

Williams, *Black American Women in the Arts and Social Sciences*, 1978.

COLEMAN, ANITA SCOTT (1890-1960)

Educator

Essayist

Poet

Short-story writer

There is only a little biographical information about this woman whose activity during the New Negro Renaissance eventually produced two volumes of poetry, *Reason for Singing* (1948) and *The Singing Bells* (1961), as well as essays and short stories. Anita Scott Coleman was the daughter of a Cuban who had originally purchased his wife as a slave. Some time later he joined the Union army and fought in the U. S. Civil War. Raised in New Mexico, Coleman states that she received an ordinary education, "though it culminated in the profession of teaching," which she engaged in "long enough to consider it the most interesting work I've ever done. . . . And then I was married." Her teaching career cut short, Coleman and her husband raised four children in their Los Angeles residence, while she ran a boarding home for children and continued to write.

Crisis, Opportunity, Half Century, and *Messenger* were among the periodicals that published her short stories, essays and poetry. Her work also appeared in anthologies including Beatrice Murphy's *Negro Voices* (1938) and *Ebony Rhythm* (1948). Coleman won several prizes for her writing: she received the $25 second prize for her essay "Unfinished Masterpieces," in the *Crisis* contest of 1926, and was awarded second place by *Opportunity* in the same year for her personal experience sketch "The Dark Horse."

Coleman is one of the short-story writers whose skill in this genre is evidenced by her ability to create an impact on the reader that goes beyond words. Her main characters are often multifaceted individuals, who change and develop with the dilemmas they encounter. Her short stories are laden with metaphors and phrases that demonstrate her daring with the English language. Opting to use the third person narrator more frequently than dialogue, Coleman exposes the thoughts and intents of her characters, enabling the reader to become acquainted with them despite the brevity of the form. Sophisticated vocabulary works reasonably into the fabric of the whole piece, with odd but at times refreshing combinations of formal English and slang. Coleman's collected poems include rhymes as well as blank verse and cover a variety of topics, although much of the verse she published in *Crisis* and *Opportunity* surge with race themes.

"Unfinished Masterpieces" in *Crisis* describes the feverish search of Afro-Americans stripped of self-esteem and condemned to wander over " roads leading away from plantations where the cotton waited to be picked. . . . Roads leading to pool halls and gambling dens. Roads beginning and roads ending in 'riding the roads,' carrying backward and forward, here and yon through the weird goblin land of the South's black belt" (14).

Her essays and short stories cover a broad spectrum of topics ranging from race issues to womens' issues and love. Though many Afro-American men were skilled at trades, they were denied access to jobs and therefore the dignity of providing for their families. Black women were constrained by the housekeeping roles assigned to them in their homes as well as in the residences where they worked. To black women, who were not afforded the white woman's "pettycoat privileges" of pampering or chivalry, being a homemaker and raising one's own children was a luxury, for they were usually forced to work outside the home for a white family. It was within the context of this tradition that the freedom of choice to be a homemaker became a privilege to the black middle class.

In "Rich Man, Poor Man," published in *Half Century*, an aspect of this controversial topic is plainly stated during an argument between black men and women; as one man says: "A black woman can always get a good (?) [sic] job in somebody's kitchen – but a black man can't get a good (?) [sic] job cleaning streets if some white man happens to want it" (6). This conversation is firmly implanted in the memory of Drusilla, the protagonist: "Race men, versus race women, was the topic of the day whenever this occurred, and one of these arguments had stuck and sprouted like a seed in fertile Drusilla's mind. . . . Now Drusilla decided that no matter what came or what went – she would not work for any man alive. . . . she would say 'my man is going to take care of me'" (6). Drusilla, accustomed to affluence, marries John Condon, who is a baker by trade but barred from practicing his vocation. John becomes ill, and the debts of the young couple begin to mount. Drusilla's love for John and her pride move her to sell most of her fancy clothes as she masterminds a way to launch a business of their own. Drusilla remains true to her own convictions, however, as she states to her husband, "I will not work for you, but with you."

In "Cross Crossings Cautiously" Sam Timons is a victim of a similar phenomenon: "Saw wood . . . clean house, paint barns, chop weeds . . . plow, anything, suh. . . . Just so it's work so's I can earn somethin'. I'm a welder by trade, but they don't hire cullud" (177). In the story, Claudia, a little white girl, implores Sam to escort her to the circus, as her parents, far too preoccupied with their own lives, have agreed to let her attend if she can find someone to take her. Three times, as he wanders down a desolate road and crosses the railroad tracks, Sam encounters signs warning "CROSS CROSSINGS CAUTIOUSLY." The admonition goes unheeded, and Sam agrees to accompany Claudia to the circus. When the parents discover this, they are outraged; the reader learns he has been lynched, while the little girl continues to wonder where her "circus man" is.

Reason for Singing (1948) expresses the author's personal experiences and thoughts. The title poem in the volume states the writer's purpose: to ponder many aspects of life and of death, of joy and of sorrow, of war and of peace, and most of all, to declare an overall optimism for the future of humanity. Coleman's poetry uses similes and metaphors in outlining relationships, as well as humor, as seen in the poem, "Definition": "Night is a velvet cloak / Wrapped 'round a gay Lothario; / Day is a flash-light / In the hand of a prude."

SELECT BIBLIOGRAPHY

Primary

Fiction

"Cross Crossings Cautiously." *Opportunity* (June 1930): 177, 189.

"The Eternal Quest." *Opportunity* (August 1931): 242-43.

"The Little Grey House." *Half Century* (July-August 1922): 4, 17, 19; (September-October 1922): 4, 21.

"The Nettleby's New Year." *Half Century* (January 1920): 4, 14-15.

"Rich Man, Poor Man." *Half Century* (May 1920): 6, 14.

"Three Dogs and a Rabbit." *Crisis* (January 1926): 118-22.

"El Tisco." *Crisis* (March 1920): 252-53.

"Two Old Women A-Shopping Go." *Crisis* (May 1933): 109-10.

UNPUBLISHED (TITLES MENTIONED ONLY)

"Annie Hawkins" (honorable mention in *Crisis*, 1926).

"The Dark Horse" (second place, personal sketch, *Opportunity*, 1926).

"Flaming Fame" (honorable mention in *Crisis*, 1926).

Nonfiction

"Unfinished Masterpieces." *Crisis* (December 1926).

Poetry

"Black Baby." *Opportunity* (February 1929): 53.

"Black Faces." *Opportunity* (October 1929): 320.

"Definition." *Opportunity* (November 1927): 340.

"The Dust of the Streets." *Crisis* (July 1927).

"Having Ears, He Heard." *Opportunity* (October 1935): 303.

"Humility." *Opportunity* (September 1933): 271.

"Idle Wonder." *Opportunity* (May 1938): 150.

"Life Is a See-Saw." *Crisis* (March 1939.

Reason for Singing, Prairie City, Ill.: Decker Press, [1948].

Singing Bells. Pictures by Claudine Nankivel. Nashville: Broadman Press, 1961.

"Wash Day." *Opportunity* (April 1927): 119.

"What Choice?" *Opportunity* (December 1933): 380.

IN ANTHOLOGIES

Murphy, *Ebony Rhythm*, [1948] 1968. "America Negra"; "Black Faces"; "The Colorist"; "Hands"; "Humility."

Murphy, *Negro Voices*, [1938] 1971. "Theme with Variations."

Secondary

Campbell, Dorothy, *Index to Black American Writers in Collective Biographies*, 1983.

Chapman, *Index to Black Poetry*, 1974.

Chapman, *Index to Poetry by Black American Women*, 1986.

Ellis, *Opportunity; A Journal of Negro Life*, 1971.

Fairbanks and Engeldinger, *Black American Fiction*, 1978.

Index to Poetry in Periodicals, 1925-1929, 1983.

Kallenbach, *Index to Black American Literary Anthologies*, 1979.

Rush, Myers, and Arata, *Black American Writers Past and Present*, 1975.

Shockley, *Afro-American Women Writers, 1746-1933*, 1988.

COOPER, ANNA JULIA (1856-1964)

Essayist

Educator

Anna Julia Cooper, born to a slave mother and a white father, was recognized as an outstanding educator, essayist, and lecturer who gave expression to the seemingly voiceless black women of America. Though her principal work, *A Voice from the South*, was published in 1892, Cooper continued to be influential and a vocal writer well into the twentieth century.

Born a slave, she became a highly educated woman. She attended St. Augustine Normal School and Collegiate Institute, a freedmen's school founded by an Episcopal clergyman, in her native city of Raleigh, North Carolina, where at the age of eleven she became a student-teacher. In 1877 she married the Reverend G. A. C. Cooper, a coworker at St. Augustine's, but she was left a widow only two years later. She then attended Oberlin College, where she received an A.B. degree and an A.M. in 1887. While at Oberlin, she taught classes composed mostly of white students. During the summer months, while still a student, she taught at various schools in Wheeling, West Virginia; Cottage City (the present-day Oak Bluffs), Massachusetts; and Jefferson City, Missouri. In 1887, she became a Latin teacher at Washington High School (later renamed M Street High School and still later Dunbar High School) in Washington, D.C., where she stayed for the next thirty years. In 1901, she was appointed principal of the school but was dropped from the staff in 1906, being then fifty years old. As principal of the M Street High School, she had stressed high academic standards. She developed a college prep program for qualified students, and her main goal was to secure positions for her students in respectable colleges. She was successful in having several admitted to Harvard, Yale, and Princeton, but she incurred sharp criticism from the board members of the M Street High School for pushing the students too hard and aspiring too highly for blacks. This was the reason she was asked to give up her position as principal.

In 1910, the school invited her back, and she resumed teaching, though not her former duties as principal. During her four years of "exile," she taught at the Lincoln Institute in Jefferson, Missouri, and spent her summers at Oberlin. In 1925, at the age of sixty-six, she took a leave to attend the Sorbonne in Paris; with her powerful intellect and proficient French, she acquired a Ph.D. with research focusing on the attitudes of the leaders of the French Revolution toward slavery. Upon her return to the United States, she founded Frelinghuysen University, a night school for employed Afro-Americans, which she ran out of her own home in Washington, D.C. A crusader for high school education, she continued writing essays until her death on 27 February 1964 at the age of 107.

Her first book, *A Voice from the South by a Black Woman of the South* (1892) sets forth her ideas on the rights of women in eight cogent essays. Clearly, Cooper considered the struggle of women as part of the overall black struggle. For her, there could be no substitute for black woman's advocacy of herself: "Our Caucasian barristers are not to blame if they cannot quite put themselves in the dark man's place, neither should the dark man be wholly expected, fully and adequately to reproduce the exact voice of the Black woman." Cooper went on to say, in vivid language, that no one else could "more accurately tell the weight and fret of the long dull pain than the open-eyed but hitherto voiceless black woman of America." Cooper championed higher education as the key to the liberation of "the sadly expectant Black Woman." *A Voice from the South* is now considered to be one of the early texts of black feminism.

Cooper's most respected work lay in the field of education. She was a champion of blacks, and particularly black women, seeking higher education. As a teacher of black students, she held Tuskegee Institute in high esteem, but on several issues disagreed with Booker T. Washington's philosophy about education, arguing that race should not be a criterion, that only ability should determine who should be allowed to continue with a higher education. She also made strong arguments that black women should be given the same opportunities in education as black men.

Her articles state her beliefs on these issues, frequently recognizing that white feminists did not necessarily include their black sisters in their struggle for equality. One of the most informative of Cooper's works is "The Third Step," which sets forth the principles that guided her life.

The Anna J. Cooper Papers are held in the Manuscript Division of the Moorland-Spingarn Research Center, Howard University.

SELECT BIBLIOGRAPHY

Primary

Drama

"Christmas Bells" [a one-act play for children; in verse].

Nonfiction

"Angry Saxons and Negro Education." *Crisis* (May 1938): 148.

L'attitude de la France a l'égard de l'esclavage pendant la révolution. Paris: Imprimerie de la Cour d'Appeal, 1925. (Measures concerning Slavery in the United States, 1787-1850. Equality in the Democratic Movement.)

Charlemagne: Voyage à Jerusalem et à Constantinople. Publié avec un glossaire par Anna Julia Cooper. Paris: A. Lahure, 1925.

"The Humor of Teaching." *Crisis* (5 November 1930): 387.

The Life and Writings of the Grimké Family. Washington, D.C.: The author, 1951.

"Social Settlement" (reprint). *Oberlin Alumnae Journal*.

"The Third Step." Howard University: Moorland-Spingarn Research Center.

A Voice from the South – By a Black Woman of the South. Xenia, Ohio: Aldine Printers, 1892. Reprint, with an introduction by Mary Helen Washington. New York: Oxford University Press, 1988.

IN ANTHOLOGIES

Shockley, *Afro-American Women Writers, 1746-1933*, 1988. "The Higher Education of Women."

Secondary

Campbell, Dorothy, *Index to Black American Writers in Collective Biographies*, 1983.

Dannett, *Profiles of Negro Womanhood*, 1964.

Davis, Thadious M., "Anna Julia Haywood Cooper," 1979.

Ellis, *Opportunity; A Journal of Negro Life*, 1971.

Giddings, *When and Where I Enter: The Impact of Black Women on Race and Sex in America*, 1984.

Harley, "Anna J. Cooper: A Voice for Black Women," 1978.

Herman, *Women in Particular*, 1984.

Hutchinson, *Anna J. Cooper: A Voice from the South*, 1981.

Loewenberg and Bogin, *Black Women in Nineteenth-Century American Life: Their Words, Their Thoughts, Their Feelings*, 1976.

Matthews, *Black American Writers, 1773-1949*, 1975.

Moorland-Spingarn Research Center, Howard University, Washington, D.C.

Oberlin College Archives, Oberlin, Ohio.

Porter, *North American Negro Poets*, 1945.

Richardson, *Black Women and Religion*, 1980.

Rush, Myers, and Arata, *Black American Writers Past and Present*, 1975.

Spradling, *In Black and White*, 1980.

Sterling, *We Are Your Sisters*, 1984.

Williams, *American Black Women in the Arts and Social Sciences*, 1978.

COPELAND, JOSEPHINE (?-?)

Poet

According to Arna Bontemps's biographical note, Josephine Copeland, the fifth child in a family of six, was born in a small resort town, Covington, just sixty miles outside of New Orleans, Louisiana. The school term was short in this rural community, and as a result she had some trouble acquiring an education. She passed the entrance exams to McDonagh 35 High School in New Orleans, but while attending had to work mornings and evenings before and after classes. She took evening classes at Dillard University in New Orleans and completed a two-year teaching course. Thereafter she moved to Chicago.

Her poem "The Zulu King: New Orleans" begins by exalting a regally costumed Zulu king, part of the Mardi Gras Carnival. With his skin "as glossy as black satin" and his retinue of "menacing" warriors, he inspires cheers from the crowd, even though the float contains "a naked pot-bellied babe / Simmering over a mock bush fire." The poem concludes with the revelation of the poet's own response to the exotic and frightening display: "The blood quickened in my pagan heart; Africa called to her own again." Like Langston Hughes and Helene Johnson,* Copeland responds passionately to the African heritage and the beauty of blackness. Her style is highly visual and descriptive, with understated emotion.

What seems to be the only other poem published by Copeland is "Negro Folk Songs," in *Crisis* of May 1940. In four unrhymed stanzas she exposes both the torment of oppression and the hidden dreams "oozing up from the fetid swamps of racial discrimination / baptized by tears of / Racial frustration."

Given Copeland's expressive power, manifest in both these poems, it is regrettable that no more of her work has been found.

SELECT BIBLIOGRAPHY

Primary

Poetry

"Negro Folk Songs." *Crisis* (May 1940): 158.

IN ANTHOLOGIES

Bontemps, *Golden Slippers*, 1941. "Zulu King: New Orleans."

Secondary

Chapman, *Index to Black Poetry*, 1974.

Chapman, *Index to Poetry by Black American Women*, 1986.

Rose Bibliography Project, *Analytical Guide and Indexes to "The Crisis," 1910-1960*, 1975.

Rush, Myers, and Arata, *Black Women Writers Past and Present*, 1975.

COWDERY, MAE VIRGINIA (1909-1953)

Poet

Visual artist

Mae Virginia Cowdery was an artist whose promise was unfulfilled because of her early death. An only child, she was born into the Afro-American middle class; her parents, Mr. and Mrs. Lemuel Cowdery, resided at 222 West Penn Street in Germantown, Philadelphia. Her mother was a social worker and the director of the Bureau for Colored Children; her father was a caterer and post office clerk.

Cowdery was intelligent as well as artistically inclined, expressing her creative spirit both in the visual and the literary arts. She received her secondary education at the Philadelphia High School for Girls, an institution for scholastically talented students. In her senior year, three of her poems were accepted for publication in the 1927 spring issue of *Black Opals*, the showcase for black literary artists in Philadelphia like Idabelle Yeiser,* Evelyn Crawford Reynolds,* Nellie Bright,* and Ottie Beatrice Graham,* but which also accepted work from outside authors including Marita Bonner,* Gwendolyn Bennett,* Gertrude P. McBrown.* After graduation from Girls' High, young Cowdery matriculated at Pratt Institute in New York to pursue design and the visual arts.

While in New York the artist became involved in the cultural festivities of the Harlem Renaissance. She was befriended by Langston Hughes and was encouraged by Alain Locke to submit her work to black magazines. Cowdery's work appeared occasionally between 1927 and 1930 in *Crisis* and *Opportunity*. The poet also made contributions to *Carolina Magazine* and *Unity*. Some of her poems appeared in anthologies like Charles S. Johnson's *Ebony and Topaz*, which featured other writers such as Alice Dunbar-Nelson,* Jessie Fauset,* Angelina Weld Grimké,* and Zora Neale Hurston,* *Braithwaite's Anthology*, and *The Negro Genius* by Benjamin Brawley. In 1927 she won the Krigwa Poem Prize for "Longings." Following this distinction, Cowdery's portrait graced the cover of the January 1928 issue of *Crisis*. She appears dressed in a masculine tailored suit, her short hair smoothly slicked back into a shiny luster on her head, giving the impression that she, like many other contemporary young intellectuals, endorsed the Bohemian life-style – confronting life with an impulsive, carefree, and reckless air, an ambience reinforced by poet Edna St. Vincent Millay's influence on the younger generation of the twenties.

According to Vincent Jubilee, Cowdery was also persuaded by Millay's literary personality and attitude – cavalier yet wistful – as expressed in the poem "Longings":

To dance
in the light of the moon
A platinum moon
Posed like a slender dagger
On the velvet darkness
Of night . . .
To dream –
'Neath the bamboo tree
On the sable breast
Of earth –
And listen to the wind . . .
To talk
With God.

Mae Cowdery belonged to the Beaux Art Club, a literary group based in Philadelphia, which was established during the 1920s but prospered from the 1930s through the 1950s. She published a volume of poetry, *We Lift Our Voices*, in 1936. The poems embrace varying themes of love, nature, and death. In many the poet frequently connects the poem's subject to natural objects with metaphors, as in "Tree . . . to . . . B.H." ("You are a tall dark tree") or "Each Night" ("I am but the smallest star"). In the introduction by William Stanley Braithwaite, Cowdery is called a "fugitive poet" because she is one of numerous Afro-American writers who published in the black periodicals of the Harlem movement and perhaps even had her work published in anthologies, but was never recognized as a contemporary American poet.

In spite of the fact that none of the other Philadelphia writers – Idabelle Yeiser,* Nellie Bright,* Evelyn Crawford Reynolds,* and Arthur H. Fauset – was published in *Crisis* or *Opportunity* after 1930, they did not consider Cowdery a peer in their craft. (In her society column, Reynolds was more interested in describing Cowdery's attire than her poetry.) They labeled her "a Bohemian," or as Jubilee says, her "intense glow . . . did not develop into the lasting flame." The poet's sporadic literary career came to an end when she took her own life in 1953.

SELECT BIBLIOGRAPHY

Primary

Fiction

"Lai-Li." *Black Opals* (Spring 1928).

Poetry

We Lift Our Voices and Other Poems. Philadelphia: Alpress, 1936.

IN ANTHOLOGIES

Johnson, Charles S., *Ebony and Topaz*, [1927] 1971. "Dusk."

Stetson, *Black Sister*, 1981. "I Sit and Wait for Beauty."

Secondary

Chapman, *Index to Black Poetry*, 1974.

Index to Poetry in Periodicals, 1925-1929, 1983.

Jubilee, "Philadelphia's Afro-American Literary Circle and the Harlem Renaissance," 1980.

Kellner, *The Harlem Renaissance*, 1984.

Matthews, *Black American Writers, 1773-1949*, 1975.

Porter, *North American Negro Poets*, 1945.

Rose Bibliography Project, *Analytical Guide and Indexes to "The Crisis," 1910-1960*, 1975.

Rush, Myers, and Arata, *Black American Writers Past and Present*, 1975.

CUTHBERT, MARION VERA (1896-1989)

Activist

Educator

Poet

Short-story writer

Essayist

Biographer

Civil and women's rights activist Marion Vera Cuthbert was one of the most confrontational and political writers of the 1930s. In her studies of the social conditions of Afro-Americans, she articulated the complex interface between race and gender, noting that women of color had neither white nor male privilege. Cuthbert understood the relationship between literacy and political power; as an executive board member of the YWCA, Cuthbert lived her convictions, engaging in race relations activities and wielding as a political weapon the written word.

Information about Cuthbert is scant and provides only a sketchy outline with many omissions concerning her early life. One of the few writers in this book from the Midwest, she was born in St. Paul, Minnesota, where she attended the local schools. She received her bachelor's degree from Boston University in 1920. Between 1920 and 1926 she became an administrator at the Burrel Normal School (location unknown) and left her position as principal there to become dean of Talladega College from 1927 to 1930. *The Interracial Bulletin* of

November 1931, a publication of the National Student Council, YWCA, noted that Cuthbert was awarded a Kent fellowship to study at Columbia University in New York where she earned her M.A. in 1931. Her doctoral dissertation *Education and Marginality: A Study of the Negro Woman College Graduate* completed at Columbia, is dated 1942. In the preface to the collective biography *Twelve Negro Americans* (1936), Mary Jenness described Cuthbert as a National Board member of the Young Women's Christian Association who was "more widely known than some of the people in this book, but [who] refused to be included, preferring to help behind the scenes as a sponsor and advisor." Cuthbert was hired as an instructor at Brooklyn College in 1945. According to the college's archives, she continued teaching there through 1960 and was eventually promoted to professor of sociology.

Cuthbert's writings, very much a part of her life and her involvement with the YWCA, include poetry, essays, and books about the history and conditions of race relations in America. *Education and Marginality: A Study of the Negro Woman College Graduate* expounds on the political, social, and economic effects of education on the lives of Afro-American women. In chapter 1 Cuthbert begins by placing the black woman in "herstory." In chapter 2, she discusses the background of the Negro college woman; in 3, the college graduates participating in the questionnaire study; in 4, their motives for going to college; in 5, their relationships with their family after college; in 6, their work life and personal living after college days; in 7, major problems in their social relationships; in 8, graduate women and the problem of leadership; and in 9, the evaluation of their college experience. She concludes with a chapter of recommendations. The statistical evidence of her study makes it difficult to deny the grim realities of black women's lives.

In all of her work, Cuthbert is skillful in pinpointing problems where race and gender intersect and where the struggles of women of color differ from those of white women and black men. The professional fields open to women were teaching and social work; for black women this meant teaching and social work in black communities. Jobs outside of the Afro-American community for women, educated or not, consisted mainly of domestic and personal service. In *Democracy and the Negro*, Cuthbert asserts:

> While the fight of black men for work can be told as part of
> the story of the gains and retreats of labor as a whole, the
> story of the Negro woman worker needs to be told as a
> separate chapter in a dark history. Belonging to the most
> exploited group in the country, she adds to the exploitation
> based upon color the exploitation based upon sex. Forced to
> work outside of her home in greater numbers than any
> other group of women in our country, she finds herself at
> the mercy of the poorest, most labor demanding and dirtiest

of industries. Her treatment at the hands of white women
who employ her are nothing short of scandalous. (20)

Written during the depression, "Problems Facing the Young Negro
Woman" expounds on the hardships of being "child bearer, homemaker and
toiler." Though it presents bleak scenarios of the situations facing young
black women, it is in general a message imbued with hope. Cuthbert assumes
that Afro-American women have the support of black men and also
encourages black women to recognize the possibility of empowerment
through unity with fellow workers and particularly with women of all colors.

Cuthbert's prose is characterized by conscience-burning rhetoric, where
she identifies discriminatory pretexts and myths. In "Church and Society," a
YWCA publication, she argues: "One of the oldest concepts was that the
Negro is an in-between man, not rightly beast or man, but inclining, if
anything, more toward the bestial side. The early days were filled with
debates as to whether or not he had a soul." Cuthbert continues, "But by far
the greater portion of our population view the Negro as a delightful
entertainer, something that must be amusing . . .Black vs. white complexion;
straight vs. kinky hair; broad vs. aquiline features–therefore some sort of
practical joke. . . all the exuberance of the New World at its best but in
caricature" (1). Finally, Cuthbert perceives that racism is motivated by fear
that Afro-Americans are contenders for "some of the honors and spoils of the
world."

Juliette Derricotte (1933) is a brief interpretive biography published in
memory of a dean of women at Fisk University and YWCA race relations
activist. Derricotte died following a car crash when she was denied admission
to hospitals in Atlanta despite her severe injuries. The introspection, internal
dialogue, and vacillation between first and third persons cause the reader to
be aware of simultaneous levels of consciousness and add a psychological
quality to the book. Cuthbert interjects some of her own thoughts and
observations into *Juliette Derricotte* in a manner that carries it beyond the
average biography.

The *Negro Yearbook* (1937-38) reviews two of Cuthbert's books: *April
Grasses* and *Juliette Derricotte*. It merely describes the contents of the books,
both published by the Woman's Press in New York. In a brief review of *April
Grasses* the critic points out that there is no mention of race. This could be
curious, considering Cuthbert's political stance; but it is also possible that she
was using her writing as a means of escape from the daily humiliation and
degradation inflicted by race and gender prejudice.

Cuthbert's poetry is not poetry on racial themes; rather, it is
inspirational, with themes devoted to the abstract. A woman of strong faith,
Cuthbert infuses a spirituality into her poetry, that essential part of herself
that was evidenced by her extended affiliation with the Young Women's

Christian Association. In *Songs of Creation*, she voices her strong faith, as in "The Life of God": "Where God stands is always here / No faint horizon line, no yonder, but only / At this place. Count two–you and I– / And He will say, "Yet Three." Cuthbert, like other female writers, used her writing as an escape and turned to God in search of a life blind to race and gender.

Given her outspoken stance on issues of race and sex discrimination it is not surprising that Marion Vera Cuthbert "escaped notice." There was a greater audience for creative writing because the reader was convinced of its purpose merely to entertain; it spoke of suffering but did not identify or condemn the oppressors. Expositors of controversial topics like racism and sexism often encountered so little interest from publishers and such hostility or indifference that they, their work, or both disappeared. This was the case with Marion Vera Cuthbert, who was a professor at Brooklyn College through the 1960s but whose literary career seems to have stopped in the 1930s.

SELECT BIBLIOGRAPHY

Primary

Fiction

"Mob Madness." *Crisis* (April 1936): 108, 114.

Nonfiction

"The Dean of Women at Work." *Journal of the National Association of College Women* 13-14 (April 1928): 39-44.

Democracy and the Negro. New York: Pilgrim Press, 1936.

Education and Marginality: A Study of the Negro Woman College Graduate. New York: Garland Publishing Co., 1987. Originally a Ph.D. thesis, Columbia University, New York, 1942.

Juliette Derricotte. New York: Woman's Press, 1933.

"Problems Facing Negro Young Women." *Opportunity* (February 1936): 47-49.

Review of *Candy*, by L. M. Alexander. *Opportunity* (December 1934): 379-80.

We Sing America. New York: Friendship Press, 1936

Poetry

April Grasses. New York: Woman's Press, 1936.

"Black Flute." *Opportunity* (May 1928).

"Hands of a Lady at Prayer." *World Tomorrow* (February 1929).

Songs of Creation. New York: Woman's Press, 1949.

Secondary

Brooklyn College Archives, Brooklyn, N.Y.

Chapman, *Index to Black Poetry*, 1974.

Deodene and French, *Black American Poetry since 1944*, 1971.

Ellis, *Opportunity; A Journal of Negro Life*, 1971.

French, Fabre, Singh, and Fabre, *Afro-American Poetry and Drama, 1760-1975*, 1979.

Herman, *Women in Particular*, 1984.

Index to Poetry in Periodicals, 1925-1929, 1983.

Jenness, *Twelve Negro Americans*, 1936.

Matthews, *Black American Writers, 1773-1949*, 1975.

Porter, *North American Negro Poets*, 1945.

Reardon and Thorsen, *Poetry by American Women, 1900-1975*, 1979.

Richardson, *Black Women and Religion*, 1980.

Rose Bibliography Project, *Analytical Guide and Indexes to "The Crisis," 1910-1960*, 1975.

Rush, Myers, and Arata, *Black American Writers Past and Present*, 1975.

Sims-Wood, *The Progress of Afro-American Women*, 1980.

Spradling, *In Black and White*, 1980.

Stetson, "Black Women in and out of Print," 1982.

DAY, CAROLINE BOND STEWART (1889-1948)

Short-story writer

Essayist

Sociologist

Educator

Caroline Stewart Day is best known for her ground-breaking sociological research, published as *A Study of Some Negro-White Families in the United States*. But this recognition somewhat overshadows her tireless efforts as an advocate for her race, particularly through drama.

Born in Montgomery, Alabama, on 18 November 1889, Caroline Bond Stewart was the daughter of Moses and Georgia Fagan Stewart. She was educated at the Tuskegee Institute in Alabama from 1901 to 1905 before attending Atlanta University from 1905 to 1912. She also studied at Radcliffe College in Cambridge, Massachusetts, from 1916 to 1919, where she received her A.B. and A.M. degrees. On 1 March 1920, Caroline married Aaron Day, Jr.

Throughout her college years, Caroline served as secretary of such organizations as the YMCA and the Circle for Negro Relief. After graduating, her first academic position was as dean of women at Paul Quinn College in Waco, Texas. In 1921, she became the head of the English department at State College of Texas in Prairie View. She then moved to Atlanta University where she was the director of dramatics and a teacher of English; she remained there until 1926 when she returned to Radcliffe as a fellow in the anthropology department.

In 1929, she undertook research under the direction of anthropology professor Dr. Ernest A. Hooton at Harvard and under the sponsorship of the Laura Spelman Rockefeller Fund, through the Bureau of International Research of Harvard/Radcliffe. Originally titled "The Sociological, Genealogical and Physiological Aspects of Negro-White Crosses in the United States," her study analyzed findings from living people in 1927-28; 2,537 adults from 346 families were surveyed by questionnaires. It was published in 1932 as *A Study of Some Negro-White Families in the United States* for the Harvard African Series by the Peabody Museum of Harvard. After completing her study, she taught at Howard University. According to Radcliffe College records, she died on 5 May 1948.

Day's summary of her findings, the most recent research on interracial mixture at the time, and of two other studies focusing on earlier periods appeared in the March 1930 issue of *Crisis*. Naturally the article views her own study most favorably, suggesting that its contemporary time frame and living subjects render hers the most relevant and accurate of the three. Day makes a pointed effort to quash the negative, unsubstantiated conclusions about black parentage put forth by the two other researchers, James H. Johnson, Jr., and George T. Dixon, particularly as Johnson and Dixon take, respectively, a historical and literary approach to the subject, relying mostly on secondary documents. Day's more scientific/genetic slant and her exclusive use of primary data give her study greater credibility.

Day's other area of interest was theater. Although she taught at the college level, she took a keen interest in developing dramatic arts programs for elementary school children, insisting that only through refinement by culture would Afro-Americans be able to advance themselves. In "Educational Fruit" (*Opportunity*, August 1933) she deplores children's abandoning of drama for "the crudest of wild-west moving pictures." As she points out, participating in a play not only promotes the memorization of "beautiful lines of poetry" but induces a sense of professionalism, cooperation, and imagination, far more lasting fruit than mere entertainment from action pictures. Earlier in *Crisis* (September 1925), Day had compiled a list of plays whose casting allowed black actors far more choice, alternatives to both classical English drama and indigenous historical plays with racial themes. Implicitly, Day suggested that a strong theater arts tradition would spawn respected Afro-American playwrights and actors to fill future demand.

Day also wrote short stories, the finest of which by far is "The Pink Hat." Seemingly autobiographical, the story recounts the adventures of a woman who "passes" by wearing a pink hat that gives her skin a rosy cast. The hat is her "magic carpet," opening up new worlds of courtesy and culture closed to blacks. Inevitably she is caught; she breaks her ankle while hurrying to leave a play before the crowd. As her ankle mends, though, so does her spirit: she concludes that her life in the black quarter of town as teacher and neighbor is more fulfilling than the perilous existence offered by the hat. Elegantly written and somewhat detached–she is more bemused than bitter–the sketch won third prize in *Opportunity*'s 1926 contest.

Disappointingly, none of her other articles or stories approaches its quality. "A Fairy Story" for children (*Crisis*, October 1919) is a well-intentioned but clumsily executed tale about the goodness of Ean, a "Hamite" princess who is "gentler and darker than the others." Although its fable format necessitates character simplification, its depiction of Ean as the best character solely because of her race is a misguided effort to address a problem reversed in real life. Although Day's intention may have been, in fact, to lampoon the real-life situation, her prose seems too straightforwardly earnest to serve that purpose.

In general, Day's essays and stories stress racial advancement independently within black society rather than through better relations with whites. For her, whites serve mainly as cultural models to which Afro-

Americans should aspire. A position that would later conflict with those advocating the beauty and legitimacy of purely black culture, it also obscures her views on gender roles.

SELECT BIBLIOGRAPHY

Primary

Fiction

"A Fairy Story." *Crisis* (October 1919). Also in Cromwell, *Readings from Negro Authors*, 1931, 124-27.

"The Pink Hat." *Opportunity* (December 1926).

IN ANTHOLOGIES

Cromwell, Turner, and Dykes, *Readings from Negro Authors*, 1931. "A Fairy Story."

Nonfiction

"Educational Fruit." *Opportunity* (August 1933).

"Race Crossings in the United States." *Crisis* (March 1930).

A Study of Some Negro-White Families in the United States. Cambridge: Peabody Museum of Harvard University, 1932.

"What Shall We Play?" *Crisis* (September 1925).

Secondary

Campbell, Dorothy, *Index to Black American Writers in Collective Biographies*, 1983.

Ellis, *Opportunity; A Journal of Negro Life*, 1971.

Kallenbach, *Index to Black American Literary Anthologies*, 1979.

Matthews, *Black American Writers, 1773-1949*, 1975.

Rose Bibliography Project, *Analytical Guide and Indexes to "The Crisis," 1910-1960*, 1975.

Who's Who in Colored America, 1927.

DELANY, CLARISSA M. SCOTT (1901-1927)

Educator

Poet

Social worker

Born in Tuskegee, Alabama, to Emmet Jay and Elenora Baker Scott, Clarissa Scott Delany was the third of five children. She was raised at Tuskegee Institute, where her father was secretary to founder Booker T. Washington. Clarissa received seven years of her education in New England, studying at Bradford Academy and then at Wellesley College, where she graduated Phi Beta Kappa in 1923. She stated in later life that her "seven years in New England (1916-1923) ... tinged [her] Southern blood with something of the austerity of that section."

Clarissa was very active during her college years, participating in Delta Sigma Theta (a black sorority), varsity field hockey, the debating team, and the Christian Association. She was also, according to Wellesley classmates, a singer and pianist of concert calibre. It was during Scott's time at Wellesley that she first encountered the ambience of the New Negro Movement. According to Boston educator Wilhelmina Crosson, she began to attend Literary Guild meetings at 464 Massachusetts Avenue in Boston, where young black people gathered weekly to listen to featured speakers such as Claude McKay give readings of their work and talks on racial issues.

After her graduation from Wellesley, Clarissa traveled through France and Germany, doing some studies in race relations. "A Golden Afternoon in Germany" is a brief sketch chronicling one European experience. Later she published her work while she taught at the Dunbar High School in Washington, D.C. Her works included poetry, book reviews, and an essay on her experiences in Europe in the National Urban League publication *Opportunity; A Journal of Negro Life*. Scott's reviews are colorfully descriptive as she expatiates on themes familiar to the Harlem literati – Pan- Africanism, superstition, the mulatto, and so on.

In 1925, Clarissa was awarded fourth prize by *Opportunity* for her poem "Solace." The four poems she published were collected shortly afterward in Countee Cullen's anthology, *Caroling Dusk* (1927). "Solace" describes the life cycle of trees as the seasons pass and "tender green give[s] way to darker heavier leaves." The poet likens the trees, defying the tumultuous winds and rain, to herself: "The summer torrents strive / To lash them into a fury / And seek to break them / But They stand." In letters of Wellesley classmates there is mention of the "The Mask" – "the anguish of her days" – that occasionally surfaced in her demeanor: "My life is fevered / and a restlessness at times / An agony – again a vague / and baffling discontent / Possesses me."

Clarissa's private struggles found only veiled expression in her poetry. The only four poems she published are somewhat mysterious; they do not refer to specific obstacles she faced as a black woman. Rather her verses are charged with a melancholy tone that attempts to embrace the hope of healing for a troubled soul. In the poem "Joy" she confesses, "Too long I have walked a desolate way, / Too long stumbled down a maze / Bewildered." However, hope appears in "Interim" when the poet declares: "Another day will find me brave, / And not afraid to dare."

Intellectual leaders, including Alice Dunbar-Nelson,* Angelina Weld Grimké,* and W. E. B. Du Bois, lauded her as a poet. Although a few drama sources list Delany as a playwright, author of *Dixie to Broadway* (1924), there is no extensive bibliographical evidence showing that she wrote plays.

In October 1926, Clarissa married Hubert T. Delany, a young lawyer, in Washington, D.C. The couple moved to New York, where Clarissa continued to do social work, gathering information for a "Study of Delinquent and Neglected Negro Children" in cooperation with the National Urban League and Women's City Club of New York. But less than a year later Clarissa Scott Delany's life and literary potential were cut short. She died, according to her death certificate, of kidney disease, which in those days was most commonly a reaction to the streptococcal infection she had been battling for six months. In her diary Alice Dunbar-Nelson wrote: "D-N, like everyone else who knew Clarissa Scott Delany considered her early death a tragedy [Tuesday, October 11]. . . . Clarissa Scott died yesterday. It made me faint when I read it [Wednesday, October 12]. . . . Poor Emmett! Shriveled and gray. [His daughter] Clarissa's death hit him hard [Saturday, December 10]."

Her potential unrealized, the life of Clarissa Scott Delany was symbolic of the plight of most black women writers of her time.

According to a Wellesley classmate of Clarissa's, a "YWCA Camp Clarissa Scott" was established on land donated by her family on Chesapeake Bay in 1931.

SELECT BIBLIOGRAPHY

Primary

Nonfiction

"A Golden Afternoon in Germany." *Opportunity* (December 1925): 277-78.

Review of *The Black Harvest*, by I. A. R. Wylie. *Opportunity* (March 1926): 104-5.

Review of *God's Stepchildren*, by Sarah G. Millin. *Opportunity* (June 1925): 181-82.

Review of *Green Thursday*, by Julia Peterkin. *Opportunity* (April 1925): 118.

Review of *Quaint Companions*, by Leonard Merrick. *Opportunity* (May 1925): 157.

Review of *Toro of the Little People*, by Leo Walmsley. *Opportunity* (December 1926): 397.

Review of *The Wooings of Jezebel Pettyfer*, by Haldane MacFall. *Opportunity* (January 1926): 26-27.

IN ANTHOLOGIES

Cromwell, Turner, and Dykes, *Readings from Negro Authors*, 1931. "A Golden Afternoon in Germany."

Poetry

"Interim." *Palms* (October 1926).

"Joy." *Opportunity* (October 1926): 321.

"The Mask." *Palms* (October): 1926.

"Solace." *Opportunity* (June 1925): 175.

"Solace" [eulogy]. *Opportunity* (November 1927): 321.

IN ANTHOLOGIES

Cromwell, Turner, and Dykes, *Readings From Negro Authors*, 1931. "The Mask"; "Solace."

Cullen, *Caroling Dusk*, 1927. "Interim"; "Joy"; "The Mask"; "Solace."

Secondary

Afro-American Encyclopedia, 1974.

Dunbar-Nelson, *Give Us Each Day: The Diary of Alice Dunbar-Nelson*, 1984.

Kellner, *The Harlem Renaissance*, 1984.

Low and Clift, *Encyclopedia of Black America*, 1981.

Randolph, "Another Day Will Find Me Brave: Clarissa Scott Delany, 1901-1927," 1988.

Rush, Myers, and Arata, *Black American Writers Past and Present*, 1975.

DICKINSON, BLANCHE TAYLOR (1896-?)

Educator

Poet

In 1926, while living in Sewickley, Pennsylvania, Blanche Taylor Dickinson received an honorable mention in the *Crisis* contest for her poem "The Hill," and a special Buckner prize from *Opportunity* for her poem "A Sonnet and a Rondeau." Her poems appeared in well-known anthologies such as Johnson's *Ebony and Topaz* and Cullen's *Caroling Dusk*. In the latter book the poet gives a short autobiographical paragraph: " I am a lover of music and divide my time between the typewriter and piano. . . . My favorite poets are Countee Cullen, Georgia Douglas Johnson, Edna St. Vincent Millay; my favorite past-time, walking along a crowded street. I have a hunch that I shall become a short story writer and my favorite exertion is trying to perfect my 'technique.'" However, sources do not reveal listings of any short stories she may have written.

Reportedly Dickinson was born on a farm near Franklin, Kentucky, on 15 April 1896, although vital statistics offices in Kentucky have no records to verify this. She attended Bowling Green Academy and Simmons University, and though she did not receive a degree, she taught for many years in Kentucky schools.

Dickinson's work was published in various Afro-American newspapers including *Franklin Favorite*, *Chicago Defender*, *Louisville Leader*, *Pittsburgh Courier*, and *Wayfarer*. Her poems encompass a variety of themes. In some of them, she subtly voices her observations about what life was like for those who were black and female in America. During an era when beauty was considered paramount for a woman, the myth of classic beauty neglected women of color. In "Revelation," a "brownskin girl" buying a beautiful dress "Draped on a bisque mannequin / So blond and slim and bold," fantasizes about her own beauty until she "stooped to drink . . . ah, to see / The cruel water reflecting me! / Dark-eyed, thick-lipped, harsh, short hair." The girl is comforted by the revelation that beauty is not necessarily virtuous: "But Lucifer saw himself, too, fair."

"Walls of Jericho" speaks of the Afro-American pursuit of the promised land, the "milk and honey" of the "American dream": 'Let me learn,' the dark ones say. / They have learned that Faith must do / More than meditate and pray / That a boulder may fall through / Making one large man size entrance / Into wondrous Jericho." The "one large man size entrance" may allude to the leadership of individuals like W. E. B. Du Bois, Harriet Tubman, Booker T. Washington, or Ida B. Wells-Barnett* which would pave the way for future generations of Afro-Americans.

Blanche Taylor Dickinson described female fortitude at a time when strength was more often identified as a male characteristic. Her poem "Fortitude" would be a fitting tribute to women of all colors whose struggles went unheeded and whose accomplishments were never recognized:

> She screamed but nobody heard her . . .
> Her body was a silencer.
> She cried and never moved a tear . . .
> Her heart was broken, tears dripped there.
> Silent, she seemed content to lay
> Her soul awhile in fresh red clay
> Proud to stand, all grief defying . . .
> We knew that she was all but dying.

SELECT BIBLIOGRAPHY

Primary

Poetry

"Chase." *American Poet* 4 (1927).

"A Dark Actress – Somewhere." *Crisis* (September 1928): 300.

"Fires." *Opportunity* (June 1929): 173

"Fortitude." *Opportunity* (February 1927): 37

"Good Wife." *Bozart* 5-6 (1929).

"A Sonnet and a Rondeau." *Opportunity* (September 1927): 263

"To One Who Thinks of Suicide." *Crisis* 1 (1928).

IN ANTHOLOGIES

Cullen, *Caroling Dusk*, 1927. "Four Walls"; "Revelation"; "That Hill"; "To an Icicle"; "The Walls of Jericho."

Johnson, Charles S., *Ebony and Topaz*, [1927] 1971. "Things Said When He Was Gone."

Secondary

Campbell, Dorothy, *Index to Black American Writers in Collective Biographies*, 1983.

Chapman, *Index to Black Poetry*, 1974.

Ellis, *Opportunity; A Journal of Negro Life*, 1971.

Index to Poetry in Periodicals, 1925-1929, 1983.

Kallenbach, *Index to Black American Literary Anthologies*, 1979.

Rose Bibliography Project, *Analytical Guide to the Indexes to "The Crisis," 1910-1960*, 1975.

Rush, Myers, and Arata, *Black American Writers Past and Present*, 1975.

DUNBAR-NELSON, ALICE RUTH MOORE (1875-1935)

Journalist

Poet

Short-story writer

Playwright

Alice Dunbar-Nelson devoted her life to the cause of social, political, and educational betterment for her fellow Afro-Americans. Her creative writing, sustained throughout her adult life, has been little known and appreciated, but it is now attracting attention owing to the efforts of scholar Gloria Hull.

Born to a middle-class family in New Orleans, Louisiana, on 19 July 1875, Alice Ruth Moore was the youngest of three children of Joseph and Patricia Wright Moore. Her father was a seaman and her mother a seamstress. After graduation from public schools in New Orleans, Alice continued her education at the city's Straight College (now Dillard University) where she graduated from the two-year teaching program in 1892. She pursued further study at the University of Pennsylvania, Cornell University, and the School of Industrial Arts, Philadelphia.

Her first volume of poetry, sketches, and short stories, *Violets and Other Tales*, was published in 1895 while she was teaching in New Orleans. "In Unconsciousness" is a mock-epic inspired by a tooth extraction and "The Woman" is a lively essay on female autonomy that assures readers that an independent woman can still be a loving wife. One of her poems, along with her photograph, was published in the Boston *Monthly Review*, catching the attention of Paul Laurence Dunbar, the most respected and widely known black poet of that time. He began a correspondence with Alice Ruth Moore that lasted for two years, culminating in their marriage on 6 March 1898.

After their marriage, the Dunbars moved to Brooklyn, New York, and Alice taught in the public schools; she also worked as a teacher of evening classes on New York's East Side and served as the secretary of the National Association of Colored Women. Meanwhile, her husband encouraged her writing, and in 1899, she published her second volume, *The Goodness of St. Rocque and Other Stories*, a collection of fourteen tales featuring French and Creole characters in a New Orleans setting. Critics note that these stories show the influence of New Orleans author and social reformer George Washington Cable (1844-1925), but add that the young author presented new types of characters not found in Cable's work. The stories are well crafted, with effective surprise endings. In addition to short stories and poetry, Dunbar wrote novelettes, autobiographical pieces, drama, political commentary, essays, and newspaper columns.

Alice and her husband moved to Washington, D.C., where she continued to teach. But their marriage was tempestuous, and in 1902, they separated. Paul died four years later of tuberculosis at the age of thirty-four. At the time of the separation, Alice moved to Wilmington, Delaware, to teach at Howard High School. She became the head of the English department, a position she held for the next eighteen years. During this time, she turned to writing historical articles for various journals and edited two anthologies for students, *Masterpieces of Negro Eloquence* in 1914 and *The Dunbar Speaker and Entertainer* in 1920.

She also continued with creative writing, contributing poems, sketches, and a play to *Opportunity* and *Crisis*. Her play *Mine Eyes Have Seen* is, according to James Hatch, a double-edged examination of the loyalty blacks owe to a nation that denies them equality. Too many characters overwhelm this short play, however, and the protagonist's sudden decision to answer a draft call is unconvincing. But her poem "I Sit and Sew," anthologized by Countee Cullen and noted by Hatch, skillfully conveys the contained frustration of the passive role imposed on women: "The little useless seam, the idle patch" is all the activity assigned to her when men go to war and die in foreign trenches. "This pretty futile seam, it stifles me / God, must I sit and sew?" the poet poignantly asks. Monroe Majors noted in *Negro Poets and Their Poems* that this poem expresses a "spirit of rebellion against confinement to the petty thing." Dunbar-Nelson herself accepted a wartime mission from the Women's Committee of the United States Council of National Defense; her duties entailed traveling about the various state divisions, surveying and advising on the organization of black women's groups.

On 20 April 1916, Dunbar married Robert John Nelson (whom she calls "Bobbo" in her diary), publisher of the *Wilmington Advocate*, a weekly newspaper devoted to the advancement of blacks. According to Hull's recent findings, this was her third marriage.

Dunbar-Nelson's political activism and outspoken nature often led to professional complications. In 1920, she was dismissed from her teaching post at Howard High School for attending a conference held at the Marion, Ohio, home of Republican presidential candidate Warren G. Harding. She had gone in order to determine the stand the party should take on racial problems. Having lost her position, she became the associate editor of the *Advocate*. In 1923, she also began writing a weekly column in the *Washington Eagle* and was associate editor of the *A.M.E. Church Review*.

In 1924, Dunbar-Nelson helped found the Delaware Industrial School for Colored Girls, a school devoted to helping delinquent black girls. She volunteered there for many years as a teacher and a parole officer. Another affiliation was with the American Interracial Peace Committee, an organization set up to enlist black support for the cause of world peace in

1928. She served as its secretary until 1931 and lectured at colleges and universities around the country on behalf of the group.

Dunbar-Nelson died in her home in Philadelphia in 1935 of a heart ailment she had suffered for three years. The diary she kept sporadically in 1921, 1926-27, 1928, 1929, 1930, and 1931 has recently been uncovered, annotated, and published by Hull. The entries reveal that Dunbar-Nelson worked tirelessly against great odds to advance the cause of equality for Afro-Americans. Hull notes the humiliations the writer suffered in an effort to recoup her lost teaching position and the penury she and her family often endured, unbeknownst to the audiences that flocked to hear her speak. Dunbar-Nelson's emotional life emerges from the diary as a complex one, in which devotion to her husband is unwavering but shared with strong romantic attachments to other women.

According to Karen F. Stein, Dunbar-Nelson was a pioneer in the black short-story tradition. She did not give up fiction, as can be seen in "Hope Deferred" (*Crisis*, September 1914, 238-44), a stirring story of a black engineer forced to work as a waiter. Nevertheless, she chose to devote herself more to journalism and political and social activities.

SELECT BIBLIOGRAPHY

Primary

Drama

"The Author's Evening at Home." September 1900.

Mine Eyes Have Seen. Crisis 15 (1918): 271.

IN ANTHOLOGIES

Hatch and Shine, *Black Theatre U.S.A.*, 1974. *Mine Eyes Have Seen*.

Fiction

"The Ball Dress." *Leslie's Weekly* 12 (December 1901).

The Goodness of St. Rocque and Other Stories. New York: Dodd, Mead, 1899.

"Hope Deferred" [short story]. *Crisis* (September 1919).

Violets and Other Tales. Boston: Privately printed, 1895.

ANTHOLOGIES EDITED BY DUNBAR-NELSON

The Dunbar Speaker and Entertainer. Napierville, Ill.: J. L. Nichols, 1920.

Masterpieces of Negro Eloquence. New York: Bookery Publishing Co., 1914.

Nonfiction

Give Us Each Day: The Diary of Alice Dunbar-Nelson. Edited by Gloria T. Hull. New York: W. W. Norton, 1984.

Paul Laurence Dunbar: Poet Laureate of the Negro Race. Philadelphia: A. M. E. Church Review, 1914.

The Works of Alice Dunbar-Nelson. Edited by Gloria T. Hull. New York: Oxford University Press, 1988.

Poetry

IN ANTHOLOGIES

Cromwell, Turner, and Dykes, *Readings from Negro Authors*, 1931. "April Is on the Way"; "Sonnet."

Cullen, *Caroling Dusk*, 1927. "I Sit and Sew"; "Snow in October"; "Sonnet."

Johnson, Charles S., *Ebony and Topaz*, 1927. "April Is on the Way."

Kerlin, *Negro Poets and Their Poems*, 1923. "I Sit and Sew."

Shockley, *Afro-American Women Writers, 1746-1933*, 1988. "I Sit and Sew"; "Tony's Wife."

Stetson, *Black Sister*, 1981. "I Sit and Sew"; "Music"; "Sonnet"; "Snow in October."

Secondary

Arata, *More Black American Playwrights*, 1978.

Arata and Rotoli, *Black American Playwrights, 1800 to the Present*, 1976.

Bakish and Margolies, *Afro-American Fiction, 1853-1976*, 1979.

Campbell, Dorothy, *Index to Black American Writers in Collective Biographies*, 1983.

Chapman, *Index to Black Poetry*, 1974.

Dannett, *Profiles of Negro Womanhood*, 1964.

Fairbanks and Engeldinger, *Black American Fiction*, 1978.

Ford, "Alice Dunbar Nelson," 1971.

French, Fabre, Singh, and Fabre, *Afro-American Poetry and Drama 1760-1975*, 1979.

Hatch and Abdullah, *Black Playwrights, 1823-1977*, 1977.

Herman, *Women in Particular*, 1984.

Hull, "Alice Dunbar-Nelson: Delaware Writer and Woman of Affairs," 1976.

Hull, *Color, Sex, and Poetry*, 1987.

Index to Poetry in Periodicals, 1925-1929, 1983.

Kellner, *The Harlem Renaissance*, 1984.

Low and Clift, *Encyclopedia of Black America*, 1981.

Matthews, *Black American Writers, 1773-1949*, 1975.

Richardson, *Black Women and Religion*, 1980.

Rose Bibliography Project, *Analytical Guide to the Indexes to "The Crisis," 1910-1960*, 1975.

Rush, Myers, and Arata, *Black American Writers Past and Present*, 1975.

Spradling, *In Black and White*, 1980.

Stein, "Alice Ruth Moore Nelson," 1981.

Whiteman, *A Century of Fiction by American Negroes, 1853-1952*, 1974.

Williams, *American Black Women in the Arts and Sciences*, 1978.

DUNCAN, THELMA MYRTLE (1902-?)

Educator

Playwright

A native of St. Louis, Missouri, Thelma Myrtle Duncan was educated at Howard University in Washington, D.C., where she penned her first play and graduated cum laude with a bachelor of music degree. Duncan was in the company of May Miller,* Georgia Douglas Johnson,* Zora Neale Hurston,* and other black women playwrights who were Howard graduates or members of the university's intellectual community. Duncan also attended Columbia University in New York City.

Her first play, *The Death Dance*, is a one-act musical with African themes. The University Players at Howard first produced the musical, which premiered on 7 April 1923, and it was produced again by a Baltimore theater. Tribal potions and dances establish the play's authentic African setting and theme. The action is set in the village of Vai, where a drug called "ordeal" is given to an accused thief, Kamo. In spite of the Medicine Man's attempt to kill Kamo in order to eliminate competition in his suit for a beautiful dancer, Asumana, Kamo survives the "ordeal" and is found innocent.

While living in North Carolina and teaching music, Duncan pursued her interest in writing. In 1930, she wrote *Sacrifice*, another one-act play. The sacrifices a mother, Mrs. Payton, and daughter, Ina, of a black family make to put Ina's brother Billy through school appear to be in vain when Billy steals a chemistry exam. The play falls into a familiar genre among black writers: the domestic drama. *Sacrifice* does not deal with the socioeconomic problems faced by a black family; instead, the playwright opts to explore themes of life-style and interaction among the members of an Afro-American family.

In 1931, Duncan published *Black Magic*, a comedy about a husband who resorts to voodoo in order to regain his wife's faithfulness. Eventually he discovers that she has not been unfaithful, but merely out looking for employment. Unlike *Sacrifice* and *The Death Dance*, this play, which made its way into *The Yearbook of Short Plays* for 1931, contains dialect. Charles Feinberg and Alex B. Feldman of the Federal Theatre Project's Play Bureau, gave *Black Magic* a favorable rating: "A hilarious comedy, admirably suited for amateur production." In the same year Duncan began to devote all her time to literary pursuits and music became an avocation in her life. There is no record of her writings after the 1930s, however.

SELECT BIBLIOGRAPHY

Primary

Drama

IN ANTHOLOGIES

Locke and Gregory, *Plays of Negro Life*, [1927] 1970. *The Death Dance.*

Richardson and Miller, *Plays and Pageants from the Life of the Negro*, 1930. *Sacrifice.*

Wise, *The Yearbook of Short Plays*, 1931. "Black Magic."

Secondary

Arata, *More Black American Playwrights*, 1978.

Arata and Rotoli, *Black American Playwrights, 1800 to the Present*, 1976.

French, Fabre, Singh, and Fabre, *Afro-American Poetry and Drama 1760-1975*, 1979.

Hatch, "Speak to Me in Those Old Words," 1976.

Hatch and Abdullah, *Black Playwrights, 1823-1977*, 1977.

Kallenbach, *Index to Black American Literary Anthologies*, 1979.

Locke and Gregory, *Plays of Negro Life*, [1927] 1970.

Rush, Myers, and Arata, *Black American Writers Past and Present*, 1975.

Wise, *The Yearbook of Short Plays*, 1931.

DUNHAM, KATHERINE (1910-)

Poet
Autobiographer
Essayist
Short-story writer
Novelist
Choreographer
Anthropologist

Katherine Dunham, best known as a choreographer, is also a writer and a woman of intercultural vision. She was born in Glen Ellyn, Illinois, in 1910. Her parents had aspirations for a teaching career for their daughter, but she had her heart set on dancing. While still in high school in Joliet, Illinois, she began organizing dance companies among her neighborhood friends. Upon graduation, Dunham entered the University of Chicago, where she studied anthropology. She was particularly interested in folklore, with an emphasis on the dance as a social custom. In 1934, while still a student, she was asked to dance at the Chicago World's Fair.

Dunham's studies in field techniques with Melville Herskovitz sparked her interest in the Maroon community of Accompong, Jamaica, and in 1935, a Rosenwald Fellowship funded a year of field study in the West Indies. Dunham's experiences with the descendants of rebel slaves (Maroons) in Jamaica is recounted in *Journey to Accompong* (1946), a day-by-day account of her search for primary data on the African-derived Koromantee war dances.

From the point of view of a sympathetic participant, Dunham intertwines her eyewitness report with a historical description of these descendants of runaway slaves who escaped to the hill country and reverted to African customs: she discusses patrilineal descent, courtship customs, and women owning and working their own fields, of which they also owned the produce. One of the first outsiders to actually live with the Maroons, Dunham accustomed herself to packed-dirt-floor houses and cooking on the ground amid lizards and mouse-bats, as she sought vestiges of West African life in the mountains of Jamaica. Noting the "meager material culture" in terms of weaving and basketmaking, Dunham nevertheless appreciated the rich oral culture of Nansi stories and folktales, some of which she transcribes in Creole English dialect. In exchange for the Cab Calloway and Billie Holiday records that Dunham played for them on her portable Victrola, the villagers were willing to share their songs.

Still, the dances remained elusive and until her last days in Accompong, Dunham had seen only European forms such as the quadrille and shay-shay. She wanted to see Koromantee dances to validate her theory on the survival of this West African rite, bound up with African religion and cosmology. Then, on the nineteenth day of her sojourn in Jamaica, a village woman died: "While I was at Moggotty this morning Mis' Mattie Cross had suddenly grown weary of this life and had joined her ancestors in that happy land which is a sweet confusion of Scotch Presbyterian and Gold Coast hereafter" (85). At the burial, some mourners under the influence of rum began to move in African rhythm. Dunham knew then that from under the "veneers of the Scotch minister and the cricket games . . . and set dances . . . the sleeping Koromantee and Eboe and Nago would come to the fore" (131). In her book she also relates how she was initiated into ancestral Obeah rites, when her Jamaican mentor, Ba' Weeyums, washed her in rum at a graveyard.

When she returned to the university, she received her B.A. degree and began work on her master's. She never finished the work for the degree, though, for she became heavily involved in theater production, choreographing such shows as *Stormy Weather, Cabin in the Sky*, and *Tropical Review*. She married John Pratt in 1941.

Katherine Dunham was not one to accept inferior treatment from any quarter. When in Cincinnati and Chicago, her company was denied hotel accommodations and she successfully sued.

As a world traveler, Dunham journeyed to Senegal, Martinique, Cuba, Trinidad, Haiti, and frequently Mexico where she published one of her nonfiction works, *Las Danzas de Haití*.

According to Leah Creque-Harris, Dunham and her company often served as cultural ambassadors for the United States, "although entirely without official backing. The State Department never sponsored a goodwill cultural tour for the Dunham Company. Dunham's request for support was flatly refused because of a dance, entitled 'Southland' that portrayed a lynching scene" (28).

Much of Dunham's writing belongs to the latter half of the twentieth century, but one short story, "Afternoon into Night," was collected in Langston Hughes's *The Best Short Stories by Negro Writers* (1967). It is the story of two bullfighters in Mexico City, and how one accepts the other's violent death. Dunham plunges her reader into the setting, her images bringing Mexico City and the bullring alive, particularly her descriptions of the crowd. Dunham depicts the Mexican atmosphere with mariachi players on the street and heavy smells of orchids and gardenias in the parks. She meticulously describes the attire of the matadors, both their professional garb and their casual dress. These descriptions form a clear image of the lithe, agile bullfighter, completing her portrait of Mexico City and its inhabitants.

Dunham's papers are in archives established at Southern Illinois University, East St. Louis. Dunham herself is artist-in-residence there, dividing her time between East St. Louis and Haiti, where she continues to take a leading part in the social and cultural life of the people.

SELECT BIBLIOGRAPHY

Primary

Fiction

Kasamance. Chicago: Third Press, 1974.

A Touch of Innocence. New York: Harcourt Brace, 1959.

Nonfiction

Las Danzas de Haiti. Mexico: Acta Anthropologica 114, 1947.

Island Possessed. Garden City, N.Y.: Doubleday, 1969.

Katherine Dunham's Journey to Accompong [autobiography]. New York: Henry Holt & Co., 1946. Reprint. Westport, Conn.: Greenwood, 1972.

Secondary

Campbell, Dorothy, *Index to Black American Writers in Collective Biographies*, 1983.

Creque-Harris, "Katherine Dunham's Multi-Cultural Influence," 1986.

Davis, Lenwood G., *The Black Woman in American Society*, 1975.

Fairbanks and Engeldinger, *Black American Fiction*, 1978.

Hatch and Abdullah, *Black Playwrights, 1823-1977*, 1977.

Herman, *Women in Particular*, 1984.

Kallenbach, *Index to Black American Literary Anthologies*, 1979.

Klotman and Baatz, *The Black Family and the Black Woman*, 1978.

Low and Clift, *Encyclopedia of Black America*, 1981.

Matthews, *Black American Writers, 1773-1949*, 1975.

Rush, Myers, and Arata, *Black American Writers Past and Present*, 1975.

Sims-Wood, *The Progress of Afro-American Women*, 1980.

Spradling, *In Black and White*, 1980.

Williams, *American Black Women in the Arts and Social Sciences*, 1978.

DYKES, EVA BEATRICE (1893-1986)

Scholar

Eva Beatrice Dykes, born in Washington, D.C., in 1893, graduated from the M Street (later Dunbar) High School and Howard University. Her uncle, Dr. James Howard, encouraged her to continue her education at Radcliffe College, where with his financial support and scholarship aid she received her A.M., A.B., and Ph.D. In 1921, she became one of the first three black women (with Sadie Alexander and Georgiana Simpson) to earn a Ph.D. in the United States. While working on her doctorate, she contacted a number of historical societies in various states. One in North Carolina responded that she would not be permitted to visit there because of her color; this is the only instance of discrimination in her life that she recalled in interviews. Her uncle, one of the first black Adventists in Washington, D.C., helped Dykes to deal with bigotry. According to her, he "always told [me] that the people who were prejudiced were victims, and not oppressors. Many of them were victims of the type of education that they had received. ... I didn't hate them."

She went on to teach at Walden University and at her alma mater, the Dunbar High School. She taught at Howard University for fifteen years (1929-44), where she was voted "best all-around teacher" by the faculty of the College of Liberal Arts.

In 1944, after converting to the Seventh-Day Adventist Church, she combined her religious beliefs with teaching by accepting a position at Oakwood College, a Seventh-Day Adventist school in Huntsville, Alabama, where she taught from 1944 to 1968. There she worked diligently to help the college expand its curriculum and attain accreditation; the school honored her by naming a library after her in 1973. After her retirement, Dykes was provided with a cottage on the campus of Oakwood.

She is the author of *The Negro in English Romantic Thought* (1942) and many articles published in such journals as *Crusader, Message, Journal of Negro History*, and *Negro History Bulletin*. Most important to Dykes was her religion: "Being a Seventh-Day Adventist, we believe that the Lord is coming soon," she said. "When Jesus was here, in Matthew 24, he did announce the signs of His coming ... and many of the signs of His coming are believed by Seventh-Day Adventists. For example, we believe that there will be, as prophesied in Revelation, a unity between church and state. ... now there is a revival of that unity. There is an attempt on the part of many people ... to sell on Sunday, the first day of the week."

Her powerful book on English romantic thought deals with that phase of romanticism that, committed to the love of freedom, "revolves around the amelioration of the condition of the lowly and the oppressed." Dykes follows this thread when examining in the writings of Wordsworth, Southey, Coleridge, Byron, and Shelley, as well as those of the period's forgotten literary figures, their opposition to the slave trade and slavery. She analyzes their portrayals of black figures and discusses historical contexts and the impact of the poetry on prevailing social attitudes in England and America. Dykes concludes that the romantic writers "were not impractical idealists, living remote from the great questions of the day. On the contrary, they were vitally interested in current social, political, and economic problems." Moreover, all the leading writers were sympathetic toward blacks, although some, like Coleridge, later became increasingly conservative and most did not go so far as to advocate social equality.

Of special interest is a chapter devoted to women abolitionists like Aphra Behn, Lady Mary Wortley Montague, Lady Middleton, Anna Seward, Dorothy Wordsworth, and Harriet Martineau. It leads to Dykes's conclusion that "literary men and women of all types were more or less active in voicing their protest against the evils of slavery," yet this is the aspect of their legacy most overlooked.

SELECT BIBLIOGRAPHY

Primary

Nonfiction

The Negro in English Romantic Thought; or, a Study of Sympathy for the Oppressed. Washington, D.C.: Associated Publishers, 1942.

IN ANTHOLOGIES

Cromwell, Turner, and Dykes, *Readings from Negro Authors*, 1931.

Secondary

Hill and King, Transcript from *The Black Women's Oral History Project*, 1987.

EPPERSON, ALOISE BARBOUR (?-CA. 1954)

Poet

Little is known of Aloise Barbour Epperson's life, except that her home was Norfolk, Virginia. Fannie Mallory Jones, also of Norfolk, describes the author in a preface to Epperson's *The Hills of Yesterday and Other Poems* (1943). She writes that Epperson was an introvert from childhood; for a child such as she, the ugly realities of life as a black in the racist South were devastating. The brutalities of her environment made her shudder and retreat into a beautiful world of poetry she created for herself. Jones concludes: "I am no critic and I have not the temerity to predict the future of this little book, but I know that a fine high spirit which was without tongue has been touched with a coal of fire."

In her own preface to *The Hills of Yesterday*, Epperson speaks of "a nameless longing, a haunting desire for the unattainable" that comes from several sources: from "the infinite sadness of loving freedom and of forever being denied its full privilege because of racial barriers," from grief over an adored daughter's death, and from "an abiding love of peace found nowhere in a war-torn world."

A sensitivity for the unspoken sufferings of Afro-Americans weaves throughout Epperson's fantasy world. In her poem "Negroes Share the Fourth," the reader hears a sharply intelligent voice, biting, but humorous, conveying attitudes of the black working community. "We do not boast or brag / 'Cept that the cotton planted by us made the flag." Her poem reveals strong pride and bitterness. She depicts angry Afro-American people unrecognized for their hard work, which benefits only their employers.

In her later collection, *Unto My Heart and Other Poems*, dedicated to the memory of her husband, James H. Epperson, several of the poems suggest that she was a mulatto. In one, "The Mulatto," an apparently biographical poem, she writes, "I have no race. / I am not white nor am I black." She goes on to tell of her loneliness born of exclusion from both races. In the end she turns to Christ, asking for "fellowship" in his land. In another insightful and possibly autobiographical poem, "My Two Grandmothers," she writes of two forebears, one white, one black:

> My milk white grandmother was lovely,
> meticulous, elegant and grand,
> My coal black grandmother was ugly
> With broad features and toil roughened hand.

Passages like this express the conflict of belonging to conflicting groups and her inability to see physical beauty in her black grandmother's face. The poem resolves this tension, however, by locating similarities between the two women: their search for pride and self-knowledge. The final stanza evinces respect for both women and celebrates their shared gender:

> I had two royal grandmothers,
> Unlike yet like were they;
> For the glory of womanhood crowned them both
> As they trod the common way.

SELECT BIBLIOGRAPHY

Primary

Poetry

The Hills of Yesterday and Other Poems. Norfolk, Va.: Printed by J. A. Brown, 1943.

Unto My Heart and Other Poems. Boston: Christopher Publishing House, 1953.

Secondary

Christopher Publishing House, Norwell, Mass.

Porter, *North American Negro Poets*, 1945.

Reardon and Thorsen, *Poetry by American Women, 1900-1975*, 1979.

Rush, Myers, and Arata, *Black American Writers Past and Present*, 1975.

Virginia Public Library, Norfolk, Va.

FAUSET, JESSIE REDMON (1882-1961)

Poet

Editor

Novelist

Like Zora Neale Hurston,* Shirley Graham (Du Bois),* Nellie Bright,* and other black women writers of this era, Jessie Redmon Fauset was the daughter of a minister. Reverend Redmon Fauset, of the A.M.E. Church, and his wife, Anna Seamon, lived in Fredericksville, New Jersey, when their seventh child, Jessie Redmon was born on 26 April 1882. She came into a family that had been free since the eighteenth century. Owing to this history, Redmon Fauset held a relatively privileged social status, enabling him to amply provide for his children and encourage their high educational aspirations. Anna Seamon Fauset died when her daughter was very young, and her father was remarried, to a woman named Belle Huff. Because of the untimely death of her mother, Jessie established a strong bond with her father, and his complete support for his daughter is seen in his efforts to help her pursue her in educational goals.

When Jessie, probably the only black student in the school, graduated from the Philadelphia Girls' High School in 1900, she was denied admission to a local teachers' college. She then applied for admission to Bryn Mawr, but the college skirted the issue of accepting a black student. When she was offered a scholarship to Cornell University because of her father's influence and her superior academic standing, Bryn Mawr encouraged her to accept it, thus avoiding having actually to enroll a black student. She received her B.A. from Cornell in 1905, the first black woman to graduate from the university; she may have been the first black woman to be elected to Phi Beta Kappa.

Fauset returned to Philadelphia to seek employment as a teacher, but its segregated schools denied her a position. She taught for a year in a Baltimore school before she began a fourteen-year tenure teaching French at the M Street High School (later Dunbar High) in Washington, D.C. Then in 1918 she decided to continue her education; she received her master's degree in French from the University of Pennsylvania in 1919. Throughout her difficulties in pursuing an education and a teaching position, Fauset kept a positive outlook, believing that racial prejudice was an obstacle that could be overcome.

While teaching at the M Street School, Fauset found an outlet for her strong commitment to helping blacks outside the classroom. In 1912, she began to publish articles in the *Crisis* (edited by W. E. B. Du Bois at the time), the publication of the NAACP. Du Bois persuaded Fauset to move to New York in 1919, where she became the literary editor of the *Crisis*. She wrote many articles on contemporary events and numerous biographical sketches. Another of Fauset's achievements at *Crisis* was to offer young writers of the Harlem Renaissance a showcase for their work. She was responsible for selecting the poetry and fiction that appeared in the magazine. According to Langston Hughes, she was "one of those who midwifed the so-called New Negro literature into being." In keeping with this role, she opened her home as a literary salon, offering young writers a forum to discuss their work and that of others.

She and W. E. B. Du Bois also published a children's magazine, *The Brownies' Book*, in 1920 and 1921; Fauset did much of the writing and editing for this publication, and again, she was able to offer opportunity to many unknown black writers, like novelist Nella Larsen.*

In 1927, Fauset joined the faculty of the De Witt Clinton High School in New York City, where she taught French, and two years later she married Herbert E. Harris, a businessman. They moved to Montclair, New Jersey, in 1939, but Fauset continued to teach in New York until 1944. After moving from New York, she ceased to take part in black cultural affairs, although she did remain in contact with some black writers and intellectuals. In 1949, she accepted a semester-long teaching position in the English department at Hampton Institute in Virginia. After a long bout with arteriosclerosis, Fauset died in 1961 of hypertensive heart disease.

Her poetry and much of her fiction is marked by French phrases (such as the poem, "La vie c'est la vie") and a sophisticated tone; her work, about the middle class, was apparently intended for an educated audience. She wrote four novels between 1924 and 1933, as well as a fifth which she worked on for many years but never completed. A recurring theme in all the novels is the struggle for fulfillment in a world of racial prejudice. In the first of these, *There Is Confusion* (1924), the main character, Joanna Marshall, meets with racial prejudice and determines to fight for autonomy and personal fulfillment. In order to emerge victorious, Joanna must forsake her own dreams to help the man that she loves attain professional status. As in most of the novels, the heroine must learn to sacrifice in order to triumph. Hugh Gloster (1948) called this novel "the trail-blazer among works in which Miss Fauset illustrates that bourgeois Negroes are interesting subjects for literary treatment" and noted that it was "the first nationally recognized novel by an American colored woman."

In her next novel, *Plum Bun* (1929), the protagonist attempts to avoid ostracism by passing as a white person; but to do so, she must shun the company of her beloved, dark-skinned sister and live an insecure existence in New York, always fearful of being discovered. Her passing functions, then, as a metaphor for the aspiration to membership in a privileged class endowed with material and emotional security. Tellingly, the white disguise proves to be a heavier burden than dark skin.

Fauset's novels portray women as suffering and sacrificing disproportionately, and her third novel, *The Chinaberry Tree* (1931), offers another variation of this motif. The novel is the story of a slave woman's feelings for her former master. When she is freed from slavery, she realizes that her love for her master has gone. After the woman comes to a new understanding of skin color, money, and marriage, her master offers to marry her. But she now has other ideals, and he is no longer a "prince" in her thoughts. As Margaret Perry comments, however, the tree of the title fails to become an effective controlling symbol and the characters do not successfully engage reader interest.

Comedy, American Style (1933) tells the tragic story of a woman's self-hate and its effects on her family. The great difficulty in attaining true happiness is the theme. Fauset concludes with a realistic assessment of black middle-class life in America. Again, passing is a metaphor for the protagonist's desperate quest, and ironically, the cost of success is loneliness, alienation, and loss of community.

Deborah McDowell, in assessing Fauset as a novelist, shows that most critics have followed the "misguided lead" of Robert Bone in cavalierly dismissing Fauset's work on the basis of its depiction of middle-class, therefore atypical, characters. McDowell argues that Fauset's genteel "novels of manners" constitute "a self-conscious artistic stratagem pressed to the service of her central fictional preoccupations, [which were] impalatable to the average reader of her day." Fauset's concerns lay in exploring female consciousness, limitations imposed on female development, and ambiguities stemming from conflict. This thematic insistence, says MacDowell, places Fauset "squarely among the early black feminists in Afro-American literary history." Fauset knew that she risked rejection from publishers and critical quarters, and this risk, McDowell convincingly argues, may have led her to channel her narrative material into the "safe" zones of genteel realism, a strategy that has gained for her the dubious distinction of being a "bourgeois" writer. Another exegete of Fauset, Mary Dearborn, asserts that Fauset's authorship was predicated on the thankless role of "mediator, bringing two cultures together by asserting their samenesses rather than their differences." Fauset naively believed that white readers would be ready to acknowledge the social criticism embedded in her fiction. Dearborn contends that Fauset's consciousness, appearances to the contrary, was informed by a tangible history of oppression and that she wrote with the ethnic woman's "sense of a divided self, of being both determined by ancestry and entirely self-made."

Though Fauset challenged sexual stereotypes, portrayed women struggling for autonomy, and exposed American hypocrisy about skin color, she has not yet received her due as a serious writer. Her novels, praised by Braithwaite and other critics in the 1930s, fell into obscurity and were subsequently excluded from the literary canon. Her exclusion can be only partially justified by lapses in her craft; Fauset's achievement thoroughly outweighs her technical flaws. She is now being recognized and placed in her proper perspective within the Afro-American literary canon.

SELECT BIBLIOGRAPHY

Primary

Drama

The Gift of Laughter

Fiction

The Chinaberry Tree: A Novel of American Life. New York: Frederick A. Stokes, 1931. Reprint. New York: AMS Press, 1969.

Comedy, American Style. New York: Frederick A. Stokes, 1933. Reprint. New York: AMS Press, 1969.

"Double Trouble." *Crisis* (August 1923): 155-59; (September 1923): 205-9.

"Emmy." *Crisis* (December 1912): 79-87; (January 1913): 134-42.

"My House and a Glimpse of My Life Therein." *Crisis* (July 1914): 143-45.

Plum Bun: A novel without a Moral. New York: Frederick A. Stokes, 1929.

There Is Confusion. New York: Boni & Liveright, 1924.

"'There Was a Time': A Story of Spring." *Crisis* (April 1917): 272-77; (May 1917): 11-15.

"The Sleeper Wakes." *Crisis* (August 1920): 168-73; (September 1920): 226-29; (October 1920): 267-74.

"When Christmas Comes." *Crisis* (December 1922): 61-63.

Nonfiction

"Impressions on the Second Pan-African Congress." *Crisis* (November 1921): 12-18.

"New Literature on the Negro." *Crisis* (June 1920): 78-83.

"The 13th Biennial of the N.C.A.C." *Crisis* (October 1922): 257-60.

"What Europe Thought of the Pan-African Congress." *Crisis* (December 1921): 60-69.

"The 'Y' Conference at Talladega." *Crisis* (September 1923): 213-15.

IN ANTHOLOGIES

Cromwell, Turner, and Dykes, *Readings from Negro Authors*, 1931. "Henry Ossawa Turner"; "This Way to the Flea Market."

Poetry

"Again It Is September." *Crisis* (September 1917).

"'Courage!' He Said." *Crisis* (November 1929): 378.

"Dead Fires." *Palms* (October 1926).

"Dilworth Road Revisited." *Crisis* (August 1922): 167.

"Here's April!" *Crisis* (April 1924): 277.

"Mary Elizabeth." *Crisis* (December 1919): 51-56.

"Oriflamme." *Crisis* (January 1920): 128.

"Rain Fugue." *Crisis* (August 1924): 155.

"Rencontre." *Crisis* (January 1924): 122.

"The Return." *Crisis* (January 1919): 118. Also in *Palms* (October 1926).

"Rondeau." *Crisis* (April 1912): 252.

"Song for a Lost Comrade." *Crisis* (November 1922): 22.

"Stars in Alabama." *Crisis* (January 1928): 14.

"To a Foreign Maid." *Crisis* (February 1923).

"La vie c'est la vie." *Crisis* (July 1922): 124.

"Words! Words!" *Palms* (October 1926).

IN ANTHOLOGIES

Cromwell, Turner, and Dykes, *Readings from Negro Authors*, 1931. "Noblesse Oblige"; "Rondeau."

Cullen, *Caroling Dusk*, 1927. "Fragment"; "Noblesse Oblige"; "Rencontre"; "The Return"; "Touche"; "La vie c'est la vie"; "Words! Words!"

Johnson, Charles S., *Ebony and Topaz*, [1927] 1971. "Divine Afflatus."

Kerlin, *Negro Poets and Their Poems* [1923] 1935. "Oriflamme."

Shockley, *Afro-American Women Writers, 1746-1933*, 1988. "Rejection."

Stetson, *Black Sister*, 1981. "Oriflamme"; "Touche."

Secondary

Bakish and Margolies, *Afro-American Fiction, 1853-1976*, 1979.

Bontemps and Hughes, *The Poetry of the Negro, 1746-1949*, 1949.

Campbell, Dorothy, *Index to Black American Writers in Collective Biographies*, 1983.

Chapman, *Index to Black Poetry*, 1974.

Dannett, *Profiles in Negro Womanhood*, 1964.

Dearborn, *Pocahontas's Daughters*, 1986.

Ellis, *Opportunity; A Journal of Negro Life*, 1971.

Fairbanks and Engeldinger, *Black American Fiction*, 1978.

Feeney, "Greek Tragic Patterns in a Black Novel: Jessie Fauset's *The Chinaberry Tree*," 1974.

Feeney, "A Sardonic, Unconventional Jessie Fauset: The Double Structure and Double Vision of Her Novels," 1979.

Herman, *Women in Particular*, 1984.

Index to Poetry in Periodicals, 1920-1924, 1983.

Index to Poetry in Periodicals, 1925-1929, 1983.

Johnson, Abby Arthur, "Literary Midwife: Jessie Redmon Fauset and the Harlem Renaissance," 1978.

Kellner, *The Harlem Renaissance*, 1984.

Low and Clift, *Encyclopedia of Black America*, 1981.

MacDowell, Deborah E., "The Neglected Dimension of Jessie Redmond Fauset," 1985.

Perry, *The Harlem Renaissance*, 1982.

Perry, *Silence to the Drums*, 1976.

Rose Bibliography Project, *Analytical Guide and Indexes to "The Crisis, 1910-1960*," 1975.

Rush, Myers, and Arata, *Black American Writers Past and Present*, 1975.

Salk, *A Layman's Guide to Negro History*, 1967.

Sims-Wood, *The Progress of Afro-American Women*, 1980.

Spradling, *In Black and White*, 1980.

Sylvander, "Jessie Redmon Fauset," 1980.

Sylvander, "Jessie Redmon Fauset," 1987.

Sylvander, *Jessie Redmon Fauset, Black American Writer*, 1981.

Wall, "Jessie Redmon Fauset," 1980.

Whiteman, *A Century of Fiction by American Negroes, 1853-1952*, 1974.

Williams, *American Black Women in the Arts and Social Sciences*, 1978.

FERNANDIS, SARAH COLLINS (1863-1951)

Poet
Essayist
Activist

Sarah Collins was born in Port de Posit (Baltimore), Maryland on 8 March 1863, the daughter of Caleb Alexander and Mary Jane Driver Collins. She graduated from the Hampton Institute in 1882 and then attended the New York School of Social Work. She became a teacher, finding positions in Tennessee, Florida, Baltimore, and at her alma mater, the Hampton Institute.

On 30 June 1902 she married John A. Fernandis, and they established a "model home" in Bloodfield, one of the poorest black districts in Baltimore. Sarah and her husband hoped thereby to create an environment conducive to comfortable living. They included in the community kindergartens, libraries, and day nurseries. They went on to improve "Scallop Town," a black neighborhood in East Greenwich, Rhode Island. Sarah also worked as a social investigator in the public health clinic in Provident Hospital in Baltimore.

Sarah Collins contributed many of her poems and articles on community service to the *Southern Workman*, published at Hampton Institute. Her work appeared from 1891 to 1936. Much of the poetry gathered in *Southern Workman* appears in her book *Poems*, written in a neoromantic style and a religiously inspired vein.

Nature and its sometimes hidden beauty predominate. She seeks to find beauty in the harsh or the unlikely: for example, she praises the first buds that push their way up through the cold breast of the earth. Rather than regard the winter and spring rains despairingly, Fernandis offers the thought that their ultimate purpose is not to bestow pain but to renew beauty. "A Blossom in the Alley" also speaks of natural beauty surviving in an environment where it is least expected. Collins reminds us that the force that pushes the blossom to the surface gives a "message of all-pervading good." The emphasis on beauty extracted from the dark and dank can be closely linked with her own work in rebuilding rundown neighborhoods in Washington, D.C., and East Greenwich. Her belief that the pains of the present are not necessarily those of the future comes out in her poetry centered around a benevolent, all-forgiving God and the struggles of the black community to attain unity.

To deal with sorrow and despair Collins advises patience and trusting belief in God's rewards. "My Thanksgiving" finds a faithful follower giving thanks for being able to withstand the abuses of a racist society. "The cruel stress" is bearable because of a belief in deliverance.

Sarah Collins Fernandis dedicated two poems to those who inspired her. The first, entitled "The Torch Bearer," is to Booker T. Washington, founder of Tuskegee Institute. She lauds his perseverance and fortitude "To lead his people till they rose to reach / The goal where progress needs must give them place." The second is for Hollis B. Frissell, a late president of her alma mater, Hampton Institute. "The Offering" concerns a black woman not wanting to give up her son to the war effort, although other women have done so gladly. She explains:

> My soul heavily pressed the galling load
> Of prejudice's mass accumulate.
> Though I had stifled bitterness and hate,
> And rendered true allegiance while the goad
> Of race-thrusts hurt, I could not give my boy.

But upon seeing that the greater good of his departure would be his becoming a part of a fight for freedom, the mother strengthens her faith and offers him "with joy!" "My Heritage" also recounts the lives of captured slaves and the cruelties that were inflicted upon her "ancestors of the ship."

SELECT BIBLIOGRAPHY

Primary

Nonfiction

"Inter-racial Activities of Baltimore Women." *Southern Workman* (October 1922): 482-84.

Poetry

Poems. Boston: R. G. Badger, 1925.

Vision. Boston: Gorham, 1925.

Secondary

Campbell, Dorothy, *Index to Black American Writers in Collective Biographies*, 1983.

Chapman, *Index to Black Poetry*, 1974.

French, Fabre, Singh, and Fabre, *Afro-American Poetry and Drama 1760-1975*, 1979.

Reardon and Thorsen, *Poetry by American Women*, 1979.

Rush, Myers, and Arata, *Black American Writers Past and Present*, 1975.

Sims-Wood, *The Progress of Afro-American Women*, 1980.

FIGGS, CARRIE LAW MORGAN (?-?)

Playwright

Poet

No biographical information is available on Carrie Law Morgan Figgs, who wrote occasional verse and plays for church and children. We glean from her books that she was both author and publisher of two of them, *Select Plays* (1923) and *Nuggets of Gold* (1921), which is marked "Price 50 cents." Her address is listed on the frontispiece of both works: "528 E. 46th Place, Chicago, Illinois."

Figgs states in the preface to *Nuggets* that an earlier book called *Poetic Pearls* had enjoyed "enormous sales." That success had inspired her to publish her new collection of nineteen poems. With noticeable self-importance, Figgs gives some extracts of letters she received complimenting her first book of poetry: "The book is a contribution to the literature of our race" and "The book is a jewel. You are the uncrowned queen of literary art." The title poem, "My Nuggets of Gold," is an ode to the poet's children: "I own three golden nuggets, / Two boys and a girl; / Who fondly call me mother; / I'm the happiest woman in the world." The abcb rhythm of the poem is frequently irregular, as is its unstressed/stressed gallop.

Figgs also includes two poems in dialect, "Whoa Mule" and "Who's You Talking To," and specifies them as dialect under their titles. In the first of the two, the speaker scolds his "country mule" for disobedience: "A city mule has got some sense / You never see him jammin de fence." The second poem is also a reprimand; an elderly person challenges his grandchild's "sass": "Why I'll break you down in the loins, sir / If you gimme any mo' talk / Don't you thing that I can't reach you / Cause I got rheumatiz and can't walk." Other poems designated "Sacred" under their titles, such as "That Eastern Star" and "I Will Trust in Jesus," emphasize the role of Jesus as the savior of all sinners. "The Negro's Upward Flight" compares the progress of the Afro-American to the skyward soar of the eagle and concludes that "His brother in white / Is no longer his peer / He is the equal of any man / Found anywhere." "The Black Queen," written in four quatrains, praises the Afro-American woman, her strength and her importance to men: "She stands bolt upright by her men, She will not let them fall." Figgs's poetry, unlike her plays, reveals her consciousness of the plight of her people.

Figgs published three short plays. *Santa Claus Land* is a Christmas fantasy in three acts for children. Alice is a young governess who on Christmas Eve takes brothers Fluffy, Stuffy, and Toughy on a journey through the woods to find Santa Claus Land. In act 1, the children meet the Queen of the Fairies, who are conjured up in rhyme by the queen and also speak in rhyme themselves. In act 2 the youngsters enter the Land of Goblins. The King of the Goblins, taken with Alice's beauty, commands her to stay with him and the others to go. Toughy is the bravest of the children and though Alice is older, he rescues her from the king. He is also the sassiest of the characters and the only one to speak in Afro-American dialect, as when he scolds Stuffy for his desire to eat one of the fairies in Fairy Land: "Boy, ain't you got no sense? Them's nothing but gals. They ain't no Fairies. Them's home-made wings; watch me catch one of 'em and take them wings off." Alice is portrayed as passively fearful of the king who desires to abscond with her and make her Queen of the Goblins.

Jepthah's Daughter is the tragic story of a biblical figure forced to offer his only child in sacrifice. The play is written in biblical English, complete with "thee's" and "Thou's" and Hebrew characters who sing gospels about Jesus. It contains anachronisms – one character "adjusts glasses" and the chorus sings "What a Friend We Have in Jesus" as well as "Jewish Heroines."

Prince of Peace is a reenactment of the angel's prophecy of Jesus' conception. Figgs's version focuses on King Herod and his queen, who plot to slay the child for fear he will grow up to overthrow their kingdom. There is much singing of Christmas carols in this play.

Figgs also wrote a "comedy drama" entitled *Bachelors'* Convention. A slapstick comedy with a faint hint of feminism, it takes place in the City of Hollygog, State of Nowhere, where some of the characters wear two or three pairs of glasses and are named "Mr. Sleepyhead" and "Mr. Womanhater." During a meeting of the bachelors at their headquarters, it is decided that none of the men will ever again associate with women. After a day of attempting to mend their clothes and cook for themselves, the men are approached by twenty-four women, survivors of a shipwreck. The women ask for lodging in return for housekeeping. A bargain is struck whereby the females agree to remain on the condition that the men "stay home at night, and take care of the babies, while WE attend our club meetings; bring home your money untouched and give us every penny; and when we have company, stay out in the kitchen or down in the cellar, and at all times be subservient to our will."

SELECT BIBLIOGRAPHY

Primary

Drama

Select Plays: Santa Claus Land, Jepthah's Daughter, The Prince of Peace, Bachelor's Convention. Chicago: The author, 1923.

Poetry

Nuggets of Gold. Chicago: Jaxon Printing Co. (by the author), 1921.

Poetic Pearls. Jacksonville, Fla.: Edward Waters College Press, 1920.

Secondary

Arata and Rotoli, *Black American Playwrights, 1800 to the Present*, 1976.

French, Fabre, Singh, and Fabre, *Afro-American Poetry and Drama, 1760-1975*, 1979.

Hatch and Abdullah, *Black Playwrights, 1823-1977*, 1977.

Porter, *North American Negro Poets*, 1945.

Reardon and Thorsen, *Poetry by American Women, 1900-1975*, 1979.

Rush, Myers, and Arata, *Black American Writers Past and Present*, 1975.

FLEMING, SARAH LEE BROWN (1875-1963)

Poet

Novelist

Teacher

Poet, novelist, and Brooklyn's first black teacher, Sarah Lee Brown Fleming was a versatile writer who explored many forms of written expression. Until recently, little biographical information existed about her, except such fragments as a note in *Jet* magazine (30 April 1964, 11) stating that in 1955, "Mrs. Sarah Fleming of New Haven, Connecticut, was cited before Congress for her work in civic and welfare organizations" and that in 1952, Fleming had been the first Negro woman elected Connecticut mother of the year. Her husband, Richard Stedman Fleming, a dentist, is listed in *Who's Who in Colored America* in 1933-37 and later volumes, although not in the 1950 edition. Their children's birth dates were 1903 and 1906. Ann Allen Shockley (1988) has recently located Fleming's descendants and has established Sarah Brown Fleming's birth and death dates as 1875 and 1963, respectively.

Hope's Highway, Fleming's only known novel, is a narrative published in 1918 whose message asserts that not only can the Afro-American achieve educational and material success despite enormously destructive obstacles but that there are Anglo-Americans who are free of racial prejudice and have dedicated their lives to working for justice for other people.

Among the prominent people to whom the book is dedicated are Booker T. Washington, W. E. B. Du Bois, Archibald Grimké, and Wright Cuney.

The sweeping style of the book is engaging and romantic. Set in Santa Maria (a mythical slaveholders' place?), the story features two principal heroes. Ironically enough, Grace Ennery, the granddaughter of humane slaveowners, is one of them. In her girlish optimism, she appears entirely unaware of the bigoted sentiment of some whites regarding blacks: "Hers was a Divine sympathy, impartial and uncolored." Because of her mother's death when Grace was a little girl "she had been removed, nearly all her life, from the world at large" and thus was ignorant of its biases and its irrational hatred of Afro-American people. Toward the latter half of the story, Tom Brinley, a young man from the South determined to fight the racism his people encounter daily, becomes the central protagonist. After being framed as a criminal, Tom escapes from a chain gang and with Grace's help is educated at Oxford University. He eventually returns to the South to rebuild a Negro college.

The plot is at times refreshingly unpredictable. One of its greatest strengths is its ability to delineate its various perspectives: the burning hatred of the racist politician, the naive idealism of the young Anglo woman, and the frustration and perseverance of the Afro-American fighting for the betterment of his people and himself. The story also introduces the idea that life is preferable for the black in Western Europe, where no apparent prejudice on the basis of physical features exists. The hero, Tom, encounters only goodwill while he studies for a degree in England and, at one point, rises, unhampered by bigotry, to the rank of a commander of a regiment of the French army.

Critics have taken almost no notice of the novel. John Milton Charles Hughes says only that *Hope's Highway* "piously resolved the race problem in religion." Yet Fleming's novel, written decades before the insurgence of the black power movement, at a time before a separate identity and independent political movements were to become prominent, examines the sentiments of Afro-Americans regarding benevolent slaveholders and their descendants and the willingness of blacks to accept the ruling class's assistance in the political, social, and educational struggle. The novel is extremely sensitive to all aspects of the racial conflict between whites and blacks in this country. One character aptly notes that white Americans were also morally demeaned by slavery: "In crushing the slave our own people were crushed, because an inferior element sprang up, an element that would never have come into existence but for the importation of slaves." *Hope's Highway* stresses that not only is it possible for the Afro-American to rise up against oppression but also that members of the white ruling class, though privileged and sheltered from hardships, are capable of seeing injustice in their society and are willing to fight against the irrational and inhumane forces that perpetuate the oppression of a people.

Clouds and Sunshine, dedicated to Fleming's children, Dorothy and Harold, is a collection of twenty-seven poems published in 1920 and divided into three categories: the first, unnamed and written in conventional poetic and mainstream English; the second, "Dialect Poems"; and the third, "Race Poems," written in the same tidy poetic style as the first section. Quatrains with aabb or abca end-rhyme patterns dominate. The poems of the first section vary from meditations on death or love to the recounting of specific anecdotes. The dialect poems consist of almost limerick-like verses, and most of the race poems deal with the history of Afro-Americans and the struggles they face in the future.

SELECT BIBLIOGRAPHY

Primary

Fiction

Hope's Highway. New York: Neale Publishing Co., 1917. Reprint. New York: AMS Press, 1973.

IN ANTHOLOGIES

Shockley, *Afro-American Women Writers, 1746-1933*, 1988. "John Vance."

Nonfiction

"Eliza A. Gardner" and "Josephine St. Pierre Ruffin" (biographical sketches). In *Our Women: Homespun Heroines*. Hallie Q. Brown, comp. Freeport, N.Y.: Books for Libraries Press, 1971.

Poetry

Clouds and Sunshine. Boston: Cornhill, 1920. Reprint. Freeport, N.Y.: Books for Libraries Press, 1971.

Secondary

Bakish and Margolies, *Afro-American Fiction, 1853-1976*, 1979.

Campbell, Dorothy, *Index to Black American Writers in Collective Biographies*, 1983.

French, Fabre, Singh, and Fabre, *Afro-American Poetry and Drama, 1760-1975*, 1979.

Matthews, *Black American Writers, 1773-1949*, 1975.

Reardon and Thorsen, *Poetry by American Women, 1900-1975*, 1979.

Rush, Myers, and Arata, *Black American Writers Past and Present*, 1975.

Shockley, *Afro-American Women Writers, 1746-1933*, 1988.

Spradling, *In Black and White*, 1980.

Whiteman, *A Century of Fiction by American Negroes, 1853-1952*, 1974.

Williams, *American Black Women in the Arts and Social Sciences*, 1978.

GAINES-SHELTON, RUTH ADA (1872-?)

Educator

Essayist

Poet

Playwright

In 1925, Ruth Ada Gaines-Shelton won second prize in the Amy Spingarn contest conducted by *Crisis* for her play, *The Church Fight*. Little is known about Gaines-Shelton, a writer whose career spans more than twenty years. Like many Afro-American playwrights, she began by writing plays for churches, clubs, and schools in the black community. These places were the forums for black playwrights who wanted to depict Afro-American life free from the stereotypes in which Broadway and other white-controlled theaters cast people of color.

Born on 8 April 1872, in Glasgow, Missouri, Ruth Ada Gaines was the daughter of the Reverend George W. and Mary Elizabeth Gaines. Her father was a minister in the A.M.E. Church for forty years and was widowed when Ruth was two years of age. In 1891, young Gaines helped her father when he directed the building of the Old Bethel A.M.E. Church on Dearborn Street in Chicago, Illinois. She earned her degree from the Normal School of Wilberforce University in Ohio, graduating in 1895. She then taught school in Montgomery, Missouri, until she and William Obern Shelton were married on 8 June 1898. Although they had three children, Gaines-Shelton continued writing dramas through the mid-1920s.

Gaines-Shelton was a grandmother at the time she won forty dollars for her play *The Church Fight*. The drama, published in *Crisis* in May 1926, does not spotlight racial issues, but demonstrates the importance of the black church. As one of the few exclusively black-controlled institutions, it was the nucleus of social, educational, religious, and political aspects of Afro-American life. One of the few comedies written by a black playwright of this time period, the play concerns the complexities of church politics and the strife among parishioners. The play is only incidentally racial in theme, however. The characters have allegorical names which may represent human nature on a universal scale and, in some cases, parallel persons mentioned in the Bible. For example, the characters Sister Sapphira and Brother Ananias resemble the biblical Ananias and his wife, Sapphira, in a chapter of The Acts of the Apostles, who deceptively withheld money and lied in an attempt to cheat their local church.

While she was enrolled at Wilberforce, Gaines-Shelton wrote for the university publication, the *Wilberforce Graduate*. "Whether your job is great or small . . . it is necessary to be firm. . . . Know your worth and carry yourself in the presence of obstacles as if all else but you were ephemeral," she wrote in her inspirational essay, "Forward Savoy." The piece begins with anecdotes of courageous individuals, including Ida B. Wells-Barnett,* Elizabeth Cady Stanton, Amanda Smith, Susan B. Anthony, and others, but a clear theme is the promotion of women's rights and suffrage.

Gaines-Shelton also wrote her class poem. It seems likely that "Hail and Farewell" is her only published poem; it was composed in honor of Wilberforce University and the graduating class of 1895. A poem of eleven stanzas with rhyming verse, it embodies a familiar exhortation given at commencement time, with the poet insisting that ". . . a stronger tie / Will bind each heart to heart / The friendships formed, as hours went by / Will ne'er from us depart."

Sources record that Gaines-Shelton wrote many plays, but it is unclear where the manuscripts, presumably most of which are unpublished, are located. Whether she wrote poetry as frequently is yet to be discovered. Some information on Ruth Gaines-Shelton is housed at Wilberforce University in Ohio.

SELECT BIBLIOGRAPHY

Primary

Drama

"Aunt Hagar's Children."

The Church Fight. Crisis 32 (May 1926): 17-21.

"The Church Mouse."

"Gena, the Lost Child."

"Lord Earlington's Broken Vow."

"Mr. Church."

"Parson Dewdrop's Bride."

IN ANTHOLOGIES

Hatch and Shine, *Black Theatre U.S.A.*, 1974. *The Church Fight.*

Poetry

"Hail and Farewell." *Wilberforce Graduate* 15 (1895).

Secondary

Arata and Rotoli, *Black American Playwrights, 1800 to the Present*, 1976.

Campbell, Dorothy, *Index to Black American Writers in Collective Biographies*, 1983.

Hatch and Abdullah, *Black Playwrights, 1823-1977*, 1977.

Hatch and Shine, *Black Theatre U.S.A.*, 1974.

Kellner, *The Harlem Renaissance*, 1984.

Rembert E. Stokes Learning Resources Center Library, Wilberforce University, Wilberforce, Ohio.

Richardson, *Black Women and Religion*, 1980.

Rose Bibliography Project, *Analytical Guide to the Indexes to "The Crisis," 1910-1960*, 1975.

Who's Who in Colored America, 1927.

Wilberforce University Archives, Wilberforce, Ohio.

GILBERT, MERCEDES (1889-1952)

Actress

Playwright

Songwriter

Novelist

Though she has undeservedly fallen into obscurity, Mercedes Gilbert was in her day a well-known actress, playwright, songwriter, and novelist and one of the few black women of her time to combine acting and writing. She appeared in many Broadway productions, on radio and television, and in one-woman shows. Her theatrical career started in such silent pictures as *The Call of His People*, *Secret Sorrow*, and *Body and Soul* with Paul Robeson. Released in 1924, *Body and Soul*, directed by Oscar Micheaux, the most prolific black filmmaker of the 1920s, concerns a virtuous but opportunistic preacher.

Gilbert's obituary in the *New York Times* lists one of her more memorable performances as that of Zipporah, wife of Moses, in the original production of *Green Pastures* (1930); she played the role throughout its five-year run. In Langston Hughes's *Mulatto*, a Broadway success during the 1935-36 season, Gilbert played Cora Lewis, common-law wife of Colonel Norwood, in a role that has beautiful and tragic monologues. She unexpectedly succeeded Rose McClendon when she was handed her script on a Saturday evening and told to prepare to go on the following Tuesday. Of her performance in *Mulatto*, Robert Garland wrote: "Mercedes Gilbert

121

pinch-hits successfully. . . . Hers is a perilous part and she makes hay with it" (*New York World Telegram,* 8 May 1936). Gilbert played the role for one year on Broadway and seven months on tour.

She was also well known for her performance of a Portuguese woman in A. E. Thomas's *Lost* (1927), as a member of the all-black casts of *Lysistrata* and *Tobacco Road,* and for her role in *How Come, Lord* (1937); among other Broadway productions, Gilbert appeared in musicals and dramatic shows such as *The Lace Petticoat* (1927); *Bamboola* (1929); *Home Bound*; *Play, Genius, Play*; and *Lula Belle*. In the 1940s she toured the country and Canada with a one-woman dramatic recital of her work; the first performance was Sunday, 16 March 1941, at the St. Martin's Community Theatre (New York?). She also performed and lectured on black history at colleges.

Her undated four-page typescript autobiography, held at the Schomburg Center for Research in Black Culture of the New York Public Library, mentions a new play, *The Searching Wind,* and another novel, *Come and Live with Me.* She says she is looking forward to returning to one-woman theater, which "I like much better than the too often maid parts we Negro actresses are relegated to." There seems to be no trace of Gilbert or her work after 1947, the date of an invitation at the Schomburg to her and her husband's twenty-fifth wedding anniversary on 19 July.

Mercedes Gilbert was a native of Jacksonville, Florida. In the autobiographical notes held at the Schomburg, Gilbert relates that her father, Daniel Marshall Gilbert, and her mother, Edna Earl Knott Gilbert, were both in business at the time of her birth: "My father owned a furniture business, and my mother a dressmaking establishment. Because of their businesses, my care was left entirely to a nurse, who also taught me at home, through my kindergarten and primary grades. I entered my first school [the Boylan Home, a seminary for girls in Jacksonville] in the fourth grade."

Gilbert began writing poems at age six and recited them "on any occasion that arose; those were many as my mother was an ardent worker in the church (African Methodist Episcopal)." When her family moved to Tampa, Florida, Gilbert attended the Catholic school there and later the Orange Park Normal and Industrial School. She continued her studies at Edward Waters College in Jacksonville. After graduation, Gilbert taught school in southern Florida for a few terms, "but wanting a definite profession, I entered The Brewster Hospital Nurses Training School and graduated three years later," remaining on the staff as assistant superintendent for two years. During her training she wrote and presented several plays and finished a book of poems entitled *Looking Backward.*

Gilbert's publisher, Christopher House, believes that Gilbert spent a short time in Chicago before moving to New York. In any case, Gilbert says she arrived in New York City in 1916, hoping to become a city nurse. She explains that since her hospital did not have the number of beds to make it a Grade One training school, she would have had to take a three-year postgraduate course at Lincoln Hospital. Instead, she worked as a private duty nurse for a short time.

At the suggestion of a friend, Gilbert found a songwriter, Chris Smith, to collaborate with her in setting her poems to music. "Strange to say," Gilbert recalled, "the first was a song about the 'sport of kings,' horse racing, entitled 'The Also Ran Blues.' This song became quite a hit and was recorded by most of the record companies." Other well-known songs recorded for Arto Records by the eight-piece jazz band and blues singer that Gilbert managed were "The Decatur Street Blues" of 1922 and "Got the World in a Jug." At this time, Gilbert was also writing for the Associated Negro Press. It was also now, on 19 July 1922, that Gilbert married Arthur J. Stevenson.

Then began Gilbert's career in vaudeville and moving pictures. Her first "real production, a big [Broadway] musical comedy," was *The Lace Petticoat*. "Daniel Haynes and a group of male singers were also in the cast, a cast of 150, all white except the singers and myself."

Gilbert was the author of three plays, *Ma Johnson's Harlem Rooming House*, *In Greener Pastures*, and *Environment*, of which we have been able to locate only *Environment*. It is a domestic drama in three acts about a mother's troubles with a fugitive husband and a wayward son.

Gilbert also compiled and edited *Selected Gems of Poetry, Comedy, and Drama*, a miscellaneous collection of her work published in 1931. It contains many monologues in dialect, such as the humorous "Talk on Evolution" as well as lyric poems (e.g., "Dreams," "Loneliness"). On the book's dust jacket, the publishers note that the monologues in *Selected Gems* have been broadcast over national radio stations "and have always amused and interested all listeners. ... This fact is what decided her to publish them in book form." They also remark that "the work is mainly in Southern dialect, because the direct appeal of this soft speech is intriguing and amusing to readers both North and South."

As a novelist, Gilbert merits an attention never accorded *Aunt Sara's Wooden God*, a work that appeared in 1938 with a foreword by Langston Hughes. He likens the novel to *Jonah's Gourd Vine* (Hurston*) and *Ollie Miss*, a pastoral love novel by George W. Henderson (born 1909), adding that Gilbert's is "an authentic every-day story of thousands of little families below the Mason-Dixon Line, bound to the soil by poverty and blackness, but living their enclosed lives always in the hope that someday some one of them may escape the family group and go on to higher things." Yet *Aunt Sara's Wooden God* goes beyond the everyday social realism that Hughes describes. Gilbert demonstrates considerable gifts for character development, particularly in William, Aunt Sara's adored son, who is torn between noble goals and self-destructive impulses. The novel's action, revolving around the Cain and Abel relationship of the brothers, William and Jim, and its painful consequences for their mother, also alternates between the communal, church-based life of tiny Byron, Georgia, and the more worldly and sometimes corrupt ways of Macon. Both settings are painted in an evocative and convincing manner. As in other works of the Harlem Renaissance, the emphasis is on ethnic material and dialect, but Gilbert transcends these confines to give us a profound exploration of individual lives and complex relationships.

Curiously, the novel had few reviews; we found only one, in the *Journal of Negro Education* (January 1939), a disdainful piece chastising Gilbert for her "touches" of social realism (like Richard Wright's), regionalism, (in the tradition of Heyward and Hurston*), and character study. The reviewer, an assistant professor of English at Howard University, faults her additionally for not emphasizing one theme, leaving no "point," no "edge," no "sociological excuse." That she intertwines all of them in her narrative is apparently overlooked by the reviewer.

New York City records show that Mercedes Gilbert Stevenson was living in Jamaica, New York, at 108-13 164th Street, at the time of her death in 1952 and that she was survived by her husband.

SELECT BIBLIOGRAPHY

Primary

Drama

Environment. Boston: Christopher Publishing House, 1931.

"In Greener Pastures."

"Ma Johnson's Harlem Rooming House." Serial, 1938. (Produced at the YMCA, Harlem, New York).

Fiction

Aunt Sara's Wooden God. Boston: Christopher Publishing House, 1938.

ANTHOLOGIES (EDITOR OF HER OWN WORK)

Selected Gems of Poetry, Comedy, and Drama. Boston: Christopher Publishing House, 1931.

Secondary

Arata and Rotoli, *Black American Playwrights, 1800 to the Present*, 1976.

Bakish and Margolies, *Afro-American Fiction, 1853-1976*, 1979.

Belcher, "The Place of the Negro in the Evolution of the American Theatre," 1975.

Campbell, *Index to Black American Writers in Collective Biographies*, 1983.

Christopher Publishing House, Norwell, Mass.

Ellis, *Opportunity; A Journal of Negro Life*, 1971.

Fairbanks and Engeldinger, *Black American Fiction*, 1978.

French, Fabre, Singh, and Fabre, *Afro-American Poetry and Drama, 1760-1975*, 1979.

Hatch and Abdullah, *Black Playwrights, 1823-1977*, 1977.

Hatch-Billops Collection, Archives of Black American Cultural History, New York City.

Herman, *Women in Particular*, 1984.

Lovell, "Excuses for Negro Novels" [review of *Aunt Sara's Wooden God*, by Mercedes Gilbert], 1939.

Matthews, *Black American Writers, 1773-1949*, 1975.

Obituary, *New York Times* (6 March 1952).

Porter, *North American Negro Poets*, 1945.

Rose Bibliography Project, *Analytical Guide to Indexes to "The Crisis," 1910 to 1960*, 1975.

Richardson, *Black Women and Religion*, 1980.

Rush, Myers, and Arata, *Black American Writers Past and Present*, 1975.

Schomburg Center, New York Public Library.

Spradling, *In Black and White*, 1980.

Stewart, Harry T., "The Poet-Actress: A Personal Interview with Miss Mercedes Gilbert," 1936.

Whiteman, *A Century of Fiction by American Negroes, 1853-1952*, 1974.

GOODEN, LAURETTA HOLMAN (?-?)

Poet

Few Afro-Americans were able to break out of local circles to attain the national recognition that publication in magazines like *Crisis* or *Opportunity* would bring. Women, particularly, were limited in scope of publication: most, like Lauretta Holman Gooden, were fated to brief local exposure, or worse, obscurity.

Born in Sulphur Springs, Texas, Lauretta Holman attended schools there until her family moved to Texarkana. With a focus in English literature and composition, she began writing verse at the age of ten, mostly to entertain herself and friends. After her marriage to John Gooden the couple resided in Dallas, owners of a grocery store. There the Goodens raised their son and the children of Gooden's deceased sister.

Gooden published two poems in *Heralding Dawn* (1936), the anthology of poetry by Afro-Americans raised and/or residing in Texas. (Sources do not indicate whether or not Gooden published in newspapers, anthologies, or magazines other than *Heralding Dawn*). In "A Dream of Revenge" the poet contemplates rejection by a loved one: "My heart feels the cold, maddened / Between the deeply suppressed conflicting passions / of wounded love and outraged pride." The speaker compares her anger to the ferocity of nature: "Ah! it suits me this savage coast and water. / I like the howling chaos of wind and water; / A plan of vengeance comes to my darkened mind." Finally she recovers with bitter determination: "Yet why should I mourn the loss of love I never possessed . . . / The passionate tenderness is gone; / I plucked it from my heart as I would have torn a thorn from my flesh."

Although Gooden does not mention race, she addressed the topic of lynching in her poem "Question to a Mob": "O, cruel mob destroying crew, / Who gave the life of man to you? / Why have you gathered, small and great, / To murder, more through sport than hate?"

John Mason Brewer, the editor of the anthology, describes Gooden's poetry as "deeply emotional, intensely feminine [?], and vitally human" in which her "well placed phraseology [is] a vivid picture of life situations as impressed upon the heart of a woman." Two poems scarcely provide material for commentary; however, Gooden's fleeting literary endeavor, joined with those of her colleagues who published in *Heralding Dawn*, indicates there was at least some New Negro Renaissance activity in Texas.

SELECT BIBLIOGRAPHY

Primary

Poetry

IN ANTHOLOGIES

Brewer, *Heralding Dawn*, 1936. "A Dream of Revenge"; "A Negro's Prayer"; "Question to a Mob"; "Richard T. Hamilton"; "Sister Many Attends the Business League."

Secondary

Kallenbach, *Index to Black American Literary Anthologies*, 1979.

GOODWIN, RUBY BERKLEY (1903-1961)

Poet

Short-story writer

Autobiographer

Hollywood publicist

Born on 17 October 1903 in DuQuoin, Illinois, Ruby Berkley Goodwin did not complete her college education until she was forty-six years old. In the period between high school graduation and matriculation at San Gabriel College (San Diego State) in California, she held two practical jobs. She wrote a syndicated column, "Hollywood in Bronze," and, from 1936 to 1952, served as secretary and publicist for screen actress Hattie McDaniel of *Gone with the Wind* fame.

In her introduction to her first book, *From My Kitchen Window* (1942), Goodwin, decrying the injustice of racism, expresses her moral philosophy: reliance on God and optimism. The eradication of injustice is vital to achieve a world that promotes "love instead of hate; helpfulness and encouragement instead of arrogance and disdain."

The injustices tackled by Goodwin in many of her sixty poems stem from a society that can easily withstand or ignore human suffering. Often God is worked into the pieces in order to ease the suffering of the lonely and the downtrodden. Goodwin describes herself as a prophetess "envisioning a perfect world order based upon the true Fatherhood of God and the brotherhood of man." "My New Year's Prayer" entreats God to strengthen her heart so that she may "know that people everywhere in every land, love sunlight more than darkness, love music more than wailing shrieks of bombs, love handclasps better than the thrust of steel."

Entrapment by a profound human loneliness–the kind caused by the withdrawal or absence of a loved one–is another prevalent theme embedded in Goodwin's works. "My Bargain" finds the desperate soul asking God

> Is this what I asked for?
> This loneliness,
> This inexpressible loneliness
> That steals through every hour of my day
> Robbing it of beauty, peace and purpose?

Though married and a mother of five, Goodwin describes loneliness with painful accuracy. Another of her poems, "My Hedge," deals with the internal blocks that arise in order to protect the vulnerable "true self."

Her themes generally encompassing universal afflictions, Goodwin writes few specifically woman-centered poems. Of the sixty poems in *My Kitchen Window* one finds only "Query to an Old Maid" and "A Barren Woman's Philosophy." "Query" connects with those poems centered around an unfaithful or hurtful lover.

> Are you so cold, so self-sufficient, maid
> That you cannot respond to man's desires;
> Or have you learned, as David did of old,
> When he said ruefully, "'All men are liars?'"

The second poem concerns a sterile woman asking herself why fate has denied her the infant touch "at my breasts." She resolves her pain with the realization that by "God['s] not entrust[ing] into my care a little soul" she will never have to see her "son stretch a hangman's rope." This bleakness echoes Grimké,* Burrill,* and other women writers who anguished over the uncertain futures of African-American children.

The remainder of the poems, roughly one-fourth of the volume, concern the "black experience" in an America that, through Goodwin's eyes, remains entrenched in racist tactics. Her central themes are racial pride and self-integrity. Trying to boost her race, Goodwin wrote "H'ist Yore Head, Black Boy" in dialect:

> H'ist your head, black boy,
> If you was born in a shack,
> In a tumble-down, weather-beaten house,
> Down by de railroad track.
> Jesus was born in a cow shed,
> On de hard rough floor;
> Lincoln was born in a cabin too,
> Buck up, don' git sore.

"A Scottsboro Victim Speaks" is similarly encouraging:

> I fight not for myself.
> I will be done when e'er the verdict's reached,
> Innocent or guilty will mean naught to me.
> I fight to save perchance another soul
> Who may some day be where one day I was.

Goodwin has been a member of many organizations in the Los Angeles area: the Los Angeles Urban League, Chaparral Poetry Society, Screen Actors Guild, and the Negro Actors Guild. In 1953 she was honored for her autobiography, *It's Good to Be Black*, receiving the Commonwealth Award for best nonfiction book by a California author. She was a member of the Christian Science Church from 1956 until her death.

SELECT BIBLIOGRAPHY

Primary

Fiction

Twelve Negro Spirituals (With Stories of Negro Life by Ruby Berkley Goodwin). With William Grant Still. New York: Handy Brothers Music Co., 1937.

Nonfiction

It's Good to Be Black [autobiography]. Garden City, N.Y.: Doubleday, 1953.

Poetry

From My Kitchen Window. New York: Wendell Malliet & Co., 1942.

A Gold Star Mother Speaks. Fullerton, Calif.: Orange County Printing Co., 1944.

IN ANTHOLOGIES

Murphy, *Ebony Rhythm*, [1948] 1968. "Guilty"; "If This Be Good-bye"; "New Year's Prayer"; "We Launched a Ship."

Murphy, *Negro Voices*, [1938] 1971. "Anxiety"; "I Dream Alone Again"; "I Sing"; "Race Prejudice in America"; "Rendezvous with God"; "Soul Suffering."

Secondary

Campbell, Dorothy, *Index to Black American Writers in Collective Biographies*, 1983.

Chapman, *Index to Black Poetry*, 1974.

Chapman, *Index to Poetry by Black American Women*, 1986.

Fairbanks and Engeldinger, *Black American Fiction*, 1978.

French, Fabre, Singh, and Fabre, *Afro-American Poetry and Drama, 1760-1975*, 1979.

Kallenbach, *Index to Black American Literary Anthologies*, 1979.

Matthews, *Black American Writers, 1773-1949*, 1975.

Porter, *North American Negro Poets*, 1945.

Reardon and Thorsen, *Poetry by American Women, 1900-1975*, 1979.

Rush, Myers, and Arata, *Black American Writers Past and Present*, 1975.

Sims-Wood, *The Progress of Afro-American Women*, 1980.

Spradling, *In Black and White*, 1980.

GORDON, EDYTHE MAE (CA. 1890-?)

Short-story writer

Poet

Edythe Mae Chapman Gordon appeared briefly as a short-story writer and a poet in the twenties and thirties. Her short story "Subversion" was included in the first (1928) volume of the *Saturday Evening Quill*, and was on the roster of "distinguished short stories" cited by the O. Henry Memorial Award Prize Stories of 1928. According to her bio-note in the *Saturday Evening Quill*, she also contributed short stories to the "*Illustrated Feature Section* of the Negro press." Gordon was educated in the public schools of Washington, D.C., where she was born. Several years after her marriage in 1916 to Eugene Gordon (who later would become president of the Saturday Evening Quill Club and editor of its magazine), she enrolled in special courses at Boston and Harvard universities. More or less coincidentally, Gordon completed her Boston University master's thesis, "The Status of the Negro Woman in the United States from 1619 to 1865" the same year her husband and Cyril Briggs coauthored a booklet entitled *The Position of Negro Women*, which contains excerpts from Gordon's work. Although this publication, pointedly socialist in tone, might appear to be propaganda for Communist party recruitment, it specifically examines the disadvantages of being black and female in a capitalist society, citing statistics to support its claims.

Gordon, in her thesis, says it is the first interdisciplinary study examining the legal, social, religious, economic, and educational status of Afro-American women. She prefaces her investigation by acknowledging that much of the material she presents also applies to black men; however, she emphasizes, "it must be remembered that for three hundred years, under both chattel slavery and wage slavery, Negro women worked under the same conditions as men. In addition to being a slave, the Negro woman was subjected to the double handicap of being a Negro and at the same time being a woman and was prostituted to the lust of slaveholders." Gordon articulates the impact of economic class as well as the double jeopardy faced by women of color. Her statistics and documentation are accompanied by testimonies of female survivors of slavery and Reconstruction days.

Gordon won greater acclaim for her short stories than for her poetry, which she apparently continued to compose through 1938 when she published a few poems in Beatrice Murphy's *Negro Voices*. Through her pensive free verse she speaks of love and human relationships, and then examines the impact of financial hardship upon them in her short stories "If Wishes Were Horses" and "Subversion."

In the latter story the terminally ill John Marley, a financially unsuccessful music teacher, strives for the love and approval of his wife, Lena. He soon discovers that his friend, the prosperous realtor Charley Delany, is having an affair with Lena, and worse, that Delany, not he, is the true father of his child. It is with dejected resignation that Marley concludes he has nothing to fear in death.

In "If Wishes Were Horses" Fred Pomeroy is perturbed by a palm reader's prediction that his wife, Rachel, will soon "be able to realize her desires" and "do some of the things she has long wished to do," adding that Pomeroy will be the one to make her dreams come true. Pomeroy, a poor clerk in a department store, is baffled, but his wife does realize her aspirations – from the $50,000 insurance check she collects after Pomeroy dies.

These two stories are so similar the reader seems to be introduced to the same protagonist twice under different names: each is a threadbare worker who is despised because of his poverty and whose value is measured by the size of his life insurance policy. Because Gordon's characters are struggling financially, they are seen by society as failures – the emotionally barren victims of unrequited love. From another point of view, the wives, financially dependent on their husbands, are partners in their economic difficulties and have no hope of earning enough to live apart from their husbands. Gordon weaves images and tones of stark reality into these brief but complex fictional sketches that explore the effects of a money-conscious society.

Like most of the women who belonged to the Saturday Evening Quill Club, Gordon seems finally to have vanished from the literary scene; perhaps she was only inspired by the cultural fervor of the moment. Her husband may have encouraged her efforts to write or, because he was president of the club, been part of the reason she was overlooked. However accomplished her writing may have been, she, like many women – particularly those with celebrated husbands, fathers, or brothers – faded into obscurity either by choice or because it was expected of her.

SELECT BIBLIOGRAPHY

Primary

Fiction

"Hostess." *Saturday Evening Quill* 3 (June 1930): 56, 57.

"If Wishes Were Horses." *Saturday Evening Quill* 2 (April 1929): 52, 53.

"Subversion." *Saturday Evening Quill* 1 (June 1928): 15, 16.

Nonfiction

"The Status of the Negro Woman in the United States from 1619 to 1865." M A. thesis, Boston University, 1935.

Poetry

"April Night." *Saturday Evening Quill* (June 1930): 32.

"Cradled Gifts." *Saturday Evening Quill* (June 1930): 59.

"Elysium." *Saturday Evening Quill* (June 1930): 55.

"I See You." *Saturday Evening Quill* (April 1929): 74.

"I Understand." *Saturday Evening Quill* (April 1929): 11.

"Let Your Rays." *Saturday Evening Quill* (June 1930): 58.

"Love Me." *Saturday Evening Quill* (April 1929): 53.

"One Summer's Day." *Saturday Evening Quill* (April 1929): 11.

"Tribute." *Saturday Evening Quill* (April 1929): 11.

"Worship." *Saturday Evening Quill* (June 1930): 55.

"Young Love." *Saturday Evening Quill* (April 1929): 76.

IN ANTHOLOGIES

Murphy, *Negro Voices*, [1938]1971. "Sonnet for June; "Buried Deep."

Secondary

Index to Poetry in Periodicals, 1925-1929,1983.

Kallenbach, *Black American Literary Anthologies*, 1979.

Mugar Memorial Library, Boston University, Boston, Mass.

Saturday Evening Quill, 1928-30

GRAHAM, OTTIE BEATRICE (1900-?)

Playwright

Short-story writer

According to Vincent Jubilee, Ottie Beatrice Graham attended the Writers' Guild dinner of 21 March 1924, an event at which literary hopefuls were introduced to white publishers, critics, and editors. As participants in the Philadelphia-based faction of the New Negro Movement, she and Arthur Huff Fauset (who was also present) had both published by 1924. Yet even their hometown newspapers omitted their names from the list of those who appeared at the event. The *Tribune* of Philadelphia noted the dinner was a reception sponsored by the NAACP in honor of Jessie Fauset,* but did not acknowledge the presence of the two local writers. And Georgia Douglas Johnson,* in her column in the *Pittsburgh Courier*, merely commented on a talk given by a Philadelphia art collector. This was an example of what Jubilee describes as the Philadelphia press' neglect of its local artists.

As a result, little is known about Graham or how her literary career began. Born in Virginia, the daughter of the Reverend W. G. Graham of Philadelphia, she attended Philadelphia public schools and continued her studies at Howard and Columbia universities. According to a bio-sketch in *Opportunity* she won prizes for her writing while at Howard, and around that time won a contest sponsored by the Alpha Kappa Alpha sorority in New York for her short story "To a Wild Rose." It was later published in the June 1923 issue of *Crisis*. The black press of Philadelphia did recognize her for this achievement, but when she published her short story "Slackened Caprice" in the November 1924 issue of *Opportunity*, it was reported that she was devoting her time to commercial art as well as literary work.

Graham never appeared in *Black Opals*, but she belonged to one of the Philadelphia literary groups participating in the New Negro Movement, and she drew attention from W. E. B. Du Bois and Jessie Fauset, editors of the *Crisis*. According to Jubilee, Graham was one of the few authors whose writing held the potential for launching a literary vocation, but she "chose for various reasons, to subdue a full-fledged literary career in favor of some other vocation or interest." With the overwhelming economic odds against her, obviously Graham could not consider supporting herself by writing.

Graham in her writing explores an issue central to the New Negro Movement: the problem of identity. She demonstrates how slavery damaged Afro-American self-esteem. The search for identity was an all-important theme in the New Negro Renaissance.

In "To a Wild Rose" Flo declares, "My blood is African! My blood is royal!" She is the beautiful and defiant bronze girl who escapes from slavery with her friend "Red Boy," who now several years later relates the story. The narrator fondly remembers their exodus to the North, where he and Flo, former slave children, are raised. Flo sustains herself by cherishing her putative identity: she is a descendant of Oroonoka, an African prince abducted and sold into slavery. It is for this reason that Flo will not marry "Red Boy": "I couldn't be your wife, 'cause you don't know what you are. It wouldn't matter, but I am African, and my blood is royal!" She marries a Moroccan, later to discover that her African blood is not pure: she is the product of her mother's rape by her owner.

"Holiday" is a complex scenario of the mixed-blood dilemma, a theme akin to the search for identity and most commonly known as the "tragic mulatto." The protagonist, Margaret Meade, abandons her brown-skinned daughter, Claire, to pass as the celebrated white stage actress, Madame Margot Cotell. She rises to fame and fortune, but the psychological pressures and isolation of passing tell on her and she begins to confuse her roles as Madame Cotell and Margaret Meade. Meade finally reveals herself to her daughter, but Claire, having suffered years of isolation and loneliness, rejects her mother in disbelief. This further devastates the already weakened actress. "Madame Cotell," hearing the waves of the ocean near her cottage, says, "it is applause. Hear how they call for me. More. I must get back to my part." She then plunges into the ocean and dies. Graham portrays the dualities of the protagonist well through her use of foreshadowing and by playing on the meanings of her characters' words; it is unfortunate that her literary talent was afforded only fleeting recognition.

SELECT BIBLIOGRAPHY

Primary

Drama

Holiday. Crisis 26 (May 1923): 12-17.

Fiction

"Blue Aloes" [short story]. *Crisis* 28 (July 1924): 156-62.

"Slackened Caprice" [short story]. *Opportunity* (November 1924): 332-35.

"To a Wild Rose" [short story]. *Crisis* 26 (June 1923): 59-63.

Secondary

Ellis, *Opportunity; A Journal of Negro Life*, 1971.

Jubilee, "Philadelphia's Afro-American Literary Circle and the Harlem Renaissance," 1980.

Rose Bibliography Project, *Analytical Guide and Indexes to "The Crisis," 1910-1960*, 1975.

GRAHAM DU BOIS, SHIRLEY LOLA (1896-1977)

Biographer

Playwright

Novelist

Although often overshadowed by the towering figure of her second husband, W. E. B. Du Bois, Shirley Lola Graham (baptized Lola Bell Graham) merits attention in her own right as a biographer and playwright. Born in Indianapolis, Indiana, on 11 November 1896 (a date recently authenticated in a family Bible by scholar Kathy A. Perkins), Graham was of Indian, Negro, French, and Scotch descent. She was the daughter of Etta Bell Graham and David Andrew Graham, a devout Methodist minister who read classics to his only daughter, not fairy tales. Her father's ministry took the family to the Deep South of New Orleans and to the West, where her father preached to immigrant black farmers and their families.

Graham later graduated from Lewis and Clark High School in Spokane, Washington, where she was class poet and prize winner for an essay on Booker T. Washington. Her family could not afford to send her to college. Upon graduation, she married Shadrach T. McCanns, but they were divorced in the mid-1920s, leaving her with two baby sons.

When Graham's father was sent to Monrovia, Liberia, to become the head of a school there, she crossed the Atlantic with her family, remaining in Paris while they went on to Africa. In Paris she studied music seriously from 1926 to 1928, and in 1929, earned a French certificate from the Sorbonne. She returned to the United States where she taught music at Morgan State College (Baltimore) for the next two years, there writing several plays for college productions. Then, in 1931, she enrolled as a sophomore at Oberlin College where she received her B.A. degree in 1934 and her M.A. in 1935.

In 1932, while a sophomore at Oberlin, Graham wrote her first musical play, *Tom-Tom*. She developed its music entirely from centuries-old African themes and rhythms, some of them brought from Liberia by her brother. Drums were an all-important element in the score and the long chant of the old-style Negro preacher replaced the traditional opera recitative. At the suggestion of Ernst Lert, director of the Cleveland Summer Opera Company, she expanded her play into an opera, a sixteen-scene dramatization of the Middle Passage from Africa to America. The opera was produced by the Cleveland company in July 1932. Kathy A. Perkins's analysis of Graham's drama career points out that *Tom-Tom* was the first all-black opera to be produced on a large scale with a professional cast, indeed, the first opera by a black female to be produced.

In 1930 Graham wrote a one-act play, *Coal Dust*, and a three-act comedy, *Elijah's Raven*. She received critical attention as a folk-poet and musician and was offered an opportunity to study music in Vienna, but she turned down the offer in order to stay in America with her young sons.

From 1935 to 1936, Graham taught music and arts at the Tennessee State College in Nashville and served as chairman of the fine arts department there. She was the director of the Negro Unit of the Chicago Federal Theatre from 1936 to 1938. In the latter year, she enrolled at the Yale University School of Drama, where she was a Julius Rosenwald Fellow; she received her degree in 1940. She then became the director of the USO at Fort Huachuca, Arizona, from 1941 to 1943. Throughout this time, she continued to write plays and musical scores.

In 1944, Graham, in her first attempt at nontheatrical writing, collaborated with George Lipscomb to write *Dr. George Washington Carver: Scientist*, a biography for teenage readers. The book was well reviewed by such publications as the *Christian Science Monitor* and the *Saturday Review of Literature* and she acquired the reputation of being a writer in a popular vein, yet with lyrical style and searching character study. In 1946, she wrote her second biography, again for the teenage reader; this time her subject was singer and actor Paul Robeson. As a result of this biography Graham's name appeared in the press in reports of congressional investigations of allegedly left-wing and subversive organizations. The book was removed from the shelves of U. S. overseas libraries by the State Department in 1953. A *New York Times* critic objected to the book's "rhapsodic style" and "too little attention to chronology." Graham's next biography, *There Once Was a Slave*, a historical novel for adults, based on the life of abolitionist leader Frederick Douglass, won the Julian Messner Award of $6,500 in December 1946 for "the best book combating intolerance in America."

In 1951, Graham married the eminent W. E. B. Du Bois. By this time, her eldest son, David, was deceased and the next, Robert Graham McCanns (who now goes by the name David Du Bois), was a veteran of World War II. Graham lived the last period of her life as an expatriate, beginning in 1961 with the couple's emigration to Ghana where the two became citizens in 1963. There she became the founding editor of *Freedomways*, and in 1964, a year after her husband's death, she became the founding director of Ghana Television. In 1968, Graham moved to Peking, China, where she served as the English editor of the Afro-Asian Writers Bureau. She died there in 1977.

Shirley Graham Du Bois was awarded the Armisfield Wolf Prize and the Academy of Arts and Letters Award for contributions to American literature and an honorary doctorate of humane letters from the University of Massachusetts in 1973.

SELECT BIBLIOGRAPHY

Primary

Drama (unpublished)

"Coal Dust." Karamu Theatre, 1938.

"Dust to Earth." 1941.

"Elijah's Raven." Karamu Theatre, 1942.

"I Gotta Home," 1940.

"It's Morning."

"Little Black Sambo." With Charlotte Chorpenning. Federal Theatre Project, Chicago, 1938.

"The Swing Mikado." Federal Theatre Project, Chicago, 1938.

"Tom-Tom." Cleveland Opera Series, 1932.

"Track Thirteen." Expression Company, Boston, Mass. 1940.

Fiction

Zulu Heart. New York: Third Press, 1974.

Nonfiction

Booker T. Washington: Educator of Hand, Heart, and Head. New York: Messner, 1955.

Dr. George Washington Carver, Scientist. With George D. Lipscomb. New York: Messner, 1944.

"Egypt Is Africa." Part 1. *Black Scholar* 1 (May 1970): 20-22.

"Egypt Is Africa." Part 2. *Black Scholar* 2 (September 1970): 28-34.

Gamal Abdel Nasser: Son of the Nile. New York: Third Press, 1972.

His Day Is Marching On: A Memoir of W. E. B. Du Bois, Philadelphia: J. B. Lippincott, 1971.

Jean Baptiste Pointe de Sable: A Founder of Chicago. New York: Messner, 1953.

Julius K. Nyerere: Teacher of Africa. New York: Messner, 1975.

"The Liberation of Africa." *Black Scholar* 2 (February 1971), 32-37.

Paul Robeson, Citizen of the World. New York: Messner, 1946.

A Pictorial History of W. E. B. Du Bois. Chicago: Johnson Publishing Co., 1976.

Rosa Parks. New York: Crowell, 1973.

"Spirituals to Symphonies." *Etude* (November 1936).

The Story of Phyllis Wheatley: Poetess of the American Revolution. New York: Messner, 1949.

The Story of Pocahontas. New York: Grosset & Dunlap, 1953.

"The Struggle in Lesotho." *Black Scholar* 2 (November 1970): 25-39.

There Once Was a Slave: The Heroic Story of Frederick Douglass. New York: Messner, 1946.

"Towards an American Theatre" [criticism]. *Arts Quarterly* 1 (October-December 1937): 18-20.

Your Most Humble Servant: The Story of Benjamin Banneker. New York: Messner, 1949.

Secondary

Arata, *More Black American Playwrights*, 1978.

Arata and Rotoli, *Black American Playwrights, 1800 to the Present*, 1976.

Bakish and Margolies, *Afro-American Fiction, 1853-1976*, 1979.

Campbell, Dorothy, *Index to Black American Writers in Collective Biographies*, 1983.

Coven, *American Women Dramatists of the Twentieth Century*, 1982.

Current Biography, 1940-[1946].

Davis, Lenwood G., *The Black Woman in American Society*, 1975.

French, Fabre, Singh, and Fabre, *Afro-American Poetry and Drama, 1760-1975*, 1979.

Hatch and Abdullah, *Black Playwrights, 1823-1977*, 1977.

Herman, *Women in Particular*, 1984.

Kellner, *The Harlem Renaissance*, 1984.

Klotman and Baatz, *The Black Family and the Black Woman*, 1978.

Matthews, *Black American Writers, 1773-1949*, 1975.

Perkins, "The Unknown Career of Shirley Graham," 1985.

Richardson, *Black Women and Religion*, 1980.

Rose Bibliography Project, *Analytical Guide and Indexes to "The Crisis," 1910-1960*, 1975.

Rush, Myers, and Arata, *Black American Writers Past and Present*, 1975.

Shockley and Chandler, *Living Black American Authors*, 1973.

Sims-Wood, *The Progress of Afro-American Women*, 1980.

Spradling, *In Black and White*, 1980.

Turner, *Afro-American Writers*, 1970.

Williams, *American Black Women in the Arts and Social Sciences*, 1978.

GRIMKÉ, ANGELINA WELD (1880-1958)

Poet

Short-story writer

Playwright

Angelina Weld Grimké, a consummate poet and gifted playwright, was born in Boston, Massachusetts, on 27 February 1880, the only child of Archibald Henry Grimké, a former slave whose father was the slaveowner, and Sarah E. Stanley, a white Bostonian. Archibald was also the nephew of Angelina Grimké Weld and Sarah M. Grimké, Quaker abolitionists and feminists, and he named his daughter after the former.

Archibald and Sarah Grimké were estranged in 1883 and Angelina lived with her mother for her first four years of life and then with her father. Sarah Stanley Grimké, who wrote philosophical essays with such titles as "Personified Unthinkables, An Argument against Physical Causation" (1884), died in 1898 without having seen her daughter again.

Owing to her unusual parentage, Angelina grew up as a light-skinned girl in aristocratic Boston circles. She attended a succession of schools: the Fairmount School in Hyde Park, Boston; the Carleton Academy in Northfield, Minnesota; the Cushing Academy in Ashburn, Massachusetts; and the Boston Normal School of Gymnastics, from which she graduated in 1902. In each of these schools, she was almost always the only African-American student.

Angelina's mother died when the daughter was eighteen, and from that point on, she grew very close to her father, a successful lawyer, diplomat, and activist who encouraged his daughter to achieve and to excel in all of her endeavors. He enveloped her with paternal love, and she was devastated by his death in 1930.

Angelina began a long career in teaching in 1902, first at the Armstrong Manual Training School and, as of 1916, at the Dunbar High School in Washington, D.C. Throughout her life, she was a writer of verse, but according to biographer Gloria T. Hull, much of her writing was "self-suppressed." Hull reveals that many of Grimké's poems were "explicitly woman-identified," and probably for this reason, much of it remained unpublished. Her strongest relationships were with other women poets and writers, such as Clarissa Scott Delany,* Georgia Douglas Johnson,* and Mary (Mamie) Burrill.*

Grimké's poem "To Clarissa Scott Delany" is a poignant elegy that repeatedly asks if the ephemeral beauties of life truly disappear when we no longer see them. The poet concludes that if such things as the "violet-lidded twilight" or "the tang of the sea" or "the shimmering note / In the shy, shy throat / Of the swaying bird" can in some sense exist, then Clarissa Scott too is not dead, "only unseen, unseen."

Hull classifies Grimké's poetry, much of which appeared in magazines and anthologies of the Harlem Renaissance, into five categories: elegies, love lyrics, nature lyrics, racial poems, and poems about life and universal human experience. The style is always delicate, musical, and pensive, its mood sad, hushed, and refined. Its depth of feeling and thought and vividly imagistic style deserve further recognition and analysis. Michael Greene points out that Grimké's poetry "has affinities with the work of other black poets like Jessie Redmon Fauset,* Anne Spencer,* Georgia Douglas Johnson,* Countee Cullen, and William Stanley Braithwaite – poets who frequently tended to avoid racial subjects and dialects, focusing instead on the subjects of a more genteel tradition." Greene believes that her poetry is also reminiscent both of that of the Pre-Raphaelites, particularly the Rossettis, and of the imagist poems of Edna St. Vincent Millay and Amy Lowell.

Grimké was also one of the first black women playwrights. Her three-act play *Rachel* was produced at the Myrtill Minor Normal School in 1916 and then published in 1921. Jessie Fauset,* writing in *Crisis,* calls it "a play as terrible, as searching and as strong as anything produced by the continental European dramatists – including the Scandinavians. Indeed, one must think of Ibsen, for the action progresses from one depth of sad dreariness to another" (64).

This was a play about lynching and its devastating psychological effects on a young black woman, who suddenly awakens to the tragic prospects black children face in life. Doris Abramson succinctly summarizes: "In the beginning, Rachel is a happy young woman to whom motherhood is sacred, a state to be desired; by the end of the play she has determined never to marry, never to bear children because she will not have them live in the racist society she has been forced to endure over the course of the four years that the play uncovers" (9). According to Barbara Molette, the performance of *Rachel* was sponsored by the drama committee of the NAACP, but some of its members objected to it, averring that "the stage was no place for propaganda." Molette comments pointedly that "for portraying Black people as she knew they existed and not how the white playwrights of that era, such as Eugene O'Neill and Ridgely Torrence, envisioned them – exotic and inarticulate creatures . . . one would think that most Black folks would have thanked [Grimké], instead very few heard what [she] had to say."

In 1919 Grimké published a short story, "The Closing Door," in Margaret Sanger's *Birth Control Review*; the story is a tragic tale of a young woman traumatized by the lynching of her brother in Mississippi and the consequent rage that she turns on her own newborn child. Michael Greene comments that a modern audience would object both to the characters' extreme sense of futility and to the cloying sentimentality of discourse, but still would be moved by the most eloquent and lyrical of its speeches.

In 1933 when Grimké retired from teaching, she moved to New York, where she lived in semi-seclusion, writing no more. She died at age seventy-eight.

Grimké's poetry, most of it still unpublished, as well as her letters, diaries, scrapbooks, and manuscripts, can be found among the Grimké family papers at the Moorland-Spingarn Research Center at Howard University, Washington, D.C.

SELECT BIBLIOGRAPHY

Primary

Drama

"Let There Be Light" [radio production script]. Lincoln Centennial Phonodisc. New York: National Council of the Churches of Christ in the United States of America Broadcasting and Film Commission, 1954.

Rachel. Boston: Cornhill Publishing Co., 1921. Reprint. Washington, D.C. McGrath Publishing Co., 1969.

IN ANTHOLOGIES

Hatch and Shine, *Black Theatre U.S.A.*, 1974. *Rachel.*

Fiction

"The Closing Door" [short story]. *Birth Control Review* (1919).

Nonfiction

"A Biographical Sketch of Archibald H. Grimké." *Opportunity* (February 1926): 44-47.

Review of *Gertrude of Denmark*, by Tillie Buffman Chase Wyman. *Opportunity* (December 1924): 378-79.

"Struggle against Racial Prejudice." *Journal of Negro History* 48 (October 1963): 277-91.

Poetry

"The Black Finger." *Opportunity* 1:343 (November 1923).

"Death." *Opportunity* 3:68 (March 1925).

"Dusk." *Opportunity* 2:99 (April 1934).

"For the Candle Light." *Opportunity* 3:263 (September 1925).

"I Weep." *Opportunity* 2:196 (September 1925).

"Little Grey Dreams." *Opportunity* 2:20 (January 1924).

IN ANTHOLOGIES

Cromwell, Turner, and Dykes, *Readings from Negro Authors*, 1931. "Dawn"; "Grass Fingers"; "Surrender"; "To the Dunbar High School – A Sonnet"; "Your Hands."

Cullen, *Caroling Dusk*, 1927. "Dusk"; "The Eyes of My Regret"; "For the Candle Light"; "Grass Fingers"; "Greenness"; "Hushed by Hands of Sleep"; "I Weep"; "A Mona Lisa"; "Paradox"; "The Puppet Player"; "Surrender"; "Tenebris"; "The Ways of Men"; "When the Green Lies over the Earth"; "A Winter Twilight"; "Your Hands."

Johnson, *Ebony and Topaz*, [1927] 1970. "To Clarissa Scott Delany."

Kerlin, *Negro Poets and Their Poems*, [1923] 1935. "At the Spring Dawn"; "El Beso"; "Dawn"; "A June Song"; "The Puppet Player"; "To Keep the Memory of Charlotte Forten Grimké"; "The Want of You"; "A Winter Twilight."

Locke, *The New Negro*, [1925] 1968. "The Black Finger."

Shockley, *Afro-American Women Writers, 1746-1933*, 1988. "At April"; "Grass Fingers"; "A Mona Lisa."

Stetson, *Black Sister*, 1981. "At April"; "For the Candle Light"; "A Mona Lisa"; "To Keep the Memory of. . . ."

Secondary

Abramson, "Angelina Weld Grimké, Mary T. Burrill, Georgia Douglas Johnson, and Marita O. Bonner: An Analysis of Their Plays," 1985.

Arata and Rotoli, *Black American Playwrights, 1800 to the Present*, 1976.

Bontemps and Hughes, *The Poetry of the Negro, 1746-1949*, 1949.

Campbell, Dorothy, *Index to Black American Writers in Collective Biographies*, 1983.

Chapman, *Index to Black Poetry*, 1974.

Ellis, *Opportunity; A Journal of Negro Life*, 1971.

Fauset, Review of "Rachel," 1920.

French, Fabre, Singh, and Fabre, *Afro-American Poetry and Drama, 1760-1975*, 1979.

Greene, Michael, "Angelina Weld Grimke," 1986.

Hatch and Abdullah, *Black Playwrights, 1823-1977*, 1977.

Hull, *Color, Sex and Poetry*, 1987.

Hull, "Under the Days: The Buried Life and Poetry of Angelina Weld Grimké," 1979.

Kallenbach, *Index to Black American Literary Anthologies*, 1979.

Kellner, *The Harlem Renaissance*, 1984.

Matthews, *Black American Writers, 1773-1949*, 1975.

Miller, Images of Black Women in Plays by Black Playwrights," 1977.

Molette, "Black Women Playwrights: They Speak. Who Listens?" 1976.

Perry, *The Harlem Renaissance*, 1982.

Richardson, *Black Women and Religion*, 1980.

Rush, Myers, and Arata, *Black American Writers Past and Present*, 1975.

Spradling, *In Black and White*, 1980.

Stetson, *Black Sister*, 1981.

HARE, MAUD CUNEY (1874-1936)

Musicologist

Playwright

Biographer

Maud Cuney Hare, playwright and early exponent of Creole and Afro-American music, was born in Galveston, Texas, on 16 February 1874. She was the daughter of Adelina Bowie and Norris Wright Cuney, a prominent businessman and leader in state and national politics. Maud wrote a biography of her father, chronicling his dedication to school reform and progressive education as well as his fight for fair practices and justice for blacks. It is, however, her path-breaking work as a musicologist and playwright that merits far more attention than it has received.

Hare's contribution as a musicologist parallels that of Zora Neale Hurston* as an anthropologist, for like Hurston she traveled to the Caribbean (Mexico, the Virgin Islands, Haiti, Puerto Rico, and Cuba) to collect folklore and elucidate African influences on New World culture. In such articles as "Negro Music in Porto Rico," Hare traces the presence of African instruments, rhythms, and dances in Caribbean culture. In Haiti she collected French Creole songs which she transcribed and published with both the original lyrics and her own English translation. Hare traced the development of various African dancers, showing that the tango of Argentina, the habanera of Cuba, and the bamboula of Louisiana all derived from ancestors in Africa. She also published *Negro Musicians and Their Work* (1936) which contains numerous references to black women whose performances or compositions include works based on religious themes.

She graduated from Galveston Central High School in 1890 and went on to study music at the New England Conservatory in Boston, where she was the private piano pupil of Emil Ludwig and Edwin Klahre. (She does not appear to have been related to Waring Cuney, then also at the New England Conservatory.) While in Boston, she studied English at the Lowell Institute at Harvard University.

Returning to Texas, Hare's first position was director of music at the Texas Deaf, Dumb, and Blind Institute for Colored Youths in Austin, Texas, from 1897 to 1898. She then went to Chicago, Illinois, to teach piano at Institutional Church; this was settlement work. In 1903, she returned to her teaching career as a music teacher at State Normal and Industrial College in Prairie View, Texas. She left this position in 1904 to return to Boston to pursue a career as a concert pianist and private instructor. On 10 August 1904, she married William Parker Hare in Boston. By the 1920s she was well known as a pianist and lecturer at such places as the Brooklyn Academy of

Music, Syracuse University, Albany Historical and Art Association, and the Harvard Music Association. In her lecture-recitals on black music she and the baritone William Howard Richardson appeared together.

A letter dated 25 September 1927 from Cuney Hare to the African feminist and educator Adelaide Casely (mother of Gladys Casely Hayford*) tells of her plans to establish an Allied Arts Center in downtown Boston. She speaks enthusiastically of the project: "If I am fortunate in securing this place, it will mean that I can put our young folks' talent and wares in a section that will be in the regular stream irrespective of race. I abhor the segregated districts." She suggests that Casely send her some "attractively dyed clothes" and "native work like ... wood carvings, bead work, basketry and [wall hangings]" from Casely's school. "I will have an exhibit of them and then keep permanently a small collection always on hand to sell. A percentage on sales to go to someone that I will have to do this." Cuney Hare's dream, the Allied Arts Center, was indeed realized and it sponsored such productions as *Dessalines, Emperor of Haiti* by the black playwright Edgar Easton.

In her later years, she established the Musical Art Studio in Boston and sponsored a little theater movement among the black community there. She directed many of the plays of this movement as well as lending her musical skills to the productions. Yet there appears to be no written record of her work. Her personal life is equally shrouded in mystery, but it would appear that as a strikingly attractive light-skinned woman of a certain class and status she was protected from some of the harsh realities of discrimination. A photograph in *Opportunity* (December 1924) shows her costumed in an Oriental-inspired beaded headdress, a handsome woman with great stage presence.

Hare's four-act romantic drama entitled *Antar of Araby* appeared in 1930; the play deals with the legendary Arab or Persian desert poet who wins the daughter of an Arab chieftain. The issue is color, for Antar is a slave whose blackness and lowly status are barriers to his success. In a lofty, epic style Cuney Hare dramatizes what is a veiled search for something more than equality. Antar's goal is preeminence and nobility, in keeping with what are revealed to be his regal antecedents.

The Message of the Trees, published in 1918, does not contain any work by Cuney Hare. Rather, it is a compilation by her of poems by nearly a hundred poets (all white except Paul Laurence Dunbar) on the subject of trees. There is no connection here with music, musicology, or Afro-American cultures, her three consuming interests, and it remains unclear why she undertook this particular project.

In addition, Hare was the editor of the music notes for *Crisis* and a contributor to such journals as the *Christian Science Monitor, Musical Quarterly, Musical Observer,* and *Music America.*

According to Boston vital statistics, Hare was living in Jamaica Plain, Boston, at the time of her death in 1936 from cancer.

SELECT BIBLIOGRAPHY

Primary

Drama

IN ANTHOLOGIES

Richardson and Miller, *Plays and Pageants from the Life of the Negro*, 1930. *Antar of Araby*.

Nonfiction

"Allied Arts Players." *Christian Science Monitor* (10 May 1929).

"Chandley Revi." *Christian Science Monitor* (21 June 1924).

"Creole Music of 1869." *Christian Science Monitor* (June 1925).

The Message of the Trees: An Anthology of Leaves and Branches. Edited by Maud Cuney-Hare. Boston: Cornhill, 1918.

Norris Wright Cuney: A Tribute of the Black People. New York: Crisis Publishing Co., 1913.

Negro Musicians and Their Music. Washington, D.C.: Associated Publishers, 1936; N.Y.: Da Capo Press, 1974.

Six Creole Songs (with original Creole and translated English text). New York, Boston, and Chicago: Carl Fisher, n.d.

"Trees" (Children's Little Theater). *Christian Science Monitor* (30 April 1927).

IN ANTHOLOGIES

Cunard, *Negro: An Anthology*, [1934] 1969. "Negro Music in Porto Rico." "Folk Music of the Creoles."

Johnson, Charles S., *Ebony and Topaz*, 1971. "Negro Music in Porto Rico."

Shockley, *Afro-American Women Writers, 1746-1933*, 1988. "Home Life."

Secondary

Arata and Rotoli, *Black American Playwrights, 1800 to the Present*, 1976.

Campbell, Dorothy, *Index to Black American Writers in Collective Biographies*, 1983.

City of Boston, Vital Statistics, Boston, Mass. [Death certificate.]

Cromwell, Adelaide M., *An African Victorian Feminist*, 1986.

Dannett, *Profiles of Negro Womanhood*, 1964.

Ellis, *Opportunity; A Journal of Negro Life*, 1971.

French, Fabre, Singh, and Fabre, *Afro-American Poetry and Drama, 1760-1975*, 1979.

Hatch and Abdullah, *Black Playwrights, 1823-1977*, 1977.

Herman, *Women in Particular*, 1984.

Kallenbach, *Index to Black American Literary Anthologies*, 1979.

Kellner, *The Harlem Renaissance*, 1984.

Opportunity (December 1924): 380. [Photograph of Hare.]

Porter, *North American Negro Poets*, 1945.

Richardson, *Black Women and Religion*, 1980.

Rush, Myers, and Arata, *Black American Writers Past and Present*, 1975.

Spradling, *In Black and White*, 1980.

HARMON, FLORENCE MARION (1880-1936)

Short-story writer

Little is known of Florence Harmon, born the same year as Angelina Weld Grimke, save that she was a member and treasurer of the Boston Quill Club, a group of young black intellectuals with literary interests during the twenties. Professionally, she worked at the *Saturday Evening Quill* and the *Boston Post*, with Quill president Eugene Gordon.

Harmon was born in Lynn, Massachusetts, and studied at the fundamentalist Gordon College of Theology and Missions near Boston. Records show that she matriculated as a first-year student in 1924 but do not indicate that she continued there. However, Harmon published a story called "The House of Mirth" in the 1924 Gordon yearbook. The story is a fable about the birth of a deformed child to a self-perceived perfect monarch. Could it possibly be read as a veiled comment on prejudice and the need for compassion?

Two more extant stories, published in the *Quill* in the late 1920s, reveal Harmon as a keen observer of human nature and of genteel middle-class mores. In "Belated Romance" two aging suitors renew their marriage proposals to an upper class spinster, at her banker's urging. Harmon presents her three main characters – the two gallant gentlemen who endeavor to rise to the occasion and the demure lady who tends to her tatting as she hears their suit – in a humorous fashion, skillfully delineating their idiosyncracies. "Attic Romance" describes an artist's attraction to his upstairs neighbor and the outcome of his pursuit, after "rain beat so incessant a tattoo on Crowther's roof window that his loneliness became unbearable." Harmon is particularly adept at conveying the texture of the life and speech of her genteel white characters. Both stories abide by the conservative guidelines established by Gordon for the *Quill* – foregoing dialect for traditional conventions.

Given her narrative skill and editorial activities, why Harmon apparently ceased her literary endeavors remains a puzzle. At the time of her death from heart failure in 1936, her mother gave Harmon's occupation as "dressmaker." She is buried in a family plot at Pine Grove Cemetery, Lynn, Massachusetts.

Florence Harmon should not be confused with another Florence Harmon, born in McAlester, Oklahoma, probably in the 1920s, who published books of poetry in 1969 and 1975.

SELECT BIBLIOGRAPHY

Primary

Fiction

"Attic Romance." *Saturday Evening Quill* (1929): 32-33.

"Belated Romance." *Saturday Evening Quill* (1928): 62-63.

"The House of Mirth." *Hypernikon* (Yearbook of Gordon College, 1924), 74-75

IN ANTHOLOGIES

Cromwell, Turner, and Dykes, *Readings from Negro Authors,* 1931. "Attic Romance."

Secondary

Campbell, Dorothy, *Index to Black American Writers in Collective Biographies,* 1983.

City of Boston, Registry of Vital Statistics.

Daniel, Walter C., *Black Journals of the United States,* 1982.

Gordon College Archives, Wrentham, Mass.

Kallenbach, *Index to Black American Literary Anthologies,* 1979.

Kellner, *The Harlem Renaissance,* 1984.

HARRISON, JUANITA (1891?-?)

Autobiographical travel writer

Juanita Harrison's writing was not a primary or lifelong activity. It was an outgrowth of her traveling experiences, which would have been unusual for any woman of modest means during the 1930s, but were especially so for a black woman domestic. She wrote her book at the suggestion of her employer, Mrs. Myra K. Dickinson. The preface tells us that Harrison had only a few months of schooling before she was ten, and then engaged in "an endless round of cooking, washing, and ironing in an overburdened household. . . . But the child at work . . . lived with a bright vision of templed cities in foreign lands which she had seen pictured in the stray pages of a magazine." Indeed, at age sixteen she began to work in far-away places like Canada and Cuba, a prelude to the grand world tour she undertook at age thirty-six and that is recorded in diary form in her only book. Having taken YMCA classes whenever she could, she acquired some conversational Spanish and French that served her well in her adventures around the world. That she was able to realize her dream during the bleak years of the depression is even more remarkable.

Though Harrison's writing style is artless and ungrammatical, her themes undeveloped, and her content mostly factual, her book, *My Great Wide Beautiful World* (originally published in *Atlantic Monthly*), is a unique document. It tells of a woman who dreamed of traveling worldwide and refused to allow anything to interfere with that dream. The existence of classism and racism are barely acknowledged in Harrison's chronicle of the years she spent circling the globe (1927-35) from California to Jerusalem, Burma, and Thailand and finally to Hawaii, where she settled. Having none of Zora Neale Hurston's* or Katherine Dunham's* scholarly qualifications, she nonetheless resembles them in her wanderlust, her appreciation of cultural differences, and her resolute autonomy.

The book seems not to have been edited; none of the grammar, spelling, or punctuation errors was corrected either by Mildred Morris, the arranger and author of the preface, or by Macmillan, the publisher. Harrison persistently used the verb "to be" in the plural with a singular subject, there are few commas and periods, and capitalization is erratic. At one point Harrison tells of an employer in Paris who thinks she should put her travels "in a book, misteakes and all. I said that if the mistekes are left out there'll be only blank."

Frequently exulting in being single, Harrison says of the Spanish women and girls she sees washing clothes: "if I was married I would be at home washing dirty clothes just as they are doing." She turns down the many advances, mostly gallant, of the gentlemen she meets along the way because she prefers to sightsee alone. And when a man dared to be "fresh" with her, she "landed an upper cut under his chin" as discouragement to the others. Whenever she sees autonomous women, she is pleased. In Rangoon, for example, she notes, "what a joy to see the wide streets and the women enjoying so much freedom, and the Burma women with their High Crown of black hair. I do not like their big cigars that are stuck in many of their mouths, but they say inside is as harmless as corn silk."

Harrison consistently celebrates self-reliance, pageantry, and the sensual delight of exotic sights, sounds, and tastes. "Paradise is not lost," she says, "it is here on earth." One of her most vivid descriptions is of the feast of the goddess Kali in India, with its procession, ablution, prostration, and sacrificing of goats. Spiritual feeling is often expressed as well – Harrison prays in Greek, Catholic, and Protestant churches. A relativist in matters of religion, she would have been "just as well pleased to be a Hindu." Equally, in matters of class, "I dont mind being a high cast but I want to be a low cast too." Upon attending the famous Passion Play in Oberammergau, performed only once every ten years, Harrison comments, like a good Californian, that it is less impressive to her than some film performances: "Where Christ ascents cannot come up to Hollywood at all."

Clearly, working her way around the world gave Harrison pure pleasure, as can be seen in some of the poetic moments of her text. At one point she watches the Alps "take off their white winter robe by July they were completely nud."

Her story concludes on Waikiki Beach in Hawaii, where she finds a yard to pitch the tent she bought with the earnings from her *Atlantic Monthly* articles and also finds a sweetheart, the first time she tells of allowing a man to kiss her. Harrison appears not to have written anymore, yet, as reviewer Katherine Woods noted in 1936, "There is nothing on our shelves, certainly, that is quite like this spontaneous, shrewd, and unselfconscious story of the Odyssey of an American negress."

SELECT BIBLIOGRAPHY

Primary

My Great Wide Beautiful World. Arranged and with a preface by Mildred Morris. New York: Macmillan, 1936. Originally published in *Atlantic Monthly* (October and November 1935).

Secondary

Brignano, *Black Americans in Autobiography*, 1984.

Chalmers, *Witnesses for Freedom*, [1959] 1976.

Klotman and Baatz, *The Black Family and the Black Woman*, 1978.

Spradling, *In Black and White*, 1980.

Woods, "Juanita Harrison Has Known Twenty-Two Countries," 1936.

Woods, "Traveling for Adventure," 1936.

HAYFORD, GLADYS MAY CASELY (AQUAH LALUAH) (1904-1950)

Poet

Dancer

This British-educated African poet and dancer was introduced to the North American public through *Atlantic Monthly*, where three of her poems were published. Gladys May Casely Hayford, an only child, was born in Axim, the Gold Coast, on 11 May 1904, to prominent West African parents: Joseph Casely Hayford the elder, a distinguished lawyer from the Gold Coast (Ghana) and an early leader in the Pan-African movement, and Adelaide Smith Casely Hayford, a prominent educator and founder of Girls' Vocational School in Freetown, Sierra Leone.

Because of a birth defect in one leg, the child was taken by her mother to England for treatment. There she learned English, while continuing to speak Fanti. Later, she would attend college at Colwyn Bay in Wales and reside for a total of five years in the British Isles. A gifted poet and musician, her mother urged her to study at Columbia University in New York, but Gladys, already in Europe, chose instead to join a Berlin jazz troupe. She also decided to forgo an opportunity to study at Radcliffe. Indeed, Gladys's spontaneous decisions and tempestuous romances greatly vexed her mother, as evidenced in the latter's *Memoirs*. Adelaide M. Cromwell, biographer of Adelaide, devotes a revealing chapter of her book to the "bittersweet" relationship of mother and daughter. This insight was based on examination of the unpublished poetry of Gladys, made accessible to Cromwell by the poet's only son, Kobe Hunter. Returning to Africa in 1926, Gladys assisted her mother at the Girls' Vocational School, teaching African folklore and literature. Gladys played an important part in strengthening the school, and her mother hoped Gladys would one day be principal. But Gladys died early, of black water fever at the age of forty-six.

In Countee Cullen's anthology, Gladys writes: "By twenty I had the firm conviction that I was meant to write for Africa. This was accentuated by the help which our boys and girls need so much and fired by the determination to show those who are prejudiced against color, that we deny inferiority to them, spiritually, intellectually and morally; and to prove it. I argued that the first thing to do, was to imbue our own people with the idea of their own beauty, superiority and individuality, with a love and admiration for our own country, which has been systematically suppressed" (196).

A lilting and sometimes plaintive simplicity gives her work unique flavor. In simple couplets she asks "But how can the Negroes play their harps, / With sorrow for intervals pain for sharps?" ("A Poem"). In "Rainy Season

Love Song" her tone is sensual, celebratory, and full of vivid, specifically African imagery: African flowers (the frangipani), African dress (the lappah skirt), and close family ties (mothers and babies) set her poetry apart from that of her Afro-American contemporaries.

An important source for future scholarship is the mother-daughter correspondence of the two Casely Hayford women, collected by Anna Melissa Graves. Cromwell states: "There is much that one could write about this fascinating, talented, and sensitive daughter of Mrs. Casely Hayford. She warrants a biography of her own." In light of the Pan-African themes of the Harlem Renaissance period, Hayford, who is contemporaneous with the women chronicled here and published in the same journals, must be included in discussions of the period.

SELECT BIBLIOGRAPHY

Primary

Poetry

"Creation." *Messenger* (May 1926).

"Mammy." *Messenger* (March 1926).

"Nativity." *Opportunity* (January 1927): 13. Also in Cullen, *Caroling Dusk*, 1927, 197.

"The Palm Wine Seller." *Journal of Negro Life* 8, no. 2 (February 1930): 41.

"A Poem." *Opportunity* (July 1928): 220. Also in *Messenger* (March 1926).

"Rainy Season Love Song." *Opportunity* (September 1927): 275.

IN ANTHOLOGIES

Bontemps, *Golden Slippers*, 1941. "The Serving Girl."

Cullen, *Caroling Dusk*, 1927. "Nativity"; "Rainy Season Love Song"; "The Serving Girl"; "Baby Cobina."

Kerlin, *Negro Poets and Their Poems*, [1923] 1935. "The Palm Wine Seller."

Secondary

Bontemps and Hughes, *The Poetry of the Negro, 1746-1949*, 1949.

Chapman, *Index to Black Poetry*, 1974.

Cromwell, Adelaide M., *An African Victorian Feminist*, 1986.

Ellis, *Opportunity; A Journal of Negro Life*, 1971.

Graves, *Benvenuto Cellino Had No Prejudice against Bronze*, 1943.

Index to Poetry in Periodicals, 1920-1924, 1983.

Kallenbach, *Index to Black American Literary Anthologies*, 1979.

Oxley, *The Black Man in the World's Literature: Gladys May Hayford (1906-), Poet*.

Rose Bibliography Project, *Analytical Guide and Indexes to "The Crisis," 1910 to 1960*, 1975.

Spradling, *In Black and White*, 1980.

HAZZARD, ALVIRA (1899-1953)

Poet

Playwright

Short-story writer

Alvira Hazzard was a member of the Saturday Quill Club in Boston. According to a bio-note in its literary publication, the *Saturday Evening Quill*, Alvira Hazzard was born in North Brookfield, Massachusetts, to John and Rosella Curry Hazzard. Her family had been in New England for three generations. She graduated from Worcester Normal School and taught in Boston public schools.

Organized in July of 1925, the Saturday Quill Club was a Boston gathering of young black intellectuals with literary aspirations. That the membership was all-black was incidental, since any qualified individual could join. Other black women involved with the club were Marion G. Conover, Alice Chapman Furlong, Edythe Mae Gordon,* Florence M. Harmon* (who was treasurer of the club and assistant editor of the *Saturday Evening Quill*), Helene Johnson,* Gertrude P. McBrown,* Florida R. Ridley,* Gertrude Schalk, and Dorothy West.* The club produced its publication annually, with 250 copies per edition. Since, as its editor admitted, *Saturday Evening Quill* was not a commercial endeavor but a publication to gratify club members, the editorial staff was not able to accommodate requests from all over the country for copies. Selections of every genre were included in the magazine, which was considered conservative but "by far the most interesting and the best," according to W. E. B. Du Bois. Hazzard, mentioned in the bio-note as "a prolific writer of one-act plays," published various poems and three plays in the magazine, "many of which [had been] acted by amateurs."

Mother Liked It is a two-act play about the lost-generation high society of the 1920s. An alleged Prince Ali Khan, noted in the character sketch at the beginning of the play as "the problem," arrives in town to give performances at the Empire Theatre. Two young women, Alta and Tess, scorn their girlfriend Meena, who, infatuated with the Indian prince, has "gazed on his oriental beauty." Alta and Tess play a prank on Meena, setting up one of their men friends "to costume and ape the Prince." Later it is discovered that Prince Ali Khan is not from India, that he is being impersonated by a "husky college halfback and one-hundred percent American," mocking another culture to pay his way through college. This apparently solves "the problem," so that Alta and Tess change their attitudes. Hazzard uses phrases, presumably the vernacular of the time, that are peculiar and occasionally divert the reader's attention from the plot.

In another play Hazzard shows that liberal northerners were often not free of racism. *Little Heads* deals with the complexity of the relationship between the burgeoning black middle class and the dominant white middle class in America. Frances, daughter of a black northern family, is elated to be invited to a party given by Delores, a wealthy white schoolmate. Frances's brother and sister, Joe and Bee, intercept the invitation, discovering that their sister has been invited to the party only to provide entertainment for the guests. Frances is expected to dress "old-fashioned" and "sing some of those delightful spirituals." The work shows that although Afro-Americans could embody white standards of education, wealth, and beauty, they still had to metaphorically if not literally ride in the back of the bus.

Present in both *Little Heads* and *Mother Liked It* is the stereotyping of persons of color as buffoons to entertain and amuse white people (still perpetuated through the legacy of Charlie Chan and Amos 'n' Andy). As explored in *Little Heads,* of all grounds for division – social, economic, political, religious – segregation by race was the most rigid.

Most of Hazzard's works were featured in the Quill Club publication, but she also published several short stories in the *Boston Post,* as did Florence Harmon* and Dorothy West,* two other black Boston women writers. Alvira Hazzard, single throughout her life, last resided in Roxbury on Akron Street. An autopsy report indicates that she died of chronic lymphatic leukemia on 10 January 1953. Despite her writing and teaching careers, Hazzard's death certificate lists her "usual occupation" as a clerk at Boston City Hospital.

SELECT BIBLIOGRAPHY

Primary

Drama

Little Heads. Saturday Evening Quill (April 1929): 42-44 .

Mother Liked It. Saturday Evening Quill (April 1928): 10-14.

Fiction

"Blind Alley." *Saturday Evening Quill* (April 1929): 73-74.

Poetry

"Alabaster." *Saturday Evening Quill* (June 1930): 69.

"Beyond." *Saturday Evening Quill* (April 1929).

"The Penitent." *Saturday Evening Quill* (June 1928): 16.

"Predestination." *Saturday Evening Quill* (April 1929): 22.

"To My Grandmother." *Saturday Evening Quill* (April 1929): 22.

Secondary

Arata and Rotoli, *Black American Playwrights, 1800 to the Present*, 1976.

French, Fabre, Singh, and Fabre, *Afro-American Poetry and Drama, 1760-1975*, 1979.

Hatch and Abdullah, *Black Playwrights, 1823-1977*, 1977.

Index to Poetry in Periodicals, 1925-1929, 1983.

Kellner, *The Harlem Renaissance*, 1984.

HOLLOWAY, LUCY ARIEL WILLIAMS (1905-1973)

Educator

Musician

Poet

Lucy Ariel Williams received national recognition when, as a Fisk University senior, she shared first and second prizes for her dialect poem "Northboun'" in the *Opportunity* contest of 1926; but the attention was fleeting.

Lucy, the third child and only daughter of Fannie Brandon of Alabama and Dr. H. Roger Williams of Louisiana, was born on 3 March 1905. The first Williams sibling died in infancy, leaving Lucy and her brother, Herschell, to form a close relationship that would endure until Herschell's death in 1949. Dr. Williams was a practicing physician and druggist in Mobile, Alabama, who passed on his interest in creative writing (especially verse) to his offspring. Lucy, called Ariel by family and friends, recollected this period of her childhood as the origin of her interest in writing, when she and Herschell offered their father help as critics of his writing.

As professionals, Williams's parents valued education, and Ariel attended Mobile's Emerson Institute until the tenth grade. After completing her secondary education in the preparatory department of Talladega College in 1923, she enrolled at Fisk University, receiving her B.A. with a major in music in 1926. To further her art, she matriculated at the Oberlin Conservatory of Music with aspirations of becoming a concert pianist. After attending the conservatory for two years, she earned the degree of bachelor of music with a major in piano and a minor in voice. In the late thirties, following her marriage to Joaquin M. Holloway and the birth of her son, Joaquin, Jr., the musician spent summers studying at Columbia and with Fred Waring.

Williams was invited to become director of music at North Carolina College in Durham following her graduation from Oberlin Conservatory. She accepted, despite her intentions of becoming a concert pianist. After this position ended in 1932, her subsequent jobs and activities distracted her from the concert stage. From 1932 to 1939 Williams moved several times. According to Oberlin College archives, Williams taught music and high school subjects at the Dunbar High School in Mobile, Alabama, from 1932 to 1936; for 1936, the year she wed mail carrier Holloway, she is listed as "homemaker"; in 1936-37 she taught at the Fessenden Academy, under the auspices of the American Missionary Association, in Florida; in 1937-38 she took maternity leave; and in 1938-39 she taught in Lincoln Academy, also under the supervision of the AMA, in Kings Mountain, North Carolina. Williams returned to Dunbar High School in Mobile from 1939 to 1945 when she assumed a newly created position as supervisor of music in the Mobile public schools. She held this post until her death in 1973.

The list of Ariel Williams's professional, civic, and local memberships attests to her various activities. They include Emanuel African Methodist Episcopal Church, Carrie A. Salvant Federated Club, Delta Sigma Theta Sorority, the Mobile County, Alabama State, and American Teachers associations, Music Educators National Conference, and the American Bridge Association. As a music educator Williams published "E for Excellent" in the January 1955 issue of the *Music Educator's Journal.*

A publication called *Live Wire: Sepia South in the News* assures us that Williams's mother was a schoolteacher and choir singer "admired for her beauty and chastity" and her father was "an intellectual giant, beloved as a physician, druggist, preacher, singer, poet, and friend of mankind." Best of all, "in spite of her talent and achievements, Mrs. Holloway maintains a sweet simplicity. She is one of the few career women who considers her home and family first. . . . [her husband and her son] know her as a thoroughly domestic wife and mother who can cook a mighty good lemon pie and who could make a living any day off of home made chocolate fudge." While these comments seem sexist and condescending, one must also keep in mind that during this period most black women had to leave their children every morning to clean, wash, and cook for and raise the children of white families across town. For black families able to live on one income, the male's, *homemaker* was an admiring term associated with the middle class.

In the scheme of the Harlem-based segment of the New Negro Renaissance, the poet's contribution was the five poems she published in *Opportunity* from 1926 to 1935. Although *Opportunity* and *Crisis* were national showcases for Afro-American creative artists, countless women were unable to use the exposure from publication in them to build literary careers. Holloway and the vast majority of women writers were shunned by publishers and their work dismissed.

The Oberlin archives disclose Williams's frustration as she tried to advance her literary career. The confidence and cheerful disposition she displayed at poetry readings on the stage and radio or at her lectures on self-discipline, art, and the writer/scholar's influence on education were less in evidence in her letters: "[I am] . . . writing poems which may or may not be as successful as "Northboun'" and "Glory" and a few others, wishing very much that I could find a publisher for a collection of poems." In 1947 she was still seeking a publisher for poems she had been compiling since the 1920s and had begun a full-length novel.

Williams was fifty years old when the Exposition Press in New York published *Shape Them into Dreams* in 1955. The volume opens with "I know how a volcano must feel," a poem typical of her thirty-five others in free verse and rhyme, some of them metaphors, emanating from her experience and introspection. Williams here is the volcano, "With molten lava / Smoldering in its breast," whose core is a woman, an Afro-American. Her "thoughts, wild thoughts" lie in the abyss of her soul. "Something beautiful" dreams, but aspirations, like molten lava, cannot be formed, and so she "must pour them out thus," burning a path to the consciousness of the reader. Another metaphor is used in "Apples," in which the author observes "Apples / spotted and scarred / On the outside / . . . are sweet and sound / under the skin / but Rosy, luscious-looking apples / some of them are rotten / at the core. / People are like apples." "My Temple" carries her reader through her self-realization that her soul is "the smallest chapel, / But the greatest communion / I have ever known."

Some of Williams's poems had racial themes. "Northboun'," one of two dialect poems published in *Shape Them into Dreams*, is about the migration of Afro-Americans north during the 1920s. "Northboun'" later appeared in anthologies by Countee Cullen, Arna Bontemps, James Weldon Johnson, and others including a textbook used at State Teachers' College in Mobile, Alabama. The other dialect poem, "A'nt Sooky Speaks" deliberates on the usefulness of educating black people. Other works are "Memory of a Jim Crow Car," "Black Magician," and "Picture of an Aged Negro." Williams also included the class poem she wrote for Fisk University's graduating class of 1926, "The Entrance Gate," one of her less intense poems.

Despite the visibility generated by the prize-winning "Northboun'" in *Opportunity*, she remained obscure both as a writer and a musician on a national level. Only small local and Afro-American newspapers (including the *Pittsburgh Courier* and the *Mobile Press Register*) celebrated the achievements of the educator, community leader, poet, and lecturer.

Interesting comparisons can be drawn between Williams's career and that of Georgia Douglas Johnson,* who also studied at Oberlin. Both women were fond of music and writing. Johnson's first love was music, but her primary vocation (in terms of money) was writing. Also a music major, Williams had intentions of becoming a concert pianist, a career that never materialized. By giving piano performances locally in Mobile, Alabama, she never relinquished her dream entirely. Unfortunately she was only remembered locally. An elementary school in Mobile was rededicated and renamed in her honor following her death in 1973.

SELECT BIBLIOGRAPHY

Primary

Poetry

Shape Them into Dreams: Poems. New York: Exposition Press, 1955.

IN ANTHOLOGIES

Bontemps, *Golden Slippers*, 1941. "Northboun'."

Cullen, *Caroling Dusk*, 1927. "Northboun'."

Secondary

Bontemps and Hughes, *The Poetry of the Negro, 1746-1949*, 1949

Bontemps and Hughes, *The Poetry of the Negro, 1746-1970*, 1970.

Campbell, Dorothy, *Index to Black American Writers in Collective Biographies*, 1983.

Chapman, *Index to Black Poetry*, 1974.

Deodene and French, *Black Poetry since 1944*, 1971.

Ellis, *Opportunity; A Journal of Negro Life*, 1971.

Fisk University Archives, Nashville, Tenn.

French, Fabre, Singh, and Fabre, *Afro-American Poetry and Drama, 1760-1975*, 1979.

Index to Poetry in Periodicals, 1925-1929, 1983.

Kallenbach, *Index to Black American Literary Anthologies*, 1979.

Kellner, *The Harlem Renaissance*, 1984.

Oberlin College Archives, Oberlin, Ohio

Reardon and Thorsen, *Poetry by American Women, 1900-1975*, 1979.

Rush, Myers, and Arata, *Black American Writers Past and Present*, 1975.

Spradling, *In Black and White*, 1980.

Stetson, *Black Sister*, 1981.

HOPKINS, PAULINE ELIZABETH (1859-1930)

Novelist

Playwright

Short-story writer

Literary editor

Pauline Elizabeth Hopkins, whose creative activities bridged the nineteenth and twentieth centuries, was so prolific and prominent at one time that it is hard to understand why for many decades she was forgotten. Her struggle, both as a black and as a woman, to become a writer is emblematic of the period and yet unique in the degree to which she triumphed. Born in Portland, Maine, in 1859, she moved to Boston at a very early age and attended public schools there. At age fifteen she won first prize (ten dollars in gold) for an essay on "The Evils of Intemperance and Their Remedies" in a competition sponsored by noted novelist, playwright, and historian William Wells Brown. This prize encouraged her to seek a career as an author after her graduation from the Girls High School.

Hopkins's desire to become a playwright was realized with the writing of her first musical drama, *Slave's Escape: Or the Underground Railroad* in 1879. She revised it later as *Peculiar Sam: or the Underground Railroad*. This play embodies one of her recurring themes – the escape of slaves – inspired by Brown's works. The Hopkins Colored Troubadours performed it in Oakland Garden, Boston, in July 1880. Pauline herself performed the role of "the pet of the plantation." Her play received favorable notices from the press and high praise from critics.

After this successful start, she performed and sang, touring with her family. The press called her "Boston's Favorite Soprano." She also completed the unpublished "One Scene from the Drama of Early Days," a dramatization of the biblical story of Daniel in the lion's den. There is no record of the play's production.

In the early 1890s financial circumstances forced her to study stenography, after which she was employed by two wealthy citizens who were members of the Republican party. On their enthusiastic recommendation, she was appointed to the Bureau of Statistics where she worked for four years. Pauline also lectured publicly during this period. For her many speaking appearances she received excellent notices from the press.

Her life as a fiction writer commenced in her forties when she began publishing short articles in *The Colored American*, published by the Colored Co-operative Publishing Company. The first issue (May 1900) carried her short story "The Mystery Within Us," a reflection of Hopkins's interest in metaphysical and spiritual phenomena. The same publishing company published her first and best known novel *Contending Forces: A Romance Illustrative of Negro Life North and South* (1900), her only fiction published in book form during her lifetime.

Contending Forces, a story of love lost and regained, fuses black themes with white literary conventions as manifested in the sentimental novel. In the preface, Hopkins urges blacks to investigate and record their personal histories. She wrote: "Fiction is of great value to any people as a preserver of manners and customs – religious, political and social. It is a record of growth and development from generation to generation. No one will do this for us: we must ourselves develop the men and women who will faithfully portray the inmost thoughts and feelings of the Negro with all the fire and romance which lie dormant in our history."

Critic Jane Campbell sees the novel as a historical romance written from a feminist perspective, "strategically designed to acquaint a large audience with black women's heroic possibilities and with their significant roles in past events." In it Hopkins denounces "the victimization of women, and her message is that black women must resist such victimization whenever possible" (184).

Hopkins does not fail to address the problems that blacks confronted during the post-Reconstruction era: lynching, expatriation to Africa, lack of employment opportunities for educated blacks, and voting disfranchisement. While arguing for social change, she also emphasizes the need for the black race to be proud of its heritage and the extended family system, which is a symbol of the unity of all blacks.

The publication of this novel became the stepping-stone from which Pauline rose to editor and frequent contributor to the *Colored American*, an important forum for black writers. Two of her short stories, "Talma Gordon" and "George Washington, a Christmas Story," appeared in the October and December 1900 issues of the periodical. In 1901, she began to publish the first of her three serialized novels in the *Colored American*. *Hagar's Daughters, a Story of Southern Caste Prejudice* ran for twelve installments (from March 1901 to March 1902) under the pseudonym Sarah A. Allen.

Her second serialized novel, *Winona, a Tale of Negro Life in the South and Southwest*, ran from May 1902 to October 1902, and her third, *Of One Blood; or, The Hidden Self*, ran from November 1902 to November 1903. Both of these novels dealt with the taboo topic of interracial love, and their publication subsequently led to subscription cancelations by white patrons. *Of One Blood* also echoed the themes found in "The Mystery within Us," emphasizing the common blood of all races.

In November of 1903, the *Colored American* published her short story "As the Lord Lives, He Is One of Our Mother's Children." She also published twenty-one biographical sketches about *Famous Men of the Negro Race* and

Famous Women of the Negro Race from February 1901 to October 1902. Among those featured were Frederick Douglass, Toussaint L'Ouverture, William Wells Brown, Sojourner Truth, Harriet Tubman, and Frances E. W. Harper. She also wrote more generally on the role of women.

According to Shockley, Hopkins resigned from *The Colored American* in September 1904. Others have suggested that the struggle between W. E. B. Du Bois and Booker T. Washington was the cause for her resignation. (With Du Bois, Hopkins believed in higher education and political participation for blacks, not the limited goal of vocational education and accommodation to segregationist practices.)

Hopkins then published with another magazine, *Voice of the Negro*, which had just appeared in January 1904. Her first contribution to the December edition of this southern journal was an illustrated article, "The New York Subway." From February to July 1905, she wrote four sociocultural survey pieces in a series called "The Dark Races of the Twentieth Century" for the *Voice*, as it later came to be known. She founded her own publishing firm, P. E. Hopkins and Company in Cambridge, and in 1905 published *A Primer of Facts Pertaining to the Early Greatness of the African Race and the Possibility of Restoration by Its Descendants, with Epilogue*, a booklet of thirty-one pages. Her last published works appeared in the February and March 1916 editions of the *New Era Magazine*, published by the New Era Publishing Company in Boston. The first was a novella entitled *Topsy Templeton*, which described the efforts of individuals to solve the race question, and the second comprised the biographies of two prominent clergymen. After 1916, she resumed work as a stenographer at the Massachusetts Institute of Technology.

Boston records show that she died on 13 August 1930 at the Cambridge Relief Hospital after suffering burns over her entire body. Her death certificate says that her "dress caught fire while she was heating water on an oil stove at her home" at 19 Jay Street. She was buried on 17 August in the Garden Cemetery in Chelsea, Massachusetts.

Mary Helen Washington sees in Hopkins an author who, like Frances Harper (1825-1911), "enlisted [her] fiction in the battle to counter the negative images of blacks and women." She "put women's lives, women's activities, women's feelings into the foreground of [her] fiction." Yet her tacit acceptance of the nineteenth-century "cult of true womanhood" hampered Hopkins so that she undermined her female characters even as she elevated them. Washington believes that Hopkins's anger is "submerged." Gwendolyn Brooks, too, focuses on the moderation of Hopkins's characters' response to racism, compared to the rage we find in authors of the 1960s. Washington agrees that Hopkins's anger is "submerged." Thus, self-censorship can be identified as the root cause of Hopkins's ambiguities. She did not allow herself to speak out as today's reader might wish she had.

Despite the brilliance and the complexity of Hopkins's literary accomplishments, she was forgotten and appears not to have had an influence on the next generation. However, the excellent essays of Campbell, Mainiero, Shockley, Tate, and Washington predict that Hopkins's work will be resurrected and that she will be celebrated as a "literary foremother." Much work still remains before such questions as her readership, contacts with other writers, and position in the American literary tradition can be illuminated.

SELECT BIBLIOGRAPHY

Primary

Drama

Slaves' Escape; or, The Underground Railroad. Boston, Oakland Garden, 5 July 1880. Edited and revised as *Peculiar Sam; or, The Underground Railroad*, n.d.

Fiction

Contending Forces: A Romance Illustrative of Negro Life North and South. Boston: Colored Co-operative Publishing Co., 1900. Reprint, with an afterword by Gwendolyn Brooks. Carbondale: Southern Illinois University Press. Reprint, with an introduction by Richard Yarborough. New York: Oxford University Press, 1988 (forthcoming).

Hagar's Daughter: A Story of Southern Caste Prejudice. A novel, under pseudonym Sarah A. Allen, serialized in *Colored American* (March 1901-March 1902).

The Magazine Novels of Pauline Hopkins. With an introduction by Hazel V. Carby. New York: Oxford University Press, 1988. Includes *Hagar's Daughters, Winona,* and *Of One Blood*.

Novels: Selections. New York: Oxford University Press, 1988.

Of One Blood; or, The Hidden Self. A novel, serialized in *Colored American* (November 1902-November 1903).

Winona: A Tale of Negro Life in the South and Southwest. A novel, serialed in *Colored American* (May 1902-October 1902).

IN ANTHOLOGIES

Shockley, *Afro-American Women Writers, 1746-1933*, 1988. "The Sewing Circle."

SHORT STORIES

"As the Lord Lives, He Is One of Our Mother's Children." *Colored American* (November 1903).

"Bro'r Abr'm Jimson's Wedding, A Christmas Story." *Colored American* (December 1904).

"A Dash for Liberty." *Colored American* (August 1901).

"George Washington, A Christmas Story." *Colored American* (December 1900).

"The Mystery within Us." *Colored American* (May 1900).

"Talma Gordon." *Colored American* (October 1900).

"The Test of Manhood, A Christmas Story." [Under pseudonym Sarah A. Allen] *Colored American* (December 1906).

"Topsy Templeton." *New Era* (1916).

Nonfiction

The Dark Races of the Twentieth Century. Series in *Voice of the Negro* (February 1905-July 1905).

Famous Men of the Negro Race. Series in *Colored American* (February 1901-September 1902).

Famous Women of the Negro Race. Series in *Colored American* (November 1901-October 1902).

"The New York Subway." *Voice of the Negro* (December 1904).

A Primer Pertaining to the Early Greatness of Africa. Cambridge: P. E. Hopkins, 1905.

"Toussaint L'Ouverture: His Life and Times." *Colored American* (November 1900).

Secondary

Arata, *More Black American Playwrights*, 1978.

Arata and Rotoli, *Black American Playwrights, 1800 to the Present*, 1976.

Bakish and Margolies, *Afro-American Fiction, 1853-1976*, 1979.

Berzson, *Neither Black nor White*, 1978.

Bone, *The Negro Novel in America*, 1965.

Campbell, Dorothy, *Index to Black American Writers in Collective Biographies*, 1983.

Campbell, Jane, "Pauline Elizabeth Hopkins," 1986.

Fairbanks and Engeldinger, *Black American Fiction*, 1978.

Gloster, *Negro Voices in American Fiction*, 1948.

Hatch and Abdullah, *Black Playwrights, 1823-1977*, 1977.

Johnson and Johnson, "Away from Accommodation: Radical Editors and Protest Journalism, 1900-1910," 1977.

Lamping, "Pauline Hopkins," 1980.

Logan and Winston, *The Dictionary of American Negro Biography*, 1982.

Loggins, *The Negro Author*, 1931.

Matthews, *Black American Writers, 1773-1949*, 1975.

Rush, Myers, and Arata, *Black American Writers Past and Present*, 1975.

Shockley, "A Biographical Excursion into Obscurity," 1972.

Sims-Wood, *The Progress of Afro-American Women*, 1980.

Spradling, *In Black and White,* 1980.

Tate, "Pauline Hopkins, Our Literary Foremother," 1985.

Turner, *Afro-American Writers*, 1970.

Whiteman, *A Century of Fiction by American Negroes, 1853-1952*, 1974.

Williams, *American Black Women in the Arts and Social Sciences*, 1978.

Yarborough, "The Depiction of Blacks in the Early Afro-American Novel," 1980.

HUNTER, JANE EDNA (HARRIS) (1882-1971)

Autobiographer

Lawyer

Nurse

Activist

In *A Nickel and a Prayer* (1940) Jane Edna Hunter chronicled her life and career as founder in 1913 of the Phyllis Wheatley Association, a training school and residence for young Afro-American women in Cleveland. Driven by her own experiences as a destitute woman in the big city, Hunter fought tirelessly for rural black women facing the perils of the city. Such conditions as "the dark little rooms under the eaves; lumpy straw mattresses, dim gas lights which had to be turned off at ten o'clock" angered Hunter and drove her to investigate even the night clubs where white men went to see Negro girls dance: "The whole atmosphere is one of unrestrained animality, the jungle faintly veneered, with civilized trappings." Hunter was quick to perceive how easily these young women could be exploited by corrupt individuals.

The pioneering program Hunter established, similar to the settlement houses of Jane Addams and others, started with nickel contributions from eighty sponsors. Starting without capital, she founded not only a residential building but a community center with employment offices, gymnasium, recreation facilities, and cafeteria. During her leadership at the Phyllis Wheatley Association, Hunter also furthered her own career, taking evening courses at Western Reserve University and then working toward a law degree at Cleveland's Baldwin Wallace College. In 1925 she graduated and was admitted to the bar, but her primary concern remained helping young black women who were struggling as she had. She observed with deep concern "how they have to struggle step by step to get from the drudgery of life into the semi-professional, and out of this channel into that of the professional one; and day after day as they pass through the mill that grinds the soul out of them."

Hunter's first profession was that of a nurse and social worker. In nursing, too, she saw a desperate need for an institution to aid and protect young lonely women, many newly arrived in Cleveland. By 1916 her organization was joined by an Efficiency Union that assisted the women in securing jobs. Another organization, the Let Us Be Friends Club, helped the women with social contacts. In 1917 a $100,000 donation from John D. Rockefeller enabled the home to expand, and several branch associations opened in other large cities, performing comparable social service tasks.

Born on Woodburn Farm, a plantation near Pendleton, South Carolina, Jane Edna Harris was educated in a one-room schoolhouse and a Baptist church school. Her father, a sharecropper, died when Jane was ten and she and a sister were sent to live with an aunt as part of a strategy to support the large family. Later she earned her room and board as a domestic with a family in Aiken, South Carolina, who treated her so poorly that neighbors (white as well as black) protested. She fared better with another family when one of the daughters taught Jane to write her name and read nursery rhymes. In 1896, when she was about fourteen, two black Presbyterian missionaries who had a school in Abbeville, South Carolina, enabled her to work her way through Ferguson Academy (later renamed Ferguson-Williams College), and she graduated from there in 1900.

At around this time, Jane's romantic hopes were thwarted "when the boy I loved made a loveless marriage." Jane, encouraged by her mother, did the same, marrying Edward Hunter, forty years her senior. In her autobiography she reflects ruefully on this rash step: "I am sure it was wrong to live in wedlock without mutual affection." This marriage lasted fifteen months.

At age seventeen, while working as a nurse in the home of attorney Benjamin Rutledge in Charleston, Jane met Mrs. Ella Hunt, a prominent black Ladies Auxiliary worker. Hunt encouraged her to pursue a career in nursing with formal training in Charleston and was instrumental in her being admitted to the training school for nurses at the Cannon Street Hospital.

Her practical experience in that city was invaluable in establishing her vocation, as she reveals in her autobiography: "Work in the horrible slums of historic Charleston was no less a privilege than the experience in the homes of the well-to-do," for the deplorable conditions there "quickened my sympathies and renewed my purpose to help my people." Indeed, Jane went on for advanced training at Hampton Institute to acquire more expertise in her field.

The decision to move to Cleveland was made on the spur of the moment, when friends of hers told her of employment opportunities for blacks. Arriving in Cleveland jobless, Jane struggled to find employment in her profession. Through contact with doctors, including John D. Rockefeller's personal physician, she eventually secured jobs with prominent physicians and surgeons in the city.

Her autobiography, *A Nickel and a Prayer* (1940), describes in vivid and painfully honest terms her intimate motivations for founding the Phyllis Wheatley Association. Chief among them was the desire "to give to the world what she had failed to give her mother." Recalling the enmity between her parents and her having sided with her father, Hunter analyzes why she identified so much with her light-skinned father and explains how she undertook her work "to atone for [her] aversion for [her] mother." Her mother's death plunged Hunter into a crisis during which she even contemplated suicide but from which she emerged with increased self-knowledge and zeal for her mission in life.

Though Hunter encountered initial opposition from club women who believed the YWCA should fill the needs of destitute and lonely black migrant women, Jane persuaded her adversaries that existing social agencies were discriminatory. In embracing the concept of "separate but equal," however, Hunter opened herself to controversy that did not abate but became increasingly bitter.

Clearly, Hunter was a disciple of Booker T. Washington and never ceased to believe in his self-help credo. Rebecca Chalmers Barton observes, however, that Hunter's story of her own life goes beyond the Booker T. Washington school of autobiographies. Though it includes tributes to uplift and progress through faith, Hunter's book delves beneath the surface of her life to examine her motivations and to analyze the source of her conflict in her early relationships with her parents. Barton nevertheless judges Hunter harshly, concluding that she acted out of a "strange mixture of self-interest and idealism" stemming from the unresolved conflict with her dark-skinned mother. Says Barton of Hunter's tendency to look to influential white patrons, "Not without profit has she sat at the feet of her hero, Booker T. Washington. Like him, she has no desire to batter at stone walls of prejudice. Like him, she selects the pleasant and sunny detours. The 'right people' will approve of her and speed her on her way. If the 'wrong people' oppose her, she can find consolation in the fact that she acts in their best welfare anyway. She is, first and last, a martyr to her mother." Thus Barton attempts to link Hunter's unabiding sense of guilt to her acceptance of Washington's ideology.

Adrienne Lash Jones's doctoral dissertation documents Hunter's eagerness to secure a position in the ranks of national Afro-American leaders. By cultivating the friendship of prominent educators Mary McLeod Bethune, Nannie Burroughs, and Charlotte Hawkins Brown,* Hunter made clear that she perceived herself as their peer. She corresponded and visited with them. Jones also points out that Hunter's choice to spend her life in female-dominated environments, helping young women, is traceable to strong female role models in her own life (not her mother, but her grandmother, aunts, and others) and also to her fear of sexual exploitation.

SELECT BIBLIOGRAPHY

Primary

Nonfiction

A Nickel and a Prayer [autobiography]. 2d ed. Nashville, Tenn.: Parthenon Press; Cleveland: Elli Kani Publishing Co., 1940.

"The Phyllis Wheatley Department of the National Association of Colored Women." *National Notes* (January 1929): 10.

"Twenty-fifth Anniversary Celebration of the Phyllis Wheatley Association." *Southern Workman* (February 1936): 37-38.

Secondary

Barton, *Witnesses for Freedom*, [1948] 1976.

Campbell, Dorothy, *Index to Black American Writers in Collective Biographies*, 1983.

Coyle, *Ohio Authors and Their Books*, 1962.

Daniel, Sadie Iola, *Women Builders*, [1931] 1970.

Jones, "Jane Edna Hunter: A Case Study of Black Leadership, 1910-1950," 1983.

HUNTON, ADDIE D. WAITES (1870-1943)

Biographer

Essayist

Activist

Both Addie Hunton and her daughter, Eunice Hunton Carter,* beneficiaries of unique educational opportunities, worked ceaselessly for the same cause: to advance women and blacks. But Hunton's contributions lay in organizational efforts to support working women, whereas her daughter, of a more literary background, stressed cultural advancement for Afro-Americans.

Born in Norfolk, Virginia, on 11 June 1870, Addie D. Waites was the daughter of Jesse and Adaline Lawton Waites. Following her graduation from public high school in Boston, she entered the Spencerian College of Commerce in Philadelphia, Pennsylvania. In 1889 she was the only black person to graduate from the institution. She married William A. Hunton of Ontario, Canada, on 19 July 1893, the same year she began her career as a teacher; she then became the principal of State Normal and Agricultural College in Alabama. The Huntons raised two children: Eunice and William Alphaeus, Jr.

From 1905 to 1906 Hunton was secretary and bursar at Clark University in Atlanta, Georgia. She then studied at Kaiser Wilhelm University in Strassburg, Germany, from 1908 to 1910. The list of Hunton's leadership positions is long. She worked extensively for the National Association of Colored Women's Clubs and the YMCA, which represented some seventeen countries. She was president of the Empire State Federation of Colored Women's Clubs, first vice president of the International Council of the Women of Darker Races, chair of the Department of Program and Literature of the National Association of Colored Women, president of the Circle of Peace and Foreign Relations, and a member of the National Board Committee for Girl Reserves.

As early as 1904 Addie Hunton was writing articles and essays on issues pertaining to women of color. Many of them were updates on the progress of women's clubs such as the YWCA and the National Association of Colored Women. Though it was segregated at the time, the national board of the YWCA began to supervise work being done for Afro-American women in 1907. Hunton addressed topics related to all women as well as specific issues concerning black women. She believed the aim of the YWCA in both its urban and its rural groups was to strengthen "the physical, social, intellectual, moral, and spiritual interests of young women" (189). Hunton's writing reflects this concern for the wholeness of women.

While single black women were expected to support themselves, many married black women also had to work as wash women, maids, or cleaning women because most black families could not survive on the husband's inadequate wages. Day care for children of working parents received little support, financially or otherwise; it was even stigmatized. But in "Women's Clubs: Caring for the Children," Hunton urged day-care facilities for working parents: "Day nurseries are generally a positive need for those communities in which any considerable number of mothers are forced to find employment outside of the home. They are a pressing need in those congested or poverty-stricken areas where, because of the cost of living or the unstable conditions of family relations, the women are driven to be wage earners" (78). Hunton also voiced the need for shelters for homeless children and told her readers about the Baltimore-based Empty Stocking and Fresh Air Circle, a group who did more than simply provide toys for children at Christmas time.

Hunton wrote a brief essay outlining her concerns in the *Crisis* symposium Votes for Women, expressing concern about women's issues, including suffrage: "Acutely suffering from the wrongs and humiliations of an unjustly restricted suffrage, it is but natural that the colored woman should feel deeply and keenly wherever the question of suffrage arises" (189). Carrie Williams Clifford,* Mary B. Talbert, Elizabeth Lindsay Davis, and Mary Church Terrell* were other Afro-American women who expressed their views in the symposium.

Hunton and another woman, Kathryn Johnson, served for fifteen months during World War I as YWCA welfare workers at a supply base in France and then at a recreation center for soldiers in the Alpine region of Savoie in southern France. Their book, *Two Colored Women with the Expeditionary Forces* (1920), uses as chapter epigraphs poems by Georgia Douglas Johnson,* Carrie W. Clifford,* Paul Lawrence Dunbar, Leslie Pinckney Hill, and James Weldon Johnson. This book reflects varying points of view on the black American war experience. Hunton notes that "some were not anxious" for the black soldier to participate in World War I, whereas others believed that if he offered his life "for a new freedom" he would be totally free from the shackles of oppression. Hunton observes that the shackles were not loosed from his body but that the war experience had to some degree "removed the fetters from his soul." She concludes that the 150,000 men who went to France "caught the vision of a freedom that gave them new hope and a new inspiration."

In 1938 Hunton published a biography of her husband, William Alphaeus Hunton, sixth son of a Virginia slave who escaped via the Underground Railroad to Ontario, Canada. W. E. B. Du Bois once referred to Alphaeus Hunton as "a pioneer prophet of young men," a designation that Alphaeus's wife takes as her subtitle. In rich historical and documentary detail, Addie Waite Hunton chronicles her husband's path to leadership as the first black official of the YMCA, dedicated to organizing black youth and to breaking down "barriers of insularity and passivity . . . recalcitrant opinions, and impotence." This biography was published twenty-two years after her husband's death. She explains that "before such a task could be undertaken, it was necessary that time should pass, and, as it seemed decreed, surcease for my loss and pain found in work on the battle-torn soil of France. In the intervening years I have re-read hundreds of letters that had their beginning three years before our marriage and that continued twenty years after." To write the biography she conducted numerous interviews with her husband's siblings and boyhood friends in Canada "among the scenes of his childhood and early manhood."

SELECT BIBLIOGRAPHY

Primary

Nonfiction

"Caring for Young Women." *Crisis* (July 1911): 121-22.

"The Club Movement in California." *Crisis* (December 1912): 90-92.

"The Detroit Convention of the National Association of Colored Women." *Voice of the Negro* (July 1906): 589-93.

"The National Association of Colored Women." *Crisis* (May 1911): 17-18. Also in Aptheker, *A Documentary History of the Negro in the United States*, 1973.

"Negro Womanhood Defended." *Voice of the Negro* (July 1904): 280-82.

"A Social Center at Hampton, Virginia." *Crisis* (July 1912): 145-46.

"The Southern Federation of Colored Women." *Voice of the Negro* (December 1905): 850-54.

Two Colored Women with the American Expeditionary Forces. Brooklyn: Brooklyn Eagle Press, 1920.

William Alphaeus Hunton: A Pioneer Prophet of Young Men [biography]. New York: Association Press, 1938.

"Women's Clubs: Caring for the Children." *Crisis* (June 1911): 78-79.

"Women's Clubs State Convention." *Crisis* (September 1911): 210-11.

"The Work of the National Board of the Young Women's Christian Association." In Trawick, *The New Voice in Race Adjustment*, 1914.

179

"YWCA." *Crisis* (August 1915): 188-89.

Secondary

Campbell, Dorothy, *Index to Black American Writers in Collective Biographies*, 1983.

Dannett, *Profiles of Negro Womanhood*, 1964.

Ellis, *Opportunity; A Journal of Negro Life*, 1971.

Herman, *Women in Particular*, 1984.

Matthews, *Black American Writers, 1773-1949*, 1975.

Rose Bibliography Project, *Analytical Guide and Indexes to "The Crisis," 1910-1960*, 1975.

Sims-Wood, *The Progress of Afro-American Women*, 1980.

Spradling, *In Black and White*, 1980.

Who's Who in Colored America, 1927.

HURSTON, ZORA NEALE (1891-1960)

Anthropologist and folklorist
Novelist
Short-story writer
Playwright
Essayist
Autobiographer
Adventurer

Zora Neale Hurston attracted attention as soon as her first novel was published by J. B. Lippincott in 1934. The *New York Times, New Republic, Saturday Review of Literature, Booklist,* and other mainstream journals commented on *Jonah's Gourd Vine* in generally admiring terms. Thereafter, each successive Hurston book was greeted with a flurry of reviews that recognized her originality while implicitly declining to view her as other than a mouthpiece of black American folklore. Hurston flourished until the 1940s but then faltered for reasons that continue to baffle,  among them her mismanagement of her personal finances, ill health, and a tendency to make pronouncements that alienated fellow Afro-Americans. Condescending descriptions of her by Langston Hughes (*The Big Sea*) and Wallace Thurman (*Infants of the Spring*) also detracted from the prestige that might have accrued to her. Thus, her work went out of print, her last manuscripts were rejected by publishers, and this most prolific of black women writers died penniless in a welfare home in her native Florida.

After a period of near oblivion, Hurston's work has been rediscovered and her achievements reevaluated. Today Hurston is gaining a secure position as an important figure in Afro-American and feminist literary history, as her books are read on college campuses and by a wide general audience. Her twin themes are (1) the vitality of the black oral tradition in folk tales, songs, and sermons, and in folk remedies, and (2) the spiritual need of humans to be unfettered. Lillie P. Howard speaks to the broader significance of Hurston: "For many of her readers, black and white, [Hurston's works] reveal life's possibilities."

Fully as much as her writings, the "Zora legend" has been built on rich anecdotal and documentary grounds. In *The Big Sea* (1940), Langston Hughes pictured her as "a perfect book of entertainment in herself." Larry Neal, writing in *Black Review* in 1972, recalled her as "very bold and outspoken – an attractive woman who had learned how to survive with native wit. She approached life as a series of encounters and challenges; most of these she overcame without succumbing to the maudlin bitterness of many of her contemporaries." Peripatetic and unconventional, Hurston touched all the frontiers that her restless intellect envisioned.

She had numerous early mentors and promoters, both male and female, white and black, among them Charles S. Johnson, Robert Wunsch, Fannie Hurst, Franz Boas, and Marjorie Kinnan Rawlings. Her contribution to the Harlem Renaissance, according to Theodore Pratt in *Negro Digest*, was considerable and her ties with such writers as Langston Hughes and Countee Cullen were strong. Hemenway, writing in 1972, noted that Hurston "helped to remind the Renaissance – especially its more bourgeois members – of the richness in the racial heritage" for, despite her education at Howard University, Barnard College, and Columbia University, she never forgot the black community from which she sprang. Foremost among the younger writers who have acknowledged her influence are Alice Walker, Toni Cade Bambara, and Shirley Ann Williams.

During her lifetime, Hurston published seven books, several plays, and numerous short stories and essays. *Jonah's Gourd Vine* (1934), written in three months while she was living in a rented house in Sanford, Florida, was her first novel. It tells of the quest of John Pearson, a poor mulatto who yearns for something better than a miserable backwoods existence under the iron hand of his stepfather. He finds innocent romance and then conjugal love with Lucy and rises to a position of prestige as preacher. But his roving eye is the tragic flaw that destroys all that he creates. Based loosely on her parents' story, this novel has an ambitious scope that embraces many moments of lyric transport in its pages. The book is dedicated to Bob

Wunsch, of the Rollins College English department, who helped Zora publish her first story in a white mainstream magazine.

Her next work, *Mules and Men* (1935), endorsed by Franz Boas, is a collection of tales framed by a semifictional Zora who guides us on a trip through central Florida and New Orleans in search of folklore. Rich in detail and full of humor, the book was written in 1929 in Eau Gallie, Florida, and established Hurston's particular blend of tradition and originality. It was attacked on political grounds by such critics as Sterling Brown and Harold Preece, who faulted it for lack of militancy. This accusation would be repeated frequently throughout Hurston's career, discouraging her in her determination to sing her own song.

Their Eyes Were Watching God (1937), a second novel written in seven weeks in Haiti, has become a pillow book for feminist readers all over the United States. The growth of Janie Crawford from girlhood and submission to adult womanhood and freedom, enduring vicissitudes of love and tragedy along the way, creates a holding center of great sustaining power. Unlike other female protagonists of the time, Janie ripens into womanhood, gaining her education through two unhappy marriages and blazing her own path regardless of the barriers. The novel is poetic and bittersweet, for Hurston shows that even the idyllic, egalitarian love enjoyed by Janie and Vergible "Tea Cake" Woods is transient. Ultimately, forces of nature (a hurricane, disease) drive the heroine to destroy the person she loves. What remains is Janie's independence and sustaining gift for telling her own tale.

In Hurston's day, such black critics as Alain Locke, Richard Wright, and Sterling Brown missed the point and once again criticized the book for absence of social content and a lack of militancy. Such attacks were consonant with the literary climate of the 1930s, when some of the brightest intellectuals were persuaded that literature must be proletarian and militant. Now Hurston's novel is viewed as a proto-feminist book, though by no means without reservations. For example, Ann L. Rayson (1974) contends that in all Hurston's novels, women live only through men and are subservient to them. Yet *Their Eyes Were Watching God* is justly considered Hurston's masterpiece: nowhere else in her work do we find such a rich fusion of inspired poetry, splendid folklore, and a sweeping yet coherent story line.

With *Tell My Horse* (1938) Hurston returned to anthropological material. This travel book contains much extraneous and inept political commentary. Most remarkable, according to Hemenway (who calls this her poorest book), is the section on voodoo and the account of zombies, which places her among the early researchers who took these spiritual manifestations seriously. Here as elsewhere, Hurston goes beyond the boundaries of scholarship because she sees the aesthetic potential of the phenomena she examines. As in her work for the Federal Writers' Project for Florida, Hurston discovers the magical realism latent in the tales and beliefs of her informants, a substance that she elaborates in works that cross the boundaries of document and fiction.

Hurston had earlier shown an interest in the biblical figure of Moses when she published the short story "The Fire and the Cloud" (1934) in *Challenge*, edited by Dorothy West.* *Moses, Man of the Mountain* (1939), in preparation for perhaps five years, presents a fictional revision of the Moses character based on an iconoclastic premise. In this novel, her third, Moses was not a Jew but an Egyptian appropriated by the Hebrews' need to believe in a redeemer. Perhaps the confusion with which the novel has been received is a reaction to her tacit proposal that Scripture is a product of folk belief rather than revealed truth. The irreverent and humorous portrayal of a Moses who practices hoodoo and speaks in Afro-American dialect, thus linking the ancient Hebrews with contemporary American blacks, was not likely to win favor among religiously orthodox critics. Yet Hurston was in earnest: she was exploring the nature of freedom and how an oppressed people, it order to achieve it, creates its own leaders. *Moses* is well regarded by Robert Bone and Darwin Turner, but at the time of its publication it was not appreciated by either Alain Locke or Ralph Ellison.

Dust Tracks on a Road (1942) is Hurston's autobiography; it is engaging and inventive but did not enhance her literary reputation. The book was completed while Hurston was employed as a story consultant at Paramount Studios in California. In it she omits discussion of the painful experiences of racism she must have encountered and the tactics by which she overcame them. There is considerable evidence that Hurston was neither naive nor devoid of rage, but she chose to camouflage this when speaking through the channels of the white publishing world. Rather, she beguiled her audiences with wit and a seeming indifference to unpleasant episodes, thus earning their goodwill but also the increasing animus of her critics. Her ignoring oppression is a statement of how she ran her life, refusing to dignify discrimination by recognizing its existence. The book was commercially successful and won a one-thousand-dollar Anisfield-Wolf award for contributions to the field of race relations.

After *Dust Tracks* Hurston devoted herself to articles and essays, some of which appeared in the *American Mercury, Saturday Evening Post, Negro Digest,* and the *American Legion Journal.* Marion Kilson (1972) notes her shift in mid-career to the essay form and her confrontation with the racial complexities in American society. As an artist, Hurston was ill prepared to address this topic, however, and came to grief. She made the mistake of publishing her articles in ultra-conservative magazines and so her views were cited by those opposing the struggle for racial equality. Looking back in 1974, Arthur P. Davis (*From the Dark Tower*) stated that Hurston's racial philosophy was one that "present-day black writers would consider incredible." She praised certain forms of segregation, for example, asserting that all-black towns like Eatonville, Florida, were good for black identity and pride.

Seraph on the Sewanee (1948), a novel that proved to be her last published book, is generally considered an unsuccessful attempt to shift to "universal" fiction, using poor white characters as protagonists. The dialogue sounds more black than white and the ending, in which an insecure woman, illsuited to marriage and motherhood, is reconciled to her lot, strikes the reader as timid and uncharacteristic of Hurston. Marilyn Mobley, in trying to explain the failure of this turgid novel, points to a tension created by Hurston's "use of her own culture as subtext and the culture of poor southern whites as text." Perhaps, Mobley speculates, Hurston wanted "to enlarge her folk esthetic into some cross-cultural statement," but the text betrays her intentions.

The Sanctified Church (1981) is an uneven posthumous collection of Hurston articles on hoodoo and institutional black religion, some of which had appeared previously in Nancy Cunard's anthology *Negro* and another in *American Mercury*. Best among these pieces is "Characteristics of Negro Expression."

Hurston's meteoric success as writer and public figure was all the more remarkable considering her humble beginnings as a black female from the small-town South. Her life story is best told in Robert Hemenway's definitive biography (1977). Her birth date, once thought to be 1901, has been pushed back by Cheryl Wall to 1891; because of a courthouse fire in which the records were lost, it is impossible to pin down the date conclusively. Hurston's now legendary origins in the town of Eatonville, Florida, in torrid rural country northeast of Orlando are entwined with the fictional world she created—one in which men congregate on the porch of the general store to tell tales and women contrive to rise above their status of "mule of the world." Eatonville was unusual. Though not the first black community in America, it was the first and oldest (incorporated in 1887), and its citizens governed themselves and elected their own officials. Some commentators, including Alice Walker, suggest that it was because of Eatonville's seclusion and self-governance that Hurston did not attack racial prejudice or espouse integration as vehemently as she might have.

The daughter of John Hurston, Baptist preacher and carpenter, and his wife, Lucy Potts, Zora remembered herself, like the child of her short story "Drenched in Light," as an adventurous and precocious girl who read avidly. She was the seventh of eight children—five boys and three girls. Zora graduated from the Robert Hungerford Normal and Industrial School, which is even today 90 percent black. Orphaned at about age thirteen, Zora lived with a succession of relatives until she ran away from a brother's house to work as maid to an actress with a Gilbert and Sullivan company. This job took her north to Baltimore. When it ended, she worked first as a maid and then as a baby-sitter and enrolled in night school at the high school division of Morgan State University. In an article published in the *Messenger* Hurston credited May Miller* with having persuaded her to study at Howard University. There from 1919 to 1924, Hurston met and studied with Georgia Douglas Johnson.* It was in *Stylus*, a Howard literary magazine, that Hurston, at about the age of thirty, published her first short story, "John Redding Goes to Sea" (1921). From Howard, Hurston went to New York and published in *Opportunity* (1925) and *Fire!!* (1926), winning recognition in the *Opportunity* literary contests and then (through President Annie Nathan Meyer) a scholarship to Barnard College in New York City as the school's first black student. She received a B.A. degree in 1928.

Hurston's studies in anthropology (1934-35) with the renowned Franz Boas enabled her to win a fellowship to collect data on black folklore in Louisiana and Florida. Another grant, a Guggenheim fellowship, enabled her to carry out fieldwork in Haiti, from which another book, *Tell My Horse*, would result. Hurston's anthropological fieldwork nourished much of her writing: *Mules and Men* (1936), *Tell My Horse* (1939), many articles and parts of novels.

For five years beginning in 1927, Charlotte Osgood Mason, a wealthy patron of black arts, sponsored Hurston's field trips and writing (as well as the work of Langston Hughes), contributing more than $15,000. Despite this support, publishers' advances, royalties, and income from articles, Hurston never had money and often found herself without soap or shoes in good repair. A born wanderer, she pursued folklore and romance up and down the Atlantic seaboard, from New York to the Caribbean, and from New Orleans to Honduras in search of an illusory Mayan city. She also traveled the country with her musical reviews, worked at a college in North Carolina, in Paramount Studios in Hollywood, and in St. Augustine, Florida, during World War II.

By 1940 Hurston was at her zenith, having published her three great novels and two books of folklore. As journalist Linda Farrar has written, "It seemed Zora – this black woman from the poverty pot of the rural South – was scaling a mountain of accomplishment, past barriers of race, sex, and poverty, destined for the heights."

Why she left New York, the artistic hub that had propelled her to recognition, had more to do with her restless nature and inability to submit to the straitjacket of discipline than with the Great Depression and its scattering effect on the Harlem Renaissance. A devastating experience in which she was unjustly accused and tried on immorality charges also left its mark. Once she was without "godmother" Charlotte Osgood Mason's assistance, Hurston, like many other writers, found an employment opportunity in the Federal Theatre and the Federal Writers' Project's Florida division.

In 1951 Hurston returned permanently to Florida, to settle in Eau Gallie (1951-56), then a small peaceful community near the Atlantic, where she had written *Mules and Men* in 1927. For four years Hurston lived in houseboats on the Indian and Halifax rivers in northern and central Florida. There she found solitude, forgetfulness, and contentment. Despite her success in the North, when Hurston returned to Florida as a middle-aged woman, she was in dire straits. In between placement of articles, she took such jobs as substitute teaching, library work, and domestic service. In 1951, when Zora was working as a domestic in Rivo Alto Island (Miami), her surprised employer discovered that her maid was the author of a story she was reading in the *Saturday Evening Post*. Her novels, however, were being rejected by her publisher now and, in failing health, she returned to Eau Gallie. After a succession of interim jobs, she entered a welfare home in St. Lucie, where she died in 1960.

Zora Neale Hurston was buried in a black cemetery in Fort Pierce. The minister's unadorned words at her funeral are worth remembering: "The Miami paper said she died poor. But she died rich. She did something." In her wandering life, she had traveled the country and the Caribbean, worked for several colleges and Paramount Studios, been a reporter and a political worker during the war. As she herself wrote in 1941, she had touched the four corners of the horizon.

A complete authoritative bibliography of Hurston's writings has yet to be assembled. Adele Newson's bibliographic reference guide permits us to follow the critical reception of Hurston's work from 1934 to 1986. Frequent reviews of her books but little in-depth consideration of her opus characterized the period from 1934 to 1960, the year of her death, by which time the literary establishment had forgotten her. The Hurston revival began with a sympathetic obituary written in 1960 by Alan Lomax, once her collaborator in field research. For Lomax, *Mules and Men* was "the most engaging, genuine, and skillfully written book in the field of American folklore."

The first of Hurston's books to be reprinted was *Their Eyes Were Watching God* (Fawcett Publications, 1965). Newson says that "critics who later reevaluated Hurston's works presumably had in their undergraduate work this reprint to whet their appetites." Other Hurston books to be reprinted were *Mules and Men* (1978), *Moses, Man of the Mountain* (1984), and *Dust Tracks on a Road* (1984).

By 1974, critics were beginning to analyze Hurston's protagonists and compare her work to that of recognized authors. Roger Rosenblatt (1974) called Janie a "true heroine in the Charlotte Bronte mold because she endures well, holds on to her decency and sense in spite of the fakery about her and triumphs over apparent defeat." After a lapse of some ten years, comparative study was renewed. Michael G. Cooke (1984) observed that

Janie Crawford, like Wright's Bigger Thomas, kills to preserve her "self" – a complication that makes her a tragic figure. Recent criticism has also made interesting comparisons between Hurston's characters and those of black male writers, on the one hand, and of black female writers, on the other. For example, Lee R. Edwards (1984) finds that Hurston's Janie and Toni Morrison's Sula are both bent "on destroying and reconstructing the assumptions" of their societies, though Sula is more destructive. Alice Fannin compares Janie to Alice Walker's Celie, protagonist of *The Color Purple*, seeing them as explorers of "self," able ultimately to survive alone. And Adele Newson suggests that Walker's Shug Avery is drawn from three female characters in Hurston's *Tell My Mule*. Marjorie Pryse (1985) feels that Hurston gave black women entry to literary power when they were excluded from other kinds and created a bridge between the primitive authority of folk life and the literary power of written testimony.

A banner year for Hurston's reputation was 1975. Hemenway in that year placed Hurston in the pastoral tradition, finding that she was caught between two conflicting impulses to celebrate the uniqueness of Eatonville and to escape from its limits. Popular magazines such as *Encore* published articles on Hurston and *Ms.* carried Alice Walker's article telling of her search for Hurston's gravesite. Walker's article can be credited with bringing Hurston to the attention of a popular female audience and with disseminating the Zora legend.

Next came a stream of scholarly work in the form of doctoral dissertations by Colleen Davidson (1975), Lillie Howard (1975), Beatrice Horn Royster (1975), Martha Hursey Brown (1976), Cheryl A. Wall (1976), and others. One line of criticism was opened by Karla Francesca Clapp Holloway (1978) in her dissertation on literary and linguistic structure in Hurston's fiction. Holloway vindicates Hurston's use of dialect (important to other black writers as well), showing that language reveals characters as no narrative commentary can and that Hurston asserts the use of dialect as a conscious choice. Through dialect, the character defines himself or herself and the novelist mediates this self-definition. Similarly, Valerie Melissa Babb (1980) finds that Hurston's writing yields a "clear definition of American literary language as a linguistic form which utilizes many techniques compounding dialect, vernacular, and borrowing."

Increased sophistication marks recent studies of Hurston – for example, Barbara Johnson's work on metaphor, metonymy, and voice in *Their Eyes Were Watching God* (1984). Another sophisticated approach is the application of new critical theory to her fiction. Elizabeth Meese (1986) employs specific terms of literary analysis in order to focus on Hurston's transforming orality into textuality.

We should be cautious about seeing Zora Neale as unique. Rather, she represents a synthesis of many of the efforts of black women writers of her time, carrying to a higher degree all their combined aspirations. She was not the only black woman novelist of the early twentieth century–Jessie Fauset,* Nella Larsen,* Mercedes Gilbert,* and Zara Wright* published fine novels, too. Nor was she the only collector of folklore–Katherine Dunham* and Maud Cuney Hare* were ethnologists as well. There were others working in each of the fields she pursued, though indeed she was the most prolific and accomplished of them all. Hurston was a feminist who set down male as well as female quest stories.

The first National Zora Neale Hurston Symposium was held in October 1981 at Morgan State University, where the Zora Neale Hurston Society is housed. Correspondence, manuscripts, and other primary source materials are held at the American Jewish Archives in Cincinnati, the American Philosophical Society in Philadelphia, Atlanta University, Boston University, Schomburg Center (New York Public Library), University of Florida at Gainesville, the Beinecke Library at Yale University, Library of Congress Manuscript Division, and Howard University's Moorland-Spingarn Research Center.

SELECT BIBLIOGRAPHY

Primary

Drama

Color Struck: A Play in Four Scenes. Fire!! 1 (November 1926): 7-14.

"Great Day," 1927. [With Langston Hughes. Unpublished musical revue.]

Mule Bone: A Comedy of Negro Life in Three Acts, 1931. *Drama Critique* (Spring 1964): 1-3-107. [Excerpts.]

IN ANTHOLOGIES

Johnson, *Ebony and Topaz*, [1927] 1941. *The First One*. [One act.]

Fiction

Jonah's Gourd Vine. Introduction by Fannie Hurst. Philadelphia: J. B. Lippincott; London: Duckworth Press, 1934.

Moses, Man of the Mountain. Philadelphia: J. B. Lippincott, 1939. London: J. M. Dent & Sons, 1941. Reprinted, with an introduction by Blyden Jackson, as *The Man of the Mountain*. Chicago: University of Illinois Press, 1984.

Seraph on the Sewanee. New York: Charles Scribner's Sons, 1948.

Spunk: The Short Stories of Zora Neale Hurston. Berkeley, Calif.: Turtle Island Foundation, 1984.

Their Eyes Were Watching God. Philadelphia: J. B. Lippincott, 1937. Reprint. London: J. M. Dent & Sons. Greenwich, Conn.: Fawcett Publications, 1965. With a foreword by Sherley Anne Williams. Chicago: University of Illinois Press, 1978.

SHORT STORIES (NOT IN Spunk)

"Drenched in Light." *Opportunity* (December 1924): 371-74.

"John Redding Goes to Sea." *Opportunity* (January 1926): 16-21.

IN ANTHOLOGIES

Cromwell, Turner, and Dykes, *Readings from Negro Authors*, 1931. "Drenched in Light."

Musical

Fast and Furious. [With Clinton Fletcher and Tim Moore.] In Burns Mantle and Garrison Sherwood, *Best Plays of 1931-1932.*

Nonfiction

Dust Tracks on a Road. Philadelphia: J. B. Lippincott, 1942. Reprint. London: Hutchinson & Co., 1944. With an introduction by Robert Hemenway, Chicago: University of Illinois Press, 1984.

"How It Feels to Be Colored Me." *World Tomorrow* 11 (May 1928).

"The Hue and Cry about Howard University." *Messenger* 11 (September 1925).

I Love Myself When I Am Laughing and Then Again When I Am Looking Mean and Impressive. Edited by Alice Walker. Introduction by Mary Helen Washington. Old Westbury, N.Y.: Feminist Press, 1979.

Mules and Men. Philadelphia: J.B. Lippincott, 1935. Reprint. London: Kegan Paul & Co., 1936. Chicago: University of Illinois Press, 1978.

The Sanctified Church. Foreword by Toni Cade Bambara. Berkeley, Calif.: Turtle Island Foundation, 1981.

Tell My Horse. Philadelphia: J. B. Lippincott. London: J. M. Dent & Sons, 1938. New ed., with an introduction by Bob Callahan, as *Voodoo Gods: An Inquiry into Native Myths and Magic in Jamaica and Haiti.* Berkeley, Calif.: Turtle Island Foundation, 1981.

"What White Publishers Won't Print." *Negro Digest* 7 (April 1950): 85-89.

Secondary

Babb, "Evolution of American Literary Language," 1980.

Barton, *Witnesses for Freedom*, [1948] 1976.

Berzson, *Neither Black nor White*, 1978.

Bone, "Zora Neale Hurston," 1970.

Burke, "Zora Neale Hurston and Fanny Hurst as They Saw Each Other," 1977.

Byrd, "Zora Neale Hurston: A Negro Folklorist," 1975.

Cantarow, "Sex, Race, and Criticism: Thoughts of a White Feminist on Kate Chopin and Zora Neale Hurston," 1978.

Edwards, *Psyche as Hero*, 1978.

Ellison, "Recent Negro Fiction," 1941.

Fannin, "A Sense of Wonder: The Patterns for Psychic Survival in *Their Eyes* and *The Color Purple*," 1986.

Farrar, "Zora Neale Hurston: Local Writer Called Literary Giant," 1986.

Giddings, "A Shoulder Hunched against a Sharp Concern: Themes in the Poetry of Margaret Walker," 1971.

Gloster, "Zora Neale Hurston: Novelist and Folklorist," 1943.

Hemenway, *Down Home*, 1975.

Hemenway, *Zora Neale Hurston*, 1977.

Hemenway, "Zora Neale Hurston and the Eatonville Anthropology," 1972.

Holloway, "A Critical Investigation of Literary and Linguistic Structures in the Fiction of Zora Neale Hurston," 1978.

Howard, *Zora Neale Hurston*, 1980.

Howard, "Zora Neale Hurston," 1987.

Johnson, Barbara, "Metaphor, Metonymy, and Voice in *Their Eyes Were Watching God*," 1984.

Jordan, "On Richard Wright and Zora Neale Hurston: Notes toward a Balance of Love and Hatred," 1974.

Kilson, "The Transformation of Eatonville's Ethnographer," 1972.

Love, "Zora Neale Hurston's America," 1976.

Meese, *Crossing the Double-Cross*, 1986.

Newson, *Zora Neale Hurston*, 1987.

Pettis, "Zora Neale Hurston," 1980.

Pinckney, "In Sorrow's Kitchen," 1978.

Pryse, "Pattern against the Sky," 1985.

Rayson, "The Novels of Zora Neale Hurston," 1974.

Reagon, "Zora Neale Hurston," 1982.

Sheffey, *Rainbow Round Her Shoulder*, 1982.

Starke, *Black Portraiture in American Fiction*, 1971.

Turner, *In a Minor Chord*, 1971.

Walker, "In Search of Zora Neale Hurston," 1975.

Wall, "Three Novelists: Fauset, Larsen, and Hurston," 1976.

Washington, "Zora Neale Hurston: The Black Woman's Search for Identity," 1972.

JEFFREY, MAURINE L. (1900-)

Educator

Poet

Maurine L. Jeffrey was a local poet who published in *Heralding Dawn*, a volume affirming the activity of a Texas literary group. It is easy to overlook poets – particularly local ones – whose work, published in newspapers, magazines and journals, seems occasional. These intermittent essays, poems, and short stories of black women writers, seldom mentioned in biblic graphies and other sources, should not necessarily be considered as "the only thing they did." There may be other work that remains to be unearthed. As was the case with most black women who published in the early twentieth century, Maurine Lawrence Jeffrey had no showcase of her own.

A native of Longview, Texas, Maurine Lawrence was born in 1900. She and her parents moved to Dallas when she was three years of age. There she attended the Dallas grammar schools, including the J. P. Stacks Elementary School. It was shortly after Jeffrey's graduation that her father died; an only child, Maurine was sent by her mother to Prairie View College. There she studied a variety of subjects but was most enthusiastic about history, English, and music. After completing four years at Prairie View with an excellent record, Jeffrey taught in the Dallas public schools. Two and a half years later she resigned to marry Jessie W. Jeffrey, the oldest son of a professor.

Jeffrey's interest in writing began as early as twelve, when she wrote her first rhymes. Her work was published for the first time in 1924, and from that time on she was on the staff of many local newspapers, including the *Dallas Express*. Critics gave favorable reviews of her poetry. Some of her verse appears in *Heralding Dawn*, J. Mason Brewer's 1936 anthology of Texas poets, which also includes Gwendolyn Bennett,* Lauretta Holman Gooden,* Lillian Tucker Lewis,* Birdelle Wycoff Ransom,* and Bernice Love Wiggins.* "My Rainy Day" is a twelve-line poem of a somewhat nostalgic nature. "Pappy's Last Song," in dialect verse, tells of a man weary of life who asks his family to usher him into eternity with a Negro spiritual:

> Raise dat hymn, Liza, daughter,
> > As you do on Sunday morn;
> Sing it soft, and slow, sorter;
> > My 'ligion's a-risin', sho's you born.
> Jimmy, son, drop in some bass,
> > Sam, come on wit' a little tenor;
> Ma, you lead dat s'prano in place,
> > While Pa moans like a sinner.

SELECT BIBLIOGRAPHY

Primary

Poetry

"My Rainy Day." *Dallas Express* [date unknown].

"Pappy's Last Song." *Dallas Express* [date unknown].

IN ANTHOLOGIES

Brewer, *Heralding Dawn*, 1936. "My Rainy Day"; "Pappy's Last Song."

Secondary

Kallenbach, *Index to Black American Literary Anthologies*, 1979.

JESSYE, EVA ALBERTA (c.1897-1992)

Poet

Columnist

Musical editor/arranger

Eva Alberta Jessye can best be described as possessing a musical talent with a literary twist. She combines both in her primary work, *My Spirituals,* a combination book and musical score. Jessye selects sixteen favorite songs which are endearing for their strong associations with past faces and experiences. Jessye explains in her introduction: "Collecting these songs has not been a difficult task. I was not obliged to delve in remote corners of the South or coax them from reluctant elders. They are the songs of my childhood and of my own people. I have sung them all my life."

Each story is thus enlivened by poignant song. In one, "Ain't Got Long to Stay Heah," she tells of the "visiting Kansans" who would board up their houses each fall and take to the cotton fields to do extra picking. Competitions for picking would naturally ensue between native and visiting pickers. To spur production each team chose a leader who "sang" the pickers into action. In this story the natives' leader, "a strapping boy of nineteen summers," sings "Goin' to Pick Dis Cotton 'Till de Sun Go Down," while his visiting counterpart, a short, overweight woman named Tiny, sings "Ain't Got Long to Stay Heah."

Jessye's words create intimate snapshots of her life. The spiritual "Bles' My Soul An' Gone" evokes Jessye's memory of sitting on the porch with her Aunt Harriet after the evening chores were through. Out of Jessye's ears we hear the silence that surrounds the house perched on the "edge of the prairie." The prairie is endless, and the only vestiges of life, as Jessye says, are to be found in the barnyard. However, "the one thing that made the spot endurable was Aunt Harriet's singing for a glorious voice dwelt in her frail body."

Although Jessye did not write these spirituals, she makes them her own with personal images, sounds, smells, and feelings. The stories themselves are intimate and warm, but the spirituals add an extra dimension of love.

Eva Alberta Jessye was born in Coffeyville, Kansas, in 1897, the daughter of former slaves. Her musical talent was recognized early and encouraged by Marion Cook, who brought his touring musical show to her hometown in 1907. On his advice Eva attended Western University in Kansas, studying choral music and musical theory. After she received her degree in 1914, she studied at Langston University for a year. Then, like many black women of the era, she became a teacher in segregated public schools of Oklahoma. Continuing to pursue her musical interests, she taught piano in Muskogee, Oklahoma, and then became director of music at Morgan State University in Baltimore, Maryland.

In 1922, Jessye worked on the editorial staff of the *Afro-American*, a Baltimore journal. After one year in that position, she decided to seek an active career in music. She moved to New York, taking many jobs singing in theaters as a warm-up act before films. In 1926 she met Marion Cook again and he encouraged her to continue to set higher goals. Shortly thereafter, Jessye formed a choral group, the Original Dixie Jubilee Singers (later called the Eva Jessye Choir). The choir gained popularity very quickly, and they appeared in many stage shows and on radio programs such as the "Major Bowles Family Radio Hour" and "General Motors Hour." The Eva Jessye Choir was chosen as the official choral group to sing at Dr. Martin Luther King's funeral.

Jessye then branched into stage and film. When King Vidor set out to make the first all-black cast musical motion picture, he asked Eva Jessye to train the choir and in 1929 invited her to be the director of music for his new film, *Hallelujah!* Throughout her career as a film and stage musical director, Jessye managed a training school for performers in New York. *Hallelujah!* earned her a favorable reputation, putting her in demand. NBC broadcast her folk oratorio of Milton's *Paradise Lost and Regained* in 1931. She later served as the choral director for original Broadway productions such as Gershwin's *Porgy and Bess* and *Four Saints in Three Acts*.

She is the author of many musical compositions including *My Spirituals* (1927), *The Life of Christ in Negro Spirituals* (1931), and *The Chronicle of Job* (1936). She is also a poet, having published in several anthologies of the era.

October 1 in Kansas has been proclaimed Eva Jessye Day. She received honorary degrees from Wilberforce University in Ohio and Allen University in South Carolina. Her papers are housed at Pittsburg State University in Kansas and at the University of Michigan.

SELECT BIBLIOGRAPHY

Primary

Nonfiction

The Chronicle of Job, 1936.

The Life of Christ in Negro Spirituals, 1931.

My Spirituals. New York: Robbins-Engel, 1927.

When the Saints Go Marching In. New York: Marks Music Co.

Poetry

"The Maestro." *Opportunity* (August 1933): 244.

IN ANTHOLOGIES

Kerlin, *Negro Poets and Their Poems* [1923] 1935. "The Singer"; "Spring with the Teacher"; "To a Rosebud."

Secondary

Bennett, Gwendolyn, Review of *My Spirituals*, by Eva Jessye, 1927.

Campbell, Dorothy, *Index to Black American Writers in Collective Biographies*, 1983.

Chapman, *Index to Black Poetry*, 1974.

Chapman, *Index to Poetry by Black American Women*, 1986.

"Daughter of ex-Slaves Who Made Good on Broadway Recalls Life." *New York Times* (7 October 1979): 76.

Ellis, *Opportunity; A Journal of Negro Life*, 1971.

Herman, *Women in Particular*, 1984.

Kallenbach, *Index to Black American Literary Anthologies*, 1979.

Kellner, *The Harlem Renaissance*, 1984.

Lanker, Brian. *I Dream a World: Portraits of Black Women who Changed America*, Stewart, Tabori & Chang, 1989.

Low and Clift, *Encyclopedia of Black America*, 1981.

Obituary, *New York Times*, Tuesday, 3 March 1992, A21.

Richardson, *Black Women and Religion*, 1980.

Rush, Myers, and Arata, *Black American Writers Past and Present*, 1975.

Spradling, *In Black and White*, 1980.

JOHNSON, DOROTHY VENA (1898-1970)

Educator

Poet

Dorothy Vena Johnson, a resident of California, could be considered one of the writers in the West Coast section of the New Negro Movement. She came to writing somewhat late, however, and her only known link to the movement is the publication of two early poems in *Golden Slippers*, Arna Bontemps's well-known anthology for children. Unbound by constraints of modesty seen in some women writers, her apparently simple poetry breaks new ground in its radically bitter, sarcastic attacks on racism.

According to her death certificate, Johnson, the daughter of James M. and Namie Plumb Vena, was born on 7 May 1898 in California. She received most of her early education at a convent and continued her studies at the University of Southern California, where she earned an A.B. degree, and the Teacher's College at UCLA. Johnson, who was an educator for forty years, remained in the Los Angeles area to teach junior high school students journalism and poetry. Her students, in turn, were consistent contributors to *Nuggets*, a magazine of poetry for and by children. Johnson married a lawyer, who ultimately became a U.S. attorney, and founded the Allied Arts League. A member and former treasurer of the Los Angeles Creative Writing Teachers Association, she also contributed two poems to the National Poetry Association's *National Anthology of Verse* (1949), written by high school and college instructors.

Johnson's poetry is simple, brief, and direct. Her abab rhyme scheme, short meter, and use of metaphors mislead some into thinking that her work is geared solely toward children. Though two poems were published in *Golden Slippers* – "Twinkling Gown" and "Palace" – her mournful tone and cutting themes squarely address adults. Even these two children's poems end on a pensive, bleak note as they contemplate nature's movements and cycles.

Johnson boldly confronts racism in a series of four poems: "Epitaph for a Bigot," "Post War Ballad," "Ode to Justice," and "Jerked to God." With raw imagery she speaks of brutalities committed against people of color: "Life to the bigot is a whip." In "Ballad" she resurrects a statue of Crispus Attucks, the first martyr of the Boston Massacre, who, seeing no other sign of Afro-American achievement, is disappointed with democracy and feels that his sacrifice has been in vain. After "hearing how Nazis / Brewed some evil deeds / And how his loyal race / Was disdained like weeds," he decides it "would [be] better to stay a stone." Such harsh, but apt, parallels sharpen to an even more stinging metaphor in "Jerked to God." This poem marks the perversion of God's gifts – Jesus, trees, people – in lynching: as "Humans /

Jerked to God." Its staccato rhythm ("A life; a tree / A rope; a rod") accentuates the message.

Johnson refers to history again in "Ode to Justice," dedicated to the Scottsboro Boys. The case, which reached the Supreme Court in two trials, focused on nine boys, ages thirteen to nineteen, who were charged with raping two white girls. All but one were sentenced to death by Alabama courts, but they appealed successfully, supported by the alleged victim, Ruby Bates. Ironically, the boys were freed on technicalities stemming from the Alabama trial procedures, not because of their innocence. The defendants were saved by their inadequate legal counsel and the documented exclusion of blacks from the county's jury pool. Johnson notes the irony of their victory as she mocks "Lady Justice [who] is often blind / . . . / And seems to be devoid of mind / Reason and virtue / . . . deaf and dumb." In her "barren earth . . . [the] soul within / Is warped and stained and buried deep / In tainted earth and vicious sin." In using the personification of justice as a lady rather than a woman, Johnson is perhaps mocking the immorality committed under the guise of protecting "white ladyhood."

Johnson's other poems are no less somber as they reflect on starving children, personal sin, mercurial success, omnipresent defeat, nature, and the toil of Afro-Americans. Only one, "The Bride," ends on a relatively light note as the narrator, who despondently watches her former lover marry, derives satisfaction from seeing that the "bride was stout." The poet was capable of purely beautiful imagery, also, as demonstrated in "Crystal Shreds" – rain, God's weeping, "release[s] absolution / In crystal shreds / Of ethereal dew." Apart from "To a Courageous Mother," none of her works considers women separately. Many of Johnson's shorter poems are collected in *Poems for Radio* (1945) for broadcast over the air. (The editors specify no basis for selection, apart from variety.) It is probably no coincidence that none of her race-related poems is included in this anthology. In 1967 Johnson suffered a cerebral hemorrhage from which she eventually died at the age of seventy-two.

SELECT BIBLIOGRAPHY

Primary

Poetry

IN ANTHOLOGIES

Bontemps, *Golden Slippers*, 1941. "Twinkling Gown."

Murphy, *Ebony Rhythm*, [1948] 1968. "Epitaph for a Bigot"; "Post War Ballad"; "Road to Anywhere"; "Success."

Murphy, *Negro Voices*, [1938] 1971. "Crystal Shreds;" "Jerked to God"; "Ode to Justice."

Secondary

Bontemps and Hughes, *The Poetry of the Negro, 1746-1949*, 1949.

Campbell, Dorothy, *Index to Black American Writers in Collective Biographies*, 1983.

Chapman, *Index to Black Poetry*, 1974.

Chapman, *Index to Poetry by Black American Women*, 1986.

Kallenbach, *Index to Black American Literary Anthologies*, 1979.

Rush, Myers, and Arata, *Black American Writers Past and Present*, 1975.

Williams, *American Black Women in the Arts and Social Sciences*, 1978.

JOHNSON, GEORGIA DOUGLAS (CAMP) (1877-1966)

Columnist

Educator

Musician

Playwright

Poet

Among black women writing during the New Negro Renaissance, Georgia Douglas Johnson is one of the best known. The author of lyrics, short stories, four volumes of verse, and several plays, she published her work in an array of periodicals: *Crisis, Messenger, Minaret, Liberator, Opportunity, Palms,* and *Voice of the Negro.* For years Johnson was overlooked by critics as they compared her with black male poets (called by J. Saunders Redding "masculine literature of the Negro") and with white female poets like Sara Teasdale. Sixty years later literary critics are beginning to accord Johnson a significant place among the writers of the early twentieth century. She is now considered an important figure in the development of Afro-American literature historically and politically.

Information concerning the poet's parentage and youth is scarce. According to Ann Allen Shockley, the Registrar's Office at the University of Atlanta confirms Johnson's birth date as 10 September 1877. The daughter of George and Laura Camp, she received her primary education in Atlanta public schools, continuing her studies at Atlanta University (Normal Program), Oberlin Conservatory of Music in Ohio and Cleveland College of Music (training in music, harmony, violin, piano and voice), and Howard University. She returned to Atlanta to teach school and serve as an assistant principal after completing her course in Cleveland. She married Henry Lincoln Johnson, a lawyer and politician, in 1903. The couple moved to Washington, D.C., in 1909 where they had two sons, Henry Lincoln, Jr., and Peter Douglas.

Johnson, as a central figure of the New Negro Movement, welcomed to her home scores of black intellectuals, including William Stanley Braithwaite, W. E. B. Du Bois, Angelina Weld Grimké,* and Zora Neale Hurston.* Mentioned by Gwendolyn Bennett* in her Ebony Flute column, the Johnson residence was also the location of the Washington, D.C., literary salon, the Round Table, which met on Saturday nights. Among those who gathered at the Johnson residence were Marita Bonner,* Mary Burrill,* Countee Cullen, Clarissa Scott Delany,* Alice Dunbar-Nelson,* Jessie Fauset,* Angelina Weld Grimké,* Langston Hughes, Zora Neale Hurston,* Alain Locke, Gertrude Parthenia McBrown,* May Miller,* Mary Effie Lee Newsome,* and Anne Spencer.* In addition, Johnson participated in civil rights activities and politics. She was involved with the Pan-African movement, minority and women's issues, human rights organizations, the Congregational church, the Republican party (like Alice Dunbar-Nelson* and Mary Church Terrell*), and various other literary organizations.

Widowed in 1925, she took government jobs to support herself and her sons while continuing her work as a writer. Poet May Miller recalls Johnson's unselfishness in permitting Zora Neale Hurston, financially distressed at the time, to reside with the author and her sons while she too was experiencing financial hardships. Johnson simultaneously maintained a full-time job and conducted energetic and interesting salon meetings. By 1927 Johnson was working for the Department of Labor as the commissioner of conciliation, a reportedly strenuous job from which Johnson was dismissed in the mid-1930s. With income from piecemeal jobs and royalties from her writing, she financed her sons' educations by herself. This was no insignificant feat, especially since black women were the lowest paid workers in the labor force.

At the age of thirty Georgia Douglas Johnson's literary output increased greatly, and she made contacts like Dean Kelly Miller at Howard University and his friend William Stanley Braithwaite, who helped promote her career. Johnson published more than two hundred poems in four collections between 1918 and 1930; some of them were also published in periodicals.

Johnson's first volume of poetry, *The Heart of a Woman* (1918), assembled with Jessie Fauset's aid, was introduced in relatively progressive terms for the times by William Stanley Braithwaite as "intensely feminine . . . which means more than anything else that [the poems] are deeply human." Since Johnson thematically uncovers the heart of a woman, her style apparently justifies criticism in terms of stereotypical female sentimentality. Her style, enhanced by her ability as a lyricist, draws on the classical, neoclassical, romantic, Victorian, and early twentieth-century traditions; today some of the vocabulary is outdated. The verses unfold in themes of love, despair, joy, peace, alienation, and other emotions, abstracted by an occasional spirituality against a backdrop of nature. The periodic use of King James English intensifies the formal effect: "God sends thee with thy soothing balms / That I may falter to thy arms."

Gloria T. Hull suggests that "*The Heart of a Woman* has been persistently locked into its designation as a book of tidy lyrics that express the love-longing of a feminine sensibility. Read afresh – that is, deeply, autobiographically, and with feminist awareness – it becomes much more than that and takes on new levels of interest and meaning" (157). The poet seeks "compassion's breast" to restore the heart of woman, which "breaks, breaks, breaks on the sheltering bars." Her search takes her from elation ("Oh I am so happy, my heart is so light, / The shades and the shadows have vanished from sight, / This wild pulsing gladness throbs like a sweet pain / O soul of me, drink, ere night falleth again!") to devastation ("O love, you have shorn me, and rifled my heart, / You have torn down the shrine from the innermost part"). Her joy is qualified by a fear of night; her dejection suggests an internal violence, with little promise of recovery. Flowing with her intermittent positive thoughts of the future is a pervading tone of alienation, lurking on the dark side of hope, particularly evident in poems like "Isolation," "Quest," "Pages from Life" and "Foredoom":

> Her life was dwarfed, and wed to blight
> Her very days were shades of night,
> Her every dream was born entombed,
> Her soul, a bud, that never bloomed.

Placing Johnson's work in proper historical context raises the difficulty she had in maintaining her identity and freedom of expression in a society and period obsessed with outward appearances. Johnson was married to a public official who believed a woman's place was in the home and disapproved of his wife's writing, but he freely quoted her poetry in some of his more memorable speeches.

In a letter Johnson wrote to Arna Bontemps on 19 July 1941, she stated: "My first book was *The Heart of a Woman*. It was not at all race conscious. Then someone said she has no feeling for the race. So I wrote *Bronze*. It is entirely race conscious."

The allegation that Johnson was not dedicated to racial uplift because she wrote of womanhood without mentioning race demonstrates the unresolved duality women of color had to endure. They were expected to identify themselves as either black or female, but never both. Beyond the formal English in Johnson's poetry is the imploring tone of a woman, and of an Afro-American, seeking an audience in a society which respected neither. Rejected by white women and ignored by black men, Afro-American women were not permitted to comfortably support both causes. Such was their legacy in a society stratified by race and gender.

Bronze was the fruit borne of this double jeopardy, out of Johnson's "bitter earth wound," as affirmed by Effie Lee Newsome's verbose but perceptive review of the second volume of verse: "It is well nigh impossible to think of this vital product from the pen of Georgia Douglas Johnson without having communicated to one some of the intense conviction that WROUGHT it into being." Laced with feminine imagery, the poem "Moods" summarizes *Bronze*: "My heart is pregnant with a great despair / With much beholding of my people's care / 'Mid blinded prejudice and nurtured wrong / Exhaling wantonly the days along." The poem "Bondage" calls to mind the title of Alice Walker's collection of essays *In Search of Our Mothers' Gardens*:

"Where unto may I wander free? / Alas, alas / My garden walks lie inwardly."

In several of Johnson's poems she connects by metaphor victims of prejudice with Christ on the Cross at Calvary, as in "The Cross," "Hegira," and "Perspective." While "Alien" and "Octoroon" deal with the sorrowful circumstances of mixed blood and heritage, Johnson reserves a section of *Bronze* to speak about women carefully within the context of race. A major theme emanating from the section labeled "Maternity" is the ambivalence of black women giving birth joyfully but with anguish: they were bringing children into a society that despised them even before they were born. This theme is paralleled by a latent one: in "Black Woman," the child denied entry into the world may symbolize the unrealized identity of the Afro-American woman.

Johnson later in life disclosed her desire to limit her writing about race in order to escape the sting of racism she suffered daily. She believed, "If one can soar, he should soar, leaving his chains behind." The two other books of poetry Johnson produced, *An Autumn Love Cycle* (1928) and the personally published *Share My World* (1962), embraced more universal topics. *Autumn* garnered something less than praise from most black critics, too absorbed with the state of race relations in America to acknowledge nonracial poetry. Johnson, however, received support from literary salon members Ann Spencer,* Marita Bonner,* and Alice Dunbar-Nelson*; the latter believed that Johnson's motivation for the volume was a love affair. Present-day critics agree that the third collection – even more autobiographical than her previous works – is her most mature work, as she ponders the autumnal years.

Johnson's plays were a more direct vehicle for protest on the various social phenomena fermenting in America. She was first-place winner of the 1927 *Opportunity* play contest and worked with the Krigwa players. She also became involved with the Federal Theatre Project, a federally sponsored theater that was part of President Franklin Roosevelt's New Deal. The Federal Theatre Project became a forum for hopeful playwrights, and Johnson submitted five plays: two historical skits of slaves in their quest for freedom and three dramas on the topics of rape and lynching. She naturally assumed that experimental and social protest dramas would be accepted.

But though technically strong, none of the plays was ever produced by the Federal Theatre – perhaps because they openly denounced brutalities committed in this country against people of color. Johnson's drama was written in a mixture of standard English and traditional black dialect. Protest and social commentary were intensified to a greater degree than in her poetry.

"Plumes" is the play for which Johnson won *Opportunity*'s first prize in 1927. Charity's daughter, Emmerline, is gravely ill, but Charity's friend, Tildy, advises her not to pay the doctor to operate since he cannot guarantee that her daughter will recover, or even survive. Tildy foresees Emmerline's death, solemnly reading the future from the coffee grounds in her cup. Charity is unsure as to whether she should risk paying the doctor to operate. The chances are slim and if Emmerline should still die, no money would remain to bury her in style. Superstition supersedes the doctor's advice. Charity hesitates; Emmerline dies. While the characterization of women who must consider a life-or-death decision in terms of money makes an interesting comment on the feminization of poverty, the element of fortune telling and superstition echo a popular Harlem Renaissance motif, "conjuring." The reader is left to judge whether poverty, superstition, or Charity's procrastination is to blame for Emmerline's death.

A Sunday Morning in the South opens as Sue, the seventy-year-old grandmother of Tom, nineteen, and Bossie, seven, calls her grandsons to breakfast. Against the background singing of a church service in progress next door, Tom is accosted by the police. He is charged with an assault that took place at 9:00 p.m. the night before, while he was at home asleep in bed. The young white woman, emotionally distraught, is not able to verify Tom as her assailant. The police nonetheless arrest him, and he is handed over to a mob to be lynched. Sue does her best to defend Tom and calls on a young white woman for whom she used to be mammy to intervene. But she is too late. Again, as in *Bronze*, and as extracted from Robert T. Kerlin's critique of *Heart of a Woman*, the parallel between Christ bearing the cross to Calvary and the oppression of a people surfaces.

In this play, Johnson again used a variety of themes to mold the plot. The atrocity of lynching, the institution of black women as mammies, and the partnership of Ku Klux Klan and police were brutal realities of the early twentieth century. Johnson uses Tom, who aspires to be a minister, to show how a community is thwarted through the destruction of its leaders. The black church was the core of the Afro-American community, providing political, social, educational, and other support systems, with the black minister its leader in all aspects. Usually the most educated individual in the community, he or she would later help mobilize Afro-Americans in the civil rights movement of the 1950s and 1960s.

The resounding protest in Johnson's drama is lacking in her first volume of poetry, which was produced during the transition from the genteel age to the era of the New Negro. According to American society in general, writing was for "naughty" women, not "ladies." At that time Johnson could not overtly advocate her beliefs; she had to veil her defiance in order to maintain her status as a lady (a word rarely used for women who were not white) and to keep an audience.

At the age of sixty-four the author had several works in progress, only one of which, *An Autumn Love Cycle*, was eventually published. Other preparations included "The Torch," which was to be a collection of inspirational pieces written by famous authors; "The Life and Times of Henry Lincoln Johnson, a Biography"; "Rainbow Silhouettes," short stories of mixed blood; a volume of prose sketches written in the black press and titled "Homely Philosophy"; and finally, a "catalogue" of twenty-eight dramas with themes of Africana, lynching, passing, miscegenation, and so on. A letter to a friend reveals the extent of her prolific production: "Have about eight books here ready to get going–three new books of poetry, thirty plays–both one and three act, thirty short stories, a novel, a book of philosophy, a book of exquisite sayings . . . twenty songs." Unfortunately, much of Johnson's work went unpublished, although she actively solicited publishers for contracts. Institutions with information on Johnson's biographical and literary profiles include Atlanta University, Fisk University, George Mason University, and the Schomburg Center for Research in Black Culture in New York.

In its various themes, Johnson's poetry may have been universal, but her personal life was kept private. Perhaps Johnson felt no need to divulge the specifics of her personal life; her poetry was for the reader, but her life was her own. Scholars speculate from her reticence over her background, coupled with her recurring themes of miscegenation, passing, and other race issues, that Johnson herself had a great deal of white blood. Through her universal themes she identified the common experiences of many, but the details of her life are limited to the memories of close friends like May Miller,* who was present when Johnson was on her death bed: she stroked her hand gently and whispered repeatedly, "Poet Georgia Douglas Johnson."

SELECT BIBLIOGRAPHY

Primary

Drama

Blue Blood. In Shay, *Fifty More Contemporary One Act Plays*, 1928.

Plumes: Folk Tragedy. New York: French, 1927.

A Sunday Morning in the South: A One-Act Play. Washington, D.C.: n.p., [1924?].

IN ANTHOLOGIES

Hatch and Shine, *Black Theatre U.S.A.*, 1974. *A Sunday Morning in the South*.

Locke and Gregory, *Plays of Negro Life*, [1927] 1970. *Plumes*.

UNPUBLISHED

"Attucks."

"Starting Point."

Poetry

An Autumn Love Cycle. Introduction by Alain Locke. New York: H. Vinal, 1928. Reprint. New York: Neal, 1938. Facsimile of 1928 ed., Freeport, N.Y.: Books for Libraries Press, 1971.

Bronze. Introduction by W. E. B. Du Bois. Boston: B. J. Brimmer, 1922.

The Heart of a Woman and Other Poems. Introduction by William Stanley Braithwaite. Boston: Cornhill, 1918.

Share My World: A Book of Poems. Washington, D.C.: The author, 1962.

IN ANTHOLOGIES

Bontemps, *Golden Slippers*, 1941. "Benediction"; "Guardianship"; "I've Learned to Sing"; "My Little Dreams"; "Tomorrow's Men"; "Youth."

Cromwell, Turner, and Dykes, *Readings from Negro Authors*, 1931. "The Heart of a Woman"; "Retrospection"; "Values."

Cullen, *Caroling Dusk*, 1927. "The Dreams of the Dream"; "The Heart of a Woman"; "Hope"; "I Want to Die While You Love Me"; "Lethe"; "Little Son"; "My Little Dreams"; "Old Black Men"; "Proving"; "Recessional"; "Service"; "The Suppliant"; "What Need Have I for Memory"; "When I am Dead."

Johnson, Charles S., *Ebony and Topaz*, [1927] 1971. "Requiem."

Kerlin, *Negro Poets and Their Poems*, [1923] 1935. "The Heart of a Woman"; "The Octoroon"; "Smothered Fires."

Locke, *The New Negro*, [1925] 1968. "Escape"; "The Ordeal"; "The Riddle"; "To Samuel Coleridge Taylor"; "Upon Hearing His."

Murphy, *Ebony Rhythm*, [1948] 1968. "Interracial Black Recruit"; "I've Learned to Sing."

Shockley, *Afro-American Women Writers, 1746-1933*, 1988. "Cosmopolite"; "The Heart of a Woman"; "I Want to Die While You Love Me"; "Old Love Letters."

Stetson, *Black Sister*, 1981. "The Heart of a Woman"; "I Want to Die"; "My Little Dreams"; "Smothered Fire."

White and Jackson, *An Anthology of Verse by American Negroes*, [1924] 1968.

Secondary

Bonner, Review of *An Autumn Love Cycle*, by Georgia Douglas Johnson, 1927.

Brawley, *The Negro Genius*, 1940.

Brawley, *The Negro in Literature and Art*, 1930.

Campbell, Dorothy, *Index to Black American Writers in Collective Biographies*, 1983.

Davis, John Preston, *The American Negro Reference Book*, 1966.

Dover, "The Importance of Georgia Douglas Johnson," 1952.

Ellis, *Opportunity; A Journal of Negro Life*, 1971.

Fletcher, "From Genteel Poet to Revolutionary Playwright: Georgia Douglas Johnson as a Symbol of Black Success, Failure, and Fortitude," 1985.

Fletcher, "Georgia Douglas Johnson," 1987.

Hull, *Color, Sex, and Poetry*, 1987.

Kallenbach, *Index to Black American Literary Anthologies*, 1979.

Kellner, *The Harlem Renaissance*, 1984.

Kerlin, *Negro Poets and Their Poems*, [1923] 1935.

Locke, Review of *Bronze: A Book of Verse*, by Georgia Douglas Johnson, 1923.

Newsome, Review of *Bronze*, by Georgia Douglas Johnson, 1923.

Opportunity (July 1927): 204.

Ploski and Kaiser, *The Negro Almanac*, 1971.

Porter, *North American Negro Poets*, 1945.

Redding, *To Make a Poet Black*, 1939.

Rush, Myers, and Arata, *Black American Writers Past and Present*, 1975.

Spencer, Review of *An Autumn Love Cycle*, by Georgia Douglas Johnson, 1929.

White and Jackson, *An Anthology of Verse by American Negroes*, [1924] 1968.

Who's Who in Colored America, 1932.

Women's Poetry Index, 1986.

JOHNSON (HUBBELL), HELENE (1907-)

Poet

Born twenty-five years after Georgia Douglas Johnson,* Helene Johnson is a representative of the younger generation of poets who were part of the New Negro Movement. Remembered as one of the youngest and brightest poets of the Harlem Renaissance, Johnson's verse captures the concern and excitement inherent in the movement.

Little has been recorded about Johnson's private life, and most of what is known comes from the brief introductions in the poetry anthologies of the period. Born in Boston, the poet was educated in the public schools there. According to Raymond R. Patterson, Johnson won a short-story first prize from the *Boston Chronicle* and an honorable mention for a poem in *Opportunity*'s first literary contest. A member of the Saturday Evening Quill Club, Johnson considered Whitman, Tennyson, Shelley, and Sandburg to be her favorite poets.

After moving to New York with her cousin Dorothy West,* she published several more poems in such magazines as *Opportunity, Fire!!,* and *Vanity Fair.* While she lived in New York, she was frequently linked with various literary circles such as A'Lelia Walker's Dark Tower. Her work reveals a strong dedication to her racial heritage and concern for Harlem's ghetto life. When Johnson married and had a daughter, she disappeared from the New York scene before the end of the Harlem Renaissance. A 1988 interview conducted by Clifton Johnson, director of the Amistad Research Center in New Orleans, revealed that Johnson dedicated herself to raising her daughter and earning a livelihood, with little energy remaining for poetry. Thus her early promise remained unfulfilled.

During her time in New York, Johnson published several award-winning poems in *Opportunity*. After winning prizes in various literary contests, she became quite well known in the New York literary scene. Wallace Thurman in his satiric novel *The Infants of Spring* gives a fictional glimpse of Johnson and Dorothy West* in their heyday:

> . . . two young girls, recently emigrated from Boston. They were the latest to be hailed as incipient immortals. Their names were Doris Westmore and Hazel Jamison. Doris wrote stories. Hazel wrote poetry. Both had become known through a literary contest fostered by one of the leading Negro magazines. Raymond liked them more than he did most of the young recruits of the movement. For one thing, they were characterized by a freshness and naivete which he and his cronies had lost. And, surprisingly enough for Negro

prodigies, they actually gave promise of possessing literary talent.

This passage reflects the general expectations that the more established members of the Harlem Renaissance had for a poet like Johnson.

While living in New York, she became a member of the Fellowship for Reconciliation, an international organization that worked for pacifist resistance to war and violence, interracial goodwill, and justice in general. Both Countee Cullen and Wallace Thurman spoke highly of Johnson, noting her "promise of possessing literary talent."

Among Johnson's award-winning poems were "My Race" and "Metamorphism," published in the March 1926 issue of *Opportunity*. The themes in these two poems are typical of Johnson: the sensuous beauty of the natural world, the injustice of racial oppression, and the need for personal freedom. Johnson's most important poem, "Bottled," was published in *Vanity Fair* in May 1927. The publication of this poem won her immediate success. Insightful and quite ingenious, the poem is written in a colloquial style, comparing a bottle of Sahara sand with a Seventh Avenue "darky." In the poem, the "darky" dances to the music of an organ-grinder, and his dancing is not the stereotypical Charleston or Black Bottom. Instead, his dancing is "dignified and proud," an extension of his African heritage. The poet notices the ambiguities in the dancing man, and discovers that, like the bottle of sand, the black man has been bottled by Western culture–he is wearing "yaller shoes and yaller gloves / And swallow-tail coat." She realizes that, naturally, were he in his ancestors' jungle, he would have on no clothes. She concludes that regardless of the "trick shoes, trick coat, trick cane, trick everything," the man is still himself, a product of his culture and heritage on the inside, much like the bottled sand.

The poet may have returned to Boston in 1929; in any case, after that year, she virtually disappeared from the literary scene and lost all prominence as a poet. In 1934, Dorothy West published *Challenge: A Literary Quarterly*, and a poem of Johnson's is included in it. In the third issue of the journal (1935), another of Johnson's poems was published as was a note about her retirement and her new marriage. Not until 1970 was her married name, Hubbell, made public. In retrospect, her talent can be considered only that of a minor poet of the period, for the bulk of her work was produced over a short time and was very similar. She never ventured further, nor did she continue with her writing long enough to grow and develop.

SELECT BIBLIOGRAPHY

Primary

Poetry

"Cui Bono?" *Harlem Magazine* (November 1928).

"Fiat Lux." *Opportunity* (December 1928): 361.

"Fulfillment." *Opportunity* (June1926): 194.

"Futility." *Opportunity* (August 1926): 259.

"I Am Not Proud." *Saturday Evening Quill* (April 1929).

"Invocation." *Saturday Evening Quill* (April 1929).

"Love in Midsummer." *Messenger* (October 1926).

"Metamorphism." *Opportunity* (March 1926): 81.

"A Missionary Brings Native." *Palms* (November 1928).

"Monotone." *Opportunity* (September 1932): 286.

"Mother." *Opportunity* (September 1926): 295.

"My Race." *Opportunity* (July 1925): 196.

"Night." *Opportunity* (January 1926): 26.

"Plea of a Plebian." *Opportunity* (May 1934): 144.

"Regalia." *Saturday Evening Quill* (April 1929).

"Remember Not." *Saturday Evening Quill* (April 1929).

"The Road." *Opportunity* (July 1926): 225.

"Rustic Fantasy." *Saturday Evening Quill* (April 1929).

"Sonnet." *Opportunity* (December 1931): 374.

"Sonnet." *Opportunity* (March 1932): 81.

"Summer Matures." *Opportunity* (July 1927): 199.

"Trees at Night." *Opportunity* (May 1925): 147.

"Vers de Societe." *Opportunity* (July 1930): 210.

"Why Do They Prate." *Saturday Evening Quill* (April 1929).

"Worship." *Saturday Evening Quill* (April 1929).

IN ANTHOLOGIES

Bontemps, *Golden Slippers*, 1941. "Bottled"; "Little Brown Boy"; "New York"; "The Road."

Cromwell, Turner, and Dykes, *Readings from Negro Authors*, 1931. "Metamorphism"; "The Road."

Cullen, *Caroling Dusk*, 1927. "Bottled"; "Fulfillment"; "Magalu"; "Poem: Little Brown Boy"; "The Road"; "Sonnet to a Negro in Harlem"; "Summer Matures"; "What Do I Care for Morning?"

Johnson, Charles S., *Ebony and Topaz*, [1927] 1971. "A Sonnet to a Negro in Harlem."

Stetson, *Black Sister*, 1981. "Bottled"; "Magalu"; "The Road"; "Trees at Night"; "Summer Matures."

Secondary

Bontemps and Hughes, *The Poetry of the Negro, 1746-1949*, 1949.

Bontemps and Hughes, *The Poetry of the Negro, 1746-1970*, 1970.

Campbell, Dorothy, *Index to Black American Writers in Collective Biographies*, 1983.

Chapman, *Index to Black Poetry*, 1974.

Ellis, *Opportunity; A Journal of Negro Life*, 1971.

Index to Poetry in Periodicals, 1925-1929, 1983.

Kallenbach, *Index to Black American Literary Anthologies*, 1979.

Kellner, *The Harlem Renaissance*, 1984.

Patterson, Raymond R., "Helene Johnson," 1987.

Rush, Myers, and Arata, *Black American Writers Past and Present*, 1975.

Spradling, *In Black and White*, 1980.

Stetson, *Black Sister*, 1981.

Williams, *American Black Women in the Arts and Social Sciences*, 1978.

LARSEN (IMES), NELLA (1891-1964)

Novelist
Librarian
Nurse

Nella Larsen's novel *Quicksand* (1928) opens with an epigraph from Langston Hughes's poem "Cross": "My old man died in a fine big house / My ma died in a shack / I wonder where I'm gonna die / Being neither white nor black?" When Nella Larsen was found dead at seventy-two years of age in her Lower East Side, Second Avenue apartment in 1964, she had not only receded into oblivion socially but was no longer remembered as a major New Negro writer. She had been employed the last twenty years of her life as a night supervising nurse at hospitals near her home.

Larsen, once considered one of the most promising writers to publish during the Harlem Renaissance between 1928 and the late 1930s, had been forgotten.

A native of Chicago, Illinois, Larsen was born of an interracial marriage; her mother was Danish, her father West Indian. Her father was deceased by the time she was two years old; her mother remarried a Danish man. Though Larsen frequently alluded to herself as a "mulatto," she did not openly discuss her natural father and mother, nor her stepfather. The only Afro-American member of her family, she attended a private elementary school in Chicago with one of her half sisters and grew up with children of predominantly Scandinavian and German heritage. Larsen did reveal, however, in a biographical sketch for one of her publishers that she rarely saw her white family members so as not to embarrass them, indicating she was ostracized and denied familial security. According to Arthur P. Davis, Larsen, who "looked Italian or Spanish" ultimately "left the race" and could not be contacted by black intellectuals. These conflicts, incurred early, echoed in her writing and in the remainder of her life.

From 1907 to 1926 Nella Larsen moved through a whirlwind of schools and careers. She finished one year (1907-8) at the high school department of Fisk University in Nashville, Tennessee. Not at ease with the predominantly black Fisk, she embarked on a journey to Denmark and audited courses from 1910 to 1912 at the University of Copenhagen. Returning to the United States in 1912, Larsen studied nursing at Lincoln Hospital in New York until 1915, when she traveled to Tuskegee to become assistant superintendent of nurses. When this position ended in 1916, Larsen went to work at Lincoln Hospital in New York, where she primarily lived throughout her life. From 1916 to 1918 Larsen was employed as a nurse at the hospital; 1918 to 1921 found her working for the New York City Department of Health; and when she finished earning her certificate from the library school of the New York Public Library (where she had also worked as a library assistant) she began a new career as a children's librarian in 1924.

Nella Larsen's association with the Harlem Renaissance and its celebrated figures began with her role as the socialite wife of Dr. Elmer S. Imes, a physicist to whom she was wed on 3 May 1919. Working at the Countee Cullen Regional Branch of the New York Public Library (which later was absorbed by the Schomburg Branch) further thrust Larsen into the cultural ferment of Harlem. Through her position there she made contacts in writing and publishing, collecting letters of recommendation from W. E. B. Du Bois, James Weldon Johnson, and others.

The novelist began her writing career as a short-story author. Under a pseudonym she published two stories whose characters and style are precursors to those in her novel: middle-class characters, introverted and restless, and "cliff-hanger" conclusions, which, to many literary critics, are Larsen's major flaws. Individuals like Carl Van Vechten, James Weldon Johnson, Jessie Fauset* (with whom she was inevitably compared), Jean Toomer, and others encouraged her literary career. In "five months in her head and six weeks on the typewriter" she completed the first draft of *Quicksand*.

Published in 1928, *Quicksand* was acclaimed by both black and white reviewers in the *Amsterdam News, New York Herald Tribune, New York Times, Saturday Review of Literature, Crisis*, and *Opportunity* as the product of a new talent. "On the whole, the best piece of fiction that Negro America has produced since the heyday of [Charles Chesnutt]," commented W. E. B. Du Bois, editor of *Crisis*. Gwendolyn Bennett* was more descriptive in her assessment of the new novel in her *Opportunity* column, the Ebony Flute:

"Nella Larsen's *Quicksand* has just arrived. And let me say that many folks will be interested to hear that this book does not set as its tempo that of the Harlem cabaret – this is the story of the struggle of an interesting cultured Negro woman against her environment. Negroes who are squeamish about writers exposing our worst side will be relieved that Harlem nightlife is more or less submerged by this author in the psychological struggle of the heroine."

Alain Locke, one of the original mentors of the Harlem Renaissance, indicated that the significance of *Quicksand* beyond its applicability as a "social document" lay in its dealing with a topic "not often in the foreground of Negro fiction. . . . Indeed this whole side of the problem which was once handled exclusively as a grim tragedy of blood and fateful heredity now shows a tendency to shift to another plane of discussion as the problem of divided loyalties and the issue of the conflict of cultures."

Helga Crane, the heroine of *Quicksand*, is perpetually gripped by divided loyalties, cultural conflict, and self-examination. Attempting to escape her psychological limbo, she moves from place to place, seeking a haven of emotional stability and a complete identity. Highly autobiographical, *Quicksand* casts its protagonist as an individual of West Indian and Danish descent, who is raised in a predominantly white community for much of her youth.

From the onset twenty-two-year-old Helga Crane is dissatisfied with her life at Naxos, a small southern black college where she teaches. Constrained by expectation, pressure to "uplift the race," and what Helga considers the white man's plan for the Negro where everything is "subjected to the paring process" tolerating "no innovation, no individualisms," Helga almost decides to stay at Naxos after speaking with the sympathetic Dr. Robert Anderson, its principal. But neither her responsibility to Afro-America nor her commitment to fiancé James Vayle can suppress Helga's restlessness or her contempt for the "Uncle Tomish" ways of Naxos.

She leaves for Chicago, hoping to get support from her mother's brother, the only American relative remotely civil to her. Helga is turned away by her uncle's new wife, who refuses to believe that her husband is related to a Negro. For several weeks the protagonist is homeless, jobless, and friendless in Chicago, until a brief traveling job lands her in New York. Helga then meets, befriends, and resides with Anne Grey, a wealthy young widow. Quickly and easily she assimilates into the upper strata of Harlem society, indulging in exotic parties, extravagant possessions, and elegant clothes. Yet Helga is again dissatisfied with her life. Not even in Harlem, a contrast to Naxos, can Helga "conform or be happy in her inconformity." A brief encounter with Dr. Robert Anderson (who has also renounced Naxos) at a gathering arouses a familiar and pleasant passion within her, but that moment is lost in her restive pursuit of security and contentment. Although ventures beyond the boundaries of Harlem remind Helga that she is not free from racial injustice, she cannot fully accept the part of her that is black. She is "closed up with that something in the racial character which had always been to her inexplicable, alien."

A five-thousand-dollar "severance" check from Uncle Peter in Chicago allows Helga to escape to Copenhagen, Denmark, to her maternal relatives. Successfully introduced to Danish society, she resigns herself to luxury and the esteem of admirers. She is at first amused that her African descent is not an object of contempt as in America, but an asset. Helga's aunt and uncle see her difference as exotic and are upset by her refusal to marry a prestigious Danish painter, in spite of her explanation. They understand neither the ramifications of racially mixed marriages nor the ordeal and insecurity suffered by its offspring. While the protagonist yearns for the understanding of her Afro-American companions, she loathes the humiliation and degradation imposed upon them in America.

Now comprehending the bond she shares with Afro-Americans as deeper than skin color, Helga returns to Harlem allegedly to attend Anne Grey's wedding to Robert Anderson. Fascinated yet frightened by Anderson for the uncontrolled, irrational emotions he evokes, Helga is painfully cognizant of the lost potential for a relationship.

Helga's discontent stifles her until one rainy night she stumbles deliriously into the middle of a church service. Caught in the frenzy of the moment, an emotional catharsis ensues. Helga marries the minister who conducted the service and returns with him to Alabama. She enjoys her "new status as a preacher's wife," but life in a rural black community gives an "anaesthetic satisfaction for her senses." Helga, having gone to one extreme of pondering and searching for peace of mind to the point of rebellion, now defers soul-searching and goes to the other extreme of numb contentment. She disregards the fact she has no affection for the gluttonous, untidy, arrogant Reverend Pleasant Green, believing she is now at peace and that somehow, even though she had "shut him out from her mind, . . . surely their two lives were one." Slowly the sense of unfulfillment creeps back into Helga's life, but by this time she has already given birth to four children. Remembering the pain and instability resulting from her parents' abandonment, she cannot bring herself to desert her children; nevertheless, she decides to leave her husband. Before this occurs, however, the novel closes as Helga, still weak from her fourth child, becomes pregnant with a fifth.

Helga Crane embodies the fractured product of a society fanatically absorbed in stratifying individuals on the basis of skin color and sex. Cheryl A. Wall explains that "Helga struggles to claim both her European and African cultural heritages. Helga also aspires to a complete womanhood that is denied to black women in her society and to white women as well" (509). As Larsen points out, there is no place for Helga Crane, a mulatto endeavoring to validate her mixed ancestry in an environment rigidly structured by race, where mulattoes receive hardly more sympathy from Afro-Americans than from whites. This dual ostracism is illustrated many times: by rejection from her uncle and his wife; by another character's warning ("I wouldn't mention that my people are white, if I were you – Colored people won't understand it"); and even by Anne Grey, who hates "white people with a deep and burning hatred." Grey particularly scorns another mulatto character whose ability to pass is apparently more valuable than Grey's wealth; Helga chooses not to inform Anne that she too is a mulatto.

How exponentially frustrating it is for Helga Crane when society refuses to let her claim both her African and Danish heritage in positive ways. The color of her skin sentences her to experience the plight of Afro-American women, with whom she cannot fully relate because of her divided loyalty to middle-class values, which to some degree reflect white middle-class privilege. As Thadius Davis has written, Larsen "refuses to celebrate the values of the black middle class or to espouse racial 'uplift' in propagandistic portraits. While it may be true that her characters do not and cannot know who they are because of their divided heritages and allegiances, Larsen seems to indicate that their best opportunity for meaningful lives lies with the world of the cultured middle class, who can, to an extent, enjoy the best of both the black and the white worlds" (189). Larsen, however, is ambivalent, as she is also unwilling to approve of their "aping of white manners and mores."

At various times Helga confronts the idea of marriage, an institution traditionally used to oppress women. Helga is free at least from financial pressure to marry after her uncle gives her five thousand dollars. Nor does she need to marry for social position; she has entry into the middle class. The rejection of her first two marriage proposals from men of social standing is due to the pain she has felt over the idea of introducing children – whether mulattoes or Afro-Americans – into a hostile and cruel society. Why then does Helga marry the Reverend Pleasant Green? Her focus is not on marriage but what it symbolizes in her moment of spiritual trauma and enlightenment: two individuals becoming one in spirit, soul, and body, the unification of two entities. It is this type of bond that Helga thinks will heal the separation of her inner self: "Hers was, she declared to herself, a truly spiritual union. This one time in her life, she was convinced, she had not clutched a shadow and missed the actuality." On the contrary, Helga has gone to the other extreme in her zeal to fuse her inner self, ignoring reality.

Passing (1929), less polished according to critics but nonetheless ensuring Larsen's reputation as a major novelist of the New Negro Movement, has a less complicated plot than *Quicksand*'s, although its major themes are also divided loyalties and cultural conflicts. Irene Redfield and Clare Kendry, once childhood friends, are two women light enough to pass as white and are in fact doing so when they meet again as adults in a restaurant one hot afternoon.

A member of the middle class in Harlem, Irene Redfield is married to Brian, a successful doctor. Brian, beset by the degradation and humiliation of racial oppression, longs to move to Brazil, but Irene refuses. She feels comfortable and safe with the privileges of the black middle class and, as the only one in her family who can pass, she can escape racial confines when she chooses. Though she disapproves of passing as a life-style, she occasionally does so when it is socially convenient. Clare Kendry, an aggressive, self-centered individual who describes herself as "not safe," has "crossed over" and married a wealthy white man, an avowed racist who naturally assumes that Clare is also white.

As the novel progresses, Larsen expounds on the divided allegiance of Irene: she understands the benefits of passing and is hesitant but willing to protect Clare's desire to do so, yet she disapproves of and resents Clare's nonchalant abandonment of her Afro-American roots and responsibilities to her race. Irene thus cannot decide whether to shun or sympathize with Clare. While she vacillates, Clare quickly imposes herself on Irene, her family, and finally her husband, Brian – to the point that Irene feels Clare is threatening her relationship with Brian and the social position he provides for her.

Clare Kendry's willingness to risk anything to be friends with Irene again marks a deeper conflict than Irene's. She is obviously endangering her economic status as a wealthy white matron, her relationship with her only child, and her marriage to a man who seethes with animosity toward Afro-Americans. However, Clare is loyal to only one person – herself – and, in spite of her genuine fondness for Irene, she would use Irene as an entrance into the world she has renounced in order to connect again with blacks.

At a party Clare's husband discovers the truth, but Clare disappears through a nearby window before he can raise a commotion. The reader is left to guess whether Clare's death is suicide or murder by Irene. The ending has been questioned by many literary critics. Thadius Davis proposes, "Larsen cannot sufficiently motivate Clare to return to her race, yet she cannot logically dismiss Clare's attraction to blacks and Harlem. At the same time, Larsen cannot wholly approve of Irene's narrow materialism, nor can she punish or condemn her for it. Her solution, unrealistic and somewhat ambivalent, is to have Clare fall, jump or be pushed from an open window" (188). Once again, as in *Quicksand*, the reader is denied a satisfactory conclusion.

An interesting contrast between Irene Redfield, Clare Kendry, and Helga Crane's experiences as women rests in the fact that while Helga Crane could not pass, Clare and Irene could. That Redfield crossed the line occasionally for social convenience and Clare practiced passing as a life-style, suggests their awareness of the courtesies afforded white women, though they are still oppressed as women. Irene, for example, feeling faint one hot afternoon, receives gracious help from a cab driver who "jumped out and guided her to his car. He helped, almost lifted her in." Helga, on the other hand, visibly of African descent, was, while job hunting in Chicago, approached by "a few men, both white and black," who offered her money for sex as she walked down the street – a frequent indignity suffered by Afro-American women, and promoted by the American stereotype of the black woman as a voluptuous seductress. And later when Helga refuses to marry the prominent Danish painter, who proposes only after he realizes marriage is the only way to "win" her, he says, "You have the warm impulsive nature of the women of Africa, but, my lovely, you have, I fear, the soul of a prostitute." There are many other examples in Larsen's work of passages that skillfully uncover the subtle complexities of race and gender – so much so that her characterizations have been lauded by Afro-American and feminist critics as valid representations of both the black and female perspectives.

Nella Larsen won a Guggenheim fellowship in 1930, marking the pinnacle of her success and popularity. However, an accusation of plagiarism, despite evidence vindicating the author, undermined her confidence in herself as a creative writer. Even though she continued with her plans to fulfill her fellowship in Europe, she did not complete the two novels she began. Her marriage also suffered, and in 1933 she was divorced from Imes, who, according to one historian, was "an adulterer." In the late 1930s, Larsen, older than many of the New Negro writers, reserved in personality, and unwilling to publish in *Opportunity* and *Crisis*, slowly began to disassociate herself from other literary artists. There are no records indicating any writing activity during this time. Larsen resumed nursing to support herself for the last twenty years of her life, living in seclusion on the Lower East Side of Manhattan until her death in 1964.

SELECT BIBLIOGRAPHY

Primary

Fiction

"The Author's Explanation." *Forum*, supplement 4, 38 (April 1930): 41-42.

Passing. New York: Alfred A. Knopf, 1929.

Quicksand. New York: Alfred A. Knopf, 1928.

"Sanctuary." *Forum* 83 (January 1930): 15-18. [Short story.]

IN ANTHOLOGIES

Shockley, *Afro-American Women Writers, 1746-1933,* 1988. "The Abyss."

Nonfiction

"Playtime: Three Scandinavian Games." *Brownies Book* 1 (June 1920): 191-92.

Review of *Black Sadie*, by Thomas Bowyer Campbell. *Opportunity* (January 1929): 24.

Secondary

Bakish and Margolies, *Afro-American Fiction, 1853-1976*, 1979.

Campbell, Dorothy, *Index to Black American Writers in Collective Biographies*, 1983.

Clark, "The Letters of Nella Larsen to Carl Van Vechten: A Survey," 1978.

Davis, Arthur P., *From the Dark Tower*, 1974.

Davis, Thadious M., "Nella Larsen," 1987.

Doyle, "The Heroines of Black Novels," 1975.

Ellis, *Opportunity; A Journal of Negro Life*, 1971.

Fairbanks and Engeldinger, *Black American Fiction*, 1978.

Herman, *Women in Particular*, 1984.

Kellner, *The Harlem Renaissance*, 1984.

Low and Clift, *Encyclopedia of Black America*, 1981.

Matthews, *Black American Writers, 1773-1949*, 1975.

Perry, *The Harlem Renaissance*, 1982.

Perry, *Silence to the Drums*, 1976.

Rush, Myers, and Arata, *Black American Writers Past and Present*, 1975.

Sims-Wood, *The Progress of Afro-American Women*, 1980.

Spradling, *In Black and White*, 1980.

Tate, "Nella Larsen's *Passing*: A Problem of Interpretation," 1980.

Thornton, "Sexism as Quagmire: Nella Larsen's *Quicksand*," 1973.

Turner, *Afro-American Writers*, 1970.

Wall, "Nella Larsen," 1980.

Whiteman, *A Century of Fiction by American Negroes, 1853-1952*, 1974.

LEWIS, LILLIAN TUCKER (?-?)

Poet

Lillian Tucker Lewis was born in Corsicana, Texas. A graduate of Prairie View College, she studied at the University of Denver and at Kansas University. For over fifteen years Lewis taught in Dallas public schools. Like Birdelle Wycoff Ransom,* Lauretta Holman Gooden,* and Maurine Jeffrey,* other poets who published in the *Heralding Dawn* anthology of Texas poets, she is one of the women for whom only a small writing sample survives.

Lewis was one of the first black women in Texas to contribute verse to newspapers and magazines, the names of which J. Mason Brewer neglected to mention in his biographical paragraph on her in *Heralding Dawn* (1936). Lewis, who had an affinity for literature and drama, was also very much involved in local organizations: the Priscilla Art Club, the Ladies Reading Circle, and the City Federation of Dallas. At the time her work was published in the anthology, she was a fraternal worker at the Henderson Wren Funeral Home.

Of Lewis's poetry in general Brewer says, "A sympathetic attitude is displayed at all times in her verse with the man lower down, the unfortunate one . . . in her portrayal of life situations." Though it is difficult for the reader to determine Lewis's style on the basis of the one poem she published in *Heralding Dawn*, one can recognize a theme also present in the writing of May V. Cowdery,* Georgia Douglas Johnson,* Grace Vera Postles,* and Clarissa Scott Delany:* unfulfilled aspirations and dashed hopes. In "Longing" the author expresses the ephemeral quality of a suspended desire:

> 'Tis like the breath of a rose
> In a fragrant state.
> Until the rose is held in hand
> Then the petals droop
> At God's command.

SELECT BIBLIOGRAPHY

Primary

IN ANTHOLOGIES

Brewer. *Heralding Dawn*, 1936. "Longing."

Secondary

Kallenbach, *Index to Black American Literary Anthologies*, 1979.

Chapman, *Index to Poetry by Black American Women*, 1986.

LIVINGSTON, MYRTLE ATHLEEN SMITH (1902-1973)

Educator

Dancer

Playwright

Born in Holly Grove, Arkansas, on 8 May 1902 to Samuel Isaac and Lula C. Hall Smith, Myrtle Athleen Smith and her family moved to Denver, Colorado, when she was eight. She received part of her education in Denver public schools. Following her graduation from Manual High School in 1920, she attended the pharmaceutical school at Howard University from 1920 to 1922. During this time Livingston was a member of the school's Rho Psi Phi medical sorority. In 1923, she returned to Colorado to study at Colorado Teachers' College in Greenly. While there, she was responsible for organizing and presenting a dance group, and participated in the writers' association, the Modern Willis. In 1924 Livingston received her teaching certificate and began teaching in Denver; on 25 June of the following year, she wed Dr. William McKinley Livingston.

In 1928 Livingston joined the faculty of Lincoln University as the sole member of the physical education and dance department and the director of women's athletics. As assistant professor of health and physical education, she helped the women of Lincoln University develop their skills in such sports as basketball, soccer, track, and hockey. According to the March 1974 issue of the Lincoln University *Alumni Bulletin*, Livingston was greatly admired by her students as a "master teacher who kept abreast of teaching innovations and creative use of the new techniques" to support women in their pursuit of athletic excellence. During her forty-four years of teaching, she also engaged in other activities, among them writing plays. And for ten years, particularly during World War II, she gave instruction in first aid. She spent various sabbaticals studying at New York and Columbia universities.

Dance was Livingston's first love, and she organized the Orchesis Group of student dancers. This ensemble, specializing in modern dance, gave indoor and outdoor performances at cities across the state, including Columbia, Wichita, and Kansas City. During one of her leaves of absence she studied further under Hanya Holmes, a prominent authority in modern dance.

In the *Alumni Bulletin* of April 1972, Livingston said that she once considered a career as a playwright and revealed her affinity for writing: "Several of the student groups have performed some of my plays and I have written skits and shows for some of the sororities [perhaps including Alpha Kappa Alpha, of which she was a member] and fraternities to perform." *For Unborn Children*, the play for which Livingston won a ten-dollar third prize in the 1925 Amy Spingarn literary contest, was published in *Crisis*. The play is unusual in that it presents a white southern woman and a black man as the protagonists, thus inverting convention. Set "Somewhere in the South," it is a plea against interracial marriage. Leroy, a lawyer, has fallen in love with Selma, a white woman, and plans to marry her. His sister Marion and his grandmother vehemently oppose. Trying to explain the penalties society inflicts on mixed marriage and its offspring, the grandmother finally tells Leroy that his mother was white and that "she never could stand the sight of you and Marion; she hated you because you weren't white!" After this confession Leroy abandons his love for Selma and decides not to marry her, but it is too late. A mob clamors outside his door with intentions of lynching him.

In the preface to this play in Hatch and Shine's *Black Theater U.S.A.*, the editor notes the treatment of miscegenation as a theme by both Afro-American and white playwrights. The general assumption of mixed marriage is that it is disadvantageous for the white spouse and advantageous for the nonwhite spouse. With few exceptions, however, both black and white theater depict miscegenation as harmful through the plight of their characters (the death of one or both of the mixed couple, the tragic mulatto, and so on.).

Jeanne-Marie A. Miller has suggested that there are subtle undertones concerning race and gender that need to be further explored in *For Unborn Children*. She notes, "An emerging theme is black women's feeling of rejection when a Black man marries a white woman"(282). Marion, the sister, cries: "There must be something terribly wrong with her, for white women don't marry colored men when they can get anybody else. . . . My God! What is to become of us when our own men throw us down? . . . intermarriage doesn't hurt them as much as it does us." Although Miller considers the play interesting, she does not believe the message is enhanced by its ending.

Livingston died on 15 July 1973, survived by her sister Ella V. Smith, a retired teacher from Kansas City with whom she was sharing a condominium in Hawaii. The two women had long dreamed of "sunning on the beaches of Hawaii." In compliance with Hawaiian custom, Myrtle Smith Livingston's ashes were scattered in the Pacific Ocean. In 1977 the physical education department of Lincoln University and the housing authority of Jefferson City, Missouri, created a park named the Myrtle Smith Livingston Park in her memory.

SELECT BIBLIOGRAPHY

Primary

Drama

For Unborn Children. Crisis, no. 32 (July 1926): 122-25.

IN ANTHOLOGIES

Hatch and Shine, *Black Theatre U.S.A.*, 1974. *For Unborn Children*.

Secondary

Arata and Rotoli, *Black American Playwrights, 1800 to the Present*, 1976.

French, Fabre, Singh, and Fabre, *Afro-American Poetry and Drama, 1760-1975*, 1979.

Hatch and Abdullah, *Black Playwrights, 1823-1977*, 1977.

Inman E. Page Library, Lincoln University, Jefferson City, Mo.

Kallenbach, *Index to Black American Literary Anthologies*, 1979.

Miller, "Black Women Playwrights from Grimké to Shange: Selected Synopses of Their Works," 1982.

"Mrs. Livingston Dies in Hawaii." *Harambee* (Lincoln University Bulletin) (March 1974): n.p. [Photograph.]

Rose Bibliography Project, *Analytical Guide and Indexes to "The Crisis," 1910-1960*, 1975.

"Three Professors to Retire." *Harambee* (Lincoln University Bulletin) (April 1972): n.p. [Photograph.]

Who's Who in Colored America, 1927.

LOVE, ROSE LEARY (1898-1969)

Children's writer

Rose Leary Love, whose work as a children's writer grew out of thirty-nine years as a teacher, was born into a North Carolina family with a rich patriotic history. Her lineage included the first black man to participate in the U.S. Senate and an uncle, Lewis Sheridan Leary, who fought alongside John Brown and was killed in the 1859 attack on Harper's Ferry. Since Lewis Sheridan Leary was the grandfather of poet Langston Hughes, Rose Leary was the latter's cousin. The Learys are also a teaching family and have been so for over a hundred years. Before the Civil War a great-grandfather, a free Negro, employed slaves in his harness shop in Fayetteville. While they earned money to buy their freedom, he taught them to read and write.

Rose Leary was brought up in Charlotte's Brooklyn section, which she remembered as a place of "shade trees and roses." "We experienced a happy life," she said. Among her childhood memories was listening to the stories of former slaves among the neighbors. Like her mother and sisters, Rose attended Barber Scotia Seminary in Concord, North Carolina, and then graduated from Johnson C. Smith University in Charlotte. When her husband, George Love, was sent with a team of technical advisers to Indonesia, Rose and their son, George, spent over a year in that country. Rose taught second grade in the International School in Djakarta, using such typical American devices as "show and tell." This activity in Indonesia brought to the classroom such items as a bird of paradise and lava from a live volcano.

As a teacher in Charlotte, Rose Leary Love wrote a children's text which includes snippets of poetry. She also wrote another children's book, *Nebraska and His Granny*, which opens with the following salutation:

> Dear Boys and Girls Everywhere:
> Nebraska and his Granny want to know you, and they want you to know them.
> I have written this book so that you may read about this little brown boy, and the Granny who was good to him. She thought that he was the finest boy in all the world, and he loved his Granny better than any one else.

The story centers closely around the relationship between the "little brown boy" Nebraska and the beloved Granny who raises him. Love divided the book into seven sections – one for each day of the week, the story commencing with Monday, a "Wash Day," and ending with Sunday, or "Church Day." Other days are set aside for ironing, sewing, housecleaning, marketing, and baking. Love opens each day/chapter with a small poem relating to that particular day's activity.

Nebraska's Granny is presented as the archetypal grandmother – well-groomed, maternal, morally strict, yet forgiving. Her interactions with Nebraska are marked by playful care and deep concern. After Granny informs Nebraska that he must construct a pen for a brooding hen who has just delivered twelve chicks, she tells him she has a surprise for him.

> "What is it, Granny?' asked Nebraska.
> 'A new duck egg, or some fuzzy-wuzzy kittens?'
> 'Oh! I can't tell,' said Granny. 'You must find out for yourself.'" (24)

After a playful search Nebraska discovers that Granny has protectively placed the twelve young chicks behind the heater.

But when Nebraska has stuffed himself sick on Granny's homemade blueberry pie, she is quick to connect his moans with his berry-stained lips and sends him to bed with a dose of castor oil. She does not chastise him for overeating, but instead promises, "This will make you well." Granny does give Nebraska "a lesson in behaving" when he and his dog upset a basket of Granny's freshly washed clothes.

Love's story was illustrated by Preston Haygood, who drew eight pictures mostly showing Nebraska doing various chores. One shows Granny sewing in her rocking chair with Nebraska sitting by her feet. The text explains that Nebraska helps her by threading her needles, and she in turn entertains him with stories. As a story within a story Love included one of Granny's tales, "How Mr. Rabbit Got a Wife."

Rose Leary Love's book captures a warm familial relationship. Beneath its simple story line lies a strength which supports many rural American black families. As black children's books were scarce during the early decades of the twentieth century, *Nebraska and His Granny* was important for presenting a black childhood perspective. Children who read such books could recognize their lives reflected in Nebraska's. Also, such works expanded the picture of American childhood.

The other book by Rose Leary Love, *A Collection of Folklore for Children*, was prompted by her realization that the oral tradition of storytelling and games was disappearing. "I realized the old stories were dying out. . . . I told the children to ask their grandmothers and grandpapas to tell them the stories they knew. Then I took them down, just as they told them." But Love carefully edited them to omit dialect, or nonstandard language, which she felt belonged to the past and hindered the teaching of English to young children. This collection, illustrated by the children themselves and published in 1964, is intended as a source book for teachers in the early grades.

SELECT BIBLIOGRAPHY

Primary

Fiction (Children's Books)

A Collection of Folklore for Children in Elementary School and at Home. New York: Vantage Press, 1964.

Nebraska and His Granny. Illustrated by Preston Haygood. Tuskegee, Ala.: Tuskegee Institute Press, 1936. Reprint. 1966.

Nonfiction

"The Leary Family." *Negro History Bulletin* (November 1946): 27-34, 47.

"Women Eligible to Be Daughters of the American Revolution," Carter G. Woodson. *Negro History Bulletin* (November 1943): 36, 39.

Secondary

Duke Power Company Archives, Charlotte, N.C.

"From Children . . . A People's Folklore," *Charlotte* (N.C.) *Observer* (28 June 1964): n.p.

Porter, *North American Negro Poets*, 1945.

Rush, Myers, and Arata, *Black American Writers Past and Present*, 1975.

Tucker, "Rose Leary Love (1898-1969)," n.d.

MCBROWN, GERTRUDE PARTHENIA (1902-1989)

Children's Playwright

Educator

Poet

Gertrude Parthenia McBrown's poetry and plays are directed toward children, especially black children, whose creativity she has sought to encourage. Like Ellen Tarry* and Rose Leary Love,* McBrown has assumed the role of nurturer and creative educator concerned with the development of a new generation of black children who need positive role models on which to pattern themselves.

McBrown was born in Charleston, South Carolina, and later went to school in Boston. As a student at Emerson College of Drama and after her graduation in 1922, she prepared herself for a unique career as educator, children's writer, and performer. She continued her studies at Boston University, where she received an M.Ed. in 1926 before embarking on her career. McBrown taught in the Boston schools and directed a choral group at the Ebenezer Baptist Church, last performing in September 1923.

In Washington, D.C., during the 1920s McBrown attended gatherings at the home of Georgia Douglas Johnson,* founded a drama studio, and directed the District of Columbia Children's Theatre and Adult Drama Workshops. She was also a member of the educational board of the *Negro History Bulletin*, where she maintained a long association with Carter G. Woodson. She began to publish verse for children in *Opportunity, Black Opals, Popular Educator,* and *International Poetry Magazine.*

When she moved to New York, she taught speech and directed drama groups at the Carnegie Hall Studio. She also wrote a weekly column, Proud Heritage, for her local newspaper, *Community Chatter,* in Jamaica, New York.

Her play *Birthday Surprise* is about the career of the eminent poet Paul Laurence Dunbar. Another play, *Bought with Cookies*, is a historical children's play about the early life of abolitionist Frederick Douglass. Her poems, also for children, are simple and fanciful; she gathered them in a 1935 volume beautifully illustrated with sketches of black children engaged in their daily activities. The scenes could be from an English bedtime story book, but the children depicted are black, an early attempt to overcome the ethnocentrism in children's literature.

McBrown's subsequent studies in Paris, London, and Africa contributed to the cultural richness she has brought to her interracial audiences in lectures, recitals, and costumed one-woman shows.

SELECT BIBLIOGRAPHY

Primary

Drama

Birthday Surprise. *Negro History Bulletin* 16 (February 1953): 102-4.

Bought with Cookies. *Negro History Bulletin* 12 (April 1949): 155, 156, 165.

Poetry

"Bubbles." *Saturday Evening Quill* 6 (1928).

"Busy Fairies." *Saturday Evening Quill* 6 (1928).

"Fairies and Brownies." *Crisis* 12 (1927).

"Fire Flies." *Saturday Evening Quill* 4 (1929).

"The Frightened Witch." *Saturday Evening Quill* 6 (1928).

"Murmuring Tulips." *Saturday Evening Quill* 6 (1928).

"The Paint Pot Fairy." *Saturday Evening Quill* 6 (1928).

The Picture-Poetry-Book. Illustrations by Lois Mailou Jones. Washington, D.C.: Associated Publishers, 1935.

"Purple Dawn." *Saturday Evening Quill* 6 (1928).

"Sing Little Birdie." *Saturday Evening Quill* 6 (1928).

"The Wise Owl." *Saturday Evening Quill* 6 (1928).

IN ANTHOLOGIES

Cromwell, Turner, and Dykes, *Readings from Negro Authors*, 1931. "Happy Faces"; "Jack Frost"; "The Painter"; "They Are Calling Me"; "Purple Dawn."

Murphy, *Ebony Rhythm*, [1948] 1968. "Bronze Queen"; "Lilacs."

Secondary

Arata and Rotoli, *Black American Playwrights, 1800 to the Present*, 1976.

Campbell, Dorothy, *Index to Black American Writers in Collective Biographies*, 1983.

Chapman, *Index to Black Poetry*, 1974.

Hatch and Abdullah, *Black Playwrights, 1823-1977*, 1977.

Index to Poetry in Periodicals, 1925-1929, 1983.

Innis and Wu, *Profiles in Black*, 1976.

Kallenbach, *Index to Black American Literary Anthologies*, 1979.

Matthews, *Black American Writers, 1773-1949*, 1975.

Porter, *North American Negro Poets*, 1945.

Reardon and Thorsen, *Poetry by American Women, 1900-1975*, 1979.

Rush, Myers, and Arata, *Black American Writers Past and Present*, 1975.

Spradling, *In Black and White*, 1980.

MCDOUGALD (AYER), GERTRUDE ELISE (OR ELSIE) JOHNSON (1885-1971)

Educator

Essayist

Feminist

Elise Johnson McDougald, in addition to working for black women's causes, published essays in *Crisis*, *Opportunity*, and *Survey Graphic* at the height of the Harlem Renaissance. Although Bruce Kellner has said that he does not consider her part of the mainstream of that movement, a closer look at her essays about women and an analysis of her contribution may alter that judgment in the eyes of future researchers. Her ideas were indeed advanced for her time – she was among the few to support both the cause of the Afro-American people and that of the woman. During the 1920s and 1930s her beauty was made famous by Winold Reiss's pastel portrait of her reproduced in the "New Negro" issue of the *Survey Graphic*. Alas, her looks attracted more attention than her ideas.

Like many black women writers of this time, McDougald entered the field of education. A native of New York City, she began teaching in the public school system in 1905, after studying at the New York Training School for Teachers (1903-5), Columbia University (vocational guidance) and City College of New York (pedagogy and management). She married and took a leave of absence to raise her two children, Cornelius W. McDougald, born in 1911, and Elizabeth J. McDougald, born in 1913. In 1924 she was chosen by competitive examination to be assistant principal of Public School 89 and remained in that position until her retirement in 1954. Divorced in 1925, McDougald was married again to Vernon Ayer in 1928.

Her interest in public service began in her childhood. Her parents were Mary E. Whittle Johnson and Peter A. Johnson, one of the founders of the National Urban League. During her leave from teaching, McDougald remained active in various endeavors, such as working women's rights. She was head of the women's department of the U. S. Employment Bureau (1918-19), worked for the Henry Street Settlement, the Manhattan Trade School, and the New York branch of the U.S. Department of Labor.

Elise McDougald's essay "The Double Task" details the struggle of the Afro-American woman of the twenties, underlining the diversity of her experience. The essay begins with a poetic depiction of the many facets of the black woman, using the tiger lily as a metaphor for social and personal diversity: "one must have in mind not any one Negro woman, but rather a colorful pageant of individuals, each differently endowed. Like the red and yellow of the tiger-lily, the skin of one is brilliant against the star-lit darkness of a racial sister." Here McDougald participates in extolling the beauty of blackness, a Harlem Renaissance theme that foreshadowed the "black is beautiful" movement of the 1960s.

Throughout her essay McDougald steadfastly holds to her thesis that the problems of the Afro-American woman "cannot be thought of in mass." She enumerates three groups of black women: a small upper-class "leisure group," an active group of professionals and business women, and the majority, "struggling on in domestic service and casual work." In the "well-appointed homes" of the first group, the luxuries of tennis, golf, and country clubs, trips to Europe and California, and other "polite activities of social exclusiveness" abound. In the second group, a "spirit of stress and struggle" characterizes its female members who are women of business, professions, and trades, and who are the "hub of the wheel of progress." For the third group, "happiness is almost impossible."

The author describes the different life-styles and social and economic challenges black women face in an elegant and vivid style. She briefly discusses her own profession and states that the nearly three hundred Negro women who are in teaching measure up to the high pedagogical requirements of city and state law, and are increasingly leaders in the community. She adds that because the need for teachers is still strong, black women cause little friction to avoid igniting white workers' "fear of competition."

McDougald also frankly depicts the struggle of the Afro-American woman with a mate who, because of his "baffled and suppressed" desires to determine his economic life and that of his family, becomes domineering at home. The author maintains that education and opportunity are the cure for this misdirected aggression, and insists that the reason there are so few outstanding black women militants for the cause of sexual equality is that "their feminist efforts are directed chiefly toward the realization of the equality of the races."

It is worthy of note that the myths discussed in the essay, such as the belief that all black women fit the Aunt Jemima stereotype or that illegitimacy is accepted within the black community, are still present today and constitute a negative force working against the struggle for Afro-American equality.

McDougald's predominating theme is that black women "are of a race which is free neither economically, socially nor spiritually," and thus as female members of the Afro-American community they incur a double struggle for survival and accomplishment. In "The Schools and the Vocational Life of Negroes," an address before the National Conference of Social Workers held in Washington, D.C., and published in the 1923 issue of *Opportunity*, the author discusses the inferior education and the lack of job opportunities the Afro-American encounters. She tells of blacks who, even if they possess a college degree, can find only menial jobs. She mentions that the women are compelled to supplement the low wages of their men, and thus must neglect their home and children during the day. Again, these are all still major problems.

The author also realizes that just as there are many facets of the black woman's experience in the United States, so too with the labor experience of blacks in this country: "To have a true picture, it is absolutely necessary to touch up the dull gray of trade life with such highlights as the following: The largest Negro community in the world – Harlem – is fairly typical as to variety of occupation." She includes much statistical information in this essay, including the numbers of physicians, dentists, and musicians among the black population in Harlem. The author emphasizes the progress of her people in terms of achieving an education and entering the job market, and maintains that the difficulties blacks encounter stem not from "a lack of innate ability" but from "limited opportunity, a lack of knowledge of the opportunities which exist and a lack of help in making the necessary adjustments."

She pays special consideration to women: "One cannot resist the temptation to pause for a moment and pay tribute to the mothers of the Negro race. And, to call attention to the service she is rendering the nation in her struggle against great odds to educate and care for one group of the nation's children." As is the case with so many other women of her generation, there is no indication that McDougald continued with her writing nor any basis for speculation as to why she disappeared from the public eye.

SELECT BIBLIOGRAPHY

Primary

Nonfiction

"Colored Women in Industry." *Survey Graphic* (1925).

"The Double Task: The Struggles of Negro Women for Sex and Race Emancipation." *Survey* 53, no. 2 (1 March 1925): 689-91.

"A New Day for the Colored Woman Worker." *Survey Graphic* (1925).

"The Schools and the Vocational Life of Negroes." *Opportunity* 1, no. 8 (11 June 1923): 8-11.

IN ANTHOLOGIES

Locke, *The New Negro*, [1925] 1968. "The Tasks of Negro Womanhood."

Secondary

Ellis, *Opportunity; A Journal of Negro Life*, 1971.

Kellner, *The Harlem Renaissance*, 1984.

Rose Bibliography Project, *Analytical Guide and Indexes to "The Crisis" 1910 to 1960*, 1975.

Sims-Wood, *The Progress of Afro-American Women*, 1980.

Spradling, *In Black and White*, 1980.

Williams, *American Black Women in the Arts and Social Sciences*, 1978.

MILLER, MAY (MRS. JOHN SULLIVAN) (1899-)

Educator
Playwright
Poet

May Miller was raised in the genteel and sheltered Howard University community. She grew up in a home frequented by intellectuals and artists like Paul Laurence Dunbar, Georgia Douglas Johnson,* William Stanley Braithwaite, and W. E. B. Du Bois, and the friends and associates of her father, sociologist Kelly Miller. This heightened young Miller's own goals. Following her graduation from Dunbar High School and Howard (with honors), Miller continued her studies at American and Columbia universities, specializing in poetry and drama.

During her career as a teacher of English and speech at the Frederick Douglass High School in Baltimore, Maryland, Miller also supervised English in the city's junior high schools, participated in the Negro Little Theatre Movement, and coedited two volumes of plays and pageants with Willis Richardson. As a drama teacher, she trained youth to tune their ears to appreciate speech sounds.

Dismayed that young people did not properly acknowledge their leaders, Miller, with Carter G. Woodson, Willis Richardson and others, saw drama both as an effective tool for educating individuals about Afro-American history and as a political medium. In a taped interview in the Hatch-Billop Collection in New York, Miller states, "We started to dramatize Negro history because it is a treasure trove and greatness has no [racial] boundaries." The dramatist also made her position clear in the controversy of whether or not black English or dialect should be taught: "In order to compete in the mainstream, one must speak the accepted language."

After her marriage to John Sullivan, Miller returned to Washington, D.C., ready to focus her attention on a literary career. Her husband, an accountant employed by the U.S. Postal Service, was supportive of her aspirations as an author and would occasionally accompany her to literary engagements. When she was appointed by Mayor Walter E. Washington to the District of Columbia Commission on the Arts and Humanities, Miller took part in many local activities, such as chairing a project for the publication of poetry by children.

Miller cultivated a vast array of friendships among the writers of the 1920s and 1930s. Although she taught in Baltimore, she continued on weekends to participate in occasional meetings of the Round Table, a literary salon at the home of Georgia Douglas Johnson.* These meetings were attended by men, including Langston Hughes and Jean Toomer, but the Round Table consisted primarily of women: Marita Bonner,* Zora Neale Hurston,* and Gertrude Parthenia McBrown.* In a 1925 issue of the *Messenger* Zora Neale Hurston revealed that it was May Miller who urged her to transfer from Morgan to Howard, the beginning of a personal and literary friendship between the two women. Miller was also befriended by Georgia Douglas Johnson. She was at Johnson's deathbed in 1966, gently stroking the hand of the dying poet, repeating "Poet Georgia Douglas Johnson."

Miller was active as a dramatist during the New Negro Movement. Individually she won third prize in an *Opportunity* contest for the play *The Bog Guide* in 1925 and also honorable mention for her play *The Curs'd Thing*. The two drama anthologies Miller coauthored with Willis Richardson, *Plays and Pageants of Negro Life* (1930) and *Negro History in Thirteen Plays* (1935), helped to meet the need for education by, for, and about Afro-Americans in celebrating their history. Many of these plays were written for youths, for historical drama had an impact other genres in literature did not; since acting and orating made education accessible to both the literate and illiterate, everyone could learn of the feats of Harriet Tubman, Sojourner Truth, and others.

Graven Images is a play based on an incident in the Old Testament in which Miriam and Aaron object to Moses' Ethiopian wife, Zipporah. In the play Miriam, quickly joined by others, openly scorns Moses' wife and son for their skin color. Eventually Miriam becomes leprous (a physical condition analogous to the spiritual destruction of sin) and is herself ostracized from the camp. More subtly drawn is the treatment of women. When a group of girls ask if they can join the boys as they playfully "worship" an idol, they are told: "We are worshipping the golden bull and he does not like girl children.

. . . I am sure he does not want women to speak." The lads finally relent but add, "Remember, you must bow lower than we, for you are girls."

Miller intended that *Riding the Goat*, her most popular play, be seen not as broad comedy but as pointed satire. Set in early Baltimore, the plot concerns a young doctor whose usefulness in the black community is overshadowed by his refusal to participate in lodge activities. Churches and lodges were central to the functions and cohesiveness of the Afro-American community. Audiences viewed *Riding the Goat* as a comedy, unaware that it was a social commentary posing the question: would a young man training to be a leader be false to stoop to all the manipulations of a community just to fit in?

Miller's dramatic and poetic imagination may have stemmed from her childhood when she would sit on the steps in the cool of the evening with friends and family while they exchanged tales. In "The Pondered Moment: May Miller's Meditative Poetry," Claudia Tate identifies Miller's poetry as largely meditative, where "the poem creates a dramatic setting and places the actor, who is the meditative speaker, within it" (30). Miller's poetry (specifically meditation on human mortality) frames the ephemeral, as "the fleeting moment of contemplation in [her] poetry is captured like a still life scene" (30), as in "Gift from Kenya" from *The Clearing and Beyond*: "I've come back many times today / To touch the pale wood antelope, / Spindle legs tucked under him / Tipping his head to danger." Tate explains that in the "momentary act of touching the figurine with her hands, the speaker's imagination stretches that pensive moment through centuries of time and miles of territory, so as to locate her racial origin on an imagined, distant, exotic landscape" (30).

Miller's meditations on the passage of time and the meaning of morality are conveyed by biblical and classical motifs; other images are often drawn from nature and an African mythological tradition. Racial themes are also present in her work, as when she evokes significant moments of black history, from both the remote past and the immediate present.

In order to channel her energy into poetry, Miller discontinued writing and producing plays in 1943. She once considered writing a play in verse, but found poetry a more rewarding avenue of expression, particularly in terms of revealing her inner self. Her themes encompass love of humanity, pride in home, friends, and ambitions. Miller's readings have reached audiences through radio, television, and public and educational institutions such as the Smithsonian, the Martin Luther King, Jr., Library, the Library of Congress, and the Folger Library.

SELECT BIBLIOGRAPHY

Primary

Drama

IN ANTHOLOGIES

Hatch and Shine, *Black Theatre U.S.A.*, 1974. *Graven Images*.

Richardson and Miller, *Plays and Pageants from the Life of the Negro*, 1930. *Graven Images*; *Riding the Goat*.

Poetry

The Clearing and Beyond. Washington: Charioteer Press, 1974.

Dust of Uncertain Journey. Detroit: Lotus Press, 1975.

Halfway to the Sun. Washington: Washington Writer's Publishing House, 1981.

Into the Clearing. Washington: Charioteer Press, 1959.

Lyrics for Three Women. With Kate Lyle and Maude Rubin. Baltimore: Linden Press, 1964.

Not That Far. San Luis Obispo, Calif.: Solo Press, 1973.

Poems. Thetford, Vt.: Cricket Press, 1962.

The Ransomed Wait. Washington: Lotus Press, 1983.

Fiction

"A Fine Market" [unpublished novel].

SHORT STORIES

"Bidin' Place." *Arts Quarterly* (April 1937): 5.

"Door Stop." *Carolina Magazine* 12 (May 1930): 1-4.

"One Blue Star." *Opportunity* 23 (Summer 1945): 142-43.

Secondary

Campbell, Dorothy, *Index to Black American Writers in Collective Biographies*, 1983.

Chapman, *Index to Poetry by Black American Women*, 1986.

Deodene and French, *Black American Poetry since 1944*, 1971.

Ellis, *Opportunity; A Journal of Negro Life*, 1971.

Hatch and Abdullah, *Black Playwrights, 1823-1977*, 1977.

Hatch-Billops Collection, Archives of Black American Cultural History, New York City.

Hurston, "The Hue and Cry about Howard University," 1925.

Index to Poetry by Black American Women, 1986.

Kallenbach, *Index to Black American Literary Anthologies*, 1979.

Kellner, *The Harlem Renaissance*, 1984.

Miller, "Black Women Writers from Grimké to Shange: Selected Synopses of Their Works," 1982.

Perry, *The Harlem Renaissance*, 1982.

Reardon and Thorsen, *Poetry by American Women, 1900-1975*, 1979.

Rose Bibliography Project, *Analytical Guide to Indexes to "The Crisis," 1910 to 1960*, 1975.

Rush, Myers, and Arata, *Black American Writers Past and Present*, 1975.

Spradling, *In Black and White*, 1980.

Sullivan, May Miller. Interviews.

Tate, "The Pondered Moment: May Miller's Meditative Poetry," 1985.

Williams, *American Black Women in the Arts and Social Sciences*, 1978.

MOODY, CHRISTINA (CA. 1896-?)

Poet

A Tiny Spark by Christina Moody is a collection of poems published when the author was only sixteen years of age, as she reveals in her preface: "This little volume is composed of verses, written at different times, in my leisure hours, as an expression of the author's varying states of mind, or for the gratification of friends . . . Christina Moody (age 16 years)." Her verses show great versatility in three dialects: Afro-American, contemporary mainstream, and traditional poetic English. The variety of themes and voices Moody embodies is impressive in its power to persuade the reader that the author's written record of experiences is vicarious. Her themes vary from a child begging the rain to go away, to poems in which the speaker is a slave escaping with her child or a soldier on his deathbed writing a letter of final farewell to his mother. Other poems emphasize faith in God and prayer, nature, and fiery pride in the accomplishments and undying struggle of the Afro-American people, such as "The Depth from Whence We Came," which praises "the progress of our race."

Most stanzas in the poems are written as quatrains. End rhymes, though sometimes not uniform, are characteristic of every poem. The first, entitled "To My Dear Reader," is written in the Afro-American dialect and seems to intentionally beguile the reader into thinking the author is less talented than she in fact is, nor does it prepare the reader for the stylistic diversity of Moody's work: "Don't criticize my writing / Cause I ain't well trained you know / I had always been so sickly / Dat I haven had much show." In "The Negro's Flag and Country" the speaker answers the challenge one of her own people made to her: "And why do you call a flag your own / To which you have not right? / I call this flag my own, because long years / ago / A war broke out for freedom and the land / was full of woe. / . . . The Negro shed his blood without a murmur / or complaint, / And though they faced many a hardship, / their brave hearts did not faint. / . . . My claim upon this country is sealed with / Negro blood."

The poem "Chillun" conveys strong feminist sentiment, portraying the hardships of a woman who must struggle as both wife and mother: "Chillun and men, chillun and men; / When a 'oman gits married / Then hur trobles begin." In Moody's "My Mother," the speaker praises emotional ties between mother and daughter as incomparable to those between daughter and father: "No! I have not forgotten my father, who is / loving, kind and good. / . . . But my mother! She's my mother you / know / No matter who else there may be, / And I just can't help from thinking / There is nobody like her to me."

In "The Little Seed," the speaker describes the unexpected bloom of an apple tree: "So the seed that was wee, grew into a tree / 'Twas a wonderful

241

sight to behold." The theme of the poem seems to parallel the title of Moody's collection, *A Tiny Spark*, and suggests that despite unimpressive appearances, a small seed can sprout into a comely tree, just as a sixteen-year-old girl can produce a collection of poems as promising as this one.

Nothing more is known of Christina Moody. Was her work lost? Could it be that she found other ways to express her creativity? Did she encounter difficulties succeeding as a poet once the appeal of her precocious age was gone?

SELECT BIBLIOGRAPHY

Primary

Poetry

A Tiny Spark. Washington: Murray Brothers Press, 1910.

Secondary

Porter, *North American Negro Poets*, 1945.

Reardon and Thorsen, *Poetry by American Women, 1900-1975*, 1979.

Rush, Myers, and Arata, *Black American Writers Past and Present*, 1975.

MORYCK (FRANCKE), BRENDA RAY (1894-1949)

Columnist
Educator
Essayist
Lecturer
Short-story writer

In her bio-sketch in the June 1926 issue of *Opportunity*, Moryck revealed the origin of her literary interest: "I have been writing since I was six years old, and have a stack of infantile efforts at story-writing. Writing is a tradition in our family. The Reverend Charles Ray, my great-grandfather, was quite a distinguished man of letters. My grandfather was editor of a Boston paper from 1850-1860 and my mother writes. I love writing, and write most of the time just for fun, burdening my friends with unwieldy letters of from 16 to 80 pages. I was educated at home, at St. Vincent's Academy and Barringer High School of Newark, N.J., my native city and state, and Wellesley College." While at Wellesley Moryck composed "Why," a story integrating themes of mixed blood, nobility, and children's reality – topics that would reappear in her later writing.

Following her graduation from Wellesley in 1916 and marriage to Lucius Lee Jordan in 1917, Brenda Ray Moryck began volunteering as a worker in the Newark Bureau of Associated Charities. She found the work interesting but sobering : "I'm not exactly slumming . . . but it is just the thing to steady a somewhat erratic and too-independent young person, the kind I was in college." Records indicate that Moryck's husband died the same year they were married.

Moryck gave a substantial amount of biographical information about herself in the *Sequel* and *Sixteen Plus*, two alumnae publications about Wellesley's Class of 1916. Unfortunately there are inconsistencies in her data – for example, about her daughters. There seems to be some discrepancy about the birth or adoption dates of Moryck's adopted daughter, Julia Wormley, and her biological child, Elizabeth Osborne, born in 1931. Even more puzzling, a friend does not recall that Moryck had any children at all. Moryck also says that from 1918 to 1924 she was tutoring Spanish and teaching English at Douglas High School in Baltimore, Maryland, yet a Newark, New Jersey, address is listed, 31 Kearney Street, until 1923. Many other such ambiguities and gaps exist. She said that in 1920 she won $150 for a short story (title unmentioned) and reported having toured France and England and taking in the Pan-American Conference in the summer of 1921. After placing first in a group of sixty-five on an English teachers' examination, Moryck moved to Washington, D.C., in search of a job.

Between 1925 and 1930 Moryck taught at the Armstrong Technical High School. May Miller* recalled that in the 1920s she and Moryck teamed up to teach the Miller-Moryck dancing class on Saturday afternoons for two years in Baltimore. Miller taught dancing to one segment of the class while Moryck, who reiterates her love of children in her writing and her autobiographical notes, told stories to another group. Brenda had a vivid and brilliant imagination with the power to convince, which sometimes got her into trouble; she was at times accused by literary acquaintances of exaggerating.

While living in Washington, the writer was inspired by other literary artists, and she received national attention for several pieces of her writing. In 1927 she won honorable mention for her essay "When a Negro Sings" in the *Opportunity* literary contest of that year. "Days" was a prize story *Crisis* published in 1928, and "A Man I Know" won second prize in the *Opportunity* contest of 1926. In this essay Moryck gives a character sketch of Charles Spurgeon Johnson, promoter of the New Negro Movement and author of the *Ebony and Topaz* anthology, which includes her autobiographical essay, "I."

In "I" Moryck speaks of her childhood in context of being black, female, and human. She discusses the notion of nobility and the socially acceptable, demanding that these qualities exist only apart from prejudice. As a little girl dreams of being a princess, she aspires to aristocracy, rudely discovering that she is part of "a despised group" hailed by common white children as "niggers" or "darkies – a practice much more common in the north" than "slightly south of the Mason-Dixon line." She tells of having to relinquish tea dishes, a "secret Santa" gift from a "Caucasian Baptist Sunday School . . . because a white infant objected to 'that little colored girl' having dishes while she only had a book." But she also remembers an incident in which being Afro-American benefited her. An exquisite woman "graciously pleased to entertain [Brenda] in her home," generously sponsored Moryck not as a hired companion but as a friend. Pretense or not, Moryck accepted, for the opportunity allowed her to "taste life utterly beyond the reach of most Caucasians."

This theme of race and social standing in Moryck's writing is seen also in her prize-winning story, "Days." The Randolphs are an Afro-American couple who have moved into a neighborhood of Irish, Greek, and Italian immigrants. A Greek landlord gives a year-long lease to Mrs. Randolph, a light-skinned, elegant woman dressed in furs and diamonds, and Mr. Randolph, a lawyer, who is not present at the signing of the contract and whom the landlord declines to meet. With the exception of an Italian shoemaker, the neighbors are livid at the prospect of living in proximity with "niggers," fearing that property values will plummet and business will drop off. But for one year the neighbors watch the dignitaries and patricians – black and white friends of the Randolphs – come and go. The popularity of the neighborhood escalates; and the neighbors end up imitating the impeccable taste of the Randolphs, "so clean and quiet and refined."

As well as being an author, teacher and columnist for the *Baltimore Afro-American* and *New Jersey Herald* newspapers, Moryck lectured on behalf of organizations she supported: "Writing is a solitary pleasure at best, but speaking is intensely social. I find it delightful even without remuneration, which, of course, is not to be overlooked." She belonged to the National Association for the Advancement of Colored People, Women's Interracial Committee of the Federal Council of Churches, National Negro Nurse's Association, National Council of Negro Women, and South Harlem Community Welfare Association. She served as vocational guidance adviser of the Harlem YWCA. When Moryck married Robert B. Francke, a lawyer and attaché in the Haitian legation (Paris) in 1930, she kept her maiden name for professional purposes.

Of her passion for writing, the author said, "I seem not to be able to lay [it] down however much I desire a respite." In her themes Moryck saw the savoir-faire of the bourgeoisie life-style as a mask – different from one a person of color might wear, but nonetheless a mask. Unfortunately Moryck's superior vocabulary and crisp descriptive style are occasionally marred by run-on sentences. Although essays and short stories make up the bulk of her work, in the 1933 issue of the *Sequel* she reported that she had completed a novel. Yet it appears she is in the company of Lucy Ariel Williams Holloway,* May Miller,* Georgia Douglas Johnson,* and others whose novels remained unpublished. According to the 1939 issue of the *Sequel* Brenda Ray Moryck's success in writing continued, perhaps until 1949, when she died of pneumonia.

SELECT BIBLIOGRAPHY

Primary

Fiction

"Days." *Crisis* 35 (June 1928): 187-88, 206-7.

"Why?" *Wellesley College Magazine* (supplement to the *Wellesley College News*) 23 (June 1915): 6-14.

Nonfiction

"About Our Children." *Metropolitan* 1 (January 1935): 44, 85-86.

"A Man I Know." *Metropolitan* 1 (January 1935): 32-33, 84-85.

"A Point of View." *Opportunity* 3 (August 1925): 246-52.

IN ANTHOLOGIES

Johnson, Charles S., *Ebony and Topaz*, [1927] 1971. "I."

Secondary

Ellis, *Opportunity; A Journal of Negro Life*, 1971.

Kallenbach, *Index to Black American Literary Anthologies*, 1979.

Wellesley College Archives, Wellesley College, Wellesley, Mass.

MURPHY, BEATRICE CAMPBELL (1908-1992)

Poet

Editor

Journalist

As with many black women writers, Beatrice Murphy's literary career began in newspapers. From 1933 to 1935 she wrote a column for the *Washington Tribune* called Think It Over, and from 1935 to 1937 she was the paper's features and children's page editor. She also wrote poetry and a special feature column for the Associated Negro Press and reviewed books for *Pulse* magazine in New York, the *San Antonio Register,* and other media. Since 1938 she has been a book review editor for *the Afro-American.*

The daughter of Benjamin and Maude Murphy, Beatrice Murphy was born in 1908 in Monessen, Pennsylvania, but has lived most of her life in Washington, D.C., where she graduated from Dunbar High School in 1928. She converted to Catholicism in 1938, married, and had a son, Alvin H. Murphy.

Beatrice Murphy's literary efforts formally embarked with "The Parting," published in *Crisis,* May 1928. Its conventional expression of regret for love lost reappears in many of the poems in her collection, *Love Is a Terrible Thing* (1945). All these poems describe "the love of a woman for a man," states the prologue. The poet expresses the gamut of the experience of love: the thrill of first love; her fear of being smothered, like a butterfly crushed in a human hand ("The Secret"); and the emptiness from love that, like a departing tenant, "moves out of the heart." In a departure from conventional modesty, "Wanton" reveals an erotic fantasy with contrasts of day, demureness, and night, abandon: "By night / I am a shameless wanton / Who haunts your dreams / And slips unbidden / Into your bed / To nestle boldly / In your arms." The last poems of *Love Is a Terrible Thing* reveal disillusionment as they speak of the withering, desiccation, and sorrow exacted as love's high price.

During the 1930s, Murphy wrote to Langston Hughes requesting some of his poems for her anthology *Negro Voices.* He willingly complied, according to a memorial note by Murphy published in *Bibliographic Survey* at the time of his death, 1967.

The poems included in *Negro Voices* go further in revealing rage at a former beloved and in voicing exultation when death frees her of him. Among Murphy's more noteworthy poems are "The Guest," in which the allegorical figure of Sorrow is portrayed as a woman "dressed in somber gown; / Weary-eyed and worn; / Wearing heavy frown" to whom the poet gives lodging in her house, and "Hatred," in which burning resentment becomes a plant "watered with my falling tears / Rooted in bitterness and pruned with care," a metaphor for the poet's determination to survive her suffering. Murphy's diction is sometimes inconsistent, but her best poetry derives force from its simplicity and sharp images.

Murphy has edited several other anthologies, including *Ebony Rhythm*, which are important as display cases for the work of black poets, both male and female.

The breadth of her career and activities has been considerable. Formerly secretary to the head of the sociology department of the Catholic University of America, she was later employed as a stenographer in the Office of Price Administration. Murphy also operated a circulating library and a public stenography shop, eventually founding the Negro Bibliographic and Resource Center, Inc., where she served as its managing editor and director.

SELECT BIBLIOGRAPHY

Primary

Nonfiction

"Interracial Language." *Our Colored Missions* (September 1939): 133-34.

"Interracial Wisdom of the Children." *Our Colored Missions* (June 1938): 93.

"One Must Be Born Again." *Interracial Review* (October 1937): 152.

"What Does the Negro Want?" *Interracial Review* (May 1937): 74-75.

Poetry

Home Is Where the Heart Is. With Nancy L. Arnez. n.p., n.d.

Love Is a Terrible Thing. New York: Hobson, 1945.

"The Parting." *Crisis* (May 1928): 158.

The Rocks Cry Out. With Nancy L. Arnez. Detroit: Broadside, 1969.

EDITED BY MURPHY

Ebony Rhythm, [1948] 1968.

Negro Voices: An Anthology of Contemporary Verse. New York: Henry Harrison, 1938; Ann Arbor, Mich.: University Microfilms, 1971.

Today's Negro Voices: An Anthology by Young Negro Poets. New York: Messner, 1970.

IN ANTHOLOGIES

Bontemps, *Golden Slippers*, 1941. "Signs."

Murphy, *Ebony Rhythm*, [1948] 1968. "Anniversary."

Murphy, *Negro Voices*, [1938] 1971. "Anniversary"; "Hatred"; "Release"; "Safeguard"; "The Guest"; "Waste."

Secondary

Bailey, *Broadside Authors and Artists*, 1974.

Giovanni, Review of *The Rocks Cry Out*, by Beatrice Campbell Murphy, 1969.

Page, *Selected Black American Authors*, 1977.

Rush, Myers, and Arata, *Black American Writers Past and Present*, 1975.

Scally, *Negro Catholic Writers, 1900-1943*, 1945.

Shockley and Chandler, *Living Black American Authors*, 1973.

MURRAY, PAULI (1910-1985)

Lawyer

Poet

Priest

Pauli Murray, poet, priest, and lawyer, was born in Baltimore in 1910 and grew up in Durham, North Carolina, in the home of her maternal grandparents, the Fitzgeralds. Her grandfather, Robert, was a black Union soldier in the Civil War who was responsible for setting up schools for free blacks in Virginia and North Carolina, and her grandmother, Cornelia, was the mulatto offspring of a prominent white family of Chapel Hill. Both of these people instilled a strong sense of pride and independence in their granddaughter. Murray's accomplishments stretched over her entire life, but her beginnings as a writer belonged to the first half of the twentieth century.

Educated in the public schools of Durham, Murray graduated from Hunter College in New York City in 1933 with a B.A. in English. The years she spent in New York as a student were culturally and artistically exciting for black people, and Murray had the opportunity to know such writers as Dorothy West,* Countee Cullen, and Langston Hughes. During this time, she published her first poem, "The Song of the Highway," in 1934 in Nancy Cunard's *Color*. While in her final year in college, the poet took a course in poetry reading; in this class she was most influenced by "John Brown's Body," Stephen Benét's poem about the abolitionist martyr. She was impressed with Benét's suggestion that all black poets should express their thoughts and feelings about John Brown and other important people and events as honestly as possible – to truly convey their sense of America and claim their place in it. Murray became friends with the Pulitzer Prize-winning poet, who, until his death in 1943, offered her the constructive criticism she needed.

Murray earned three law degrees: an LL.B. from Howard University, an LL.M. from the University of California, and a D.J.S. from Yale University. She was a member of the bar in California and New York, and became the first black deputy attorney general for the state of California. Then followed several years as a Yale University tutor of law and a senior lecturer at the University of Ghana Law School. Murray was named the Louis Stulberg professor of law and politics at Brandeis University in 1973.

She was involved in other professions and activities. In 1977, Murray became the first black woman priest ordained by the Episcopal church, among the first ten American women ordained that year. She was an administrator of Benedict College in South Carolina and one of the founding members of the National Organization for Women. For a short time she worked as a field representative for the National Urban League.

She published two major works: *Proud Shoes: The Story of an American Family* (1956) and *Dark Testament and Other Poems* (1970), a collection that Murray wrote from 1933 to 1969. Murray was also the first black woman to be selected for residence at the MacDowell Colony in New Hampshire.

Dark Testament is a reflection of Murray's belief that all minority groups share the same dreams. The poems are diverse, ranging from racial poems and tragedies of the poor and powerless to general contemplations on nature and human nature. Murray started writing the title poem of the collection in the 1930s and completed the lengthy poem in 1943, the same year as the Harlem riot and Benét's death.

"Dark Testament" recounts the history of the blacks in Africa and in America. She tells of all the displaced peoples of America, and their quest for freedom and a place in the society. In the poet's eye, white Americans have been responsible for the violent history of America, yet she knows that they also have the power to restore the original promise of their land. While she respects the American dream and the country's accomplishments, she stills sees the flaws and how they affect black Americans particularly. She writes: "One hand thrusting us out to the stars, / One hand shoving us down in the gutter."

Murray sees white Americans as breaking, or attempting to break, the spirit of their black slaves by "grinding proud men to cringing slaves." Historically, she recounts the path of Afro-Americans accurately and effectively:

> Sell a man's brain for a handful of greenbacks,
> Mark him up in Congress – he's three-fifths human,
> Mark him down in the record with mules and mortgage,
> Sell him long! Sell him short! Cotton's a-boomin'.

She goes on to show how Afro-Americans dealt with the religious oppression of the whites: "Take a black's manhood, give a white god." The Afro-Americans then used this God to their own advantage: "black man . . . Sent his prayer straight to the white God's throne, / built him a faith, built a bridge to this God / And God gave him hope and the power of song."

At the end of the poem, Murray makes a plea for help and mercy and reiterates her ideals of equality by comparing the great heroes of both races:

> In coffin and outhouse all men are equal,
> And the same red earth is fed
> By the white bones of Tom Jefferson
> And the white bones of Nat Turner.

She sets an example of the two races living in harmony in the commonality of death, then she commands: "Listen, white brothers, hear the dirge of history, / And hold out your hand – hold out your hand."

Murray's use of history in her poem "Dark Testament" is linked to her other literary work, *Proud Shoes: The Story of an American Family*. This genealogical tracing of her own family shows how heavily she relied on the past and her heritage. She used both as a touchstone for the future and as a method of understanding the present. Much like Alex Haley's *Roots*, Murray's *Proud Shoes* encourages Afro-Americans to look for a positive meaning in their white America experience. In her own personal history she examines the tangled history of both races, showing how their crossing produced such remarkable individuals as herself. At the heart of the book is Murray's philosophy that black Americans must first accept the past. She believes that true emancipation can come only from their deriving strength from a painful past, and that learning to accept both the pride and the degradation of one's ancestors is the key to accepting oneself. Murray integrates the many aspects of her life in all her work. She uses her inspiring heritage as a source for work such as *Proud Shoes*. Her poetry holds strong to the ideals and virtues her grandparents instilled in her, and she lived out her many dreams and visions, fulfilling the strength that her roots gave her.

SELECT BIBLIOGRAPHY

Primary

Nonfiction

"All for Mr. Davis." The Story of Sharecropper Odell Waller. New York: Workers Defense League, n.d.

"The Fourth Generation of Proud Shoes." *Southern Exposure* (Winter 1977): 4-9.

Pauli Murray: The Autobiography of a Black Activist, Feminist, Lawyer, Priest, and Poet. Knoxville: University of Tennessee Press, 1989.

Proud Shoes: The Story of An American Family. New York: Harper & Row, 1956.

Song in a Weary Throat: An American Pilgrimage. New York: Harper & Row, 1978.

Poetry

Dark Testament and Other Poems. Norwalk, Conn: Silvermine, 1970.

"Mulatto's Dilemma." *Opportunity* (June 1938): 180.

"The Newer City." *Opportunity* (February 1934): 56.

"Youth." *Opportunity* (July 1934): 199.

IN ANTHOLOGIES

Stetson, *Black Sister*, 1981. "Dark Testament"; "Inquietude"; "Song."

Secondary

Bontemps and Hughes, *The Poetry of the Negro, 1746-1970*, 1970.

Campbell, Dorothy, *Index to Black American Writers in Collective Biographies*, 1983.

Chapman, *Index to Black Poetry*, 1974.

Deodene and French, *Black American Poetry since 1944*, 1971.

Ellis, *Opportunity; A Journal of Negro Life*, 1971.

Herman, *Women in Particular*, 1984.

Kallenbach, *Index to Black American Literary Anthologies*, 1979.

Low and Clift, *Encyclopedia of Black America*, 1981.

Matthews, *Black American Writers, 1773-1949*, 1975.

Reardon and Thorsen, *Poetry by American Women, 1900-1975*, 1979.

Richardson, Marilyn, *Black Women and Religion*, 1980.

Rose Bibliography Project, *Analytical Guide and Indexes to "The Crisis," 1910-1960*, 1975.

Salk, *A Layman's Guide to Negro History*, 1967.

Sims-Wood, *The Progress of Afro-American Women*, 1980.

Spradling, *In Black and White*, 1980.

Stetson, *Black Sister*, 1981.

Williams, *Black American Women in the Arts and Social Sciences*, 1978.

NEWSOME, MARY EFFIE LEE (1885-1979)

Editor

Poet

Effie Lee Newsome is best known for her work for children through her poetry, a children's column in *Crisis* and *Opportunity* magazines, and the Boys of Birmingham (Alabama) Club which she organized in 1925. Perhaps because of her focus on children, Newsome has not received the recognition given equally talented and proficient writers of this period. The more than one hundred poems she published should appeal to anyone who appreciates clear, sparkling verse. Newsome also contributed articles and reviews to magazines geared to adults.

Newsome's personal biography beyond childhood is sketchy, with only her post-high school education and wedding clearly dated, but a colorful description of her early life can be found in her biographical entry in *Golden Slippers* (1941), Arna Bontemps's anthology for children. Mary Effie Lee was born in Philadelphia, Pennsylvania, on 19 January 1885, the elder daughter of Benjamin Franklin Lee and Mary Elizabeth Ashe Lee. Her father, originally the editor of a black newspaper, became a bishop and moved the family to Texas. Bishop B. F. Lee was then transferred to Ohio, where Effie and her sister, Consuelo, attended school and began writing. Bontemps's biographical note tells of a happy childhood in Texas, with romps in the fields where white poppies grew and the amusement of hitching horned toads to match boxes. Effie and Consuelo also wrote and won prizes for the poems and drawings they sent to children's pages of magazines. After attending Wilberforce University from 1901 to 1904, and Oberlin College from 1904 to 1905, Effie went on to the Philadelphia Academy of Fine Arts (1907-8) and completed her education at the University of Pennsylvania from 1911 to 1914. (No sources indicate what degrees she earned at any of these institutions.) On 4 August 1920, she married the Reverend Henry Nesby Newsome. They apparently moved from Philadelphia to Birmingham, Alabama, where she started the Boys of Birmingham Club. After returning to Wilberforce, Ohio, Newsome served as librarian for the elementary school at Central State College. Ann Allen Shockley (1988) gives her death date as 1979.

Throughout their moves, Newsome steadily wrote poems and articles, mostly for children. She edited a children's column for *Opportunity*, as well as "The Little Page" in *Crisis*. Meanwhile, one of her more somber poems, "The Bird in the Cage," won an honorable mention in the 1926 Krigwa contest sponsored by *Crisis*. Interestingly, she entered the poem under the pseudonym "Johnson Ward."

Her poems published in *Crisis* from 1917 to 1934 number over a hundred. Only a few are collected in her only volume of poetry, *Gladiola Garden* (1940), beautifully illustrated with ink drawings of black children at play. All Newsome's poems are short and in simple meter. Sunny, optimistic, and sustained by muted religious tones, they are more complex than is at first obvious and they do not omit the bitter truths of discrimination and racism. The poem "Morning Light" develops the terrible image of the African child sent naked before the explorer into jungle grasses to draw out wild beasts, converting it to a religious symbol of a "fresh dawning after the dews of blood."

Likewise, a short story, "Little Cornish, the Blue Boy," is the tale of a black child who wanders into a church and is taunted by two workmen. "I shall not tell you what he called the bewildered child with the pretty brown face," says Newsome, attenuating for her young readers the impact of a cruel slur. The sexton's daughter, seeing the child bathed in the blue light of the stained glass, retorts: "He isn't what you said at all. He's a blue boy. Blue all over." The boy's mother is dying and the church lily he brings to her is her last pleasure, but the story ends optimistically with the revelation that the boy grows up to be a famous physician who takes care to bring solace to his patients in the form of flowers. The antithesis of the dark view of a Marita Bonner* or an Alice Dunbar-Nelson,* Newsome's idealism cannot be attributed only to the fact that her audience was juvenile. Rather, it seems to spring from her own spirituality and deeply rooted hopes for an enlightened future.

Curiously, Newsome's only book, *Gladiola Gardens*, does not measure up to the uncollected work. Its poems do not touch on any profound themes.

SELECT BIBLIOGRAPHY

Primary

Poetry

"Bluebird." *Crisis* (March 1925).

"The Bronze Legacy (To a Brown Boy)." *Crisis* (October 1922).

"Cricket's Wooing." *Crisis* (June 1925).

"Exodus." *Crisis* (January 1925).

"Fantasy." *Crisis* (June 1925).

"Garden So Bright." *Crisis* (June 1925).

Gladiola Gardens: Poems of Outdoors and Indoors for Second Grade Readers. Illustrated by Lois Laillou Jones. Washington, D.C.: Associated Publishers, 1940.

"A Killdeer." *Crisis* (June 1925).

"Kites." *Crisis* (March 1925).

"Magnificat." *Crisis* (December 1922).

"March Hare." *Crisis* (March 1925).

"Mild Mistress Moon." *Crisis* (June 1925).

"O Sea, That Knowest Thy Strength." *Crisis* (February 1917).

"Red Indians of Dawn." *Crisis* (June 1925).

"Sun Disk." *Crisis* (May 1923).

"Wild Roses."*Crisis* (June 1925).

IN ANTHOLOGIES

Bontemps, *Golden Slippers*, 1941. "The Baker's Boy"; "Bats"; "The Cotton Cat"; "The Cricket and the Star"; "Quoits"; "Sassafras Tea"; "Sky Pictures."

Cullen, *Caroling Dusk*, 1927. "The Baker's Boy"; "Morning Light"; "Pansy"; "Sassafras Tea"; "Sky Pictures"; "The Quilt"; "Quoits"; "Wild Roses."

Secondary

Bontemps, *American Negro Poetry*, 1969.

Campbell, Dorothy, *Index to Black American Writers in Collective Biographies*, 1983.

Chapman, *Index to Black Poetry*, 1974.

Ellis, *Opportunity; A Journal of Negro Life*, 1971.

Herman, *Women in Particular*, 1984.

Index to Poetry in Periodicals, 1920-1924, 1983.

Index to Poetry in Periodicals, 1925-1929, 1983.

Kallenbach, *Index to Black American Literary Anthologies*, 1979.

Kellner, *The Harlem Renaissance*, 1984.

Matthews, *Black American Writers, 1773-1949*, 1975.

Porter, *North American Negro Poets*, 1945.

Reardon and Thorsen, *Poetry by American Women, 1900-1975*, 1979.

Rose Bibliography Project, *Analytical Guide and Indexes to "The Crisis," 1910-1960*, 1975.

Rush, Myers, and Arata, *Black American Writers Past and Present*, 1975.

Spradling, *In Black and White*, 1980.

PETRY, ANN LANE (1908-)

Novelist
Short-story writer
Children's writer
Essayist

Ann Petry can be considered a bridge figure between the Harlem Renaissance and the black writers who came to prominence after mid-century. First published in the 1940s, Petry's writing has been sustained, creating a cohesive and unique fictional world. Coming upon the literary scene just after the Harlem Renaissance of the 1920s, she benefited from the literary experiments of that period. Though she unstintingly depicts the harsh realities confronted by Afro-Americans, the forced comparisons with Richard Wright and Chester Himes advanced by some critics do not do Petry justice. Her writing, for all its naturalism and social critique, has a poetic breadth all its own, and she can be considered a precursor of Toni Morrison and Gloria Naylor. If only because so few other of her female contemporaries were novelists, Petry must be studied as one of the major black women novelists of the 1940s and 1950s.

Writing short stories was an avocation for Ann Lane: like her father, uncle, and aunt, her profession was pharmacy. A fourth-generation New Englander born in Old Saybrook, Connecticut, on 12 October 1908, Ann was the daughter of Peter C. and Bertha James Lane. Petry, in speaking of her female relatives, noted: "My mother and her sisters . . . abandoned the role of housewife in the early part of the twentieth century. All three of them became successful businesswomen, financially independent" (*Contemporary Authors . . .*, 261). After graduating from Old Saybrook High School in 1931, Ann entered the Connecticut College of Pharmacy (now part of the University of Connecticut.) After her 1934 graduation, she worked as a registered pharmacist in her family's drugstores in Old Saybrook and Old Lyme, Connecticut. After she married George David Petry in 1938, the couple moved to Harlem. There she began to look for jobs that would give her the opportunity to write. Petry worked for such Harlem papers as the *Amsterdam News* and *People's Voice*, writing stories and selling advertising space. As a member of the American Negro Theatre, Petry also did some acting.

In November 1943, she published a short story ("On Saturday the Siren Sounds at Noon") in *Crisis*. An editor at Houghton Mifflin read the story and suggested that Petry submit a novel for entry in its fellowship competition. Later she submitted the first five chapters and a complete synopsis of *The Street*; she was awarded the Houghton Mifflin Literary Fellowship for 1945, a twenty-four-hundred-dollar prize. The following year Petry was a Best American Short Story Award recipient for her story "Like a Winding Sheet."

In Harlem Ann Petry was exposed to a way of life markedly different from that of rural Connecticut. While working as a journalist, she covered stories about murders, fires, political rallies, and various forms of protest. She became familiar with all the daily experiences that made up life in Harlem: the problems of finding jobs, adequate housing, and nutritious food. Petry was most disturbed by the children in Harlem – they were the helpless victims of segregation compounded by poverty. In 1944, she accepted a nine-month position with the New York Foundation which was planning to engage in an experimental study of the effects of segregation on black children. All of her experiences gathered while living in Harlem gave her the insights that made her first novel so powerful. She lived there for just six years before returning to Old Saybrook in rural Connecticut, but those years left an indelible imprint on her writing. Her extraordinary ability to receive and convey the impressions of the city comes through in much of her work.

The Street is not a sociological novel; Petry made a special effort to not make the blacks in her story the statistics and faceless beings of scholarship and sociology. She set out to show the inhabitants of Harlem "as people with the same capacity for love and hate, for tears and laughter, and the same instincts for survival possessed by all people." *The Street* moves swiftly, immediately capturing the attention of the reader. The novel uses situational encounters to show what life is like for people who live in overcrowded tenements; by extension, it explains the high crime and death rates among the black population of Harlem. The novel also makes comprehensible to the reader the difficulties that many black communities face in attempting to maintain cohesive bonds while living in a large, dehumanized northern city.

Through the encounters of Lutie Johnson, newly arrived to Harlem, Petry gives shape to the elements that create and perpetuate debilitating circumstances and ultimately overpower the protagonist. At first Lutie is only an observer, but the maelstrom draws her in. Fleeing from her life as a maid in suburban Connecticut, Lutie struggles to create a new life for herself and her small son, Bub. Surrounding her and Bub in their two-room family flat are a quartet of unsavory characters: Mrs. Hedges, a procuress; Mr. Jones, the superintendent, who tends the furnaces and who later attempts to seduce Lutie; Boots Smith, a musician whom Lutie, in rejecting his advances, bludgeons to death. Lutie is offered a job with the band in which Boots Smith plays, but the band is owned by Junto, the white landlord, who is ultimately trying to get to Lutie through Smith. Angered by the fact that he is being used to orchestrate Junto's link-up with Lutie and perceiving that he should be the one to enter the scene, Boots Smith approaches Lutie himself. For Lutie this is the final straw that impels her violent retaliation. With every killing blow that she delivers upon Boots she is releasing her anger and frustration. The novel ends as Lutie exits the environment that has thwarted her. She leaves behind her son who has fallen prey to "the street." None of the issues and problems are resolved, for the same conditions remain.

Petry remarks that "the sad and terrible truth about *The Street* is that now [1987] I could write that same book about Harlem or any other ghetto. Because life hasn't changed that much for black people."

In *Country Place* Petry exposes the corruption of a small New England town and its inhabitants, both white and black, during the era of the McCarthy persecution of alleged Communists. Through her narrator, the town druggist, Petry establishes that "wheresoever men dwell there is always a vein of violence running under the surface quiet." Color is less important than the exploration of human nature. Also, socioeconomic forces do not loom as large as in the first book – rather, chance can shape personal tragedy. Somewhat less pessimistic than *The Street*, this novel reverses all social hierarchies when a New England aristocrat wills her estate to her black maid, the Catholic church, and others who had previously been discriminated against in the town. The impossible love of a black "preppie" man and a white heiress harks back to the novels of Pauline Hopkins* and Zara Wright.*

Petry's fiction continues into the second half of the twentieth century, with *The Narrows* (1953), a volume of short stories (1971), and numerous books for children. Though critical interest in her work has increased, little attention has been paid to this later work.

As Mary Helen Washington has shown, critics such as Carl M. Hughes (1953), Theodore Gross (1980), and Addison Gayle (1975) have viewed Petry as an adherent to the tenets of naturalist fiction or a social critic who allows the cityscape to overwhelm her characters. At the same time, feminist critics find that Petry favors the "male quest" and is ambivalent about bestowing power on her female characters. Bernard Bell counters this view, demonstrating that Petry "moves beyond the naturalistic vision of Richard Wright and Chester Himes," as she debunks cherished American beliefs, especially those of the American Dream, the city and small town, and black character. Washington herself finds Petry at her peak as a portrayer of the New England social landscape, "its rugged individualists, its eccentrics, its highly motivated aspiring black community." She praises Petry for moving away from Harlem and toward the New England setting that she delivers so convincingly.

Why are critics made so uncomfortable by Petry's work? Foremost among their objections are that her characters seem to suffer irredeemably and are shown to be powerless, as economic and social forces consistently overwhelm their free will. Finally, the reader who seeks "strong women" with voices of their own is often disappointed, for Petry's females, caught in the tangled web of loaded circumstances, often capitulate and seek escape rather than confront their adversaries.

Like many other black women writers under consideration here, Petry has devoted herself to writing for children. In Clara O. Jackson's *Twentieth-Century Children's Writers* (1978) Petry explains: "Because I was born black and female I write about survivors (especially when I write for children): a bad-tempered little cat (*The Drugstore Cat*); a slave indicted for witchcraft (*Tituba of Salem Village*); a runaway slave who risks her life in order to guide other slaves to the North and freedom (*Harriet Tubman*); men and women persecuted for their religious beliefs *(Legends of the Saints)*" (*Contemporary Authors . . .*, 253).

In addition to writing, Petry was one of the founders of Negro Women Incorporated in 1941. The organization was primarily a consumer educational group designed to advance the cause of women as consumers in terms of jobs, food, housing, clothing, and the like. It is no longer in existence. Ann Petry continues to live in Connecticut. Some of her papers are held at Mugar Memorial Library, Boston University. The Petrys' only daughter, Elizabeth Petry Gilbert, is an attorney practicing in Philadelphia.

SELECT BIBLIOGRAPHY

Primary

Fiction

Country Place. Boston: Houghton Mifflin Co., 1947.

Legends of the Saints. Illustrated by Anne Rockwell. New York: Crowell, 1970.

The Narrows. Boston: Houghton Mifflin Co., 1953.

The Street. Boston: Houghton Mifflin Co., 1946.

FOR CHILDREN AND YOUNG ADULTS

The Drugstore Cat. Illustrated by Susanne Suba. New York: Crowell, 1949.

SHORT STORIES

"The Bones of Louella Brown." *Opportunity* (Fall 1947): 189-92, 226-30. Also in *Miss Muriel and Other Stories.*

"Doby's Gone." *Phylon* (4th Quarter 1944): 361-66. Also in *Miss Muriel and Other Stories.*

"Has Anyone Seen Miss Dora Dean?" *New Yorker* (25 October 1958): 41-48. Also in *Miss Muriel and Other Stories.*

"Like a Winding Sheet." *Crisis* (November 1945): 317-18, 331-32. Also in *Miss Muriel and Other Stories.*

"The Migraine Workers." *Redbook* (May 1967): 66-67, 125-27. Also in *Miss Muriel and Other Stories.*

Miss Muriel and Other Stories. Boston: Houghton Mifflin Co., 1971.

"The Moses Project." *Harbor Review*, no. 5-6 (1986): 52-61.

"The Necessary Knocking at the Door." *'47 Magazine of the Year* (August 1947): 39-44. Also in *Miss Muriel and Other Stories.*

"The New Mirror." *New Yorker* (May 1965): 28-55. Also in *Miss Muriel and Other Stories.*

"Olaf and His Girl Friend." *Crisis* (May 1945): 135-37, 147. Also in *Miss Muriel and Other Stories.*

"On Saturday the Siren Sounds at Noon." *Crisis* (December 1943): 368-69.

"Solo on the Drums." *'47 Magazine of the Year* (October 1947): 105-10. Also in *Miss Muriel and Other Stories.*

"The Witness." *Redbook* (February 1971): 80-81, 126-34. Also in *Miss Muriel and Other Stories.*

Nonfiction

Harriet Tubman: Conductor on the Underground Railroad. New York: Crowell, 1955. Reprinted as *A Girl Called Moses: The Story of Harriet Tubman*. London: Methuen, 1960.

Tituba of Salem Village. New York: Crowell, 1964.

Secondary

Bakish and Margolies, *Afro-American Fiction, 1853-1976*, 1979.

Bell, Bernard, "Ann Petry's Demythologizing of American Culture and Afro-American Character," 1985.

Bone, *The Negro Novel in America*, [1958] 1965.

Contemporary Authors Autobiography Series, vol. 6, 1987.

Current Biography, 1947.

Fairbanks and Engeldinger, *Black American Fiction*, 1978.

Herman, *Women in Particular*, 1984.

Jackson, *Twentieth-Century Children's Writers*, 1978.

Kallenbach, *Index to Black American Literary Anthologies*, 1979.

Kunitz and Haycraft, *Twentieth-Century Authors*, 1955.

Littlejohn, *Black on White*, 1966.

Low and Clift, *Encyclopedia of Black America*, 1981.

MacDowell, Margaret B., "The Narrows: A Fuller View of Ann Petry," 1980.

Matthews, *Black American Writers, 1773-1949*, 1975.

O'Brien, John, *Interviews with Black Writers*, 1973.

Page, *Selected Black American Authors*, 1977.

Pryse, "Pattern against the Sky: Deism and Motherhood in Ann Petry's *The Street*," 1985.

Richardson, *Black Women and Religion*, 1980.

Salk, *A Layman's Guide to Negro History*, 1967.

Shinn, "Women in the Novels of Ann Petry," 1974.

Sims-Wood, *The Progress of Afro-American Women*, 1980.

Spradling, *In Black and White*, 1980.

Weir, "The Narrows: A Black New England Novel," 1987.

PITTS, LUCIA MAE (1904-1973)

Poet

Playwright

Soldier

Lucia Mae Pitts was born in Chattanooga, Tennessee, to Janie Jones and Jarriett Pitts, both natives of Tennessee, and grew up in Chicago. She also worked as a secretary in Springfield, Illinois; Tuskegee Institute, Alabama; Atlanta; and New York City before moving to Washington D.C.in 1933. Back in Chicago, she conducted columns in the *Chicago Defender* and the Scott Newspaper Syndicate Papers, and edited the poetry page of a Chicago magazine. Her poetry was read over radio stations throughout the country.

The earliest known poems by Pitts, which appeared in *Challenge*, edited in Boston by Dorothy West,* and later in *Negro Voices* (1938), are two daring love poems that give voice to the need for erotic passion. "Challenge" praises a suitor's "timid tenderness" but insists that the speaker is "clay, my sweet, to earth hard-bound; / I cry for passion's breath hot on my cheek. / Demands I make may frighten and confound, / For these are what I need and what I seek; / A burning love that deepest depths can plumb; / A love that adds and heightens inborn fire– / That leaves the breathless body tired and numb / When it has catered warmly to desire."

The second poem in *Challenge* ("Promise") speaks of love that lasts beyond the grave and vows never to be overcome by bitterness: "I shall pluck moments from the days / As I would pluck the loveliest flowers from their bed. / These I will keep for my remembering– / Forgetting fingers that the thorns have bled. / Love and beauty, these I will hold, / And dancing hours, with music in my ears. / This is my vow: when I go down at last to death, / Who leans near me will catch the sweetness of my breath."

Pitts also contributed to *Opportunity* with "Brown Moon." Dedicated to the Ninety-ninth Pursuit Squadron of Tuskegee Institute, the poem asks the "silver-brown moon" to light the way for the young men who leave "the tranquil gardens of home" to answer the call of defense "against the stalking mob."

Pitts's next work, included in the coauthored collection *Triad*, is virtually inaccessible. The poems included in the anthology *Ebony Rhythm* (Beatrice Murphy Campbell, ed., 1948) lean toward rage at the indignities suffered by her people ("Let Them Come to Us" and "Never, Never, Never"). There she speaks of the torment that her soul has "for its daily bread" and begs for a "ladder of hope" that her arms cannot reach.

In her essay "One Negro WAC's Story," Pitts tells that while working for the Treasury Department's Bureau of Public Debt in Chicago (which, because it was under heavy fire for its segregationist policies, employed her as its first black personnel official), she decided to enlist in the WACs. At the time she was still living at home with brothers Roy, Edgar, Harrison, and Ralph. Her family, especially her older brother Roy, opposed this, so she slipped out of the house to fulfill a dream of service which she had held ever since the Women's Army Auxiliary Corps came into being in May of 1942. Her orders to report for active duty came just before Christmas of 1944.

Soon after her arrival at Fort Huachuca, Arizona, the *Apache Sentinel*, the post paper, carried her photograph and a story about her. It also printed two of her poems, one of which, "A WAC Speaks to a Soldier," she read over the loudspeaker system. Langston Hughes was one of the celebrities who visited the post. He asked to meet Pitts and autographed for her a copy of his poem, "The Negro Mother." She then became part of the first group of black WACs to volunteer for and be assigned to overseas stations. Her first assignment was in Birmingham, England, a peaceful city untouched by the war.

In the essay, Pitts recalls receiving excellent treatment from the English, though they had never seen black soldiers, much less black women soldiers. Then she was sent to Rouen, France, where she saw gutted buildings and rubble everywhere and was reunited with her beloved nephew, Lt. Thomas L. Pitts. Her play, *Let Me Dream*, was written for and performed by Company B., 6888th CPD, WAC, in Rouen. She served until June of 1945, when she requested discharge. The rest of her unit returned to the States in February 1946. Mary McLeod Bethune was scheduled to greet them at the docks in New York but could not; she asked Pitts to go in her place, and Pitts did. After the war Lucia Mae Pitts used the administrative skills she had acquired in the service to establish Pitts Personnel Service in Los Angeles.

Los Angeles County records show that at the time of her death from arteriosclerosis, Pitts, who had remained single, was executive secretary to the director of U.S. Public Housing in Los Angeles. Her remains were cremated and her ashes interred at the Angeles Abbey Cemetery.

SELECT BIBLIOGRAPHY

Primary

Nonfiction

"One Negro WAC's Story." Los Angeles: The author, 1968.

Poetry

"Brown Moon." *Opportunity* (November 1942): 336.

"Challenge." *Challenge* (May 1935).

"The First Kiss." *Challenge* (March 1934).

Triad: Poems by Helen C. Harris, Lucia Mae Pitts, Tomi Carolyn Tinsley. Washington, D.C.: The authors, 1945.

IN ANTHOLOGIES

Murphy, *Ebony Rhythm*, [1948] 1968. "Never, Never, Never"; "Let Them Come to Us"; "One April"; "If Ever You Should Walk Away"; "Afternoon Off"; "Poets."

Murphy, *Negro Voices*, [1938] 1971. "Challenge"; "Declaration"; "Moment in Paradise"; "Promise"; "Requiem"; "This Is My Vow."

Secondary

Campbell, Dorothy, *Index to Black American Writers in Collective Biographies*, 1983.

Chapman, *Index to Black Poetry*, 1974.

Ellis, *Opportunity; A Journal of Negro Life*, 1971.

French, Fabre, Singh, and Fabre, *Afro-American Poetry and Drama, 1760-1975*, 1979.

Hatch and Abdullah, *Black Playwrights, 1823-1977*, 1977.

Kallenbach, *Index to Black American Literary Anthologies*, 1979.

Rush, Myers, and Arata, *Black American Writers Past and Present*, 1975.

Sims-Wood, *The Progress of Afro-American Women*, 1980.

POPEL (SHAW), ESTHER A. B. (1896-1958)

Educator

Poet

Esther Popel grew up in Harrisburg, Pennsylvania, where the Popels had lived since 1826, her paternal grandfather having been brought there at age six by his free-born parents. She received her high school training at Central High School in Harrisburg and graduated Phi Beta Kappa from Dickinson College in Carlisle, Pennsylvania, with the Class of 1919. According to Dickinson College archives, she was a day student and probably the first Afro-American woman to attend Dickinson. Her yearbook designation, all too typical for the black students of these years, says that "if not in class she is tucked away in some far remote corner, her mind intensely concentrated on the subject matter before her, usually Browning. We do not know very much about her, as she comes from Harrisburg each day."

Popel first went into government service in the War Risk Insurance Department and also taught for two years in Baltimore before going to Washington D.C. While at Dickinson she had excelled in four languages – French, German, Latin, and Spanish. In Washington she taught French and Spanish at Shaw Junior High School and Francis Junior High School. Langston Hughes mentions her in his autobiography, *The Big Sea* (1940), as one of the writers who went to the home of Georgia Douglas Johnson* "to eat her cake and drink her wine and talk poetry and books and plays."

Popel published poems with some regularity in *Opportunity* from 1925 to 1934. Her poetry may be grouped under three headings: lyrical, religious, and political. In the poem "Kinship" the poet affirms her belief in the biblical story of creation and describes tongue-in-cheek the proponents of Darwinism: "I have no quarrel with those who claim / There is no God; who idly boast / That man has come from things akin / To apes; who point with pride / And proof to family trees whereon / Sit chattering all their simian ancestry!" Popel Shaw may well have been prompted by her religious beliefs to poke fun at the evolutionists.

Among her lyrical compositions are the poem "Night Comes Walking," which contains vivid images of night and a personification of the moon as an old woman taunted by tall trees that plunder her jewels. "Little Grey Leaves" has the brevity and the force of a haiku – fall leaves are transformed into chattering old women clinging to the branches of life. Racial feeling is manifested in "Flag Salute," where the salute to the American flag is presented in ironic counterpoint to the lynching of a young black. Popel also wrote six plays for junior high school students. Her work is almost inaccessible today, save the poems that appeared in *Opportunity*.

In Washington, Popel was a member of the Lincoln Memorial Congregational Temple. She also was a popular speaker, frequently addressing women's clubs in the Washington and New York areas. An address on race relations delivered at the Woman's Club in Lawrenceville, New Jersey, was of such interest that the Women's Press of the YMCA in New York undertook to publish it. Popel's husband, William A. Shaw, died in 1946. They had a daughter, Patricia Shaw Iversen, who lives in Norway.

SELECT BIBLIOGRAPHY

Primary

Nonfiction

"Our Thirteenth–in Ohio, 1936." *Journal of the National Association of College Women*, no. 13 (1936): 61-63.

Personal Adventures in Race Relations. 2d ed. New York: Woman's Press, National Board of the Young Women's Christian Association, 1946.

"The Tenth Milestone." *Journal of the National Association of College Women*, no. 11 (1933-34): 29.

Poetry

"Bagatelle." *Opportunity* (November 1931): 336.

"Blasphemy American Style." *Opportunity* (December 1934): 368.

"Credo." *Opportunity* (January 1925): 5.

"Flag Salute." *Crisis* (August 1934): 231.

A Forest Pool. Washington, D.C.: Modernistic Press, 1934.

"Kinship." *Opportunity* (January 1925): 5.

"Little Grey Leaves." *Opportunity* (September 1925): 382.

"Night Comes Walking." *Journal of Negro Life* (August 1929).

"October Prayer." *Opportunity* (October 1933): 295.

"Reach Down, Sweet Grass." *Opportunity* (April 1934): 110.

"Theft." *Opportunity* (April 1925): 100.

Thoughtless Thinks by a Thinkless Thoughter. N.p., n.d. [1920?].

IN ANTHOLOGIES

Cromwell, Turner, and Dykes, *Readings from Negro Authors*, 1931. "Little Grey Leaves"; "Symphonies"; "Theft."

Secondary

Campbell, Dorothy, *Index to Black American Writers in Collective Biographies*, 1983.

Cromwell, Turner, and Dykes, *Readings from Negro Authors*, 1931.

Dickinson College Archives.

Ellis, *Opportunity; A Journal of Negro Life*, 1971.

French, Fabre, Singh, and Fabre, *Afro-American Poetry and Drama, 1760-1975*, 1979.

Index to Poetry in Periodicals, 1925-1929, 1983.

Kallenbach, *Index to Black American Literary Anthologies*, 1979.

Matthews, *Black American Writers, 1773-1949*, 1975.

Porter, *North American Negro Poets*, 1945.

Reardon and Thorsen, *Poetry by American Women, 1900-1975*, 1979.

Rose Bibliography Project, *Analytical Guide and Indexes to "The Crisis,"* 1975.

Rush, Myers, and Arata, *Black American Writers Past and Present*, 1975.

Sims-Wood, *The Progress of Afro-American Women*, 1980.

PORTER, DOROTHY LOUISE BURNETT (1905-)

Bibliographer

Essayist

Librarian

Until 1973, Dorothy Porter was curator of the Moorland Library of Negro Life and History (now the Moorland-Spingarn Research Center) in the Founders Library at Howard University. She is well known as a black studies bibliographer, editor, historian, and educator, and her works as essayist and author are diverse and numerous. Among her bibliographies are "Early American Negro Writings: A Bibliographic Study," and *North American Negro Poets: A Bibliographical Checklist of Their Writings, 1760-1944*, published in 1945. She has also considered other nationalities of the African diaspora—for example, in her work on the Brazilian abolition movement in her article entitled "Padre Domingos Caldas Barbosa: Afro-Brazilian Poet."

She pioneered in interpreting little-known local records on black women, such as in her essays "Negro Women in Our Wars," which appeared in the 1945 issue of the *Negro History Bulletin* and "Selected Writing by Negro Women," in the 1968 issue of *Women's Education*.

The philosophy behind her writing can be found in her preface to *North American Negro Poets*. She writes that the principal objective of her checklist is to "reflect the richness of American holdings" in the sphere of Afro-American poetry. In the same preface she raises the question of whether poetry is "racial." She states that a poem can be racial in content while remaining poetic in form, and her bibliography is intended for "those who may wish to study the facets of race consciousness in Negro expression as well as the aesthetic factors."

Dorothy Burnett was born in Warrenton, Virginia, on 25 May 1905. She received a B.A. degree from Howard University in 1928 and married artist and author James A. Porter the following year. In 1931 she received her B.S. degree from Columbia, and in 1932 was the first black woman to receive a master's degree in library science from the same university. Her second husband was Charles H. Wesley.

SELECT BIBLIOGRAPHY

Primary

Nonfiction

"Early American Negro Writings: A Bibliographic Study." *Papers of the Bibliographic Society of America* 39 (1945).

"Negro Women in Our Wars." *Negro History Bulletin* 7 (June 1944): 195-96.

North American Negro Poets: A Bibliographic Checklist of Their Writings, 1760-1944. Hattiesburg, Miss.: Book Farm, 1945.

"The Organized Educational Activities of Negro Literary Societies 1826-1846." *Journal of Negro Education* 5 (October 1936): 555-76.

"Padre Domingos Caldas Barbosa: Afro-Brazilian Poet." *Phylon* (Third quarter 1951): 569-70.

"Selected Writings by Negro Women." *Women's Education* 7 (December 1968): 4-5.

A Working Bibliography on the Negro in the United States. Ann Arbor, Mich.: University Microfilms, 1968.

EDITED WITH OTHERS

Early Negro Writing, 1760-1837. Boston: Beacon, 1971.

The Negro in the United States: A Select Bibliography. Washington, D.C.: Library of Congress, 1970.

Negro Protest Pamphlets: A Compendium. New York: Arno, 1969.

Secondary

Bakish and Margolies, *Afro-American Fiction, 1853-1976*, 1979.

Campbell, Dorothy, *Index to Black American Writers in Collective Biographies*, 1983.

Lubin, "An Important Figure in Black Studies: Dr. Dorothy B. Porter," 1973.

Matthews, *Black American Writers, 1773-1949*, 1975.

Rush, Myers, and Arata, *Black American Writers Past and Present*, 1975.

Sims-Wood, *The Progress of Afro-American Women*, 1980.

Spradling, *In Black and White*, 1980.

Who's Who in Library Service, 1955, 390.

Williams, *American Black Women in the Arts and Social Sciences*, 1978.

POSTLES, GRACE VERA (1906-)

Educator

Poet

Grace Vera Postles, originally of Philadelphia, Pennsylvania, was secretary of the Saturday Evening Quill Club, organized in Boston in 1925. During the time, she was earning her bachelor of literary interpretation at the Emerson College of Oratory. The literary group's publication, the *Saturday Evening Quill*, was started in 1928 with the purpose of printing the best of their original work for themselves and was not for sale until 1930. The Saturday Evening Quill Club included at least twenty-three black writers from ages "21 to 60-odd." Born on 2 January 1906, Postles could have been its youngest member.

Archives at Emerson College reveal some information concerning Postles's education and career. The daughter of David W. Postles, she attended the William Penn High School for girls and the "Normal Academic Course" at Cheyney Training School for Teachers, both in Philadelphia. Postles completed about forty hours of credit at Cheyney and in May of 1927 entered Emerson College of Oratory where she received a bachelor of literary interpretation degree in May of 1929.

An interesting pictorial commentary on the flapper era is the tiny photograph in the *Emersonian* yearbook of 1928 which shows Postles in a jaunty pose, wrapped in what appears to be furs and draped against a stair railing. The caption under her name reads: "Music in her voice and in her heart." Perhaps this quote is indicative of the artistic aspirations she nurtured while she participated in the Saturday Evening Quill Club.

Most of the verse Postles wrote for the *Quill* are short poems of free verse. Her themes range from the simple observation of natural surroundings of "Blue Ridge Mts."–"A delicate blue / Silken veil / Is draped over / Abrupt elevations"–to the more pensive outpourings of a woman whose day-to-day living is so intense that she cannot distinguish between the pain and the joy in "Life." Other poems that lament over hopes met with disappointment are "A Lighted Candle," "Expectations," and "Golden Sorrow": "the heart that beats with gladness" must also "throb with affliction" eventually to "drink the bitter tonic / And live another life."

Grace Vera Postles kept in touch with her alma mater. The *Emerson College Alumni Bulletin* noted in the summer of 1932 that she was dramatic counselor at Camp Guilford Bower in New Paltz, New York, and head of the Department of English at Avery Institute, Charleston, South Carolina, in 1933. In November of 1935 the *Bulletin* reported that Postles was "teaching English and dramatics in Voorhees Institute, Denmark, South Carolina." A

January 1937 entry announcing the vocational whereabouts of the educator said she was "heading the Department of Speech and Drama, State Agricultural and Mechanical College, South Carolina," with the notation "Miss Postles will spend the coming summer in London doing special work in the Department of Speech at London University."

Postles continued writing after her involvement with the Saturday Evening Quill Club which published its annual from 1928 to 1930. According to the Emerson archives she wrote articles for the Associated Negro Press as late as 1933, under the caption of "Drama Grams."

SELECT BIBLIOGRAPHY

Primary

Poetry

"The Blue Ridge Mts." *Saturday Evening Quill* (June 1928).

"Golden Sorrow." *Saturday Evening Quill* (April 1929).

"In Winter." *Saturday Evening Quill* (April 1929).

"Life." *Saturday Evening Quill* (April 1929).

"A Lighted Candle." *Saturday Evening Quill* (April 1929).

"Moonlight." *Saturday Evening Quill* (June 1928).

"Prayer." *Saturday Evening Quill* (June 1928).

"Prisoner." *Saturday Evening Quill* (June 1928).

"Sans Words." *Saturday Evening Quill* (June 1928).

"The Scar." *Saturday Evening Quill* (June 1930): 16.

"Song." *Saturday Evening Quill* (April 1929).

Secondary

Emerson College Library, Archives, Boston, Mass.

*Index to Poetry in Periodicals, 1925-1929,*1983.

Saturday Evening Quill

PRICE, DORIS D. (?-?)

Playwright

Almost nothing is known of Doris Price, not even her birth or death dates. She is known to have written four plays, two of which (*The Bright Medallion* and *The Eyes of the Old*) were published in 1932 by George Wahr in Book 3 of *University of Michigan Plays*. The Wahr collection contains plays selected from the work of students in Professor Kenneth Thorpe Rowe's English 149 class, a course in dramatic writing. Kenneth Rowe, co-editor of the collection, describes Price's work as a "Negro folk play." Lennox Robinson, who wrote the book's introduction, praises "the high technical qualities that shine out in every play" of the collection, and adds that one or two of the plays "have moved me deeply – in particular "The Bright Medallion." He notes that since all the plays are limited to one act "they will have little or no chance in the commercial theatre." Another play called *Sokta*, though not included in the volume, was produced in the University Laboratory Theatre with a Negro cast by the Detroit chapter of Delta Sigma Theta, who also produced *The Bright Medallion* and *The Eyes of the Old*.

All of Price's plays deal with various facets of the Afro-American experience, and all portray the central character as a rebel against societal rules and standards. In *The Bright Medallion*, a black man named Samuel Hunt, labeled a coward, finds a lost medal from World War l and claims he won it for bravery. The play takes place in the Negro district of a suburban town in Texas in 1919 where gossip flourishes and the people seem uneducated, yet not in desperate material need. Sammy is threatened by Ed Crocket, the town bully, who is competing for Consy Jones, Sammy's lover and by the end of the play his widowed wife. In order to improve his bad reputation, Sammy rescues a baby from a burning house and afterward dies in Consy's arms. The humorous character of the illiterate preacher, who pretends to read from the Bible much to the amusement of the townspeople, is offset by the death of Sammy from smoke inhalation. The play is written in dialect except for the (apathetic?) white doctor who arrives too late to save Sammy's life.

The Eyes of the Old takes place in the South (in an unstated year) in the lower-class home of seventeen-year-old Carrie Jackson, her mother, Lillian, and her blind grandmother. Grandma Matthews, although not sighted, divines her young granddaughter's secret plan to drop out of high school and elope with a young man who according to Lillian "ain worth a dime." Nevertheless, the old woman does not attempt to stop Carrie, for fatalistically, she sees the elopement as inevitable, as was her own daughter's elopement and subsequent single motherhood. From Lillian's point of view, life is a self-perpetuating cycle and "we all got ter suffer en jes keep on sufferin' en all for nothin' but mo sufferin'." In Grandma Matthews's opinion, the only ones that can break the vicious circle of teen pregnancy and abandonment are those "dat kin see ter live, young folks born wid der eyes of der ole."

Two Gods: A Minaret is a play in dialect featuring characters with a strong religious involvement. The central conflict is between religious faith and a sense of betrayal by a God who inflicts loss and hard conditions. A house shutter that constantly bangs in the wind throughout the play seems to function as a reminder of past and present hardships in the protagonist's life as well as of the inner struggle she experiences between rejecting Christian religion and adhering to a cult.

The play takes place near the Alabama and Texas border around 1890. Corinne, a tall, slender woman in her twenties, lives alone in seclusion on a farmhouse after the death of her husband. Her friend Amy, a heavy middle-aged woman, spends most of the scene in the kitchen with Corinne attempting to convince her to come back to the church and take an interest in the Reverend Simpson. Simpson has shown interest under the guise of trying to bring Corinne back "ter der fold."

Instead, we discover at the play's end that Corinne has joined an atheistic cult that requires her to shave off her long black hair and wear a green scarf around her head. Amy and the Reverend Simpson consider its followers "debbil worshippers," but Corinne finds in it an outlet for her bitterness and an opportunity to spite the God who took her mother, father, sisters, brothers, and husband away in spite of her faithfulness to the church. Price's criticism of the church and apparent favoring of Corinne's character is surprising, a departure from the solidarity expressed by many of her black women writer contemporaries.

SELECT BIBLIOGRAPHY

Primary

Drama

The Bright Medallion. In Row, *University of Michigan Plays*, 1932.

The Eyes of the Old. In Row, *University of Michigan Plays*, 1932.

Two Gods: A Minaret. *Opportunity* (December 1932).

Secondary

French, Fabre, Singh, and Fabre, *Afro-American Poetry and Drama, 1760-1975*, 1979.

RANSOM, BIRDELLE WYCOFF (1914-)

Poet

Birdelle Wycoff Ransom was one of six women poets to be included in *Heralding Dawn*. The others were Gwendolyn Bennett,* Lauretta Holman Gooden,* Maurine L. Jeffrey,* Lillian Tucker Lewis,* and Bernice Love Wiggins.* Bennett and Wiggins were the best known of the six. Bennett wrote poetry, did art work for *Crisis* and *Opportunity*, and was editor of the Ebony Flute column for *Opportunity*; Wiggins published a volume of poetry, *Tuneful Tales* (1925). It is uncertain whether the other four had literary aspirations beyond the local audience. One can get a feel for the style of these poets by reading the one or two samples of each woman's work in *Heralding Dawn*. More research needs to be done on this "Texas Group."

The only biographical information available on Birdelle Wycoff Ransom, is in *Heralding Dawn*. Born in Beaumont, Texas, she was four years old when her family moved to Houston. She received her primary education at the Gregory Elementary School. When Ransom was sixteen she graduated as salutatorian from the Washington High School. In 1931 she attended Houston Junior College, graduating as valedictorian in 1933. The following spring she began writing a poetry column in the *Houston Informer* called Lines of Life; however, when she married in Galveston, Texas, she relinquished this position the same year. Apparently, her interests in literature did not wane, however, for in 1956 she completed a master's thesis, "Charles Dickens as a Social Reformer," at Texas Southern University.

Like Lillian Tucker Lewis,* Ransom published only one poem in *Heralding Dawn*, an anthology of Afro-American poets from Texas. In the poem "Night," the poet greets the night time as a friend whose "infinite shade was manifest" and "into [whose] grandeur all were blended." Perhaps Ransom is suggesting that the darkness of the night hides all color (be it skin or otherwise) from sight. J. Mason Brewer, the editor of *Heralding Dawn*, says: "Birdelle Ransom speaks in the terms of race without mentioning race. Her verse portrays in a very vivid manner, race consciousness, which she weaves into her verse with accuracy and skill."

SELECT BIBLIOGRAPHY

Primary

Nonfiction

"Charles Dickens as Social Reformer." M.A. thesis, Texas Southern University, 1956.

Poetry

IN ANTHOLOGIES

Brewer. *Heralding Dawn*, 1936. "Night."

Secondary

Kallenbach, *Index to Black American Literary Anthologies*, 1979.

REYNOLDS, EVELYN CRAWFORD [EVE LYNN] (ca. 1900-?)

Poet

Columnist

Evelyn Crawford Reynolds, who also wrote under the pseudonym "Eve Lynn," was a member of the Beaux Arts Club, a group of black writers and artists of Philadelphia, to which Mae V. Cowdery* and Bessie Calhoun Bird* also belonged. Reynolds could be called a "vanity poet." Though some are pleasing, few of her poems are memorable and she tended to publish books containing poems already published in her first collection, *No Alabaster Box* (1936). But Reynolds knew how to promote herself, as seen in the rather innocuous forewords she obtained from such notables as Mary McLeod Bethune and Marian Anderson.

Her themes are nature, God, and country, with occasional indignant references to racial discrimination and calls for harmony: "In this world are all sorts of folks / Of every kind and hue, / So why should we think white supreme / When black is magnificent too?" ("God's Children"). In "No Alabaster Box" Reynolds declares her wish to be loved and honored during her lifetime: "Let me have my flowers now, / Those you'll pile upon my grave; / Let me know their sweetness / While the love of life I crave." Like Mazie Earhart Clark,* Reynolds used poetry as a means for achieving social recognition and uniting people.

Vincent Jubilee has explained that during the 1920s Afro-Americans in Philadelphia read two weekly newspapers: the *Philadelphia Tribune* and *Pittsburgh Courier*. During that time Evelyn Crawford was a community services social worker, an occasional poet, and a resident of Philadelphia's South Side St. Albans Street. She also wrote a column of social, civic, and cultural events for the *Pittsburgh Courier*. According to Jubilee, the young writer was probably not deemed "a 'working reporter' at the functions [she] attended and wrote about, since [she herself] was a *bona fide* member of the elite clique whose activities were reported weekly to the public." Reynolds, a graduate of Girls' High and a special physical training course at Temple, was also a teacher for four years in the Bureau of Recreation. She began writing a column for the *Tribune* soon after she was appointed to the Armstrong Association as neighborhood secretary.

Reynolds married Hobson Richmond Reynolds, a mortician who rose to prominence as a member of the Pennsylvania state legislature and court judge magistrate. He was named by *Ebony* magazine as one of the most influential Afro-Americans in the country. A photograph of Evelyn appears in *Ebony* (June 1949). It shows a light-skinned woman in apron,

"Philadelphia's prominent Evelyn Reynolds, wife of Judge Hobson Reynolds," demonstrating how to prepare bacon dishes "for lunch, teatime, and supper." That she had published two volumes of poetry is noted parenthetically, as is her newspaper column.

Reynolds's column, "Eve Lynn Chats 'bout Society and Folks," was essentially focused on the professional and entrepreneurial class. She reported on local people attending social events in other cities; visiting non-Philadelphians of social prominence; the apparel worn by fashionable women; social club events including the food that was served; and occasional visits by such figures as Chandler Owen of the *Messenger* or Alain Locke.

Reynolds's first book of verse, *No Alabaster Box* (1936), was compared by Benjamin Brawley to Mae V. Cowdery's *We Lift Our Voices and Other Poems* (1936). Brawley found Reynolds's verse to be beautiful but Cowdery's as "burning with the more intense glow." In terms of publications, however, Reynolds's career superseded that of Cowdery. She eventually published two more volumes of poetry: *To No Special Land: A Book of Poems* (1953) and *Put a Daisy in Your Hair* (1963).

SELECT BIBLIOGRAPHY

Primary

Poetry

No Alabaster Box. Philadelphia: Alpine Press, 1936.

Put a Daisy in Your Hair. Philadelphia: Dorrance, 1963.

To No Special Land: A Book of Poems. New York: Exposition, 1953.

Secondary

Brawley, *The Negro Genius*, 1940.

Deodene and French, *Black American Poetry since 1944*, 1971.

Ebony (June 1949): 48.

French, Fabre, Singh, and Fabre, *Afro-American Poetry and Drama*, 1979.

Jubilee, "Philadelphia's Afro-American Literary Circle and the Harlem Renaissance," 1980.

Matthews, *Black American Writers, 1773-1949*, 1975.

Porter, *North American Negro Poets*, 1945.

Reardon and Thorsen, *Poetry by American Women, 1900-1975*, 1979.

Rush, Myers, and Arata, *Black American Writers Past and Present*, 1975.

RIDLEY, FLORIDA RUFFIN (1861-1943)

Educator

Essayist

Historian

Journalist

Short-story writer

Social worker

Florida Ruffin Ridley won second prize for her personal experience sketch/essay "An Experience" in the *Opportunity* contest of 1925. She occasionally published in *Opportunity* during the 1920s as well as in the *Saturday Evening Quill*, the annual produced by the Boston-based Saturday Quill Club. *Our Boston*, a local periodical, also published Ridley's work.

The daughter of women's rights and civil rights activist Josephine St. Pierre Ruffin, Florida Ruffin was born and raised in Boston, Massachusetts, where she resided for most of her life. She was married to Ulysses A. Ridley after completing her studies at Boston Teachers' College and taught at Grant School in that city from 1880 to 1888.

Ridley – like her mother, a founder of the black woman's club movement and suffragist – was active in national and local organizations concerned with the status of Afro-Americans and women, often one of the pioneers. She was one of the founders of the Society for the Collection of Negro Folklore in Boston, established in 1890. From 1894 to 1910 she coedited and copublished with her mother *Woman's Era*, a monthly devoted to the interests of black women. During her term as corresponding secretary of the Woman's Era Club she participated in the first Convention of Colored Women to be held in Boston, June 1895. From 1916 to 1919 Ridley joined in the war effort when she enrolled in a 1916 secretarial war course at Boston University and served as executive secretary of the Soldier's Comfort Unit from 1917 to 1919. According to a telegram addressed to her residence at 131 Kent Street, Brookline, Massachusetts, Ridley was offered a position in War Camp Community Service of New York on 29 August 1919, with a salary of $1,200 per year. Ridley was later appointed corresponding secretary of the first national organization, the National Federation of Afro-American Women. In 1923 she directed and promoted a Boston Public Library Exhibit of Negro Achievement and Abolition Memorials. She endorsed the Democratic party in the 1924 presidential campaign under the auspices of an organization called the Flying Squadron; women (including Alice Dunbar-Nelson*) from five states gathered to give talks about "Keeping Klear of the

Klan" and being "Devoted to Davis." Ridley spoke on "Why colored women are supporting J. W. Davis," the Democratic nominee that year. In 1928 she served as editor of Social Service News, organ of the Cooperative Social Agencies. Also a member of the Twentieth Century and Women's City clubs of Boston and the League of Women for Community Service, Ridley presided over the Society of Descendants, Early New England Negroes, from 1931 through 1940.

Ridley's preoccupation with the Society of Descendants, Early New England Negroes, and its goal to restore and preserve early Afro-American history permeates her writing. The Heslip-Ruffin family papers (1833-1943) housed at Amistad Research Center in New Orleans, Louisiana, provide interesting data on Ridley and her family; the documentation not only includes genealogical information but hints at a source of inspiration for her stories and essays. An African prince, abducted and brought to America, landed at Newport, Rhode Island, but escaped to Rehoboth, Massachusetts. Taking the American name David Hill, he married an Indian girl in the early eighteenth century. Pseudo-anonymously, Ridley expounds on this portion of her heritage in the essay "Preface: Other Bostonians."

In this essay, Ridley relates details drawn from documents (now contained in the Heslip-Ruffin papers) of instances of participation in early New England life by her ancestors and others. Records from the Thanksgiving Day Governor Andrew "came down to Beacon Hill to dine with colored people in one of their homes" to announcements of an anti-slavery anniversary promoted by "women who invited social ostracism and challenged physical and financial dangers by sponsoring the cause of the negro" provide a dim scenario of race relations in New England during the 1800s. Ridley also describes her involvement in "a parlor gathering in 1890 of a half dozen Boston colored women, who met to consider some possible way to bring the millions of Negro women into touch with one another for a common helpfulness and encouragement – a successful movement begun only thirty years after the Emancipation Proclamation!"

The topics central to Ridley's writing are Afro-American life and race relations in New England. In her stories and essays she captures well the novelties and hypocrisies of a segment of American society that purports to favor freedom for all peoples. Demanding respect for the multiethnic heritage that American society wants to denounce, the author refutes the assumption that Afro-Americans did not play a role in the founding of America, and muses, "It is surprising to find how definite a part of accepted technique has been the closing of eyes and ears and minds to phases of Negro life and character." Realizing that to disassociate blacks from the birth of America would be to disenfranchise them from American society, Ridley begins to fill in the gaps caused by the exclusion of white women and people of color from American history.

Ridley confronts one of the fears that racists of any color employ in an attempt to justify their stance: that the race, through intermarriage, will no longer be "pure." Ridley suggests that few Americans have "pure blood." People of color were not uncommonly seen as aliens intent on a mission to taint "American" society. The short story "He Must Think It Out" illustrates the psychological trauma caused by the dialectic of racism – a system of political stratification that transcends the spoken word or even conscious thought, affecting the spirit, soul, and body, and condemning those whose racial features are not visibly clear. In this story Henry Fitts, a financially struggling lawyer who covets wealth, becomes heir to a substantial fortune. But Fitts, white and culturally European American, discovers that receiving his inheritance depends on his publicly acknowledging his mixed blood. Not only is he shocked at the revelation that he is of Afro-American and Native American descent, as well as Anglo-Saxon heritage; he becomes frenzied as he realizes what the repercussions would be on him and his family: "If this thing proved to be true, what was he, and where did he belong? Where would he look for friends? . . . He would shoot, kill! Let any one dare insult his daughter! . . . But how absurd to imagine that Irene would be treated like a common black girl! And he laughed again, and again the laugh broke." A stifling intensity surrounds Fitts at the moment when he must "think it out"; he is assaulted by thoughts racing through his mind as he begins to consider the political implications and the doors of opportunity that will close. In a moment's time his life and his thinking have changed; he has now become a victim of a system that earlier granted him white privilege.

"Maria Peters: A Peculiar Woman" is the bio-sketch of a native New Englander of Afro-American, Native American, and Anglo-Saxon descent, who endeavored to raise her sons free of the values of a color-conscious society. With a "passion for freedom – not only the freedom of the body, but freedom of the spirit" she was "convinced that the forced consideration of every matter from a racial standpoint, did not contribute towards developing nobility of character." Maria Peters wanted to bond her children, heirs of the blood of many races, to all of humanity. For this idealism, Peters, a widow, outlived her sons. Her two oldest sons, taught to "know no color difference but to be men among men," were segregated from their friends when they went off to World War I, and their bodies were never sent home. The remaining son was "riddled with bullet wounds" when he responded to a politician who was insulting black voters and who "for good measure let loose the full force of his vituperation on the black women of America"; he called the politician a liar.

Like Olivia Ward Bush-Banks,* Ridley took pride in the ethnic diversity of her background, but in her works she warns that there is a price to pay if the guardians of "racial purity" feel threatened. Her sensitivity to the struggles of women, particularly women of color, is apparent in her stories and essays – perhaps because, as she says in "Preface": "Those phases that are richest in suffering and heroism are not always recorded in collections."

SELECT BIBLIOGRAPHY

Primary

Fiction

"He Must Think It Out." *Saturday Evening Quill* 1 (June 1928): 5-8.

"Two Gentlemen of Boston." *Opportunity* 3 (January 1926):12-13.

"Two Pairs of Gloves." *Saturday Evening Quill* 3 (June 1930): 28-32.

Nonfiction

"An Experience." (Unpublished?), awarded second prize by *Opportunity*, July 1925: 221.

"Maria Peters." *Saturday Evening Quill* 2 (April 1929):12-13.

"Preface: Other Bostonians." *Saturday Evening Quill* 1 (June 1928): 54-56.

Secondary

Ellis, *Opportunity; A Journal of Negro Life,* 1971.

Heslip-Ruffin Papers, Amistad Research Center, New Orleans, La.
Dr. Maude T. Jenkins [relative of Ridley].

Moorland-Spingarn Research Center, Howard University, Washington, D.C.

Saturday Evening Quill

Who's Who in Colored America, 1927.

ROBESON, ESLANDA CARDOZA GOODE (1896-1965)

Biographer

Travel writer

Eslanda Cardoza Goode is best known as the wife of singer Paul Robeson (1898-1976), but in addition to managing her husband's career, she established herself as a persuasive expository writer with a global outlook that was unusual in her time. She came from a highly respected biracial family of statesmen and educators. As Eslanda herself reveals in *American Argument*, the family lineage included Spanish, English, Scottish, Jewish, American Indian, and "a large majority of Negro blood." Her father, John Goode, of West Indian descent, worked as a clerk for the War Department. Her mother, Eslanda Cardoza, belonged to a prominent Sephardic Jewish family in Charleston, South Carolina. Francis Lewis Cardozo (the spelling varies), her grandfather, was a statesman who had been secretary of state and secretary of the treasury in South Carolina during Reconstruction. Throughout his life, Cardozo was a pioneer in education for blacks.

Eslanda was born in Washington, D.C., but three years after her father died in 1902, her mother took her and her two brothers to New York City where they lived in a cold-water Harlem flat. Eslanda attended the New York public schools and took a course in domestic science at Illinois State University. She transferred to Columbia University Teachers' College and received a B.A. in chemistry in 1920. She was a surgical technician and chemist at Presbyterian Hospital of Columbia University, probably the first woman of Afro-American descent to hold this position.

She met Paul Robeson, a college football hero, in Harlem in 1920, while he was a student at Columbia University Law School, and they married in August 1921. It was Eslanda who, seeing little future for him as a black attorney, influenced Paul to pursue a career in music and theater. In 1925, she left medical school and her position at Presbyterian Hospital to manage his acting career.

Her only son, Paul, Jr., was born in 1927, and Eslanda's mother cared for him during his first few years, thus enabling Eslanda to continue to focus her efforts on her husband's blossoming career. Her first book, *Paul Robeson, Negro*, was a biography of her husband. Not surprisingly, and though it is a rather simplistic portrait, it was instrumental in making him known to the public. Eunice Hunton Carter* reviewed it for *Opportunity*: "Eslanda Robeson's style is surprisingly good for a first book. ... Her pictures are clear cut and if she puts a bit more of herself into the latter chapters than perhaps she realized, shall we say that the radiance of love meeting the dazzling glory that emanates from Paul's shining success blinded her and she lost her way a bit."

In 1928, the Robesons moved to London, where they found less racial tension than in the United States. Shirley Graham Du Bois* (then using the surname McCanns) visited the Robesons there in 1931: "In a vine covered brick house in Hampstead, one of the most beautiful and exclusive suburbs of London . . . facing the famous Heath, with grounds sloping from the back to a lovely park, swept by cool breezes from the Channel and shadowed by old oaks and Chestnut trees, here I found 'the little brown boy [Paul Robeson, Jr.] who lives at Hampstead.'" Graham describes admiringly the pleasure Eslanda derived from her role as "general manager, booking agent, secretary and advisor to her illustrious husband," still finding time "to direct her household with its staff of servants and to oversee the activities of her little son."

Graham does not say so, but it was also true that the Robesons lived apart for periods of time, during which each pursued separate interests. Martin Duberman's recent biography of Paul Robeson sheds light on the complex relationship Paul and Essie had. But despite difficulties and problems, including Paul's relationships with other women, the Robesons shared a political and social activism that grew strong over the years, as did their devotion to each other.

Studies in anthropology and economics at the London School of Economics stimulated Eslanda's own interests. In 1938 she took her son on a six-month tour of Africa. *African Journey*, a personal diary of this field visit, was published in 1945. This book, which contains photographs she took with the Rolliflex camera given her by Paul, describes in simple discursive style the rural and urban life-styles and the economic situations of the various countries, with special emphasis on the herdspeople of Uganda. Robeson compares the patriarchal attitudes of South Africans to those of white southerners: "This traveling about Africa reminds me of traveling through the Deep South in America: you are passed from friend to friend, from car to car, from home to home, often covering thousands of miles without enduring the inconvenience and humiliations of the incredibly bad Jim Crow train accommodations and lack of hotel facilities for Negroes." She was one of the first Americans to speak out for the withdrawal of all colonial powers from Africa. In Robeson's view, no one could be free until all people were free.

Robeson paints her impressions of the dusty South African landscape with these words: "mists of [dust], fogs of it, clouds of it . . . floods of thick red-brown and clay-colored dust swirling everywhere." Mindful that she cannot change any of what she sees, she allows herself to admire the unhurried, timeless rhythms of Africa and be changed by this contact with a different civilization.

Throughout this time, Robeson observed the worsening political situation in Europe. Like many intellectuals of her time, she became an ardent antifascist and supporter of the Soviet Union. Both Robesons, increasingly radicalized, went to Spain during the Civil War (1936-39) to show their support for the Spanish Republic.

Another book by Robeson, *American Argument,* is a dialogue with Pearl Buck, to whom she was introduced by Carl Van Vechten, the white intellectual who played a role in the Harlem Renaissance. In this intertwined autobiography in which the two women compare their views on American life and the status of women, Buck reflects on her upbringing as a white child in China, while Robeson looks back on her own childhood as a black in white America. Buck characterizes Robeson as a person "with a fine mind, the ability to laugh, a triumphant person in herself, [without] inner morbidities."

After World War II, the Robesons settled in Connecticut, and Eslanda studied anthropology at the Hartford Seminary. Her lectures on African colonialism were popular with audiences. In subsequent years she became increasingly involved in politics. She joined the Progressive party, campaigning for Henry A. Wallace in his quest for the presidency and running for secretary of state in Connecticut on the Progressive ticket in 1948; in 1950, she also sought a congressional position from that state.

In 1953, Eslanda Robeson was called before Senator Joseph McCarthy's Committee on Un-American Activities. Citing both the Fifth Amendment and the Fifteenth Amendment, which guarantees equal rights regardless of color and race, she refused to discuss her political convictions. In a challenge to the committee, she stated that she had been fighting all of her life against racial discrimination. At one point she said to Senator McCarthy, "You're white, and I'm colored, and this is a very white committee." She was not cited for contempt, however, out of "special consideration."

Legislation that would guarantee racial equality became a prime concern as Robeson began to work with Dr. Martin Luther King in the 1950s. They both spoke out for the implementation of the 1954 Supreme Court decision on *Brown* v. *The Board of Education,* outlawing segregation in public schools.

She lived abroad for the next five years, but continued in her support of all civil rights causes. In 1965 she died of cancer in New York City.

SELECT BIBLIOGRAPHY

Primary

Nonfiction

African Journey. New York: John Day Co., 1945. Reprint. Westport, Conn.: Greenwood Press, 1972.

American Argument. With Pearl S. Buck. New York: J. Day Co., 1949.

Paul Robeson, Negro. New York: Harper & Brothers, 1930.

"What Do the People of Africa Want?" New York: Council on African Affairs, 1945.

Secondary

Campbell, Dorothy, *Index to Black American Writers in Collective Biographies*, 1983.

Carter, Review of *Paul Robeson, Negro*, 1930.

Duberman, *Paul Robeson*, 1988.

Ellis, *Opportunity; A Journal of Negro Life*, 1971.

French, Fabre, Singh, and Fabre, *Afro-American Poetry and Drama, 1760-1975*, 1979.

Herman, *Women in Particular*, 1984.

Kallenbach, *Index to Black American Literary Anthologies*, 1979.

Kellner, *The Harlem Renaissance*, 1984.

McCanns, "A Day at Hampstead," 1931.

Matthews, *Black American Writers, 1773-1949*, 1975.

New York Times, obituary, 14 December 1965, 46.

Robeson, Susan, *The Whole World in His Hands*, 1981.

Spradling, *In Black and White*, 1980.

Sullivan, "Eslanda Cardozo Goode," 1980.

Who's Who in Colored America, 1927.

Williams, *American Black Women in the Arts and Social Sciences*, 1978.

ROWLAND, IDA (1904-)

Poet

Educator

Born in Texas in 1904, Ida Rowland was one of nine children in a family of Indian, African, and European descent that moved to Oklahoma when she was thirteen. Her single volume of verse, dedicated to her parents, was published in Philadelphia in 1939, the same year she received a master's degree from the University of Nebraska. She went on to earn a Ph.D. in social sciences at French-language Laval University, Quebec, in 1948, becoming Oklahoma's first black woman Ph.D. In 1936 she had received a B.A. degree in sociology with minors in philosophy and English. Rowland married A. D. Bellegarde, the son of a Haitian diplomat exiled by Duvalier. Bellegarde taught agriculture at Langston University, Oklahoma. For many years Rowland taught social sciences at Arkansas A, M, and N (now the University of Arkansas at Pine Bluffs). Retired from teaching, she now has her own company, Bell Enterprises, which publishes instructional books on blacks for young people.

Rowland's idealism and dedication to a dream of equality as an Afro-American is obvious in her poetry. *Lisping Leaves* is a collection of forty-seven poems whose themes range from the celebration of life and nature to the social struggle of the Afro-American people. Most of the poems do not exceed fifteen lines, and there is a pattern of quatrains and rhymes throughout the work. Rowland's style is simple and lyrical, frequently alliterative, with a few poems written in traditional poetic English. Irony appears in many poems as the poet recoils at being judged not by her inner soul but by outer appearance.

Several poems, such as "Autumn Rain" and "Wind among Leaves" describe various aspects of the nature theme introduced in the title of the collection. Most of the poems utilize the natural environment as personification and metaphor, even when nature is not a central theme. Such is the poem "Confession": "Wandering winds have caressed my skin, / I long for spaces far and wide." Other poems in *Lisping Leaves* deal bitingly with the social aspects of the Afro-American experience.

In "Negroid Things," the speaker protests the expectations regarding behavior and emotions that the dominant classes impose on Afro-Americans and ironically demands: "Do souls of men have different shades? / Must we always love with an ebony heart?" In the poem "Unadjustment" imagery of incarceration abounds, where the speaker is encircled by "Tall black walls" and "darkness / That smells of mold and life that is stagnant." In the last half of the piece, the speaker dreams of a day when she will find a small hole and will be able to escape: "I shall pound the walls with my hands / Until the earth and crumbling stones / Fall upon my feet, / . . . Then I shall run forth, and with a cry of triumph / I shall embrace my world." This poem is perhaps an allusion to the impossibility of adjusting to mainstream society, and represents the effects of the various impediments the author experiences as a woman, a writer, and an Afro-American. "Our Heritage" calls for "a right to a life that is full, / A life that is useful and happy and gay," maintaining strong ties and pride in the history of Afro-Americans.

The most prominent tone in Rowland's work is optimism and love of nature, but these elements always blend with her social conscience and ironic allusions to the treatment of dark-skinned people in America as less than equal.

SELECT BIBLIOGRAPHY

Primary

Nonfiction

"An Analysis of Negro Ritualistic Ceremonies as Exemplified by Negro Organizations in Omaha." Master's thesis, University of Nebraska at Omaha, 1939.

Poetry

Lisping Leaves. Philadelphia: Dorrance & Co., 1939.

Secondary

Morgan, Gordon D., University of Arkansas at Fayetteville.

Porter, *North American Negro Poets*, 1945.

Reardon and Thorsen, *Poetry by American Women, 1900-1975*, 1979.

Rush, Myers, and Arata, *Black American Writers Past and Present*, 1975.

University of Nebraska, Registrar's Office.

SMITH, J. PAULINE (?-?)

Poet

Some of the poems included in the volume *Exceeding Riches and Other Verse* (1922) suggest that J. Pauline Smith lived in Detroit and was a member of the Bethel Church, whose eightieth anniversary she celebrates in a poem dated 29 May 1921. An anniversary hymn in honor of the one hundredth anniversary of the founding of the A.M.E Church by Richard Allen at Philadelphia confirms her affiliation with that religious denomination. But letters to the Bethel Church in Detroit and the Azalia Hackley Collection of the Detroit Public Library have yielded no information on the identity of J. Pauline Smith.

Exceeding Riches and Other Verse is dedicated to her mother, "whose lullaby songs were all from the Methodist Church Hymnal." Its poems appeared first in the following magazines and religious and secular papers: *Detroit Young Women*, organ of the YMCA, *Detroit Club Woman*, *Detroit Leader*, *Detroit Free Press*, and the *Christian Recorder*, Philadelphia. The foreword, by Theresa Smith, B. Pd.(?), states that the crying need of the world today is the preservation of the life of the spirit. Quoting from the summer 1918 issue of *Le livre contemporain*, she emphasizes the crisis of materialism and the disillusionment with scientific progress in the wake of World War I.

The majority of Smith's poems, inspired by lines of Scripture, stress the joys of faith and the power it bestows to rise above physical pain and emotional grief. While she expresses opposition to war in a poem called "The Source of Wars," based on James 4:1, other poems voice patriotic sentiment and warm support of the Red Cross and its medical and humanitarian work. Among her nonreligious poems is one to Robert Browning on the centennial of his birth (7 May 1917). Her admiration for Browning is also shown in her compilation "Olive Prints: A Yearbook of Quotations from Robert Brown's Poems."

In "A Prayer," religious feeling merges with racial consciousness: "Use me, Lord, use me for my race, / To send their status up a pace, / To make their merits better known; / Hasten their coming to their own!" (54).

SELECT BIBLIOGRAPHY

Primary

Poetry

Exceeding Riches and Other Verse. Philadelphia, Pa.: A. M. E. Book Concern, 1922.

Secondary

French, Fabre, Singh, and Fabre, *Afro-American Poetry and Drama, 1760-1975*, 1979.

Porter, *North American Negro Poets*, 1945.

Reardon and Thorsen, *Poetry by American Women, 1900-1975*, 1979.

Rush, Myers and Arata, *Black American Writers Past and Present*, 1975.

SPENCE, EULALIE (1894-1981)

Playwright

Critic

Eulalie Spence entered the United States through Ellis Island as a small girl, after her father's occupation as a sugar planter in Nevis, British West Indies, had been destroyed by a hurricane. Eulalie was the oldest of six daughters; a seventh was born after the family came to the United States. The Spences first settled on 135th Street at the corner of Fifth Avenue in Harlem and then moved to Brooklyn, opposite St. Mary's Hospital. In a 1973 audiotape interview for the Hatch-Billops Collection, Spence recalled: "One of the interesting things about our survival was that we didn't know we were poor and unfortunate. . . . My mother insisted that we were very important people and she never gave that up. We were sustained by the fact that my mother was a well-educated woman. She loved to read – she had us get books for her from the library. She told us tales, and they were always tales of adventure." Her father, too, was a deep believer in education who often said, "When lands are gone and money spent, then learning is most excellent." Two of the sisters – Eulalie and Dora – developed an interest in theater. Dora, with Eulalie's coaching, was understudy for Rose McClendon in a production of Paul Green's *In Abraham's Bosom*.

In 1914 she began teaching English and elocution at Eastern District High School in Brooklyn. Around 1926 Spence, who had written a number of "little skits," met W. E. B. Du Bois and was inspired to become involved in the emerging black theater movement. Her comedy, *Fool's Errand*, produced by the Krigwa Players, Little Negro Theater of Harlem, won second prize at the National Little Theatre Tournament at the Frolic Theatre, New York, in 1927. The performance won the drama prize, although, according to Spence, it "didn't suit Dr. Du Bois." Spence recalls that "Dr. Du Bois wanted a propaganda play and I wrote a comedy." *Fool's Errand* is a lively one-act piece involving the pressures put by lady church members on a young man to marry his girlfriend when they suspect a pregnancy. Spence neatly reverses the situation – it is the bride's mother who is expecting, but the boyfriend has shown his true love by his willingness to marry the girl. This play shows Spence's considerable skill in drawing character and handling dialect. The righteous church sisters, in their "ill-fitting garments," emerge as both amusing and sympathetic characters, each with her own quirks. It is interesting to compare this play with Ada Gaines-Shelton's *Church Fight*.

Spence wrote other comedies, including *Foreign Mail*, awarded a second prize in the Krigwa Players contest sponsored by *Crisis* in October of 1926, and *The Starter* (1926), in which a young woman tries to get her boyfriend to marry her. This play prompted fan letters from as far west as California. In 1929 Spence directed the Dunbar Garden Players in Eugene O'Neill's *Before Breakfast* and her own *Joint Owners of Spain.*

According to Spence, "the only money I ever made from writing" came from the play *The Whipping.* It was based on a novel of the same name by Ray Flanagan which Spence saw reviewed in a newspaper. She contacted the publisher and the author, proposing a satirical play. Upon their agreement, she chose an agent (Century Play Company) from the phone book. The play was announced in *Variety* and would have opened in Bridgeport, Connecticut, in 1933, but at the last minute the production was canceled. Then the play was optioned and sold to Paramount Pictures but never produced.

Another play, *Undertow,* a one-act play set in a Harlem rooming house deals with a troubled marriage and infidelity. According to James Hatch, this play "belongs to no particular culture. . . . Not many black playwrights attempted what Eulalie Spence did: to write a play whose characters were undeniably black, but whose problem within the play was not ethnic." Hatch surmises that "she may be one of the first to write black characters into a non-racial plot." Hatch asks, "Should she be praised for extending the black experience on the stage, or censored for avoiding it?" Spence claims that *Undertow* is the only noncomedy she wrote. Unlike W. E. B. Du Bois, she believed that "a play should never be for propaganda; it cannot depend on propaganda for success." Throughout this period, Spence was an avid theatergoer, never missing one of Eugene O'Neill's plays.

Unfortunately, most of Spence's scripts have vanished. Despite our efforts, including inquiries to Samuel French, Inc., of Hollywood and Baker's Plays, Boston, we have located only *Fool's Errand, The Starter,* and *Undertow.* A play entitled *Help Wanted* by Joseph S. Mitchell (*Boston Saturday Evening Quill,* April 1929) is ascribed by Arata and Rotoli to Spence, but we do not believe that this pedestrian piece could have come from her spirited pen. A play called *Episode,* listed by Arata and Rotoli as appearing in *Archive,* April 1928 is not there.

Spence's work does not reflect the sociopolitical concerns current among other Afro-American women dramatists of the 1920s. Rather, she aspired to write whimsical comedy that could play to both black and white audiences. It hardly needs to be said that such a goal was almost unattainable in the segregated world of the 1920s and 1930s and it could have been this that led to Spence's later silence. She appears to have ceased writing plays after *The Whipping.*

She did go on to earn a B.A. degree from New York University in 1937 and an M.A. from Columbia in 1939, majoring in speech. Spence recalled that at Columbia she was a member of a drama group and was always being cast in male parts or old ladies "because I was very thin."

Spence, who did not marry, taught speech and drama at the Eastern District High School in Brooklyn, New York, until her retirement in 1958. She was a dedicated and demanding teacher, constantly taking her students, one of whom was Joseph Papp, to New York performances and even backstage. The New York City Teachers' Retirement System reports that she died on 7 March 1981.

In her capacity of drama critic writing for *Opportunity*, Spence deplored the weak quality of plays written by blacks, calling for dramas that "portray the life of people, their foibles . . . and their sorrows and ambitions and defeats." What was needed, she believed, was "a little more laughter, if you please, and fewer spirituals!" In another article, "Negro Art Players in Harlem" she gave a negative review of this drama company's production of Ridgely Torrence's *The Rider of Dreams*.

SELECT BIBLIOGRAPHY

Primary

Drama

"Being Forty."

"Brothers and Sisters of the Church Council." 1920s.

"La Divina Pastora." 1929.

"Episode." *Archive* (April 1928).

Fool's Errand. New York: Samuel French, 1927. (Samuel French Prize of $200 for an unpublished manuscript).

Foreign Mail. New York: Samuel French, 1927. (Second prize in 1926 *Crisis* contest. First performed 1927, New York City).

"Her" (one act). 1927.

"Hot Stuff." 1927 (third prize, shared with "Undertow," *Crisis* contest, December 1927).

"The Hunch" (one act). 1927. (Comedy of Harlem life; second prize, 1927 *Opportunity* contest).

The Starter (third prize, shared, *Opportunity* Contest, 1927)

"Undertow" (third prize, shared with "Hot Stuff," *Crisis* contest, December 1927).

Undertow. *Carolina Magazine* 59 (April 1929): 5-15.

"The Whipping" (three-act comedy based on a novel by Ray Flanagan).

IN ANTHOLOGIES

Hatch and Shine, *Black Theatre U.S.A.*, 1974. *Undertow*.

Locke and Gregory, *Plays of Negro Life* [1927] 1970. *The Starter*.

Nonfiction

"A Criticism of the Negro Drama As It Relates to the Negro Dramatist and Artist." *Opportunity* 6, no. 6 (June 1928): 180.

"Negro Art Players in Harlem." *Opportunity* 6, no. 12 (December 1928): 381.

Secondary Works

Arata, *More Black American Playwrights*, 1978.

Arata and Rotoli, *Black American Playwrights, 1800 to the Present*, 1976.

Belcher, "The Place of the Negro in the Evolution of the American Theatre," 1945.

Ellis, *Opportunity; A Journal of Negro Life*, 1971.

French, Fabre, Singh, and Fabre, *Afro-American Poetry and Drama*, 1979.

Hatch and Abdullah, *Black Playwrights, 1823-1977*, 1977.

Hatch-Billops Collection, New York City (audiotaped interview with Spence, 1973).

Hicklin, The American Negro Playwright, 1920-1964," 1965.

Kallenbach, *Index to Black American Literary Anthologies*, 1979.

Kellner, *The Harlem Renaissance*, 1984.

Matthews, *Black American Writers, 1773-1949*, 1975.

Mitchell, *Black Drama*, 1967.

Mitchell, *Voices of the Black Theatre*, 1975.

Monroe, "A Record of the Black Theatre in New York City: 1920-1929," 1980.

Perry, *The Harlem Renaissance*, 1982.

Rush, Myers, and Arata, *Black American Writers Past and Present*, 1975.

Walrond, Review of "Being Forty," 1924.

Williams, *American Black Women in the Arts and Social Sciences*, 1978.

SPENCER, ANNE BETHEL BANNISTER SCALES (1882-1976)

Poet

Librarian

Horticulturist

Anne Spencer was a major poet of the early twentieth century, but only thirty of her poems have been published. Upon her death, more poems and historical writings were left in varying states of completion and other pieces were lost when the garden house where she kept her papers was vandalized. It is hoped that the future may bring a definitive edition of her writings and detailed study of her life and career, for Spencer's art is both wideranging and complex.

The only child of divorced parents, Annie Bannister received no formal education until she was eleven years old. Her parents, Joel Cephus and Sarah Louise Scales Bannister, made a marriage of discordant personalities: Sarah was the daughter of a former slave woman and a wealthy Virginia aristocrat, and Joel was of Afro-American and Seminole ancestry. Annie's mother was overly concerned with manners and morals, and her father's only interest was securing economic independence. Joel Bannister opened a saloon in Martinsville, Virginia, and Annie spent a good deal of time there with him; he always insisted that the little girl entertain the male customers by parading up and down the long bar, charming everyone with her beauty. Sarah did not approve of the saloon, especially when her daughter was providing most of the entertainment. In 1887, she took Annie, and they moved to Bramwell, West Virginia.

Annie's mother then placed her as the foster child of Mr. and Mrs. William Dixie while Sarah worked to support herself and the child. In this segregated town, Annie nevertheless found a friend in Elsie Brown, a white girl who was a few years her senior. The townspeople came to accept their friendship, and Annie was able to cross the color barrier and live with no racial or social restrictions. This experience gave her the confidence to develop a personal philosophy that told her never to love or hate anything because of color.

Annie lived in Bramwell for six years, and during that time she acquired two passions that would follow her through her life. First, she came to love nature and the beauty of gardens, a feeling frequently reflected in her poetry. Second, she discovered reading. Mr. Dixie would frequently bring magazines home from his barber shop, and his wife would read stories from them to the children. When Annie was about eight or nine years old, she became determined to learn how to read the stories for herself. All the adults around her offered support, and by the time she was ten, she could read. However, her skills were rudimentary and did not compensate for the lack of a formal education.

Sarah would not allow her daughter to attend the free school for blacks that was located on the outskirts of Bramwell because most of the pupils there were children of miners. When her father discovered that his daughter had not been to school, he was outraged and insisted that Sarah enroll Annie in the free school. Sarah continued to protest, but when she learned of a boarding school for blacks in Lynchburg, her problem was solved. Joel agreed to pay the tuition, and in September 1893, Sarah boarded a train for Lynchburg. She was the youngest student at the school when she enrolled under the name Annie Bethel Scales, taking her mother's maiden name.

Annie had many problems in her first months at the Virginia Seminary owing to her lack of early education, but she quickly overcame these difficulties and graduated as the valedictorian of her class in 1899. Her six short years of formal education had been intensive and highly sophisticated, giving her an uncommon depth of knowledge and wisdom. While at the seminary, she met Edward Spencer through an exchange of tutoring, and they were married in 1901. Edward had worked on a buffet car between New York and Montreal, but after their marriage he won a bid as first parcel postman in Lynchburg. The Spencers bought a house and remained there for the rest of their lives.

Unlike most housewives, Annie was not burdened with the traditional duties of housewife and mother (she had three children: Bethel, Alroy, and Chauncey); her husband provided housekeepers, and in the early 1920s, Annie's mother came to live with the family, taking over management of the household. During this time, Annie was free to read, write, and tend to her elaborate garden. Edward not only helped his wife plant and tend her garden but built her a small one-room cottage, Edankraal, at its edge. It was in this house that she wrote most of her poetry and in the garden that she found peace and solace on such occasions as the death of her friend James Weldon Johnson. As she expresses it in the poem "For Jim, Easter Eve":

> Peace is here and in every season a quiet beauty.
> The sky is falling about me
> evenly to the compass . . .
> What is sorrow but tenderness now
> in this earth-close frame of land and sky
> falling constantly into horizons
> of east and west, north and south.

With the exception of "White Things" racial themes are absent from Spencer's poetry, though certainly not from her consciousness. Most of her poems are very restrained and intimate in tone, showing her moral and aesthetic strengths. Through her garden and her poetry, she sought to transcend mortality and escape the limitations society placed on her as a black woman. Few of her poems express her outspoken nature. (Spencer fought Jim Crow in Lynchburg, conducting a one-woman boycott of segregated public facilities and transportation.) She was active in volunteer community projects, such as building a library for the black citizens of Lynchburg. In December 1923, she gave up her leisurely life in order to help her fellow citizens; she went to work at the Jones Memorial Library (white) before becoming librarian at the Dunbar High School branch, which opened in 1924. Because Spencer refused to use the Jim Crow facilities in public transportation, she walked the two miles from her house.

Spencer met James Weldon Johnson through her association when he came to Lynchburg to establish a chapter of the NAACP. Johnson sent a poem of Spencer's ("Before the Feast of Shushan") to H. L. Mencken and then arranged for its publication in *Crisis* in 1920. Spencer was forty years old at the time. From this point, she became a well-known poet, publishing in such journals as *Opportunity* and *Palms*. Her poems were included in several of the anthologies published as representative of the Harlem Renaissance. Throughout, Spencer remained very modest about her talents, never publishing a collection. Only once did she herself submit a poem for publication; otherwise, her literary friends were responsible for the recognition given to her poems. She has been called a "sophisticated genteel lady poet" (in *Black and White*). Spencer experienced rejection as well, when she submitted an article and a story she hoped would be printed by the *New Republic or Dial.*

After she became known as a poet and an intellectual, Spencer opened her home to other literary figures, most of whom were traveling from northern to southern cities. Such notables as Paul and Eslanda Robeson,* W. E. B. Du Bois, Roland Hayes, Langston Hughes, and Georgia Douglas Johnson* used Spencer's home as a stopover point in their travels.

In 1945, Spencer retired from the Dunbar Library after twenty years of service. After this she sharply decreased her public and community activities. The death of her husband, Edward, at age eighty-eight in 1964 was, according to her biographer and critic J. Lee Greene, "almost more than she could bear," for Edward had been husband, lover, father, and friend to her. She continued to write and edit poems, though near the end of her life, she was stricken with cancer and her eyesight deteriorated. She died on 27 July 1975, at age ninety-two.

That Spencer was a feminist can be claimed based on the poem "Letter to My Sister" (Spencer was an only child). This poem begins boldly, "It is dangerous for a woman to defy the gods" and then enumerates a series of pitfalls she must avoid if she is to conserve pride and dignity, all the while making herself nearly invisible. This poem can be read as a recommendation for self-sacrifice, but only if one ignores the arch irony of its tone. Gender philosophy also appears in the poems "Before the Feast at Shushan," "Po' Little Lib" and "The Lemming: O Sweden."

According to Greene, Spencer's constant themes are the search for beauty, love, and humanity: "as a poet [Spencer] probably has more in common with nineteenth-century American writers than she does either with twentieth-century American poets or with the general development of black American literature." In analyzing the poems, Greene finds a pattern: they begin "with a clash, doubt, or agony but then take an elevated course that ends in triumph of hope and affirmation connected with defiance."

But Spencer's poetry is more complex than Greene's excellent and detailed analyses demonstrate. In "Lines to a Nasturtium" we find alliterations and oxymorons that create intricate patterns of sound and meaning. With a syntax that has a slightly archaic flavor, Spencer produced poems that are often hermetic, always mesmerizing in their subtle combinatory art.

Erlene Stetson, calling Spencer a methodical and meticulous artist, points out the predicament of the woman writer at the time of the Harlem Renaissance: beset by the tacit demand that she be a genteel versifier, that she minister to the needs of the male writer, that she conform to the code of "true Negro womanhood," it was a narrow space indeed that remained for her art. Stetson rightly concludes that "Spencer's poetry, while it abounds in an array of stylistic devices, both imagistic and metaphorical, begs to be explored for its polished diction, its sense of subtle humor, and its quality."

The garden and home of Anne Spencer have been designated as a Virginia historic landmark and recognized in the National Register of Historic Places.

SELECT BIBLIOGRAPHY

Primary

Poetry

"Before the Feast of Shushan." *Crisis* (February 1920).

"Dunbar." *Crisis* (November 1920).

"Grapes: Still Life." *Crisis* (October 1929).

"Lady, Lady." *Survey Graphic* (March 1935).

"Lines to a Nasturtium." *Palms* (October 1926).

"Requiem." *Lyric* (Spring 1931).

"Rime for a Christmas Baby." *Opportunity* (December 1927).

"White Things." *Crisis* (March 1923).

IN ANTHOLOGIES

Cullen, *Caroling Dusk*, 1927. "At the Carnival"; "Creed"; "Dunbar"; "I Have a Friend"; "Innocence"; "Life-long, Poor Browning"; "Lines to a Nasturtium"; "Neighbors"; "Questing"; "Substitution."

Johnson, Charles S., *Ebony and Topaz,* 1927. "Letter to My Sister" (a revised version of "Sybil Warns Her Sister."

Kerlin, *Negro Poets and Their Poems,* [1923] 1935. "At the Carnival."

Locke, *The New Negro* [1925] 1968. "Lady, Lady."

Stetson, *Black Sister,* 1981. "At the Carnival"; "Before the Feast of Shushan"; "Lady, Lady"; "Letter to My Sister"; "Substitution."

Secondary

Bontemps, *American Negro Poetry*, 1969.

Bontemps and Hughes, *The Poetry of the Negro, 1746-1970,* 1970.

Campbell, Dorothy, *Index to Black American Writers in Collective Biographies,* 1983.

Chapman, *Index to Black Poetry,* 1974.

Chapman, *Index to Poetry by Black American Women,* 1986.

Ellis, *Opportunity; A Journal of Negro Life,* 1971.

Greene, J. Lee, "Anne Spencer of Lynchburg," 1978.

Greene, J. Lee, *Time's Unfading Garden: Anne Spencer's Life and Poetry*, 1977. [Appendix contains forty-two of Spencer's poems, those listed above and the following: "1975"; "We Remember the Rev. Philip I. Morris"; "Never Underrate the Courage"; "Sybil Speaks"; "God Never Planted a Garden"; "Change"; "Thou Art Come to Us, O God, This Year"; "He Said"; "Black Man o' Mine"; "For E.A.S."; "Any Wife to Any Husband: A Derived Poem"; "Dear Langston"; "Ascetic"; "Liability"; "Failure"; "Luther P. Jackson"; "The Sevignes"; "The Lemming: O Sweden"; [Untitled]; "Po' Little Lib"; "Epitome"; "Earth, I Thank You."

Index to Poetry in Periodicals, 1920-1924, 1983.

Index to Poetry in Periodicals, 1925-1929, 1983.

Kallenbach, *Index to Black American Literary Anthologies*, 1979.

Kellner, *The Harlem Renaissance*, 1984.

Perry, *The Harlem Renaissance*, 1982.

Rose Bibliography Project, *Analytical Guide and Indexes to "The Crisis," 1910-1960*, 1975.

Rush, Myers, and Arata, *Black American Writers Past and Present*, 1975.

Sims-Wood, *The Progress of Afro-American Women*, 1980.

Spradling, *In Black and White*, 1980.

Stetson, "Anne Spencer," 1978.

Williams, *American Black Women in the Arts and Social Sciences*, 1978.

TARRY, ELLEN (1906-)

Journalist
Autobiographer
Children's writer

Ellen Tarry, sensitive to the evils of stereotyping and the need for black children to have positive literary models, pioneered the creation of a children's literature that transcends the familiar white middle-class framework and deals with the life and experiences of black inner-city children. Her work as a journalist and a Catholic activist has also aimed toward interracial understanding. According to correspondence we received from Tarry, she continues to be active as a writer and lecturer.

Ellen Tarry, the eldest of three girls, was born to John Barber and Eula Meadows Tarry on 26 September 1906 in Birmingham, Alabama, where she attended public schools. Christened in the Methodist Episcopalian church, at age twelve she joined the Congregational church of which her father was a deacon. But after attending St. Francis de Sales School in Rock Castle, Virginia, Tarry became increasingly interested in Catholicism and on 8 December 1922, made her First Holy Communion. Her Catholicism has continued to be a motivating force in her life.

Tarry went on to State Normal School (later Alabama State University) and a succession of teaching positions in the Birmingham schools and Knights of Columbus Evening School. She also found a job with the *Birmingham Truth*, the organ of the Knights of Pythias and the Court of Calanthes, which she held from 1927 to 1929. Her column, Negroes of Note, was a mine of information on the heritage of the Negro. Inspired by articles on the life of Harriet Tubman, she spoke out in editorials against segregation and discrimination.

In 1929, Ellen left Birmingham for New York. Her goal was to attend Columbia University, but the depression intervened. Employment was scarce, but she found work waitressing. Her autobiography reveals that she could easily have passed for white, but she refused "to sail under false colors." As a result she was forced to postpone her plans for writing.

Tarry then joined the Negro Writers' Guild, a group of journalists and creative writers where she met Sterling Brown, E. Simms Campbell, and Claude McKay, who introduced her to Augusta Savage, James Weldon Johnson, and his wife, Grace Nail Johnson. She learned from children's librarian Augusta Baker that the Bureau of Educational Experiments (later Bank Street College) was offering a scholarship to a Negro writer with teaching experience. Tarry applied and with it she attended the Cooperative School for Student Teachers (1937-39), specializing in children's literature. Tarry credits Lucy Sprague Mitchell, founder of Bank Street College, as her mentor.

Another mentor was the Baroness Catherine de Hueck who was in charge of Friendship House, a Harlem Catholic Center. This connection began for Tarry a fruitful career of research, public speaking, and writing. Here she conducted a story hour for the neighborhood children. Many of her children's books were inspired by her experiences at the house.

In 1940, she began to sell articles to the *Catholic World* and *Commonweal* while working on two of her juvenile manuscripts. Responding to Richard Wright's *Native Son*, Tarry published an essay, "Native Daughter," in *Commonweal* in 1940. The article was an indictment by a colored woman of segregation and discrimination in white America. In her autobiography, Tarry compares her sociopolitical stance to that of her friend Richard Wright: He "was from Mississippi and I was from Alabama, but the difference between us was that the Catholic Church had extended open arms to me and only the Communist Party had offered Wright the opportunity at that time to fight the injustices heaped upon his people. But for the Sisters of the Blessed Sacrament, I too might have become a Communist."

Janie Bell, her first children's book, was published in 1940. It is the story of a Negro baby, abandoned by her parents in a garbage can and eventually adopted by a white nurse. One of the earliest attempts to include the black experience in mainstream literature it suggested the need for interracial harmony and love. In her autobiography Tarry speaks of the dearth of books portraying blacks constructively: "A quarter of a century ago when I criticized Claude McKay's *Home to Harlem*, there were few published books in which a Negro protagonist was depicted as a man or woman with whom the American reading public could identify, or whom they could love or respect.

A few courageous editors and publishers have changed this. . . . In the juvenile field, when I started my teaching career, there were almost no books for young readers which showed the Negro as other than Uncle Remus or Little Black Sambo."

Her second manuscript, *Hezekiah Horton*, was published in 1942 by the Viking Press. Hezekiah is a black boy living in Harlem who longs for a red automobile. When Mr. Ed, the owner of the car, tells him that he will teach him to drive and one day employ him as his chauffeur, Hezekiah is highly motivated to do his homework, in such a hurry is he to grow up to drive that car. That a black child protagonist was portrayed with appeal and dignity was historically significant at a time when virtually no black role models, save stereotypes, appeared in children's literature. Also notable is the depiction of the interracial friendship between Hezekiah and Mr. Ed. To celebrate *Hezekiah Horton*'s publication, the James Weldon Johnson Literary Guild held an autographing party for Tarry at the Hotel Theresa in Harlem.

As a journalist, Tarry did investigative reporting for the *Amsterdam News*, often attacking discrimination, especially in the armed forces. Between 1943 and 1944, she became the assistant director of the USO Club in Anniston, Alabama. There she met and married Rudolph Maurice Patton, but immediately left him when she discovered that "the contract had not been made in good faith." Tarry's daughter, Elizabeth Tarry Patton, was born on 16 November 1944.

In 1945, Tarry continued her activist career as the regional director of the New York National Catholic Community Services Club (NCCS-USO) and at the same time began collaborating with Marie Hall Ets on a picture book, *My Dog Rinty*.

My Dog Rinty has a more complex plot than Tarry's earlier books, as it recounts the efforts of little David to overcome all obstacles and keep his dog, Rinty. Young children can identify not only with David but with the spirited dog whose behavior upsets adults. The story emphasizes the values of socially acceptable behavior, hard work, and ingenuity. It is illustrated with original photographs of a Harlem family and Harlem landmarks such as the Harlem River Apartments, the 135th Street Library, the Hotel Theresa, and other sites. Tarry recalls in her autobiography that getting permission to take these pictures was an enormous task, owing to community suspicion of "anything connected with the white man's world." These photographs are now part of the James Weldon Johnson Memorial Collection at Yale University.

In 1950, Tarry published another Hezekiah Horton story, *The Runaway Elephant*, which was based on the actual escape of a bull elephant from a zoo. Hezekiah becomes a hero when he leads Mr. Ed, the newspaperman, to the elephant's former trainer. Mr. Ed and Hezekiah provide the thirty loaves of bread and multiple jars of peanut butter that aid in the elephant's safe return to the Bronx Zoo. Again, ingenuity and hard work are rewarded monetarily and a black child becomes a positive role model for young readers.

Tarry tells the details of her career, including her encounters with discrimination and the positive rewards for persistence in her absorbing book, *The Third Door: The Autobiography of an American Negro Woman* (1955). Tarry's recollections are richly descriptive and detailed, portraying the lurid contradictions of segregation and the sweet taste of her own professional success, and the satisfaction of living to see social betterment for her people.

According to Sylvia Dannett, Ellen Tarry "has not allowed prejudice to warp her perspectives or dim her optimism. On the final page of *The Third Door*, she looks ahead to a time when "there will be no door in America marked 'colored' and no door marked 'white.' Instead there will be the third door, free from racial designations–through which all Americans, all of God's children, will walk in peace and dignity."

Tarry's books for teenage readers include *Katherine Drexel: Friend of the Neglected* (1958), *Martin de Porres, Saint of the New World* (1963), *Young Jim: The Early Years of James Weldon Johnson* (1967), and *The Other Toussaint: A Post-Revolutionary Black* (1981).

SELECT BIBLIOGRAPHY

Primary

Fiction

CHILDREN'S BOOKS

Janie Bell. New York: Garden City Publishing Co., 1940.

Hezekiah Horton. New York: Viking, 1942.

My Dog Rinty. With Marie Hall Ets. New York: Viking, 1946.

The Runaway Elephant. New York: Viking, 1950.

Nonfiction

"The City of St. Jude." *Catholic World* (October 1941): 73-76.

"I Found Peace." *Missionary* (July 1942): 299-305.

Katherine Drexel: Friend of the Neglected. New York: Farrar, Straus & Cudahy, 1958.

"Know Thyself, America!" *Catholic Digest* (June 1942): 298-303.

"Lest We Forget Our Heritage." *Inter-Racial Review* (May 1940): 74-76.

Martin de Porres, Saint of the New World. New York: Farrar, Straus & Cudahy, 1963.

"Native Daughter." *Commonweal* (April 1940): 524-26.

The Other Toussaint: A Post-Revolutionary Black. Boston: Daughters of St. Paul, 1981.

"They Called Her Moses." *Catholic World* (June 1941): 314-20.

The Third Door: The Autobiography of an American Negro Woman. New York: David McKay Co., 1955. Reprint. New York: Guild, 1966; New York: Negro Universities Press, 1971.

"Why Is Not the Negro Catholic?" *Catholic World* (Fall 1940): 542-46.

Young Jim: The Early Years of James Weldon Johnson. New York: Dodd, Mead, 1967.

Secondary

Campbell, Dorothy, *Index to Black American Writers in Collective Biographies*, 1983.

Dannett, *Profiles of Negro Womanhood*, 1964.

Ellis, *Opportunity; A Journal of Negro Life*, 1971.

French, Fabre, Singh, and Fabre, *Afro-American Poetry and Drama, 1760-1975*, 1979.

Herman, *Women in Particular*, 1984.

Hopkins, *Books Are by People*, 1969.

Lerner, *Black Women in White America*, 1972.

Locher, *Contemporary Authors*, 1978.

Low and Clift, *Encyclopedia of Black America*, 1981.

Matney, *Who's Who among Black Americans*, 1978.

Matthews, *Black American Writers, 1773-1949*, 1975.

Page, *Selected Black American Authors*, 1977.

Richardson, *Black Women and Religion*, 1980.

Rush, Myers, and Arata, *Black American Writers Past and Present*, 1975.

Scally, *Negro Catholic Writers, 1900-1943*, 1945.

Sims-Wood, *The Progress of Afro-American Women*, 1980.

Spradling, *In Black and White*, 1980.

Turner, *Afro-American Writers*, 1970.

TERRELL, MARY ELIZA ("MOLLIE") CHURCH (1863-1954)

Journalist

Activist

Though we are focusing on her writings, Mary Terrell is best known as a forceful leader, both in the nineteenth and the twentieth centuries, in the movements for civil rights, women's rights, and world peace. A contemporary of Booker T. Washington, she was more outspoken than he on discrimination; she believed in breaking segregation by crossing Jim Crow lines at every opportunity.

Terrell was born at the end of the Civil War in Memphis. Her paternal grandfather was Captain C. B. Church, a benevolent slaveholder who sympathized with the Union. Her mother, who spoke French as well as English, had been a slave but never spoke to her daughter of the fact. From a comfortable home Mary was sent north for her secondary and higher education. When she received her B.A. degree from Oberlin College in 1884, there had been only two colored women to receive a B.A. degree in the United States.

Her first job was teaching reading, writing, mineralogy, and French at Wilberforce University, Ohio. She declined the post of registrar at Oberlin College and settled in Washington, D.C., where she taught Latin and German at Colored High School. There she met Robert Heberton Church, an 1884 graduate of Harvard, who was later a municipal judge in Washington, D.C., for twenty years; they married in 1891.

Marriage brought her teaching career to a close – married women were not permitted to teach in most schools in the country. In 1895 she was appointed to the District of Columbia Board of Education, the first black woman in the country to hold such a position. In Washington, she also enlisted in club work among women and campaigned for women's suffrage, becoming a friend of Susan B. Anthony. (Her husband, too, believed ardently in woman suffrage at a time when few men took that stand.) The Terrell's daughter Phyllis, named after Phyllis Wheatley, the early American black poet, was born in 1898. In 1905 the Terrells adopted a second daughter, niece Mary Church.

For a long time Mary Terrell was a member of the Booklovers' Club and the Bethel Literary and Historical Society, the oldest organization established by colored people in this country. She was a charter member and the first president of the National Association of Colored Women (1896-1901) and a founding member of the NAACP. As a U.S. delegate to the Geneva International Congress of Women in Berlin (1904), she was the only American who could address the assembly in fluent German, French, and English. After World War I she worked with the War Camp Community Service to establish educational programs for black girls nationwide. In 1919 she was a delegate, as was Jane Addams, to the International Peace Congress in Zurich. Once more, she addressed the assemblage in German. Through the 1920s, Mary Church Terrell continued to fill her days with people and causes. She served on the executive committee for the Women's International League for Peace and Freedom and was president of the Southwest Community House, a settlement house in Washington. She was widowed in 1925.

Later she went to Chicago to head Ruth Hanna McCormick's campaign for the U. S. Senate (1930). Although Chicago black women, including Ida B. Wells, protested mightily because an "outsider" had been brought in, Mrs. Terrell spent the months before the election traveling through the state lining up votes for McCormick. Three years later she was in New York to work for the reelection of Herbert Hoover under the auspices of the Republican National Committee. In 1920, when women voted for the first time, Terrell was appointed by the Republican National Committee (during the Harding administration). Through the 1930s she was director of Work among Colored Women in the East and continued to appear before committees in Congress to urge the necessity of passing an antilynching bill. She visited every president of the United States, from Harrison (whom she saw with Frederick Douglass) to Wilson urging them to speak out against lynching.

During the depression of the 1930s she worked for six months as a clerk in the Emergency Relief Administration, losing her job after her supervisor discovered that she was not white. In 1953 she headed a group opposing segregation in the District of Columbia that succeeded in abolishing it in Washington's public accommodations.

For many years she hoped to become a "successful writer" but the *Washington Post* was the only newspaper in which one of her stories appeared ("Venus and the Night Doctors") – "my very first was also my last which managed to burst into print." Because she was a black writer whose subject matter was race ("All of my stories were based on the Race Problem") and whose point of view ran counter to the popular images of blacks as delinquents or buffoons, she could find no publisher. As she revealed in her autobiography, "The editors objected to having certain conditions which obtain in the United States broadcast to the world. . . . It has been a bitter disappointment to me that I did not succeed as a story writer."

Terrell's writing set a benchmark for impassioned, fiery, and factual indictment of the evils of racism. She was unrestrained in denouncing wrongs and in her political advocacy, as in her support for the presidential candidacy of Coolidge in 1924. In her column for the *Chicago Defender* (November 10 (?), 1939) she aired opinions such as these: "The white ministers of this country roll up their sleeves and wade right into practically any subject – prize fights, politics, and everything else except the injustice and the outrages perpetrated upon a group of citizens numbering at least one tenth of the population of the country." Elsewhere in the same column she reports on a play dealing with the Sacco-Vanzetti trial and execution, *Gods of the Lightning*, reviewed by a British critic. She quotes his comment: "If I were an American, I should hate to think of any foreigner seeing this play." Terrell observes that Sacco and Vanzetti were deliberately murdered by process of law because they engaged in a strike, and then adds, "I wonder what this Englishman would say if he knew how many people in a certain group were shot, beaten, burned to death by mobs, while the murderers not only escape punishment but are allowed the correctness of the results which were reached."

The personal papers of Terrell, on microfilm at the Boston Public Library, indicate that she wrote numerous articles in such black publications as the *Chicago Defender, North American Review, Washington Tribune, Norfolk Journal and Guide, Howard Magazine, New Era* (Boston), *A.M.E. Church Review* (Philadelphia), *Southern Workman* (Hampton, Virginia), *Freeman* (Indianapolis), and *Afro-American* (Baltimore). Also, she published in the *Washington Evening Star, Washington Post*, and *Sunday Boston Globe*.

Terrell, Mary Eliza Church

SELECT BIBLIOGRAPHY

Primary

Nonfiction

A Colored Woman in a White World [autobiography]. Washington, D.C.: Ransdell, 1940. Reprint. New York: Arno Press, 1980.

Secondary

Barton, *Witnesses for Freedom*, [1948] 1976.

Campbell, Dorothy, *Index to Black American Writers in Collective Biographies*, 1983.

French, Fabre, Singh, and Fabre, *Afro-American Poetry and Drama, 1760-1975*, 1979.

Herman, *Women in Particular*, 1984.

Low and Clift, *Encyclopedia of Black America*, 1981.

Matthews, *Black American Writers, 1773-1949*, 1975.

Salk, *A Layman's Guide to Negro History*, 1967.

Sherman, *Invisible Poets*, 1974.

Sims-Wood, *The Progress of Afro-American Women*, 1980.

Spradling, *In Black and White*, 1980.

Sterling, *Black Foremothers: Three Lives*, 1979.

Williams, *American Black Women in the Arts and Social Sciences*, 1978.

THOMPSON, CLARA ANN (1869-1949)

Poet

Born at Rossmoyne (presently the Silverton, Deer Park, area of Cincinnati) Ohio, to John Henry and Clara Jane Thompson, both of whom were born slaves in Virginia, Clara Ann Thompson attended the Amity School (in a log cabin sixteen feet square) and studied with private tutors, preparing to teach. She taught for a short time in the public schools, but her principal work was as a public reader. She also contributed numerous poems to newspapers. Clara Ann was a member of the Baptist church and later of St. Andrew Episcopal Church in Mount Healthy, the NAACP, and the YWCA. She died at the home of a niece in Rosemont, having lived all of her eighty years in the Cincinnati area. She and her sister never married. Photos of her in her books, *Songs by the Wayside* and *A Garland of Poems*, show an intense and unsmiling dark-skinned woman in a lace-collared dress.

The Thompson children included several poets: a brother, Aaron Belford Thompson (5 April 1873-26 January 1929) and a sister, Priscilla Jane Thompson* (1871-1942). Between 1899 and 1926, the three published seven volumes of poetry. The eldest brother, Garland Yancy, to whom Clara was devoted, was a sculptor in wood.

Her first collected work was *Songs by the Wayside*, published by her at her brother Aaron's small private printing press in Rossmoyne, Ohio, in 1908. Another volume, *A Garland of Poems*, was published in Boston eighteen years later. Thompson's poems deserve an attention they have never received. The only critic to devote comment to them is Newman Ivey White, who finds them "of better quality than those of her brother and sister. She has more restraint." But White unfairly judges that Thompson "has no breadth of view, or intensity, or much imagination, and not much culture." His harsh opinion should be revised in the broader context of Afro-American and women's literary history.

In *Songs by the Wayside*, poems of a simple, pious nature alternate with lyrics dealing with the enduring nature of grief ("To My Dead Brother"), time flowing into eternity ("The Dying Year"), regret for lost love and friendship ("If Thou Should'st Return," "Parted") and beauty in nature ("An Autumn Day"). Especially interesting are the poems that, in the guise of a folk character, Uncle Rube, offer wry and ironic comments in dialect on how quickly whites fault blacks, but fail to acknowledge their achievements ("Uncle Rube's Defense," "Uncle Rube on the Race Problem," "Uncle Rube to the Young People"). In another poem, "The Easter Bonnet," a black maid disdains the outmoded hat given her by her employer, while her husband laughingly chides her for "hinting for the white-folks' cast-off clothes." Thompson's humor appears in other poems: "Johnny's Pet Superstition,"

"Mrs. Johnson Objects." Religion is more prominent than in her brother's or sister's work.

A Garland of Poems features many poems written for religious or civic occasions, such as "Easter, 1919," "The New Schoolhouse: Mount Healthy, Ohio," and "Our Heroes," composed for the return of the black troops to Cincinnati from the First World War. There is another "Uncle Rube" poem commenting on church behavior and more poems in which hope is counterposed to abiding pain and gloom. In a more lyrical vein, Thompson alludes to a romantic loss ("Temptation.") Her most outspoken poem is "What Mean This Bleating of the Sheep"; it rails against "that other slavery" which endures beyond physical emancipation. Thompson's foreword to this collection says, "I sometimes tell my friends that the writing of poetry has been thrust upon me – I write it because I must – and in presenting this little volume to the public, I do it, not so much with the wish for popularity or fame, but with the satisfaction that I have obeyed the commands of my somewhat despotic Muse." Her consciousness of racial tensions in her times comes through when she adds that "I have endeavored to present both sides of the subject, knowing that no problem can be truly solved in any other way."

SELECT BIBLIOGRAPHY

Primary

Poetry

A Garland of Poems. Boston: Christopher Publishing House, 1926.

Songs by the Wayside. Rossmoyne, Ohio, 1908.

IN ANTHOLOGIES

Sherman, *Collected Black Women's Poetry*, vol. 2, 1988.

Shockley, *Afro-American Women Writers, 1746-1933*, 1988. "Uncle Rube on the Race Problem."

Stetson, *Black Sister*, 1981. "His Answer"; "Mrs. Johnson Objects."

UNPUBLISHED

"There Came Wise Men," 1923.

Secondary

Campbell, Dorothy, *Index to Black American Writers in Collective Biographies*, 1983.

Chapman, *Index to Black Poetry*, 1974.

Cincinnati Enquirer (20 March 1949): 3:2.

Coyle, *Ohio Authors and Their Books*, 1962.

Dabney, *Cincinnati's Colored Citizens*, 1926.

French, Fabre, Singh, and Fabre, *Afro-American Poetry and Drama, 1760-1975*, 1979.

Kallenbach, *Index to Black American Literary Anthologies*, 1979.

Matthews, *Black American Writers, 1773-1949*, 1975.

Porter, *North American Negro Poets*, 1945.

Reardon and Thorsen, *Poetry by American Women, 1900-1975*, 1979.

Rush, Myers, and Arata, *Black American Writers Past and Present*, 1975.

Sherman, *Invisible Poets*, 1974.

Stetson, *Black Sister*, 1981.

White and Jackson, *Anthology of Verse by American Negroes*, [1924] 1968.

Williams, *American Black Women in the Arts and Social Sciences*, 1978.

THOMPSON, ELOISE ALBERTA VERONICA BIBB (1878-1928)

Poet

Journalist

Short-story writer

Playwright

Eloise Bibb Thompson and her husband were members of a California-based group of writers on racial concerns who called themselves the Ink Slingers. According to a letter in Gwendolyn Bennett's Ebony Flute column in the December 1926 issue of *Opportunity*, the organization came into existence with the help of Charles Spurgeon Johnson.

Eloise Alberta Veronica Bibb was born in New Orleans, Louisiana, on 29 June 1878. She was the daughter of U.S. Customs inspector Charles H. and Catherine Adele Bibb. Bred and educated in New Orleans during her early years, Bibb published her first volume of poetry at the age of seventeen. *Poems* (1895) is a collection of sentimental poems whose epic subjects – inspired by history, classical mythology, and Judeo-Christian legend – drown in romantic treacle. The only poem addressing black history, apart from the more affecting eulogies, is "Eliza, in *Uncle Tom's Cabin*," which resolves the trauma of the sale of Eliza's baby by reuniting them in heaven. Thompson dedicated one of the poems in this book to her literary colleague and friend Alice Dunbar-Nelson.*

For two years (1899-1901) she attended the Oberlin Academy preparatory school and taught in the New Orleans public schools for two years. In 1903, Bibb entered Howard University and graduated from the Teachers' College in 1908. After holding a position as head resident of the Colored Social Settlement in Washington, D.C., until 1911, Eloise Bibb, a Catholic, was wed to Noah D. Thompson, a Negro journalist and himself a Catholic. Upon moving to Los Angeles in 1911, the Thompsons became involved in church activities. Eloise also wrote special feature articles for the *Los Angeles Sunday Tribune* and the *Morning Sun*, as well as articles and poems for popular magazines and local diocese publications.

The Thompsons actively spoke out on racial issues in front of multicolored audiences. During the stirrings of the Harlem Renaissance, Eloise Bibb Thompson began writing dramas to reflect this voice. Controversy surrounded her first play, *A Reply to the Clansman*. Though the play was optioned for production, "complications" soon arose and Eloise was forced to hire a lawyer for its return. The play was reviewed by nine theatrical and film professionals (including D. W. Griffith) – some producers, some critics. Though each agreed that Thompson's drama was "profoundly interesting," "excellent material," and "a historical masterpiece," they all declined the opportunity to produce it – even those who had already invested money in anticipation of staging it. They were obviously dissuaded by the fact that Thompson's play was a response to Thomas Dixon's novel, *The Clansman*, an account glorifying the Ku Klux Klan, which was later made into D. W. Griffith's film *The Birth of a Nation* in 1915. As Cecil B. DeMille, one of the nine, said, "The public intent on pure entertainment would scarcely be in the mood." Of Thompson's other plays, three were produced: *Caught* (1920), performed by the Playcrafters at the Gamut Club, *Africans* (or *Africannus*) (1922), produced at the Los Angeles Grand Theatre, and *Cooped Up* (1924), which was staged at the New York City Lafayette Theatre and for which she won an honorable mention in the May 1925 issue of *Opportunity*. *Cooped Up*, produced by the Ethiopian Art Players, was universally lauded.

Thompson also published two short stories dealing with Afro-Americans in New Orleans Creole society in *Opportunity*. "Masks" and "Mademoiselle 'Tasie – A Story" are interesting mixtures of cultural examination and dialogue. In paragraphs of rambling narrative Thompson discusses the history of blacks in Creole society, particularly focusing on race prejudice between darker-skinned and lighter-skinned Afro-Americans; some black Creole families not only believed themselves superior to black Americans but also held Afro-Americans as slaves.

Early in "Mademoiselle 'Tasie – A Story" the author declares "Be pleased to know . . . that there are colored Creoles as well as white Creoles, just as there are Creole eggs and Creole cabbages." Mademoiselle 'Tasie, "of an exceptional Creole family," is a thirty-seven-year-old woman with crinkled red hair who must not be seen on the streets with "an American Negro with big ears" – a dreaded spectacle for a Creole of her aristocratic stature. "A perfect picture of poverty trying to be genteel," she is humbled when she must work for a former slave of her family because she is not able to earn a living. Pressured by her high society peers, Mademoiselle 'Tasie fearfully but definitively casts aside her snobbery to marry dark-skinned, forty-year-old Titus, a prosperous businessman who promises to take care of her.

In "Masks" the psychological complexities of passing and color surface as the author places two mulattoes, Julie (a quadroon) and Paupet (an octoroon), in the context of the quadroon quarter of Old New Orleans. Julie's grandfather, also a quadroon but with discernible African features, excels at many things. Frustrated at the limitations racism puts on his freedom, he likens it to a mask that his oppressors attach to him, beyond which he cannot and will not see – a mask he cannot escape. One day he announces, "I have found a formula for greatness! It reads, Thou shalt be seen wearing a white man's face." This declaration leads him to set up a workshop to make masks out of paper, trying to imitate Nature's version of the white man's face. Moved by her grandfather, Julie goes further with the idea of passing. She intentionally marries "the whitest octoroon she has ever seen," with the hope that her children may wear "the mask" of passing and escape the injustices she has suffered because of her skin color.

Mystery surrounds both the whereabouts of Thompson's published plays and the circumstances of her death. A eulogy in the February 1928 issue of *Opportunity* praises her talent and forthright approach, regretting how abruptly death ended her potential.

SELECT BIBLIOGRAPHY

Primary

Drama

"Africans," 1922.

"Caught," 1920.

"Cooped Up," 1924.

A Friend of Democracy, 1920.

A Reply to the Clansman, 1915.

Poetry

Poems. Boston: Monthly Review Press, 1895.

IN ANTHOLOGIES

Sherman, *Collected Black Women's Poetry*, vol. 4, 1988.

Shockley, *Afro-American Women Writers, 1746-1933*, 1988. "Gerarda"; "Tribute."

Fiction

"Mademoiselle 'Tasie – A Story." *Opportunity* (September 1925): 172-276.

"Masks." *Opportunity* (October 1927): 300-2.

Secondary

Arata and Rotoli, *Black American Playwrights, 1800 to the Present*, 1976.

Beasley, *Negro Trailblazers of California*, 1919.

Campbell, Dorothy, *Index to Black American Writers in Collective Biographies*, 1983.

Ellis, *Opportunity; A Journal of Negro Life*, 1971.

Fairbanks and Engeldinger, *Black American Fiction*, 1978.

Hatch and Abdullah, *Black Playwrights, 1823-1977*, 1977.

Molette, *"Black Women Playwrights: They Speak. Who Listens?"* 1976.

Porter, *North American Negro Poets*, 1945.

Rush, Myers, and Arata, *Black American Writers Past and Present*, 1975.

Scally, *Negro Catholic Writers 1900-1943*, 1945.

Sherman, *Invisible Poets*, 1974.

THOMPSON, ERA BELL (1906-1986)

Editor

Journalist

Autobiographer

Feminist

Though her autobiography was published only in 1946, Era Bell Thompson was born on 10th August 1906, and was therefore a contemporary of such writers as Dorothy West.* Her autobiography relates that she grew up in Des Moines, Iowa, the only girl in a family of six. Later, her family moved to North Dakota where she braved the harsh and bitterly cold winters of the prairies and learned about farming from her father who had formerly been a waiter, cook, and coal miner. She lost her mother at a young age, but matured quickly under the guidance of her father and other relatives and neighbors.

Era Bell attended elementary school and high school in North Dakota, and it was then that she realized her ambition to go to college. She enrolled at North Dakota State University in Grand Forks. A bright student, she worked hard at her studies while paying her way by doing housework and babysitting. Thompson was also a member of the basketball team and ran track. She established five state records and tied two national intercollegiate women's track records.

She started writing while in the university, with articles for a class in rhetoric. Then she wrote a column for the lovelorn in the university's newspaper, the *Student*. By the end of the year, she was the women's sports editor and all-varsity in soccer.

Thompson had to give up sports and the university because of ill health, and work was hard to find. She tried her luck in Chicago, working first as a temporary stenographer in a law office and then at a magazine office, proofreading, writing advertising copy, and reviewing books written by Negroes. As she recounts in *American Daughter*, her autobiography, "I earned an extra dollar for each book I reviewed. It was during the height of the Negro renaissance in literature, in the late twenties, when the Claude McKays, the Langston Hugheses, the Rudolph Fishers, and others were in the midst of their writing. Du Bois' *The Dark Princess* impressed me more than did any of the others, for never before had I heard black beautified. . . . His words sang, giving off a haunting cadence, a mystic something that set him on a separate hill."

She later returned to Grand Forks where she met a Dr. Riley, a minister who was very involved with the issue of education for Afro-Americans and who would in the future help her go back to college. Meanwhile she found a job as a typist for the *Bugle*, a black Minneapolis weekly, where she later wrote features and advertising copy as well as reported straight news.

When the minister was elected the president of Dawn College in Iowa, she moved with the family from North Dakota to that state where she finished work for her degree. After her graduation in 1933, she moved to Chicago once more to look for a job. After months of searching, she found a job with the Department of Public Works as a senior typist. During that time she became increasingly aware of antiwhite prejudice among black people that seemed to her as deplorable as white bias against blacks.

Thompson continued her journalism studies with night classes at Northwestern University. At work there was discontent because people were being laid off. Banking on her fine sense of humor, she began a one-page newspaper, "poking fun at the higher-ups and flattering her best friends." The paper was named the *Giggle Sheet*, and about a year later, she had saved enough money to travel in the eastern United States. After three years, when the newspaper had grown to ten pages, she traveled throughout the West.

After she returned she worked as an interviewer for the Illinois and the United States Employment services for five years. With the support of a fellowship in midwestern studies from the Newberry Library, Thompson published her autobiography *American Daughter* (1946), written with the tongue-in-cheek humor and gentle self-deprecation that had become her trademark. In 1947, she began to work with the *Negro Digest* as an editor and then became the associate editor for *Ebony*. She held this position for about four years and then in 1951 rose to become co-managing editor. By 1964, she had been promoted to international editor of the magazine, a position she held until her death.

In 1954, Thompson published her second book, *Africa: Land of My Fathers*. Among her published articles is one on Mahalia Jackson entitled "Love Comes to Mahalia" (in *Ebony,* November 1964), in which she tells about the relationship that blossomed into marriage between Mahalia and Minters Sigmund Galloway. In the August 1966 issue, she wrote an article entitled "What Weaker Sex?" In it, she decries the treatment of women by men even though women outnumber men by about two million. She looks forward to a time when women will straighten out the chaos that male leaders have created. This article is evidence that Thompson was also an ardent feminist. In November 1965, she wrote "Instant Hair," an article that reflects her wit. In it, she addresses the wig craze of those days, mentioning both its benefits and its drawbacks.

She was featured in the April 1968 column "Backstage." We learn that she was a "well-seasoned traveller" who visited all five continents. The article reported her most recent trip to the Far East where she interviewed His Holiness Maharishi Mahesh Yogi, the world's most famous guru. In April 1969, the column again focused on her recent trip to the University of North Dakota where she received an honorary doctorate. In November 1970, the same column contained a brief account of how she came to work for *Ebony* and reported that Thompson, having worked there for twenty-three years, was planning to do some more stories for the magazine in what she called a "partial retirement." In September 1971, she wrote another article, "I Was a Cancer Coward," in which, hoping to help others face radical mastectomy, she told her own story of struggle with breast cancer.

In October 1972, she is again featured in "Backstage." This time the article reported on another trip she made back to North Dakota to be honored by the town of Driscoll, for an award she received earlier in the year. In July 1976, an article informs the reader of her induction into the North Dakota Hall of Fame when she was invited back to North Dakota by Governor Arthur Link. After the induction, the magazine reports, "Ms. Thompson will receive the State's Theodore Roosevelt Rough Rider Award."

As the international editor for the magazine, she did many features including one on the canonization of twenty-two Ugandan martyrs as saints in St. Peter's Cathedral in Rome, one on a safari in Tanzania where she had shot a Thompson gazelle, and one on a Vaughan family, who had started in Nigeria and migrated to Camden, South Carolina. In this article, "The Vaughan Family: A Tale of Two Continents," she tells how African and American descendants of a former slave kept in touch for more than a century.

The March 1987 issue of *Ebony* reported that "her study of the amalgamation of the races in Brazil was one of the best stories ever done on the 'race problem'" in a country that was not supposed to have one, and that she was one of the first to look into the problems of "brown babies"–the offspring of black soldiers in Europe and Asia.

In her autobiography, she expresses her hope that the barrier between whites and people of color will some day be destroyed. In the closing lines of the autobiography she writes, "I know there is still good in the world, that way down underneath, most Americans are fair, that my people and your people can work together and live together in peace and happiness, if they but have the opportunity to know and understand each other. The chasm is growing narrower. When it closes, my feet will rest on a united America."

Thompson was interviewed and photographed by the Black Women's Oral History Project, "Women of Courage," conducted by the Schlesinger Library. The Fisk University's Black Oral History Project also interviewed her.

Era Bell Thompson died on 29 December 1986 in her home and was buried according to her wishes in the family plot in Driscoll, North Dakota. Her papers are preserved in the Carter G. Woodson Regional Library and the Chicago Public Library.

SELECT BIBLIOGRAPHY

Primary

Nonfiction

Africa: Land of My Fathers. New York: Doubleday, 1954.

American Daughter [autobiography.] Chicago: University of Chicago Press, 1946; Reprint. New York: Follett, 1967.

"Girl Gangs of Harlem." *Negro Digest* 9 (March 1951): 38-42.

"Love Comes to Mahalia." *Ebony* (November 1964): 50-61.

"Negro Publications and the Writer." *Phylon* 11:304-6.

"The Vaughan Family: A Tale of Two Continents." *Ebony* (February 1975): 53-58.

White on Black. Coeditor, Herbert Nipson. Chicago: Johnson Publishing Co., 1963.

Secondary

Campbell, Dorothy, *Index to Black American Writers in Collective Biographies*, 1983.

Ellis, *Opportunity; A Journal of Negro Life*, 1971.

Herman, *Women in Particular*, 1984.

Hill and King, Transcript from *The Black Women's Oral History Project*, 1987.

Low and Clift, *Encyclopedia of Black America*, 1981.

Matney, *Who's Who among Black Americans*, 1978.

Matthews, *Black American Writers, 1773-1949*, 1975.

Page, *Selected Black American Authors*, 1977.

Salk, *A Laymen's Guide to Negro History*, 1967.

Shockley and Chandler, *Living Black American Authors*, 1973.

Sims-Wood, *The Progress of Afro-American Women*, 1980.

Spradling, *In Black and White*, 1980.

Turner, *Afro-American Writers*, 1970.

Williams, *American Black Women in the Arts and Social Sciences*, 1978.

THOMPSON, PRISCILLA JANE (1871-1942)

Poet

Priscilla Jane was the sister of poets Clara Ann Thompson* and Aaron Belford Thompson, all children of John Henry and Clara Jane Thompson, former slaves from Virginia. Only the brother, Aaron, received recognition (James Whitcomb Riley encouraged his work and wrote a preface to one of his volumes of poetry). Priscilla's birth and death dates have been established by Ann Allen Shockley, who found them inscribed on the family tombstone in the old Colored Cemetery, Cincinnati, Ohio, now the United American Cemetery.

Priscilla prepared for teaching, but because of ill health she devoted herself to literature and public recitals of her poems. Like her sister, Clara Ann, Priscilla printed her poetry privately and did not marry, but remained in Rossmoyne with an elder brother, Garland Yancey Thompson, after her brother Aaron married and moved to Indianapolis. Garland was a cementer and molder by trade, a sculptor in wood by avocation. Priscilla was a devoted worker in her church, Zion Baptist, and was the Sunday school teacher of longest continuous service. She was known for her wit, polish, and stage presence.

In a brief introduction to *Ethiope Lays*, the author says her purpose is to present a true and just picture of her race. There are thirty-one poems, in which, according to Ivy Newman White, she shows greater rhythmic facility and metric variety than does her brother. The volume is filled with a keen racial consciousness. More militant than her sister, she exhorts blacks to rise against oppression and patronage ("Address to Ethiopia") and denounces lynching. There are some religious verses as well. Representative titles are "To a Little Colored Boy," "The Old Saint's Prayer," "The Precious Pearl," "Evelyn," and "A Winter Night."

In the introduction to her second volume, *Gleanings of Quiet Hours*, the author announces that her purpose is to elevate her race, if only in the mind of the reader. She uses dialect frequently, as in *Ethiope Lays*. There are forty poems in all, some of them repeated from *Ethiope Lays*. Representative titles are "A Home Greeting," "A Christmas Ghost," "The Interrupted Reproof," "The Examination," "Lines to Emma," "The Muse's Favor," and "Insulted." There are occasional humorous touches, as in her sister's work.

SELECT BIBLIOGRAPHY

Primary

Poetry

Ethiope Lays. Rossmoyne, Ohio: Privately printed, 1900.

Gleanings of Quiet Hours. Rossmoyne, Ohio: Privately printed, 1907.

IN ANTHOLOGIES

Sherman, *Collected Black Women's Poetry*, vol. 2, 1988. "Ethiope Lays"; "Gleanings of Quiet Hours."

Shockley, *Afro-American Women Writers, 1746-1933*, 1988. "Knight of My Maiden Love"; "The Muse's Favor."

Secondary

Campbell, Dorothy, *Index to Black American Writers in Collective Biographies*, 1983.

Coyle, *Ohio Authors and Their Books*, 1962.

Dabney, *Cincinnati's Colored Citizens*, 1926.

French, Fabre, Singh, and Fabre, *Afro-American Poetry and Drama, 1760-1975*, 1979.

Matthews, *Black American Writers, 1773-1949*, 1975.

Porter, *North American Negro Poets*, 1945.

Reardon and Thorsen, *Poetry by American Women, 1900-1975*, 1979.

Rush, Myers, and Arata, *Black American Writers Past and Present*, 1975.

Sherman, *Invisible Poets*, 1974.

Shockley, *Afro-American Women Writers, 1746-1933*, 1988.

White and Jackson, *Anthology of Verse by American Negroes*, [1924], 1968.

Williams, *American Black Women in the Arts and Social Sciences*, 1978.

TURNER, LUCY MAE (1884-?)

Poet

Lucy Mae Turner's only known book is a collection of thirty-eight poems entitled *'Bout Culled Folkses*, written mostly in the Afro-American dialect, with a good number of poems in traditional poetic English. The use of end rhyme (abab or aabb) is consistent throughout. Those poems written in dialect tend to be longer and embody the humorous storytelling tradition of the Afro-American culture. Turner shows a gift for wit and vivid description, but she occasionally uses a melancholy tone. Social activism does not appear to enter into her work, which is surprising since she was descended from Nat Turner, the slave rebel who was executed for his leadership in a famous insurrection in Virginia.

"The Secret Hours 'Ere Dawn" is an introspective poem in which the lonely speaker, gazing from her attic room, wonders "if the city at its rest / Were all so lone as I, / So foiled by fate in every quest, / So prone to sit and sigh?" In her sleep, the speaker is guided by a spirit who leads her through the city showing her that the "struggles" and the "woes" of other people are indeed deeper than her own. The spirit "in garments white" leaves her with this advice: "So in your attic peaceful rest, / Molested by no harm; / Many the soul has stood the test, / Been bathed in life blood warm."

The struggle of the Afro-American working woman figures prominently in this collection. In "Matilda at the Tubs," the speaker and her friends work as cooks, nursemaids, or washerwomen in a wealthy "white world":

> Yes, I goes down to Mis' Mary's
> Evah single Monday mawnin',
> Sta'tin 'long but six or seben,
> W'en de day is jest a dawnin'.

Here the speaker is able to maintain high spirits in her slavelike working conditions by reminiscing about "de ol' plantation" where she grew up independent "'mid de sugah cane an' cotton." In the poem "Ebony" the speaker works as a waiter in a big hotel in "rich fo'ks lan'"; despite his treatment as inferior, he caters politely to them and feels "important": "If dey calls me Ebenezer, / Or jes' plain ole 'Ebony,' / I feels still, like Julius Caesar, / Dat I'se a place in history."

The surprise is that little irony is to be found in Turner's poems on the working-class Afro-American of the period. In "Tar Paper Bungalow," the speaker compares his life-style to that of affluent people and concludes that as long as he has adequate shelter and plenty of food, he is content. The title poem of the collection, "'Bout Culled Folkses," begins with a misleading quatrain which seems to harbinger irony: "Does you want to know de method / To keep joy aroun' de place? / All I says is 'Watch de antics / Ob de good ole culled race.'" The speaker continues by praising the survival skills of his people and encourages not a false veneer of contentment but cheerful acceptance.

Women figure as strong personae in Turner's work. In "Sassy," the speaker falls in love with a "rank sinnah," and when she strolls into church one morning with him, the elder scolds her from the altar and attempts to convince her to turn from "dat gay deceiver" and marry the preacher himself. Sassy Cassy, standing up to the elder, retorts in defense of her beau and herself: "Now Bob Brown, he likes his pleasure, / But he's young an' strong an' gay / But yo' faults is pas' redemption, / You's dried up to blow away."

The briefest poem in the collection is the last one, entitled "Nat Turner": "Nat Turner was a slave who stood / For a supreme great brotherhood / Where men did not each other buy; / But, missing that, he chose to die!" Despite a dominant theme in Turner's poems that the best method of survival for Afro-American people is to be content and seek the positive in everything, her last poem recognizes another response to oppression. Thus, we find a suggestion of militancy that causes us to reread her poems with a new perspective.

As the granddaughter of Nat Turner, Lucy had a vivid consciousness of the past. Her father, Gilbert, born into slavery as well, was liberated by his mistress and made his way to free Ohio. Turner relates the family history in a moving historical and autobiographical article, "The Family of Nat Turner, 1831 to 1954." She recounts the wrenching moment of separation when her father, as a young child, said goodbye to his mother and siblings on the slave auction block, but also accentuates her father's determination to succeed in life.

As she tells it, Lucy Mae was born on 13 November 1884 in Zanesville, Ohio (Muskingum County), two years after her sister Fannie. Through hard work in a foundry, Gilbert saved enough money to buy for his wife and children "a palatial brick house at 99 Eight Street in Zanesville" later destroyed by fire. When she graduated from high school in 1903 Lucy Mae was eager to accept a tuition scholarship to attend Ohio State University in Columbus. But the family, now poor, could not afford the room and board costs. Instead, Lucy attended the more affordable Wilberforce University, a black institution in Xenia, graduating in 1908. The degree started Turner on a teaching career in East St. Louis, Illinois. With her sister Fannie, also a teacher, she bought a home in East St. Louis, and their mother joined them there. But Lucy hungered for more education.

Deeply interested in government and world affairs, Turner later resumed her studies, earning a B.S. from Ohio State University in 1934. "I felt that, even though, because of poverty, I could not take advantage of the Ohio

State University scholarship I had earned from high school in 1903, I would show myself worthy of such a course by paying my own tuition and expenses, and by obtaining the degree over thirty years later, in 1934." By the same method she earned a master's degree from the University of Illinois in 1942.

In September 1946, St. Louis University opened the doors of its law school to black students and, according to Turner, was the first university in Missouri to allow colored students to take a law course. "I entered the Evening School on the opening night, and never missed a session and was never tardy at a session, until I graduated from the Law School, with the degree of Bachelor of Law, in June, 1950." During all this time (1910 to 1954) she had taught in the public schools of East St. Louis, Illinois.

Thus was her disappointment more bitter when she did not succeed in being admitted to the bar to practice law. As a high school graduate, she had discovered two strikes against her: race and sex. Now, though a law school graduate, "I find that there are three strikes against me – I am black, I am a woman, and I have no influence in high places." Turner consoles herself with her faith in God and her roles in church, teaching, and home, recalling, somewhat unconvincingly, the motto of Nat Turner "Trust in the Lord, And you'll overcome, Somehow / Somewhere, Someday!"

SELECT BIBLIOGRAPHY

Primary

Nonfiction

"The Family of Nat Turner, 1831-1954." *Negro History Bulletin* (March 1955): 127-32, 145; (April 1955): 155-58.

Poetry

'Bout Culled Folkses. New York: Harrison, 1938.

IN ANTHOLOGIES

Murphy, *Negro Voices*, [1938] 1971. "A Bird Is Singing."

Secondary

Campbell, Dorothy, *Index to Black American Writers in Collective Biographies*, 1983.

Coyle, *Ohio Authors and Their Books*, 1962.

Kallenbach, *Index to Black American Literary Anthologies*, 1979.

Porter, *North American Negro Poets,* 1945.

Reardon and Thorsen, *Poetry by American Women, 1900-1975,* 1979.

Rush, Myers, and Arata, *Black American Writers Past and Present,* 1975.

WALKER, MARGARET ABIGAIL ALEXANDER (1915-)

Poet
Novelist
Essayist
Professor

Having written since the age of twelve, Walker published *For My People* in 1942, when she was twenty-seven. This highly successful book of poetry was the beginning of a long string of awards and distinctions. *For My People*, written in a poetic idiom based on experiments with jazz and blues rhythms, was the winner of the Yale University Younger Poets Award, thus making Walker the first black to win such an honor. In 1944, Walker received a Rosenwald fellowship for creative writing and in 1953, she was a Yale University Ford Fellow for work on the advancement of education.

Clearly, Walker has been one of the most recognized and successful black woman writers of her generation. Anthologies in which her poems appear are too numerous to list. In the civil rights movement of the 1950s and 1960s, Walker began to produce more politically aware works. For her most famous book, the novel *Jubilee*, published in 1966, she received a Houghton Mifflin Literary Fellowship award. *Jubilee* has been translated into French, German, and Swedish and in 1976, was transformed into an opera at Jackson State College.

Now in the latter part of the twentieth century Walker has published two new volumes of verse, including *Prophets for a New Day*, dedicated to her father and to her friend and mentor, Langston Hughes. This work, a collection of twenty-two poems, provides a clear window into the rebellion and outrage of the American 1950s and 1960s. Walker compares the spiritual fortitude of such biblical prophets as Isaiah, Amos, Joel, Micah, and Hosea (the poems are entitled as such) to that of people in Montgomery, Louisiana, and Mississippi who sat in jails silently praying and who fought for the cause of freedom.

From her works it becomes apparent that Margaret Walker is dedicated to writing about struggle – more precisely the struggle of black Americans. With a lyricism born of her religious background and her own historical insight Walker has successfully brought the often obscured image of the black American into clear focus.

Before completing *Jubilee*, her best-known work, Margaret Walker had put thirty-four years of research into its making. The pre- and post-Civil War portions of the novel tell the real-life story of her great-grandmother Elvira (Vyry) Dawson. The precision and clarity that she brings to *Jubilee* help to create a picture of American life during slavery and Reconstruction.

Walker leads us through the intimate details of Vyry's life: the loss of her loved ones, the development of her strong determination not to succumb to the degradation imposed on her by her owners, and her unwavering dedication to her family. Vyry clings to the dream that such torment must come to an end. Walker demonstrates, too, Vyry's strong belief in a pain-free afterlife.

Walker uncovers the differing convictions of enslaved people with respect to the concept of freedom. On the one hand, she portrays those who believe that God's will be done and that each day must be lived with that belief in mind. Walker also depicts the iron will of Randall Ware, Vyry's first husband, who as a freed man takes an active stand in bringing down the slavery that still binds him and his family. In an earnest heart-to-heart talk Vyry and Ware discuss their polar viewpoints. In this scene Vyry never wavers from the belief that "I knows all my peoples going free someday. Mister Lincoln is our Moses and God done told him to make old Pharaoh set my people free."

Adrianne Baytop points to a feminist strain in Walker when she states that Vyry passes simultaneously from slavery to freedom and from girlhood to womanhood. Says Baytop, "Walker frees her epic from the traditional male-oriented sense of the heroic, structuring her novel around Vyry, her maternal great-grandmother. Vyry's first husband ... functions only in a supportive role, and underscores Vyry's heroism" (316).

Born on the campus of Central Alabama Institute in Birmingham on 7 July 1915, Walker was the daughter of the Reverend Sigismund Walker, a professor at the institute, and Marion Dozier Walker, a musician and third-generation teacher. Like many other women writers who lived through the depression, Margaret found work with the Federal Writers' Project. She later married interior decorator Firnist James Alexander in 1943 and became the mother of two daughters and two sons.

Margaret Walker's literary career has always gone hand in hand with an academic career. She earned her bachelor's degree from Northwestern University (1935) and her master's and doctorate degrees from the University of Iowa (1940 and 1965). She taught English at Livingstone College in North Carolina and West Virginia State College, and in 1949, joined the staff of Jackson State College in Mississippi. Margaret Walker was appointed full professor in 1965 and three years later assumed the position she held until retirement as director of the college's Institute for the Study of History, Life, and Culture of Black People.

SELECT BIBLIOGRAPHY

Primary

Nonfiction

"Black Studies: Some Personal Observations." *Afro-American Studies Journal* (1970).

"Chief Worshippers at All World Altars." *Encore* (June-July 1975): 67-68.

How I Wrote "Jubilee." Chicago: Third World Press, 1972.

Jubilee. Boston: Houghton Mifflin, 1966.

"The Legacy of Phillis Wheatley." *Ebony* (March 1974).

"Nausea of Sartre." *Yale Review* (1952): 251-71.

"New Poets." *Black Expression* (1969).

A Poetic Equation: Conversations between Nikki Giovanni and Margaret Walker. New York: Amistad; Warner, forthcoming.

"Religion, Poetry, and History: Foundations for a New Educational System." In Gladys Curry, *Viewpoints from Black America.* Englewood Cliffs, N.J.: Prentice-Hall, 1970.

"Richard Wright." *New Letters* (University of Missouri) (1971).

Richard Wright: Daemonic Genius: A Portrait of a Man, A Critical Look at His Work. New York: Warner Books, 1988.

"Willing to Pay the Price." *Many Shades of Black* (1969): 119-30.

Poetry

For My People. New Haven: Yale University Press, 1942.

October Journey. Detroit: Broadside Press, 1973.

Prophets for a New Day. Detroit: Broadside Press, 1970.

IN ANTHOLOGIES

Stetson, *Black Sister*, 1981. "Ballad of the Happy Toad"; "Gilbert and Gubar"; "Kissie Lee"; "Lineage"; "Molly Means."

Secondary

Bakish and Margolies, *Afro-American Fiction, 1853-1976*, 1979.

Baytop, "Margaret Walker," 1982.

Bennett, Lerone, "The Shaping of Black America," 1975.

Bontemps and Hughes, *The Poetry of the Negro, 1746-1949*, 1949.

Bontemps and Hughes, *The Poetry of the Negro, 1746-1970*, 1970.

Campbell, Dorothy, *Index to Black American Writers in Collective Biographies*, 1983.

Chapman, *Index to Black Poetry*, 1974.

Chapman, *Index to Poetry by Black American Women*, 1986.

Dance, "Black Eve or Madonna: A Study of the Antithetical Views of the Mother in Black American Literature," 1975.

Deodene and French, *Black American Poetry since 1944*, 1971.

Fairbanks and Engeldinger, *Black American Fiction*, 1978.

French, Fabre, Singh, and Fabre, *Afro-American Poetry and Drama, 1760-1975*, 1979.

Giddings, "A Shoulder Hunched against a Sharp Concern: Themes in the Poetry of Margaret Walker," 1971.

Herman, *Women in Particular*, 1984.

Hill and King, Transcript from *The Black Women's Oral History Project*, 1987.

Hull, "Black Women Poets from Wheatley to Walker," 1975.

Kallenbach, *Index to Black American Literary Anthologies*, 1979.

Littlejohn, *Black on White*, 1966.

Low and Clift, *Encyclopedia of Black America*, 1981.

Matthews, *Black American Writers, 1773-1949*, 1975.

Page, *Selected Black American Authors*, 1977.

Randall, "The Black Aesthetic in the Thirties, Forties, and Fifties," 1971.

Richardson, *Black Women and Religion*, 1980.

Rowell, "Interview with Margaret Walker," 1975.

Rush, Myers, and Arata, *Black American Writers Past and Present*, 1975.

Salk, *A Layman's Guide to Negro History*, 1967.

Sims-Wood, *The Progress of Afro-American Women*, 1980.

Spradling, *In Black and White*, 1980.

Whiteman, *A Century of Fiction by American Negroes, 1853-1952*, 1974.

Williams, *American Black Women in the Arts and Social Sciences*, 1978.

WEEDEN, LULA LOWE (1918-)

Educator

Poet

This Lynchburg, Virginia, girl was nine years of age at the time Countee Cullen included six of her poems in his 1927 anthology, *Caroling Dusk*. (She had by then written some thirty or forty short verses.) Cullen notes that Lula Lowe's mother, Mrs. Lula L. Weeden, was herself a poet of ability. A photograph of little Lula with her two sisters appears along with her poems in *Opportunity*, May 1927 (154). Her poems are delicate verses drawn from the realms of nature and fantasy; some have the delicate grace of haikus.

The Weedens, including Dr. Henry P. Weeden, a dentist, Mrs. Weeden, and their three daughters lived on the property adjoining that of Anne Spencer* and her family. Chauncey Spencer, Anne's son, recounted in a telephone conversation with us that Lula spent long hours at the Spencers, always showing her work to Anne for improvements in phrasing and rhyme schemes.

Cullen observed in the foreword (p. x) to his anthology that the Harlem Renaissance movement had "awakened to a happy articulation many young Negro poets who had hitherto lisped only in isolated places in solitary numbers." Each writer's group of poems commenced with a detailed biographical – often autobiographical – note supplying not only professional statistics but often cogent observations about the nature of black poetry and the Harlem Renaissance. Naturally, the collection commenced with work by Paul Laurence Dunbar, whose turn-of-the-century dialect pieces generally mark the advent of a modern, self-aware black literature; it concluded with Weeden's poems.

A letter dated 31 March 1989 from Lula Lowe Weeden to us explains that she ceased writing poetry in her early teens when "I became too conscious that my peers did not appreciate that kind of poetry. And, my father thought that my mother should encourage me to be a 'more well-rounded person' and not to spend so much time apart from other children – writing. I was not dedicated enough to continue. I wrote words to class and school songs that were simple rhymes." Weeden's career continued in the realm of art education in Denver, Colorado, until her retirement. Subsequent to *Caroling Dusk*, two later publications included poems by her: *We Too Sing America*, a book written during the 1940s for elementary school-age children, and an anthology of black poets issued in Holland, in Dutch, during the 1950s. Weeden says, "I am proud to be considered a part of the Negro Renaissance. The creative thrust of that period continues to influence Black artists."

SELECT BIBLIOGRAPHY

Primary

Poetry

IN ANTHOLOGIES

Cullen, *Caroling Dusk*, 1927. "Dance"; "Have You Seen It"; "The Little Dandelion"; "Me Alone"; "Robin Red Breast"; "The Stream."

Davis, Arthur P., *From the Dark Tower*, 1974.

Secondary

Campbell, Dorothy, *Index to Black American Writers in Collective Biographies*, 1983.

Chapman, *Index to Black Poetry*, 1974.

Ellis, *Opportunity; A Journal of Negro Life*, 1971.

Kallenbach, *Index to Black American Literary Anthologies,* 1979.

Kellner, *The Harlem Renaissance*, 1984.

WELLS-BARNETT, IDA BELL [IOLA] (1862-1931)

Journalist

Activist

Ida B. Wells, crusader against that most virulent form of racism, lynching, was born in Holly Springs, Mississippi, the oldest of eight children born of slave parents. Her mother, Lizzie Bell, the child of a slave mother and an Indian father, had come from Virginia; she married James Wells, a carpenter with her master. After emancipation they continued to work for him as carpenter and cook.

Ida Bell was educated at Rust University, a high school and industrial school for freed people established in Holly Springs in 1866. Upon the death of her parents and three siblings in a yellow fever epidemic, she assumed the support of the family, though friends offered to care for the youngest four children. Just fourteen years old, she began teaching at a rural school near Memphis and took summer courses at Fisk University. On one occasion Ida refused to accept a seat in a Jim Crow railroad car and she was dragged from the train. She filed a successful lawsuit for assault against the Chesapeake and Ohio Railroad, but the judgment was later reversed by the Tennessee Supreme Court. Because of her militant articles published under the pen name "Iola" criticizing inadequate schools for blacks, the Memphis school board dismissed her.

Her early writing appeared in the *Gate City Press* of Kansas City, the *Detroit Plaindealer*, and in religious periodicals such as the *American Baptist* and *Christian Index*. For a time she wrote for the Afro-American weekly,

Living Word. In 1891 she used her schoolteacher salary to buy half-interest in the *Memphis Free Speech and Headlight*, a small newspaper. Eventually she bought out her partner and began writing about inequality in education, urging blacks to boycott streetcars and to migrate West. A year later (May 1882), after she revealed the identity of the lynchers of three Memphis Afro-Americans in an inflammatory editorial, a mob of whites demolished her printing press and office.

Wells, unable to return to Memphis, fled to New York City, where she was hired by T. Thomas Fortune of the *New York Age*. Fortune helped her secure lecture engagements for her crusade against lynching. As northern newspapers did not give full or objective coverage to lynchings, she began to compile *A Red Record*. It accounted for 1,217 murders by burning, lynching, and shooting between 1892 and 1894. Prefaced by Frederick Douglass, *A Red Record* was the first statistical pamphlet on lynching. None of the offenders was ever brought to trial. Her 1895 lecture tour to England prompted one British clergyman to say that nothing since *Uncle Tom's Cabin* had aroused public opinion to such an extent. Her style was fiery, yet concrete, documented, and quantitative, like that of a journalist who is also a social scientist. Clearly, her writing was an extension both of her social activism and of her personal rage. The unparalleled courage she showed ties her to such contemporaries as Mary Church Terrell,* whom she met on several occasions. Wells usually supported W. E. B. Du Bois in opposition to the accommodationist policies of Booker T. Washington, but she criticized Du Bois for being dilatory with regard to lynching.

In 1895 Wells married Chicago lawyer and editor of the *Chicago Conservator*, Ferdinand Barnett, and settled in Chicago. She began to write for many Chicago newspapers. The Barnetts had four children: Charles A., Herman K., Ida B. Wells, and Alfreda (Duster), who later published her mother's autobiography under the title *Crusade for Justice*.

From 1913 to 1916, aided by her husband, Wells-Barnett served as adult probation officer for the Chicago municipal court. In 1918, she traveled to East St. Louis, Illinois, to investigate and report on the widespread race riots going on then, as well as to seek legal aid for the black victims. In a letter to the *Chicago Tribune* (7 July 1919), she urged the city to prevent other explosions of violence and to "set the wheels of justice in motion before it [was] too late." But the city's leadership took no action, and one of the bloodiest race riots in the nation's history soon followed.

Wells-Barnett encouraged black women to organize. She was lifelong president of the Ida B. Wells Club, the first organization of black women in Chicago. She also founded the Negro Fellowship League, a social center with reading rooms as well as a dormitory for job-seeking black men.

As part of her effort to achieve suffrage for women she founded the Alpha Suffrage Club of Chicago, one of the first suffrage organizations for

Afro-American women. She marched in the famous suffrage parade in Washington, D.C., on the eve of Woodrow Wilson's first inauguration in 1913 and in another parade in June 1916. In December of 1918, she was one of eleven blacks chosen by a group of 250 in Washington as representatives to the Versailles Peace Conference in France. They were denied passports, however, and only Boston newspaper editor Monroe Trotter was able to attend the conference.

Wells-Barnett was one of two black women (Mary Church Terrell* was the other) to sign "The Call" on 12 February 1909, the centennial of Lincoln's birth, for a meeting "to discuss means for securing political and civil equality for the Negro." She, Mary Church Terrell, and Maria Baldwin were members of the Committee of Forty formed in New York (1909), a predecessor of the NAACP (which was founded in 1910).

In 1929 Wells-Barnett began to write her autobiography, at about the same time that her concern shifted to unemployment in black ghettos. She ran for state senate as an independent but lost to the incumbent. Her work with Jane Addams to block the formation of separate schools for blacks in Chicago was successful; however, by the time of her death in 1931, resegregation had begun.

In 1987, the Tennessee Historic Commission honored Wells-Barnett with a commemorative marker on famous Beale Street in Memphis, the city that had once exiled her.

SELECT BIBLIOGRAPHY

Primary

Nonfiction

Crusade for Justice. Edited by Alfreda Duster. Chicago: University of Chicago Press, 1970.

Mob Rule in New Orleans: Robert Charles and His Fight to Death. The Story of His Life, Burning Human Beings Alive (and) Other Lynching Statistics. Chicago, 1900.

A Red Record: Lynchings in the United States, 1892-1893-1894. Chicago: Donohue & Henneberry, 1894. Reprint. New York: Arno Press, 1971.

IN ANTHOLOGIES

Shockley, *Afro-American Women Writers, 1746-1933*, 1988. "The Case Stated."

Secondary

Campbell, Dorothy, *Index to Black American Writers in Collective Biographies*, 1983.

Dannett, *Profiles of Negro Womanhood*, 1964.

Giddings, "Woman Warrior: Iba B. Wells, Crusader-Journalist," 1988.

Herman, *Women in Particular*, 1984.

Kellner, *The Harlem Renaissance*, 1984.

Lamping, "Ida B. Wells-Barnett," 1979.

Logan and Winston, *Dictionary of American Negro Biography*, 1982.

Low and Clift, *Encyclopedia of Black America*, 1981.

Majors, *Noted Negro Women*, [1893] 1971.

Matthews, *Black American Writers, 1773-1949*, 1975.

Sterling, "Mary Church Terrell," 1980.

Williams, *American Black Women in the Arts and Social Sciences*, 1978.

WEST, DOROTHY (1907-)

Novelist

Short-story writer

Editor

Dorothy West is known for her association with such writers of the Harlem Renaissance as Langston Hughes, Wallace Thurman, Zora Neale Hurston,* Claude McKay, and Countee Cullen. In her own right, she is recognized as the founder of *Challenge* (later *New Challenge*) and author of the novel *The Living Is Easy* (1948).

West's birth date is often mistakenly given as 1912, but city of Boston records show that she was born in 1907. Brought up in Boston, Massachusetts, she attended the prestigious Girls' Latin School. As the only child of Rachel Benson and Ike West, Dorothy was fairly privileged, taking dancing lessons and spending summer vacations in the family cottage at Oak Bluffs on Martha's Vineyard Island, Massachusetts.

When her short story "The Typewriter" placed second in the June 1926 contest sponsored by *Opportunity*, she departed for New York with her cousin Helene Johnson,* the same age as she. West took bit parts on the stage and worked as a relief investigator in Harlem (an experience reflected in her story "Mammy").

In 1932 she was part of a group of black intellectuals and artists, including Langston Hughes, which traveled to the Soviet Union with the "Black and White," a project to make a film about race relations in Alabama. The film did not materialize, and West, learning that her father had died, returned to the United States.

She then founded a new magazine, *Challenge*. According to Walter C. Daniel, her intention was to recapture, in the mid-1930s, the vitality characterizing the Harlem Renaissance before its decline during the depression. In its three years of existence (1934-37), *Challenge* published some prestigious writers, but it was criticized for its moderate political stance. West made Richard Wright the associate editor, and his "Blueprint for Negro Writing" was published in *New Challenge*. West was not able to maintain her magazine for two reasons: insufficient young talent and criticism from radicals of her "pale pink tongue." Daniel points out that *New Challenge*, despite its failure, foreshadowed the fusion of art and politics that would find a stronger expression in *Black World* and similar journals a generation later. Since 1958, West, who never married, has resided on Martha's Vineyard, Massachusetts. She writes a weekly social column about the town of Oak Bluffs and occasional vignettes for the island newspaper, the *Vineyard Gazette*.

West's short stories span the years from 1926 to 1940. In them she explores subtleties of character, ironies of fate, and poignant moments of childhood. Those published in *Opportunity*, the *Daily News*, and the *Saturday Evening Quill* confirm West's power to frame dramatic narrative situations of black life. "An Unimportant Man" unravels the story of a black man's struggle for career, marriage, and progeny, and his failures at all three. "Prologue to Life" also shows men and women at cross-purposes, unable to communicate. The tragic outcome, here as elsewhere in West's work, has a multiplicity of meanings for the reader.

Her novel, *The Living Is Easy* (1948), dedicated to her father, came after the Harlem Renaissance's decline. It was reviewed far more widely than the work of earlier black women novelists such as Zara Wright* and Mercedes Gilbert,* a sign of growing interest in the Afro-American woman writer (by this time Gwendolyn Brooks had published *A Street in Bronzeville*). Reviews, many quite favorable, appeared in the *New York Herald Tribune*, the *New York Times*, the *New Yorker, Chicago Sun Book Week, Commonweal*, and *Opportunity*. In her novel West draws the portrait of a black middle-class woman whose ambitions take a cruel toll on her family. Cleo disdains southern blacks, men, and northern liberals. Classist and racist, she is unconcerned that her move up to genteel neighborhoods depends on white flight. Reviewers, while pointing out the stylistic and structural flaws, hailed this novel as the first on Boston's black community and also one of the first to portray the pernicious effects of middle-class striving for money and social status. West writes in the realistic tradition, with a slightly antiquated flavor. Despite some clichés and a potboiler subplot, the reader's interest is held by word play and agile dialogue. West's originality lies in incisive characterization and the ability to transfix the dramatic moment.

Reissued, West's novel has introduced her to a new generation, prepared to understand her work from a feminist perspective. N. Jill Weyant comments that Cleo, the protagonist of *The Living Is Easy*, "has been called a 'predatory woman' and a 'castrating female' by a generation unused to strong women characters. On closer examination, she can be related to Hedda Gabler, a clever woman whose energies have no legitimate outlet and so must be spent in molding the lives of others."

West's papers, including story manuscripts and correspondence, are housed at Boston University, Atlanta University, and Yale University libraries. An oral history of West is at the Schlesinger Library, Radcliffe College.

SELECT BIBLIOGRAPHY

Primary

Fiction

"The Black Dress." *Opportunity* 12 *(*May 1934):140, 158.

"Funeral."*Saturday Evening Quill 3* (June 1930): 18-24.

"Hannah Byde." *Messenger* (July 1926): 197-99.

The Living Is Easy. Boston: Houghton Mifflin, 1948. Reprint. New York: Arno Press, 1969. New York: Feminist Press, 1982.

"Mammy." *Opportunity* (October 1940): 298-302.

"Prologue to a Life." *Saturday Evening Quill* (April 1929): 5-10.

"The Typewriter." *Opportunity* (July 1926): 220-23, 234.

"An Unimportant Man." *Saturday Evening Quill* (June 1928): 21-32.

Nonfiction

"Elephant's Dance: A Memoir of Wallace Thurman." *Black World* (November 1970): 77-85.

Secondary

REVIEWS OF *The Living is Easy*

Bontemps, Arna. *New York Herald Tribune Weekly Book Review (*13 June 1948): 16.

Codman, Florence, *Commonweal* (25 June 1948): 264.

*Kirkus (*15 March 1948): 149.

Krim, Seymour, *New York Times* (16 May 1948): 5.

Moon, Henry Lee, *Crisis* (October 1948): 308.

*The New Yorker (*15 May 1948):122.

Thompson, E. B., *Chicago Sun Book Week* (29 June 1948): 8.

Bakish and Margolies, *Afro-American Fiction, 1853-1976,* 1979.

Bardolph, *The Negro Vanguard*, 1959.

Bone, *The Negro Novel in America*, 1965.

Campbell, Dorothy, *Index to Black American Writers in Collective Biographies*, 1983.

Daniel, Walter C., *Black Journals of the United States*, 1982.

Ellis, *Opportunity; A Journal of Negro Life*, 1971.

Fairbanks and Engeldinger, *Black American Fiction*, 1978.

Hughes, *The Negro Novelist*, 1953.

Kallenbach, *Index to Black American Literary Anthologies*, 1979.

Kellner, *The Harlem Renaissance*, 1984.

Matthews, *Black American Writers, 1773-1949*, 1975.

Perry, *Silence to the Drums*, 1976.

Roses, "An Interview with Dorothy West," 1985.

Rush, Myers, and Arata, *Black American Writers Past and Present*, 1975.

Salk, *A Layman's Guide to Negro History*, 1967.

Schraufnagel, *From Apology to Protest*, 1973.

Spradling, *In Black and White*, 1980.

Turner, *Afro-American Writers*, 1970.

Weyant, "Dorothy West," 1982.

Whiteman, *A Century of Fiction by American Negroes, 1853-1952*, 1974.

Whitlow, *Black American Literature*, 1973.

Williams, *American Black Women in the Arts and Social Sciences*, 1978.

WIGGINS, BERNICE LOVE (1897-)

Poet

Wiggins's work was published in newspapers including the *El Paso Herald* and the *Chicago Defender* and in magazines like *Half Century*. Her only volume of poetry appeared in 1925, entitled *Tuneful Tales*. J. Mason Brewer, the editor of *Heralding Dawn*, an anthology in which Wiggins's best-known poem, "Church Folks," appears, claims the poet's best work is done in dialect, and that Bernice Love Wiggins surpassed her contemporaries in writing dialect. Of the Texas group that published in *Heralding Dawn*, which also included Gwendolyn Bennett,* Lauretta Holman Gooden,* Maurine L. Jeffrey,* Lillian Tucker Lewis,* and Birdelle Wycoff Ransom,* Wiggins is the only female poet who published her own volume of verse.

Bernice Love was only five years old when her mother died and left her an orphan. She then resided with her aunt in El Paso, Texas. She attended primary and secondary school in El Paso and graduated from the Douglass High School. Bernice enjoyed expressing herself through poetry and creating original verse. One of the young poet's teachers, Alice Lydia McGowan (to whom Wiggins dedicates *Tuneful Tales*), encouraged her to pursue this avenue of literature.

In the introduction written by William Coleman, principal of the Douglass School, he seems to apologize for Wiggins growing up in the absence of a home library and many of the "other environments conducive to a refining, cultural, intellectual development." Perhaps he did so because some intellectuals/ literary artists of the New Negro Movement found the use of dialect a controversial issue: could it be detrimental to the advancement of black writers? Or was it a valid means of expressing the Afro-American experience? Whatever the case, it is explained that Wiggins's poetic expression–the "poverty, the sorrows, the sufferings, the restricted opportunities of her Race"--is "unembellished with learned allusions, figures of speech, or other conceits. . . . these poems are the natural breathings of an inspired soul."

Tuneful Tales is a volume of over one hundred poems that seem to have as many themes, many of them rooted in the author's spiritual beliefs. Wiggins often connects her faith in God with the topics of her poems. While she does not separate herself from the Afro-American experience, she does not rest on that alone as the source for her identity. Poverty, racism, women's rights, love, and the black church are a few of the poems' subjects. A significant number of the poems, but not all, are in dialect. These tend to be stories or monologues in verse form with a narrator, usually in the first person. An example is the poem "Mammy's Pride," which is ambivalent in its tone:

Dere now, kiss me yo' ole "Buggah,"
I jus' loves you thru an' thru,
Yo's as helpless as a baby
But yo' mammy's proud ob yo.
Wonder if yo'll miss yo mammy
When yo tak' yo'self a wife,
Ain't no 'oman gw'ine to spile yo'
Lak I has all yo' life.

In the other rhymes Wiggins offers thoughts, sometimes committing herself to an opinion, as in the poem "Society":

Where all the bad is counted good
And all the right is wrong
Where gossip is the chief asset
And slander floats in song.

In "Ethiopia Speaks" the poet responds to the atrocities of lynching with "Ethiopia forgives, but remembers still / And cries unto God with uplifted hands / Innocent bloods bathe the lands." According to sources, Wiggins moved to Los Angeles sometime after the publication of *Tuneful Tales*.

SELECT BIBLIOGRAPHY

Primary

Poetry

Tuneful Tales. El Paso, Tex.: The author, 1925.

IN ANTHOLOGIES

Brewer, *Heralding Dawn*, 1936. "Church Folk."

Secondary

Chapman, *Index to Black Poetry*, 1974.

Porter, *North American Negro Poets*, 1945.

Reardon and Thorsen, *Poetry by American Women, 1900-1975*, 1979.

Werden, "Bernice Love Wiggins," 1982.

WOOD, LILLIAN E. (?-?)

Novelist

Lillian Wood's only known novel bears an introduction by Robert E. Jones of the M.E. Church. The bishop noted that Wood had been a teacher for twenty years, thus gaining the confidence of people who told her their stories of lynching and terror.

The plot of *Let My People Go* revolves around the love story of Bob McComb and Helen Adams as they progress from their student days to the army, for him, and nursing, for her, during the First World War. Politicized by racial violence, the McCombs move to Chicago where Bob is elected to Congress and promptly introduces antilynching legislation which is passed.

Shockley comments that Wood's novel "is filled with messages about coping with injustice, forgiveness, and raising the masses; she insists that there are good and bad people in both races." Shockley also notes Wood's emphasis on the emerging black woman and the changes Wood believed women could bring about by combining "the virtue of the nineteenth century with the progressivism of the twentieth." A more in-depth study of this obscure author seems warranted.

SELECT BIBLIOGRAPHY

Primary

Fiction

Let My People Go. Philadelphia: A. M. E. Book Concern, 1922.

IN ANTHOLOGIES

Shockley, *Afro-American Women Writers, 1746-1933*, 1988. "The Cloud with a Silver Lining."

Secondary

Bakish and Margolies, *Afro-American Fiction, 1853-1976*, 1979.

Fairbanks and Engeldinger, *Black American Fiction*, 1978.

Matthews, *Black American Writers, 1773-1949*, 1975.

Shockley, *Afro-American Women Writers, 1746-1933*, 1988.

Whiteman, *A Century of Fiction by American Negroes, 1853-1952*, 1974.

Williams, *American Black Women in the Arts and Social Sciences*, 1978.

WRIGHT, ZARA (?-?)

Novelist

Nothing is known of Zara Wright save what she reveals through the preface and introduction to her only known novel and the book itself. Curiously, no mention is made of her in works on the black novel, such as those of Schraufnagel and Gloster.

Black and White Tangled Threads, published in 1920 by a house no longer in existence, is dedicated to her "dear, departed husband J. Edward Wright" and written in the hope that it will inspire "those who are too weak to do their duty" and "too cowardly to do what is just and right for fear of criticism." In the preface, the author expresses the idealistic belief that to live in peace and harmony is not only possible in "this great and beautiful world" but can be realized simply by loving "our neighbor as ourselves." In the introduction Wright praises the heroine of the novel as one who "sacrifices her principles of right and wrong to save those near and dear to her from imaginary shame and humiliation." The *Chicago Defender*, in a one-paragraph review, praised the book as a "realistic portrayal of individuals and events [that] lifts one to the heights of earthly ambitions."

Black and White Tangled Threads and its sequel, *Kenneth*, found under the same cover, takes place before and during World War I in the South. The heroes of the story are wealthy plantation owners (such as Paul Andrews), who have been benevolent to their slaves, and members of upper-class families (such as Zoleeta Andrews, who discovers early in life "a taint of slavery clinging to her ancestors"). All the characters in the novel who are aware of their African ancestry are proud of it and one, the heroine, even dedicates her life to working for the education of lower-class Afro-Americans and enlightenment of racist whites. With one exception, none of the characters who intermarry allows the ancestry of the "passing" spouse to dissolve the marriage or diminish love.

The novel revolves around Zoleeta Andrews, the strikingly beautiful niece of Paul Andrews, who discovers through the malice of her jealous cousin Catherine that her mother was a mulatto who married Paul's younger brother Harold. Although she constantly feels she is "sailing under false colors," Zoleeta is never ashamed of her descendants and dedicates her life to "uplifting the race." Believing the missionaries to be wrong, Zoleeta sacrifices her family life to educating "the hearts of the Southern whites," for "to uplift that race of people, despised and mistreated because their skin is black, we must first change the attitude of the Southern whites and the calm indifference of the prejudiced Northerner."

The novel is rather clouded by its large cast of characters and complex lineage. Written in the florid language characteristic of the nineteenth-century sentimental novel, it is anachronistic for its 1920 publication date. There is great emphasis by the narrator on physical beauty and the self-sacrifice of the heroine and her exaggerated unrealistic abnegation. The strength of the story lies in its brave assertion that love can overcome societal barriers to mixed marriage and in its portrayal of some white characters as humane and nonpaternalistic, in contrast to others debased by their racist leanings.

The attitude projected by the narrator toward physical beauty implies a European bias. For example, the blacks in the novel, like Zoleeta Andrews, are attractive only because they have mixed blood, or as in one character's case, because "he had not that mixed blood that is characteristic of the American negro, yet he was a handsome man." Like Pauline Hopkins, Zara Wright was constrained by the need to counter negative stereotypes of blacks and compelled to create characters conforming to standards that would appeal to a white audience.

The question is why Wright, who comes later, responded as women writers did at the turn of the century. Shockley comments that Wright's books are "fairy tales created by a fanciful imagination building on nineteenth-century models and adding a few twists of her own." This judgment, however, should be tempered with more analysis of her complex tales and their underlying meaning. Also, more documentary evidence remains to be uncovered regarding their mysterious author.

SELECT BIBLIOGRAPHY

Primary

Fiction

Black and White Tangled Threads. Chicago: Barnard & Miller, 1920. Reprint. New York: AMS Press, 1975.

IN ANTHOLOGIES

Shockley, *Afro-American Women Writers, 1746-1933*, 1988. "The Little Orphan."

Secondary

Bakish and Margolies, *Afro-American Fiction, 1853-1976*, 1979.

Chicago Defender (25 December 1920): 8.

Matthews, *Black American Writers, 1773-1949*, 1975.

Rush, Myers, and Arata, *Black American Writers Past and Present*, 1975.

Wright, Zara

Shockley, *Afro-American Women Writers, 1746-1933*, 1988.

Whiteman, *A Century of Fiction by American Negroes, 1853-1952*, 1974.

Williams, *American Black Women in the Arts and Social Sciences*, 1978.

WYNBUSH, OCTAVIA BEATRICE (1894-ca. 1972)

Short-story writer

Poet

Children's writer

Octavia Wynbush's major contribution to Afro-American literature came in the form of short stories appearing in *Crisis* and *Opportunity*. She received little recognition beyond the headline on the cover of *Crisis*, March 1936, which reads "A New Story by Octavia B. Wynbush." She published one imaginative but not very innovative children's book in 1941. After her last publication in *Crisis* (1945), Wynbush drops out of sight. The content of her stories suggests a southern, perhaps Louisiana, background. The eight stories, written between 1931 and 1945, center on themes of belief in the occult, wayward offspring, religious conversions, and revenge. Octavia Wynbush published only two poems. The first, "The Song of Cotton," illustrates the dual message of pain and beauty that King Cotton delivers. Although the cotton is delicate looking and soft, the toil behind its production is onerous. Wynbush speaks of the tears that fall on the cotton, "Hot tears of hope deferred, that maketh sick the heart" and that are "woven into the poet's song." The image of the gatherer's tears draws attention to the pain underlying beauty and the anguish that goes unsung.

The frailty of promises and the spoken word is closely examined in two of her short stories. In "Bride of God" a broken vow forces a bride to turn her desire away from men and place it instead with God. "Conjure Man" portrays the use of a witch doctor to eliminate the presence of an adversary in love. As the conjure man summarily advises his customer, "de chahms you already has is 'versible. Dey kin wu'k against you ef de one what gave 'em to you wills, as well as fo' you, you knows." As the story concludes, the conjure man stealthily connives his customer out of her fortune. Using blackmail, the conjure man proves that the only black magic involved in his art is the ability to outwit. Like Zora Neale Hurston,* Wynbush found rich thematic material in the African-derived lore of conjuring, though she exhibits skepticism of hoodoo.

"The Noose" is another of Wynbush's stories that centers around trickery and the inevitable revelation of the truth. The character King, who lives down among the twisting vines and ferns of Devil's Swamp in Louisiana, starts having dreams of a hangman's noose. This occurs after he witnesses the hanging of a man convicted of murder. The executed man was also responsible for taking King's wife away from him. From subtle details, such as an ill-placed laugh or an "unmistakable satisfaction in his whispered response," one gleans that King is responsible for his enemy's conviction and wrongful death. Following his dreams involving nooses, King is found dead with a wisp of a spider web circling his neck.

Most of Wynbush's characters speak in dialect, for many of them are inhabitants of small rural towns. At times Wynbush intermingles the southern dialect with standard English to demonstrate the contrast between her characters and their backgrounds. Building up the environments to give shape to her stories, she emphasizes the contrasts between settings of lush humid spots filled with towering trees and groves of scented flowers and those of tight yellow roads filled with sun-baked dust.

The two protagonists in "The Return of a Modern Prodigal" and "Ticket Home" must undergo emotional journeys along these Louisiana roads in order to recapture a past they relinquished years earlier. In both of these stories Wynbush attempts to rejoin her characters to an all-but-forgotten past. The thirteen-year trek back home for the wrongfully imprisoned son in "Modern Prodigal" ends with his parents never recognizing him. He departs once again without ever having revealed his identity. The same outcome is reached in Wynbush's later story "Ticket Home." After deciding to meet the daughter she abandoned fourteen years earlier, Margaret undertakes the physical transformation from country to city to finally face what has plagued her all this time. Before her journey is finished, she coincidentally meets a young woman who unknowingly provides her with information proving that she is in fact her daughter. The two women talk about the unknown mother and Margaret reassures her daughter that she is sure her mother loves her. The women part and the secret is left untold.

Octavia Wynbush's short stories deal primarily with the black community. In "Black Streak" she approaches the issue of color consciousness among blacks, a theme also developed by Marita Bonner.* Wynbush establishes dialogue between a race-conscious mother and her daughter who abhors her mother's restrictive attitudes. Through the two women's conversation Wynbush examines the fear centered on the birthing process and ultimately the perpetuation of a dark lineage. The mother lectures: "'Keep 'em on their own side of the fence, girl. If you once let the bars down, you can't put 'em back up again. You can't rub a black streak out.'" It might, at any time, show up in some child. Lucia, the daughter, returns: "'Look mother! All that was good in your day. . . . Color must have been about all there was to make a distinction, wasn't there? . . . it must have been that the people who had the best chance get it because of color.'"

While Lucia's mother unsuccessfully tries to change her seemingly rebellious daughter's viewpoint, the opposite is also the case. Wynbush maintains the differing women's opinions and leaves the story with each woman sticking firmly to her personal plane of thought.

Since Wynbush's literary activities appear to have ceased after 1945, she has escaped notice and no biographical information is published about her.

However, contributor notes in *Opportunity* identify her as a graduate of Oberlin College. The college reports that Wynbush, born in July of 1894 (or perhaps 1897) in Washington, Pennsylvania, was a member of the class of 1920 and received a B.A. with a major in German. Her parents were Abraham and Mary Sheppard Wynbush; her mother continued to live in Washington, Pennsylvania until at least 1925.

It is not easy to piece together Wynbush's employment history from the information she sent to the Alumni Office of her alma mater. She held a long succession of teaching jobs, from 1920 until her retirement in 1969. One early position was at Straight College, New Orleans (one year), perhaps in the early 1920s, followed by another at Scottville, Louisiana (two years). Other posts were at Pine Bluff, Arkansas, Arkansas State College, and Philander Smith College in Little Rock (around 1930). By the time she published "The Noose" in *Opportunity*, December 1931, she was at Columbia University working toward an M.A. in English (degree received in 1934). For her juvenile book *The Wheel That Made Wishes Come True* (1941) she won membership in the International Mark Twain Society and honorary membership in the Eugene Field Society. She taught at Sumner High School and Junin College in Kansas City, Kansas, but had a Gary, Indiana, address. As of 1936 she was at Lincoln High School, Kansas City, Missouri, and was still in Kansas City in October of 1938 and probably until her 1969 retirement. Another piece of surprising information is found in the Oberlin archives – Wynbush married in April 1963, at age sixty-seven, becoming Mrs. Lewis Strong. Geographic mobility does not seem to have been accompanied by professional advancement for Wynbush. From college teaching she went to a secondary school and apparently wrote no more after the mid-1940s.

SELECT BIBLIOGRAPHY

Primary

Fiction

JUVENILE

The Wheel That Made Wishes Come True. Philadelphia: Dorrance & Co., 1941.

SHORT STORIES

"The Black Streak." *Crisis* (October 1945): 286-87, 301.

"Bride of God." *Crisis* (October 1938): 325-26, 340-42.

"Conjure Man." *Crisis* (March 1938): 71-73, 82, 89-90.

"The Conversion of Harvey." *Crisis* (March 1936): 76-78, 93-94.

"The Noose." *Opportunity* (December 1931): 369-71.

"The Return of a Modern Prodigal." *Crisis* (October 1937): 300-1, 306, 311.

"Serena Sings." *Crisis* (October 1935): 296-97, 313.

"Ticket Home." *Crisis* (January 1939): 7-8, 29-30.

Poetry

"Beauty." *Opportunity* (August 1930): 243.

"The Song of the Cotton." *Opportunity* (June 1925): 184.

Secondary

Ellis, *Opportunity; A Journal of Negro Life*, 1971.

Fairbanks and Engeldinger, *Black American Fiction*, 1978.

Matthews, *Black American Writers, 1773-1949*, 1975.

Rose Bibliography Project, *Analytical Guide and Indexes to "The Crisis," 1910-1960*, 1975.

YANCEY, BESSIE WOODSON (1882-1958)

Poet

Bessie Woodson was born in New Canton, Buckingham County, Virginia, the daughter of James Henry and Anne Eliza (Riddle) Woodson. She was a younger sister of Carter G. Woodson (1875-1950), the noted historian and founder of the *Journal of Negro History*. She attended until 1892 the five-month rural school taught alternately by her uncles, John Morton Riddle and James Buchanan Riddle.

In 1892 the Woodsons moved back to West Virginia, where they had lived before from 1870 to 1874 when the father worked as a laborer in constructing the Chesapeake and Ohio Railroad through the center of the state. In the rapidly growing city of Huntington, which sprang up on the banks of the Ohio when the railway reached that waterway, Bessie attended the Douglass High School. Her brother Carter was one of her teachers at this school; he also served as principal and signed her diploma when she graduated in 1901. Unlike her brother, who went on to the University of Chicago, the Sorbonne, and Harvard, Bessie Woodson was to live the rest of her life in Huntington.

She started her career as a teacher in a mining camp school near Montgomery, West Virginia, and later at Guyandotte, a part of Huntington. She married and had two daughters, Ursula and Belva. Belva became the mother of Bessie Woodson's grandchildren, Nelson and Joan Bickley. Bessie was divorced from her first husband, remarried, and subsequently widowed.

The publisher of her volume of poetry *Echoes from the Hills* (1939) noted that "as a widow her main concern has been to hold together in Huntington the remnant of her family and that of her oldest brother, Robert

H. Woodson." The Beatrice Murphy anthology of 1968 reports of Bessie Woodson Yancey only that "she is occupied at present with nothing definite." Yet her grandchildren say they have reason to believe that she did continue to write poetry on a limited basis. One poem, "The Forgotten Boys," which was found among her papers, was published by the *Pittsburgh Courier*, edited by the noted author George S. Schuyler.

It seems that in her later life, Yancey wrote more prose than poetry. She was concerned about race and public affairs and expressed herself concerning them in letters to the editor which frequently appeared in her hometown Sunday newspaper, the *Herald-Advertiser*. The letters were sometimes published under the pseudonym "Bronze" or "The Yank." She was advised to use a pseudonym by the editor of the paper because of the frequency of her letters. Apparently, the editor did not want readers to feel that one person's material was dominating the column. Her letters were really mini-editorials and on at least one occasion provoked an anonymous threat by a conservative reader. She also appears to have received some support for her opinions from liberal readers, and the newspaper on occasion seems to have recognized the quality of the material she wrote. As a case in point, among her papers is a letter from the editor advising her of a small monetary prize she had won through the submission of a letter.

Some of the poetry included in *Echoes from the Hills* was first published in newspapers and magazines. Its themes are the poet's love for West Virginia and its mountain streams, and the invigorating chill of wind and winter. She also alludes to the need for "tribe and clan" to reach greater understanding. "Your strength is mine / Your weakness too. I free myself – / When I liberate you," she says in "Harmony." She celebrates her race in the poem "Ambassador" with this: "I am a Negro, / Dusky / As my native jungles, / Subtle as the creatures that move therein, / Rollicking / Like the noon-day sun." Other such celebrations are "A Toast to Colored Girls" and "The Negro Woman." She also wrote many poems in dialect such as the humorous "Backslidin'" which portrays a church meeting called to judge a sister engaged in the prohibited activity of dancing.

SELECT BIBLIOGRAPHY

Primary

Poetry

Echoes from the Hills. Washington, D.C.: Associated Publishers, 1939.

IN ANTHOLOGIES

Murphy, *Ebony Rhythm*, [1948] 1968. "Knee Deep."

Secondary

Bickley, Ancella R. [relative]. Letter, 9 June 1987.

Kallenbach, *Index to Black American Literary Anthologies*, 1979.

Porter, *North American Negro Poets*, 1945.

Reardon and Thorsen, *Poetry by American Women, 1900-1975*, 1979.

Rush, Myers, and Arata, *Black American Writers Past and Present*, 1975.

YEISER, IDABELLE (ca. 1897-?)

Educator

Essayist

Poet

Short-story writer

Awarded first prize for her personal experience sketch "Letters" in the literary contest held by *Opportunity* in 1927, Idabelle Yeiser participated in the cultural ferment of Philadelphia's New Negro Movement. Vincent Jubilee maintains that Yeiser represents "one of the pronounced talents that chose, for various reasons, to subdue a full-fledged literary career in favor of some other vocation or interest and who is not found in any periodicals except *Crisis* and *Opportunity*, and is not discussed by any critics today." It may well be that the "various reasons" were obstacles common to black women seeking literary careers. Yeiser, in a bio-sketch *(Opportunity,* July 1927), revealed, "As to my career, I love writing, but up to now it has been my avocation rather than my vocation. I do it rather spasmodically, but hope to make it my vocation."

Yeiser's parentage and childhood and how she cultivated her affinity for writing are little known. Library of Congress records show that she was the daughter of Rev. John G. Yeiser, who lived from 1845 to 1911. Idabelle compiled and edited her father's sermons. Two sources that do render a little biographical information, Jubilee's dissertation and *Opportunity,* make it clear that Yeiser enjoyed the privileges of Afro-American middle-class life. She graduated from Montclair, New Jersey, State Normal School, continuing her studies at the University of Pennsylvania. Specializing in languages and proficient in French, Italian, and Spanish, she eventually earned her Ph.D. in French from Columbia University. During 1925 and 1926 she traveled abroad, afterward returning to Philadelphia to teach.

Yeiser was active in one of Philadelphia's literary groups during her teaching career, but her concerns went beyond the pastimes of the elite. She was absorbed in promoting the social and educational welfare of the Afro-American community. Described by her peers as an "intellectual poet" she was an innovative educator whose zeal for her work and outgoing personality impelled her to encourage and inspire her students. Yeiser recognized that one of the means of diffusing prejudice was to develop culturally nonbiased programs of science, math, social studies, language arts/literature, and so on, beginning at the grade-school level. She later published a paper presented at the Harvard Workshop in Intercultural Education in the summer of 1943, *The Curriculum as an Integrating Force for Ethnic Variations.*

Yeiser, like Evelyn Crawford Reynolds,* Mae V. Cowdery,* Bessie Calhoun Bird,* and other women involved in the Philadelphia literary groups, produced volumes of poetry in the 1930s or thereafter. The poet published in *Crisis* and *Opportunity*; according to Jubilee, her only appearance in *Black Opals*, a local magazine showcasing the artistic/literary endeavors of Philadelphia's New Negro Movement groups, was in the Christmas 1927 issue. Yeiser wrote a letter giving accounts of her travels in Spain. Perhaps these notes were the inspiration for her award-winning essay, "Letters."

Superficially, "Letters" seems to be a description of the author's experiences during visits to the cities of Algiers, Biskra, and Tunis. It is a cultural escapade wherein the narrator conjures an image or defines a term. In it Africa is described, but not the beating of drums or natives half-clothed or living in huts; it is an Africa laden with tales of a culture with traditions superseding those of America.

On another level the essay is a clever vignette on the essence of Afro-American history, best captured in a profound moment: "Once we saw a group of women approach the guide, and point toward me while jabbering something in their Arab dialect. I grew alarmed, and asked the cause. The guide said, smilingly, 'They think you are one of them, so I told them you were taken away when a baby and had now come back to visit your native land.'" Here Yeiser redefines race in terms of a culture unifying the person with a heritage – a basic foundation of self-esteem. This was a major theme spawned by the spirit of the New Negro Movement.

Moods (1937), Yeiser's first volume of poetry, is divided into five parts: Nature, Children, Miniatures (poems most likely collected under this heading because of their length), Love, and Philosophy. At first glance the book seems a mediocre collection of poetry, with generic themes and fluctuation of poetic style from sonnets to quatrains, from rhyme to free verse. Yeiser, however, occasionally invites the contemplation of the reader. In "Fool's Gold" she unveils her contempt for pretentious society leaders whose "Bland words / Served from the silver tongue / Of a flatterer" are nothing more than "Kisses / From the lips of a Judas." In "Sons and Daughters" the poet, subconsciously perhaps, wonders how or if society properly values women. She questions a mother's preference for her "wayward, thoughtless" son whose errant ways will "cause the tears / to flood his mother's eyes" over the daughter who "may do her mother's every bid, / And often sacrifice her innermost wishes / That her mother may be free from care and want."

Because she was a survivor of World War II and the Depression it is understandable that a major theme in Idabelle Yeiser's second volume of poetry, *Lyric and Legend* (1947) is world peace and understanding. In this collection (which includes twenty-five poems reprinted from *Moods*), she expresses a desire for love to be shared among humankind in "The World Tomorrow" and in "What Price Peace," which was published in the February 1944 issue of *Unity* magazine. A number of poems, like "A Teacher Speaks of Retirement" and "Recompense," appear to be autobiographical.

One of the poems in *Lyric and Legend* (dedicated to an H. F.) is "The Mask." Clarissa Scott Delany,* Eloise Bibb Thompson,* and other black women writers also wrote about and titled work after the phenomenon known as "the mask." Yeiser brings a universal approach to this theme. She declares that the reserved friendliness – "the mask" – caused by "Heartaches, longings, broken idols / Disillusionment, shattered dreams / need to be woven / Into a forceful new pattern."

SELECT BIBLIOGRAPHY

Primary

Fiction

"An Echo from Toulouse, France." *Crisis* 29 (July 1926).

Nonfiction

The Curriculum as an Integrating Force for Ethnic Variations. Paper presented at the Harvard Workshop in Intercultural Education, Summer 1943. Cambridge: Harvard Graduate School of Education.

"Letters." *Opportunity* (July 1927): 206-7.

Poetry

Lyric and Legend. Boston: Christopher Publishing House, 1947.

Moods: A Book of Verse. Philadelphia: Colony Press, 1937.

Secondary

Deodene and French, *Black American Poetry since 1944*, 1971.

Ellis, *Opportunity; A Journal of Negro Life*, 1971.

Jubilee, "Philadelphia's Afro-American Literary Circle and the Harlem Renaissance," 1980.

APPENDIX A
WOMEN WRITERS BY GENRE

Autobiographers

Adams, Elizabeth Laura
Dunham, Katherine
Goodwin, Ruby Berkley
Harrison, Juanita
Hunter, Jane Edna
Hurston, Zora Neale
Pitts, Lucia Mae
Tarry, Ellen
Terrell, Mary Church
Thompson, Era Bell
Wells-Barnett, Ida B.

Biographers

Brown, Hallie Quinn
Cuthbert, Marion Vera
Graham Du Bois, Shirley Lola
Hare, Maud Cuney
Hunton, Addie D. Waites
Robeson, Eslanda Goode

Children's Writers

Love, Rose Leary
McBrown, Gertrude Parthenia
Petry, Ann Lane
Tarry, Ellen
Wynbush, Octavia Beatrice

Editors of journals or anthologies

Clifford, Carrie Williams
Fauset, Jessie
Hopkins, Pauline Elizabeth
Murphy, Beatrice Campbell
Newsome, Effie Lee
Thompson, Era Bell
West, Dorothy

Essayists

Bennett, Gwendolyn B.
Bright, Nellie Rathborne
Brown, Charlotte Hawkins
Fernandis, Sarah Collins
Carter, Eunice Hunton
Coleman, Anita Scott
Cooper, Anna Julia
Cuthbert, Marion Vera
Day, Caroline Bond
Dunham, Katherine
Fernandis, Sarah Collins
Gaines-Shelton, Ruth Ada
Hunton, Addie D. Waites
Hurston, Zora Neale
Love, Rose Leary
McDougald, Gertrude Elise
Moryck, Brenda Ray
Murray, Pauli
Petry, Ann Lane
Porter, Dorothy Louise Burnett
Ridley, Florida Ruffin
Walker, Margaret
Wells-Barnett, Ida B.
Yeiser, Idabelle

Journalists

Beasley, Delilah Leontium
Butler, Anna Mabel Land
Dunbar-Nelson, Alice
Murphy, Beatrice Campbell
Reynolds, Evelyn Crawford
Ridley, Florida Ruffin
Tarry, Ellen
Terrell, Mary Church
Thompson, Eloise Bibb
Thompson, Era Bell
Wells-Barnett, Ida B.

Literary Critics

Bennett, Gwendolyn B.
Bonner Marita
Carter, Eunice Hunton
Delany, Clarissa Scott
Fauset, Jessie
Newsome, Effie Lee
Spence, Eulalie

Novelists

Dunham, Katherine
Fauset, Jessie Redmon
Fleming, Sarah Lee Brown
Gilbert, Mercedes
Graham Du Bois, Shirley Lola
Hopkins, Pauline Elizabeth
Hurston, Zora Neale
Larsen, Nella
Petry, Ann Lane
Walker, Margaret
West, Dorothy
Wood, Lillian E.
Wright, Zara

Playwrights

Andrews, Regina M. Anderson
Bonner, Marita Odette
Burrill, Mary
Bush, Olivia Ward
Dunbar-Nelson, Alice
Duncan, Thelma Myrtle
Figgs, Carrie Law Morgan
Gaines-Shelton, Ruth Ada
Gilbert, Mercedes
Graham, Ottie Beatrice
Graham Du Bois, Shirley Lola
Grimké, Angelina Weld
Hare, Maud Cuney
Hazzard, Alvira
Hopkins, Pauline Elizabeth
Hurston, Zora Neale
Johnson, Georgia Douglas

Livingston, Myrtle Athleen Smith
Miller, May
Pitts, Lucia Mae
Price, Doris D.
Spence, Eulalie
Thompson, Eloise Bibb

Poets

Bennett, Gwendolyn B.
Bird, Bessie Calhoun
Bright, Nellie Rathborne
Bush, Olivia Ward
Butler, Anna Mabel Land
Caution-Davis, Ethel
Clark, Mazie Earhart
Clifford, Carrie Williams
Coleman, Anita Scott
Copeland, Josephine
Cowdery, Mae Virginia
Cuthbert, Marion Vera
Delany, Clarissa Scott
Dickinson, Blanche Taylor
Dunbar-Nelson, Alice
Dunham, Katherine
Epperson, Aloise Barbour
Fauset, Jessie
Fernandis, Sarah Collins
Figgs, Carrie Law Morgan
Fleming, Sarah Lee Brown
Gaines-Shelton, Ruth Ada
Gilbert, Mercedes
Gooden, Lauretta Holman
Goodwin, Ruby Berkley
Gordon, Edythe Mae
Grimké, Angelina Weld
Hayford, Gladys May Casely
  (Aquah Laluah)
Hazzard, Alvira
Holloway, Lucy Ariel Williams
Jeffrey, Maurine L.
Jessye, Eva Alberta
Johnson, Dorothy Vena

Johnson, Georgia Douglas
Johnson, Helene
Lewis, Lillian Tucker
McBrown, Gertrude Parthenia
Miller, May
Moody, Christina
Murphy, Beatrice Campbell
Murray, Pauli
Newsome, Mary Effie Lee
Pitts, Lucia Mae
Popel, Esther A. B.
Postles, Grace Vera
Ransom, Birdelle Wycoff
Reynolds, Evelyn Crawford
Rowland, Ida
Smith, J. Pauline
Spencer, Anne Bethel
Thompson, Clara Ann
Thompson, Eloise Bibb
Thompson, Priscilla Jane
Turner, Lucy Mae
Walker, Margaret
Weeden, Lula Lowe
Wiggins, Bernice Love
Wynbush, Octavia Beatrice
Yancey, Bessie Woodson
Yeiser, Idabelle

Scholars

Beasley, Delilah
Cooper, Anna Julia [History]
Cuthbert, Marion Vera
  [Education]
Day, Caroline Bond [Sociology]
Dykes, Eva [English literature]
Gordon, Edythe Mae [History]
Hare, Maud Cuney [Musicology]
Hurston, Zora Neale
  [Anthropology and Folklore]
Jessye, Eva [Musicology]

Livingston, Myrtle Athleen Smith
  [Health and Physical
  Education]
Porter, Dorothy [Literary
  Bibliography]
Yeiser, Idabelle [Education]

Short-Story Writers

Bennett, Gwendolyn B.
Bonner, Marita Odette
Bright, Nellie Rathborne
Brown, Charlotte Hawkins
Campbell, Hazel Vivian
Carter, Eunice Hunton
Caution-Davis, Ethel
Coleman, Anita Scott
Cowdery, Mae Virginia
Cuthbert, Marion Vera
Day, Caroline Bond
Dunbar-Nelson, Alice
Dunham, Katherine
Goodwin, Ruby Berkley
Gordon, Edythe Mae
Graham, Ottie Beatrice
Grimké, Angelina Weld
Harmon, Florence Marion
Hazzard, Alvira
Hopkins, Pauline Elizabeth
Hurston, Zora Neale
Moryck, Brenda Ray
Petry, Ann Lane
Ridley, Florida Ruffin
Thompson, Eloise Bibb
West, Dorothy
Wynbush, Octavia Beatrice
Yeiser, Idabelle

Travel Writers

Dunham, Katherine
Harrison, Juanita
Robeson, Eslanda Goode

APPENDIX B
WOMEN WRITERS BY GEOGRAPHIC LOCATION

Although many of the writers resided in various locations throughout their lives, some were closely associated with particular places. Below is a partial listing of these cities or states. The purpose of this roster is to encourage further study on locations of literary productivity other than New York City.

Boston, Massachusetts

Ethel Caution-Davis
Edythe Mae Gordon
Florence Marion Harmon
Alvira Hazzard
Pauline Elizabeth Hopkins
Helene Johnson
Gertrude Parthenia McBrown
Grace Vera Postles
Florida Ruffin Ridley
Dorothy West

Los Angeles, California

Elizabeth Laura Adams
Delilah Beasley
Anita Scott Coleman
Dorothy Vena Johnson
Eloise Bibb Thompson

Ohio

Hallie Quinn Brown
Mazie Earhart Clark
Ruth Ada Gaines-Shelton
Jane Edna Hunter
Clara Ann Thompson
Priscilla Jane Thompson
Lucy Mae Turner

Philadelphia, Pennsylvania

Gwendolyn B. Bennett
Bessie C. Bird
Nellie R. Bright
Mae V. Cowdery

Ottie B. Graham
Evelyn Crawford Reynolds
Idabelle Yeiser

Texas

Gwendolyn B. Bennett
Lauretta Holman Gooden
Maurine L. Jeffrey
Lillian Tucker Lewis
Birdelle Wycoff Ransom
Bernice Love Wiggins

Washington, D.C.

Gwendolyn B. Bennett
Marita Bonner
Mary Burrill
Carrie Williams Clifford
Anna Julia Cooper
Clarissa Scott Delany
Alice Dunbar-Nelson
Jessie Redmon Fauset
Angelina Grimké
Zora Neal Hurston
Georgia Douglas Johnson
Gertrude Parthenia McBrown
May Miller
Brenda Ray Moryck
Beatrice Campbell Murphy
Effie Lee Newsome
Esther Popel (Shaw)
Dorothy Burnett Porter
Anne Scales Spencer
Mary Church Terrell

367

APPENDIX C
WOMEN WRITERS BY DATE

Brown, Hallie Quinn
(1845?/1860?-1949)
Cooper, Anna Julia (1856-1964)
Hopkins, Pauline Elizabeth (1859-
1930)
Ridley, Florida Ruffin (1861-
1943)
Clifford, Carrie Williams (1862-
1934)
Wells-Barnett, Ida Bell (1862-
1931)
Fernandis, Sarah Collins (1863-
1951)
Terrell, Mary Church (1863-1954)
Bush, Olivia Ward (1869-1944)
Thompson, Clara Ann (1869-
1949)
Hunton, Addie D. Waites (1870-
1943)
Beasley, Delilah Leontium (1871-
1934)
Thompson, Priscilla Jane (1871-
1942)
Gaines-Shelton, Ruth Ada
(1872-?)
Clark, Mazie Earhart (1874-1958)
Hare, Maud Cuney (1874-1936)
Dunbar-Nelson, Alice Ruth
Moore (1875-1935)
Fleming, Sarah Lee Brown (1875-
1963)
Johnson, Georgia Douglas (1877-
1966)
Thompson, Eloise Alberta
Veronica Bibb (1878-1928)
Caution-Davis, Ethel (ca. 1880-
1981)
Grimké, Angelina Weld (1880-
1958)

Harmon, Florence Marion (1880-
1936)
Brown, Charlotte Hawkins (1882-
1961)
Burrill, Mary (ca. 1882-1946)
Fauset, Jessie Redmon (1882-
1961)
Hunter, Jane Edna (1882-1971)
Spencer, Anne Bethel Bannister
Scales (1882-1976)
Yancey, Bessie Woodson (1882-
1958)
Turner, Lucy Mae (1884-?)
McDougald, Elise Johnson (1885-
1971)
Newsome, Mary Effie Lee (1885-
1979)
Day, Caroline Bond (1889-1948)
Gilbert, Mercedes (1889-1952)
Coleman, Anita Scott (1890-1960)
Gordon, Edythe Mae (ca. 1890-?)
Harrison, Juanita (1891?-)
Hurston, Zora Neale (1891-1960)
Larsen, Nella (1891-1964)
Dykes, Eva Beatrice (1893-1986)
Moryck, Brenda Ray (1894-1949)
Spence, Eulalie (1894-1981)
Wynbush, Octavia Beatrice (1894-
ca. 1972)
Cuthbert, Marion Vera (1896-)
Dickinson, Blanche Taylor (1896-)
Graham Du Bois, Shirley Lola
(1896-1977)
Moody, Christina (ca. 1896-?)
Popel (Shaw), Esther A. B. (1896-
1958)
Robeson, Eslanda Cardoza
Goode (1896-1965)
Jessye, Eva Alberta (1897-)

Wiggins, Bernice Love (1897-)
Yeiser, Idabelle (ca. 1897-?)
Bonner, Marita Odette (1898-1971)
Johnson, Dorothy Vena (1898-1970)
Love, Rose Leary (1898-1969)
Carter, Eunice Roberta Hunton (1899-1970)
Hazzard, Alvira (1899-1953)
Miller, May (1899-)
Graham, Ottie Beatrice (1900-)
Jeffrey, Maurine L. (1900-)
Reynolds, Evelyn Crawford (ca. 1900-?)
Andrews, Regina M. Anderson (1901-)
Butler, Anna Mabel Land (1901-1989)
Delany, Clarissa Scott (1901-1927)
Bennett, Gwendolyn B. (1902-1981)
Bright, Nellie Rathborne (1902-1976)
Duncan, Thelma Myrtle (1902-)
Livingston, Myrtle Athleen Smith (1902-1973)
McBrown, Gertrude Parthenia (1902-)
Goodwin, Ruby Berkley (1903-)
Hayford, Gladys May Casely (1904-1950)
Pitts, Lucia Mae (1904-1973)
Rowland, Ida (1904-)
Holloway, Lucy Ariel Williams (1905-1973)
Porter, Dorothy Louise Burnett (1905-)
Bird, Bessie Calhoun (ca. 1906-?)
Postles, Grace Vera (1906-)
Tarry, Ellen (1906-)
Thompson, Era Bell (1906-1986)
Johnson, Helene (1907-)

West, Dorothy (1907-)
Murphy, Beatrice Campbell (1908-)
Petry, Ann Lane (1908-)
Adams, Elizabeth Laura (1909-)
Cowdery, Mae Virginia (1909-1953)
Dunham, Katherine (1910-)
Murray, Pauli (1910-1985)
Ransom, Birdelle Wycoff (1914-)
Walker, Margaret Abigail Alexander (1915-)
Weeden, Lula Lowe (1918-)

BIRTH DATES UNKNOWN

Campbell, Hazel Vivian
Copeland, Josephine
Epperson, Aloise Barbour (?-ca. 1954)
Figgs, Carrie Law Morgan
Gooden, Lauretta Holman
Lewis, Lillian Tucker
Price, Doris
Smith, J. Pauline
Wood, Lillian E.
Wright, Zara

APPENDIX D
INDEX TO TITLES

The following lists titles of primary works cited in the Selected Bibliography at the end of each chapter. The author is identified after each title.

371

BIBLIOGRAPHY

Abajian, James de T. *Blacks and Their Contributions to the American West: A Bibliography and Union List of Library Holdings through 1970*. Boston: G. K. Hall & Co., 1974.

Abramson, Doris E. "Angelina Weld Grimké, Mary Burrill, Georgia Douglas Johnson, and Marita O. Bonner: An Analysis of Their Plays." *Sage* (Spring 1985): 9-13.

Adoff, Arnold, ed. *The Poetry of Black America: Anthology of the 20th Century*. New York: Harper & Row, 1973.

Afro-American Encyclopedia. 10 vols. Miami, Fla.: Educational Book Publishers, 1974.

Anderson, Jervis. *This Was Harlem: A Cultural Portrait, 1900-1950*. New York: Farrar, Straus, 1982.

Aptheker, Herbert, ed. *A Documentary History of the Negro in the United States*. Secaucus, N.J.: Citadel Press, 1973, 32-36.

Arata, Esther Spring. *More Black American Playwrights: A Bibliography*. Metuchen, N.J.: Scarecrow Press, 1978.

Arata, Esther Spring, and Nicolas John Rotoli. *Black American Playwrights, 1800 to the Present: A Bibliography*. Metuchen, N.J.: Scarecrow Press, 1976.

Babb, Valerie Melissa. "The Evolution of American Literary Language." Ph.D. diss., University of Buffalo, 1980.

Bailey, Leonard, comp. *Broadside Authors and Artists: An Illustrated Biographical Dictionary*. Detroit: Broadside Press, 1974.

Baker, Houston A. *Afro-American Poetics: Revisions of Harlem and the Black Aesthetic*. Madison: University of Wisconsin Press, 1988.

Baker, Houston A. *Modernism and the Harlem Renaissance*. Chicago: University of Chicago Press, 1987.

Bakish, David, and Edward Margolies. *Afro-American Fiction, 1853-1976*. Detroit: Gale Research Co., 1979.

Bardolph, Richard. *The Negro Vanguard*. New York: Rinehart, 1959.

Barton, Rebecca Chalmers. *Witnesses for Freedom: Negro Americans in Autobiography*. New York: Harper & Co., 1948. Reprint. Oakdale, N.Y.: Dowling College Press, 1976.

Baytop, Adrianne. "Margaret Walker." In Mainiero and Faust, *American Women Writers*, vol. 4, 1982.

Beasley, Delilah Leontium. *Negro Trailblazers of California*. Los Angeles: Times Mirror Printing and Binding House, 1919.

Belcher, Fannin Saffore, Jr. "The Place of the Negro in the Evolution of the American Theatre." Ph.D. diss., Yale University, 1945; University Microfilms, 1975.

Bell, Bernard. "Ann Petry's Demythologizing of American Culture and Afro-American Character." In Pryse and Spillers, *Conjuring*, 1985.

Bell, Roseann P., Bettye J. Parker, and Beverly Guy-Sheftall, eds. *Sturdy Black Bridges: Visions of Black Women in Literature*. Garden City, N.Y.: Doubleday, Anchor Press, 1979.

Bennett, Gwendolyn. Review of *My Spirituals*, by Eva Jessye. *Opportunity* (November 1927): 338-39.

Bennett, Lerone. "The Shaping of Black America." *Freedomways* (Fourth quarter 1975): 280-82.

Berry, Linda S. "Georgia Douglas Johnson." In Mainiero and Faust, *American Women Writers*, vol. 2, 1980.

Berzson, Judith R. *Neither Black nor White: The Mulatto Character in American Fiction*. New York: New York University Press, 1978.

Blassingame, John W. "The Afro Americans: Mythology to Reality." In Cartwright and Watson, *The Reinterpretation of American History and Culture*, 1973.

Bone, Robert. *Down Home: A History of Afro-American Short Fiction from Its Beginnings to the End of the Harlem Renaissance*. New York: G. Putnam's Sons, 1975.

_____. *The Negro Novel in America*. 1958. Rev. ed. New Haven: Yale University Press, 1965.

_____. "Zora Neale Hurston." In Hemenway, *The Black Novelist*, 1970.

Bonner, Marita Odette. Review of *An Autumn Love Cycle*, by Georgia Douglas Johnson. *Opportunity* 7 (April 1927): 130.

Bontemps, Arna. Review of *The Living Is Easy*, by Dorothy West. *New York Herald Tribune Weekly Book Review* (13 June 1948): 16.

_____, ed. *American Negro Poetry*. New York: Hill & Wang, 1969.

_____, ed. *Golden Slippers*. New York: Harper, 1941.

_____, Bontemps, Arna, ed. *The Harlem Renaissance Remembered*. New York: Dodd, Mead & Co., 1972.

Bontemps, Arna, and Langston Hughes, eds. *The Poetry of the Negro, 1746-1949*. Garden City, N.Y.: Doubleday & Co., 1949.

_____, eds. *The Poetry of the Negro, 1746-1970*. Garden City, N.Y.: Doubleday & Co., 1970.

Book Review Digest (1948). Ten reviews of *The Living Is Easy*, by Dorothy West.

Boris, Joseph J., ed. *Who's Who in Colored America*. New York: Who's Who in Colored America Corp., 1927.

Braithwaite, William Stanley, ed. *Anthology of Magazine Verse*. Boston: B. J. Brimmer, 1927.

Braithwaite, William Stanley, ed. *Yearbook of American Poetry*. Boston: B. J. Brimmer, 1927.

Brawley, Benjamin. *The Negro Genius: A New Appraisal of the Achievement of the American Negro in Literature and the Fine Arts*. New York: Dodd, Mead, 1940.

Brawley, Benjamin. *The Negro in Literature and Art*. New York: Duffield, 1930.

Brewer, John Mason, ed. *Heralding Dawn: An Anthology of Verse*. Dallas: Superior Typesetting, 1936.

Brignano, Russel C. *Black Americans in Autobiography: An Annotated Bibliography of Autobiographies and Autobiographical Books Written since the Civil War*. Rev. and expanded ed. Durham, N.C.: Duke University Press, 1984.

Brown, Sterling, Arthur Davis, and Ulysses Lee, eds. *The Negro Caravan*. New York: Arno Press, 1970.

Burke, Virginia M. "Zora Neale Hurston and Fanny Hurst as They Saw Each Other." *CLA Journal* 20, no. 4 (June 1977): 435-47.

Byars, J. C., ed. *Black and White*. Washington, D.C.: Crane, 1927.

Byrd, James W. "Zora Neale Hurston: A Negro Folklorist." *Tennessee Folklore Society Bulletin* 21, no. 2 (June 1975): 37-41.

Calverton, Victor. *An Anthology of American Negro Literature*. New York: Modern Library, 1929.

Campbell, Dorothy. *Index to Black American Writers in Collective Biographies*. Littleton, Colo.: Libraries Unlimited, 1983.

Campbell, Jane. "Pauline Elizabeth Hopkins." In Harris and Davis, *Dictionary of Literary Biography*, vol. 50, 1986.

Cantarow, Ellen. "Sex, Race, and Criticism: Thoughts of a White Feminist on Kate Chopin and Zora Neale Hurston." *Radical Teacher* 9 (September 1978): 30-33.

Carter, Eunice. Review of *Paul Robeson, Negro. Opportunity* 8, 9 (September 1930): 280.

Cartwright, William H., and Richard L. Watson, Jr., eds. *The Reinterpretation of American History and Culture*. Washington, D.C.: National Council for the Social Studies, 1973.

Chalmers, Rebecca Barton. *Witnesses for Freedom*. Foreword by Alain Locke. New York: Harper, 1959. Reprint. Oakdale, N.Y.: Dowling College Press, 1976.

Chapman, Dorothy H. *Index to Black Poetry*. Boston: G. K. Hall & Co., 1974.

Chapman, Dorothy H. *Index to Poetry by Black American Women*. Westport, Conn.: Greenwood Press, 1986.

Chateauvert, M. Melinda. "The Third Step: Anna Julia Cooper and Black Education in the District of Columbia, 1910-1960." *Sage: A Scholarly Journal on Black Women* (Student Supplement), Summer 1988: 7-13.

Chicago Defender (25 December 1920): 8

Cincinnati Enquirer (20 March 1949): 3:2.

Clark, William Bedford. "The Letters of Nella Larsen to Carl Van Vechten: A Survey." *Resources for American Literary Study* 8 (Fall 1978): 193-99.

Clarke, John Henrik. *Harlem: Voices from the Soul of Black America*. New York: New American Library, 1970.

Contemporary Authors Autobiography Series. Detroit, Mich.: Gale Research Co., 1984-.

Coven, Brenda. *American Women Dramatists of the Twentieth Century: A Bibliography*. Metuchen, N.J.: Scarecrow Press, 1982.

Coyle, William. *Ohio Authors and Their Books*. Cleveland: World Publishing Co., 1962.

Creque-Harris, Leah. "Katherine Dunham's Multi-Cultural Influence." *Tiger Lily* 1 (1986) 2:26-29.

Cromwell, Adelaide M. *An African Victorian Feminist: The Life and Times of Adelaide Smith Casely Hayford, 1868-1960*. London: Frank Cass & Co., 1986.

Cromwell, Otelia, Lorenzo Dow Turner, and Eva B. Dykes. *Readings from Negro Authors*. New York: Harcourt, Brace & Co., 1931.

Cullen, Countee, ed. *Caroling Dusk: An Anthology of Verse by Negro Poets*. London and New York: Harper, 1927.

Cunard, Nancy. *Negro; an Anthology*. London: W. Cunard, 1934. Reprint. New York: Negro Universities Press, 1969. New York: Unger, 1970.

Current Biography. Bronx, N.Y.: H. W. Wilson Co., 1940-.

Curry, Gladys J. *Viewpoints from Black America*. Englewood Cliffs, N.J.: Prentice-Hall, 1970.

Dabney, Wendell P. *Cincinnati's Colored Citizens: Historical, Sociological and Biographical*. Cincinnati: Dabney Publishing Co., 1926.

Dance, Daryl. "Black Eve or Madonna: A Study of the Antithetical Views of the Mother in Black American Literature." In Johnson and Green, *Perspectives on Afro-American Women*, 1975.

Daniel, Sadie Iola. *Women Builders*. 1931. Reprint. Washington, D.C.: Associated Publishers, 1970.

Daniel, Walter C. *Black Journals of the United States*. Westport, Conn.: Greenwood Press, 1982.

Daniel, Walter C., and Sandra Y. Govan. "Gwendolyn Bennett." In Harris and Davis, *Dictionary of Literary Biography*, vol. 51, 1987.

Dannett, Sylvia G. *Profiles of Negro Womanhood*. 2 vols. Yonkers, N.Y.: Educational Heritage, [1964-66].

"Daughter of Ex-Slaves Who Made Good on Broadway Recalls Life." *New York Times* (7 October 1979): 76.

David, Jay. *Growing Up Black*. New York: Simon & Schuster, 1968.

Davis, Arthur P. *From the Dark Tower: Afro-American Writers, 1900-1960*. Washington, D.C.: Howard University Press, 1974.

Davis, Arthur P., and Saunders Redding, eds. *Cavalcade: Negro American Writing from 1790 to the Present*. Boston: Houghton Mifflin Co., 1971.

Davis, Elizabeth Lindsay. *Lifting As They Climb*. [Washington, D.C.]: National Association of Colored Women, 1933.

Davis, John Preston. *The American Negro Reference Book*. Englewood Cliffs, N.J.: Prentice-Hall, 1966.

Davis, Lenwood G. *The Black Woman in American Society: A Selected Annotated Bibliography*. Boston: G. K. Hall & Co., 1975.

Davis, Lenwood G., and Janet Sims. *The Black Family in the United States: A Selected Bibliography of Annotated Books, Articles, and Dissertations on Black Families in America*. Westport, Conn.: Greenwood Press, 1978.

Davis, Marianna W. *Contributions of Black Women to America*. 2 vols. Columbia, S.C.: Kenday Press, 1982.

Davis, Nathaniel, comp. and ed. *Afro-American Reference: An Annotated Bibliography of Selected Resources*. Westport, Conn.: Greenwood Press, 1985.

Davis, Thadious M. "Anna Julia Haywood Cooper." In Mainiero, *American Women Writers*, 1979.

_____. "Nella Larsen." In Harris and Davis, *Dictionary of Literary Biography*, vol. 51, 1987.

_____. "Shirley Graham [Du Bois]." In Mainiero and Faust, *American Women Writers*, vol. 2, 1980.

Dearborn, Mary V. *Pocahontas's Daughters: Gender and Ethnicity in American Culture*. Oxford and New York: Oxford University Press, 1986.

Deodene, Frank, and William P. French. *Black American Poetry since 1944: A Preliminary Checklist*. Chatham, N.J.: Chatham Bookseller, 1971.

Dillon, Richard N. *Humbugs and Heroes: A Gallery of American Negro Biography*. Garden City, N.Y.: Doubleday, 1970.

Dodson, Jualyne E., and Cheryl Townsend Gilkes. "Something Within: Social Change and Collective Endurance in the Sacred World of Black Christian Women." In Ruether and Keller, *Women and Religion in America*, vol. 3. San Francisco: Harper & Row, 1981.

Dover, Cedric. "The Importance of Georgia Douglas Johnson." *Crisis* 59 (December 1952): 633, 636, 674.

Doyle, Sister Mary Ellen. "The Heroines of Black Novels." In Johnson and Green, *Perspectives on Afro-American Women*, 1975.

Duberman, Martin Bauml. *Paul Robeson*. New York: Knopf, 1988.

Dunbar-Nelson, Alice. *Give Us Each Day: The Diary of Alice Dunbar-Nelson*. Edited by Gloria T. Hull. New York: W. W. Norton & Co., 1984.

Dunlap, Mollie E. "A Biographical Sketch of Hallie Quinn Brown." *Alumni Journal* (Central State University) (June 1963).

Edwards, Lee R. *Psyche as Hero: Female Heroism and Fictional Form.* Middletown, Conn.: Wesleyan University Press, 1984.

Ellis, Ethel M., comp. *Opportunity; A Journal of Negro Life: Cumulative Index, Volumes 1-17, 1923-1949.* New York: Kraus Reprint Co., 1971.

Ellison, Ralph. "Recent Negro Fiction." *New Masses* 40, no. 6 (5 August 1941): 22-26.

Evory, Ann, ed. *Contemporary Authors.* Rev. ed. Detroit, Mich.: Gale Research Co., 1979.

Fairbanks, Carol, and Eugene A. Engeldinger. *Black American Fiction: A Bibliography.* Metuchen, N.J.: Scarecrow Press, 1978.

Fannin, Alice. "A Sense of Wonder: The Patterns for Psychic Survival in *Their Eyes* and *The Color Purple.*" In *Zora Neale Hurston Forum* 1, no. 1 (Fall 1986): 1-11.

Farrar, Linda. "Zora Neale Hurston: Local Writer Called Literary Giant." *Florida Today* (2 February 1986): 1F-4F.

Fauset, Jessie Redmon. Review of "Rachel," by Angelina Weld Grimké. *Crisis* 21 (1920): 24.

Federal Theatre Project. *Federal Theatre Plays.* New York: Random House, [c1938.]

Feeney, Joseph J. "Greek Tragic Patterns in a Black Novel: Jessie Fauset's *The Chinaberry Tree.*" *CLA Journal* 28, no. 3 (December 1974): 211-15.

Feeney, Joseph J. "A Sardonic, Unconventional Jessie Fauset: The Double Structure and Double Vision of Her Novels." *CLA Journal* 22, no. 4 (June 1979): 365-82.

Fisher, Dexter, ed. *The Third Woman.* Boston: Houghton Mifflin Co., 1979.

Fletcher, Winona. "From Genteel Poet to Revolutionary Playwright: Georgia Douglas Johnson as a Symbol of Black Success, Failure, and Fortitude." *Theatre Annual* 40 (February 1985): 40-64.

Fletcher, Winona. "Georgia Douglas Johnson." In Harris and Davis, *Dictionary of Literary Biography,* vol. 51, 1987.

Flynn, Joyce. "Marita Bonner Occomy." In Harris and Davis, *Dictionary of Literary Biography,* vol. 51, 1987.

Flynn, Joyce, and Joyce Occomy Strickland, eds. *Frye Street and Environs: The Collected Works of Marita Bonner Occomy.* Boston: Beacon Press, 1987.

Ford, Nick Aaron. "Alice Dunbar Nelson." In James, James, and Boyer, *Notable American Women 1607-1950*, 1971.

Ford, Nick Aaron, and H. L. Faggett. *Best Short Stories by Afro-American Writers (1925-1950)*. Boston: Boston Meador Publishing, 1950. Reprint. Kraus Reprint Co, 1969.

France, Rachel, ed. *A Century of Plays by American Women*. New York, N.Y.: Richards Rosen Press, 1979.

French, William, Michael J. Fabre, Amritjit Singh, and Genevieve Fabre. *Afro-American Poetry and Drama, 1760-1975*. Detroit: Gale Research Co., 1979.

"From Children . . . A People's Folklore." *Charlotte* (N.C.) *Observer* (28 June 1964): 980.

Gates, Henry Louis, Jr. *Black Literature and Literary Theory*. New York: Methuen, 1984.

Gayle, Addison, Jr., ed. *The Black Aesthetic*. Garden City, N.Y.: Doubleday, 1972.

Giddings, Paula. "A Shoulder Hunched against a Sharp Concern: Themes in the Poetry of Margaret Walker." *Black World* (December 1971): 20-25.

Giddings, Paula. "A Special Vision, a Common Goal." *Encore* 4, no. 12 (23 June-4 July 1975): 44, 46, 48.

Giddings, Paula. *When and Where I Enter: The Impact of Black Women on Race and Sex in America*. New York: Morrow, 1984.

Giddings, Paula. "Woman Warrior: Iba B. Wells, Crusader-Journalist." *Essence* (Feburary 1988): 76, 142, 146.

Gilbert, Sandra, and Susan M. Gubar. *The Norton Anthology of Literature by Women*. New York and London: W. W. Norton & Co., 1985.

Giovanni, Nikki. "Review of *The Rocks Cry Out*, by Beatrice Campbell Murphy." *Negro Digest* (August 1969): 97-98.

Gloster, Hugh M. *Negro Voices in American Fiction*. Chapel Hill: University of North Carolina Press, 1948.

Gloster, Hugh M. "Zora Neale Hurston: Novelist and Folklorist." *Phylon* 3 (April-June 1943): 153-56.

Graves, Anna Melissa. *Benvenuto Cellino Had No Prejudice against Bronze: Letters from West Africa*. Baltimore, Md.: Waverly Press, 1943.

Greene, J. Lee. "Anne Spencer." In Harris and Davis, *Dictionary of Literary Biography*, vol. 51, 1987.

Greene, J. Lee. "Anne Spencer of Lynchburg." *Virginia Cavalcade* 27, no. 4 (Spring 1978): 178-85.

Greene, J. Lee. *Time's Unfading Garden: Anne Spencer's Life and Poetry*. Baton Rouge: Louisiana State University Press, 1977.

Greene, Michael. "Angelina Weld Grimké." In Harris and Davis, *Dictionary of Literary Biography*, vol. 50, 1986.

Guillaume, Bernice F. "Olivia Ward Bush: Factors Shaping the Social and Cultural Outlook of a Nineteenth-Century Writer." *Negro History Bulletin* 43 (April-June 1980): 32-34.

Guy, Patricia A. *Women's Poetry Index*. Phoenix, Ariz.: Oryx Press, 1985.

Harley, Sharon. "Anna J. Cooper: A Voice for Black Women." In Harley and Terborg-Penn, *Afro-American Women: Struggles and Images*. Port Washington, N.Y.: Kennikat Press, 1978.

Harley, Sharon, and Roslyn Terborg-Penn, eds. *Afro-American Women: Struggles and Images*. Port Washington, N.Y.: National University Publications, 1978.

Harris, Trudier. *Exorcising Blackness: Historical and Literary Lynching and Burning Rituals*. Bloomington: Indiana University Press, 1984.

_____. *From Mammies to Militants: Domestics in Black American Literature*. Philadelphia: Temple University Press, 1982.

Harris, Trudier, and Thadious M. Davis, eds. *Dictionary of Literary Biography*. Vol. 50, *Afro-American Writers before the Harlem Renaissance*. Detroit, Mich.: Gale Research Co., 1986.

Harris, Trudier, and Thadious M. Davis, eds. *Dictionary of Literary Biography*. Vol. 51, *Afro-American Writers from the Harlem Renaissance to 1940*. Detroit, Mich.: Gale Research Co., 1987.

Hartman, Joan E., and Ellen Messer-Davidow, eds. *Women in Print*. New York: Modern Language Association of America, 1982.

Hatch, James. "Speak to Me in Those Old Words, You Know, Those La-La Words, Those Tung-Tung Sounds." *Yale/Theatre* 8 (Fall 1976): 27.

Hatch, James V., and Omanii Abdullah, eds. *Black Playwrights, 1823-1977: An Annotated Bibliography of Plays*. New York and London: R. R. Bowker Co., 1977.

Hatch, James V., and Ted Shine, eds. *Black Theatre U.S.A: Forty-five Plays by Black Americans, 1847-1974*. New York: Free Press, 1974.

Hayden, Robert, ed. *Kaleidoscope: Poems by American Negro Poets*. New York: Harcourt, Brace & World, 1967.

Hemenway, Robert. *The Black Novelist*. Columbus, Ohio: Charles E. Merrill Publishing Co., 1970.

_____. *Zora Neale Hurston: A Literary Biography*. Foreword by Alice Walker. Urbana: University of Illinois Press, 1977.

_____. "Zora Neale Hurston and the Eatonville Anthropology." In Bontemps, *The Harlem Renaissance Remembered*. New York: Dodd, Mead, & Co., 1972.

Herman, Kali, ed. *Women in Particular: An Index to American Women*. Phoenix, Ariz.: Oryx Press, 1984.

Heslip-Ruffin Papers. Amistad Research Center, New Orleans, La.

Hicklin, Fannie E. F. "The American Negro Playwright, 1920-1964." Ph.D. diss., University of Wisconsin at Madison, 1965, pt. 2, 225-26.

Hill, Roy. *Rhetoric of Racial Revolt*. Denver: Golden Bell Press, 1964.

Hill, Ruth Edmonds, and Patricia Miller King, eds. Transcript from *The Black Women's Oral History Project*. Cambridge, Mass.: Schlesinger Library, Radcliffe College, 1987.

Hoffmann, Leonore, and Deborah Rosenfelt. *Teaching Women's Literature from a Regional Perspective*. New York: Modern Language Association of America, 1982.

Holloway, Karla Francesca Clapp. "A Critical Investigation of Literary and Linguistic Structures in the Fiction of Zora Neale Hurston." Ph.D. diss., Michigan State University, 1978.

Hopkins, Lee Bennett. *Books Are by People: Interviews with 104 Authors and Illustrators of Books for Young Children*. New York: Citation Press, 1969.

Howard, Lillie P. "Zora Neale Hurston." In Harris and Davis, *Dictionary of Literary Biography*, vol. 51, 1987.

Howard, Lillie P. *Zora Neale Hurston*. Boston: Twayne Publishers, 1980.

Huggins, Nathan. *Harlem Renaissance*. New York: Oxford University Press, 1971.

Huggins, Nathan. *Voices from the Harlem Renaissance*. New York: Oxford University Press, 1976.

Hughes, John Milton Charles. *The Negro Novelist: A Discussion of the Writings of American Negro Novelists, 1940-1950.* 1953. Reprint. Freeport, N.Y.: Books for Libraries Press, 1967.

Hughes, Langston. *The Best Short Stories by Negro Writers.* Boston: Little, Brown, 1967.

Hull, Gloria T. "Alice Dunbar-Nelson: Delaware Writer and Woman of Affairs." *Delaware History* 17, no. 2 (1976): 87-103.

_____. "Black Women Poets from Wheatley to Walker." *Negro American Literature Forum* 9 (Fall 1975): 91-96. Also in Bell, Parker, and Guy-Sheftall, *Sturdy Black Bridges*, 1979.

_____. *Color, Sex, and Poetry: Three Women Writers of the Harlem Renaissance.* Bloomington: Indiana University Press, 1987.

_____. "Under the Days: The Buried Life and Poetry of Angelina Weld Grimké." *Conditions: Five* 2, no. 2 (Autumn 1979): 17-25.

Hull, Gloria T., Patricia Bell-Scott, and Barbara Smith. *All the Women Are White, All the Blacks Are Men, But Some of Us Are Brave: Black Women's Studies.* Old Westbury, N.Y.: Feminist Press, 1982.

Hurston, Zora Neale. "The Hue and Cry about Howard University." *Messenger* 11 (September 1925): 315-316.

Hutchinson, Louise Daniel. *Anna J. Cooper: A Voice from the South.* Washington: Smithsonian Institution Press, 1981.

Hutson, Jean Blackwell. "Eunice Hunton Carter." In Sicherman et al., *Notable American Women*, 1980.

Index to Poetry in Periodicals, 1920-1924. Great Neck, N.Y.: Granger Book Co., 1983.

Index to Poetry in Periodicals, 1925-1929. Great Neck, N.Y.: Granger Book Co., 1983.

Innis, Doris Funnye, and Juliana Wu, eds. *Profiles in Black.* New York: CORE Publications, 1976.

Jackson, Clara O. *Twentieth- Century Children's Writers.* New York: St. Martin's Press, 1978.

James, Edward T., Janet Wilson James, and Paul S. Boyer, eds. *Notable American Women, 1607-1950: A Biographical Dictionary.* Cambridge, Mass.: Harvard University Press, Belknap Press, 1971.

Jenness, Mary. *Twelve Negro Americans.* New York: Friendship Press, 1936.

Johnson, Abby Arthur. "Literary Midwife: Jessie Redmon Fauset and the Harlem Renaissance." *Phylon* 34, no. 2 (June 1978): 143-53.

Johnson, Abby Arthur, and Ronald Mayberry Johnson. "Away from Accommodation: Radical Editors and Protest Journalism, 1900-1910." *Journal of Negro History* 62 (October 1977): 325-29.

Johnson, Barbara. "Metaphor, Metonymy, and Voice in *Their Eyes Were Watching God.* In Gates, *Black Literature and Literary Theory*, 1984.

Johnson, Charles S. *Ebony and Topaz: A Collectanea.* New York: Opportunity; National Urban League, 1927. Reprint. Freeport, N.Y.: Books for Libraries Press, 1971.

Johnson, James Weldon, ed. *The Book of American Negro Poetry.* 1922. Rev. ed. New York: Harcourt, Brace, 1931.

Johnson, Willa D., and Thomas Green, eds. *Perspectives on Afro-American Women.* Washington, D.C.: ECCA Publishers, 1975.

Jones, Adrienne Lash. "Jane Edna Hunter: A Case Study of Black Leadership, 1910-1950." Ph.D. diss., Case Western Reserve University, 1983.

Jordan, June. "On Richard Wright and Zora Neale Hurston: Notes toward a Balance of Love and Hatred." *Black World* 23, no. 10 (August 1974): 4-8.

Joyce, Donald F., comp. *Blacks in the Humanities, 1750-1984: A Selected Annotated Bibliography.* New York: Greenwood Press, 1986.

Jubilee, Vincent. "Philadelphia's Afro-American Literary Circle and the Harlem Renaissance." Ph.D. diss., University of Pennsylvania, 1980.

Kallenbach, Jessamine S., comp. *Index to Black American Literary Anthologies.* Boston: G. K. Hall & Co., 1979.

Kellner, Bruce. *The Harlem Renaissance: A Historical Dictionary for the Era.* Westport, Conn.: Greenwood Press, 1984.

Kerlin, Robert T., ed. *Negro Poets and Their Poems.* 1923. Washington, D.C.: Associated Publishers, 1935.

Kilson, Marion. "The Transformation of Eatonville's Ethnographer." *Phylon* 33, no. 2 (Summer 1972): 112-19.

Klotman, Phyllis Rauch, and Wilmer H. Baatz, eds. *The Black Family and the Black Woman: A Bibliography.* New York: Arno Press, 1978.

Kramer, Victor, ed. *The Harlem Renaissance Re-Examined.* New York: AMS Press, 1988.

Kunitz, Stanley J., and Howard Haycraft, eds. *Twentieth-Century Authors: A Biographical Dictionary of Modern Literature*. New York: H. W. Wilson, 1942.

Kunitz, Stanley J., and Howard Haycraft, eds. *Twentieth-Century Authors, First Supplement: A Biographical Dictionary of Modern Literature*. New York: H. W. Wilson, 1955.

Lamping, Marilyn. "Hallie Quinn Brown." In Mainiero, *American Women Writers*, 1979.

_____. "Ida B. Wells-Barnett." In Mainiero, *American Women Writers*, 1979.

_____. "Pauline Hopkins." In Mainiero and Faust, *American Women Writers*, vol. 2, 1980.

Lane, Pinkie Gordon, ed. *Poems by Blacks*. Fort Smith, Ark.: South and West, 1975.

Lee, Robert A., ed. *Black Fiction: New Studies in the Afro-American Novel since 1945*. London: Harper & Row, 1980.

Lerner, Gerda. *Black Women in White America*. New York: Random House, Vintage Books, 1972.

Lewis, David Levering. *When Harlem Was in Vogue*. New York: Knopf, 1981.

Littlejohn, David. *Black on White: A Critical Survey of Writing by American Negroes*. New York: Grossman, 1966.

Locher, Frances, ed. *Contemporary Authors: A Bio-Bibliography*. Vols. 73-76. Detroit: Gale Research Co., 1978.

Locke, Alain, ed. *The New Negro: An Interpretation*. New York: Albert and Charles Boni, 1925. Reprint. New York: New York Times Co., Arno Press, 1968.

_____. Review of *Bronze: A Book of Verse*, by Georgia Douglas Johnson. *Crisis* 25 (1923): 161.

Locke, Alain, and Montgomery Gregory, eds. *Plays of Negro Life: A Sourcebook of Native American Drama*. New York: Harper & Brothers, 1927. Reprint. Westport, Conn.: Greenwood Press, 1970.

Loewenberg, James, and Ruth Bogin. *Black Women in Nineteenth-Century Amerian Life: Their Words, Their Thoughts, Their Feelings*. University Park: Pennsylvania State University Press, 1976.

Logan, Rayford W., and Michael R. Winston. *Dictionary of American Negro Biography*. New York: W. W. Norton & Co., 1982.

Loggins, Vernon. *The Negro Author: His Development in America to 1900*. New York: Columbia University Press, 1931.

Lomax, Alan, and Raoul Abdul, eds. *3000 Years of Black Poetry*. New York: Dodd, Mead, 1970.

Love, Theresa R. "Zora Neale Hurston's America." *Papers on Language and Literature* 12, no. 4 (Fall 1976): 422-37.

Lovell, John, Jr. "Excuses for Negro Novels." Review of *Aunt Sara's Wooden God*, by Mercedes Gilbert. *Journal of Negro Education* 8 (January 1939): 73-74.

Low, W. A., and Virgil Clift. *Encyclopedia of Black America*. New York: McGraw-Hill, 1981.

Lubin, Maurice A. "An Important Figure in Black Studies: Dr. Dorothy B. Porter." *CLA Journal* 16 (June 1973): 514-51.

McCanns, Shirley Graham. "A Day at Hampstead." *Opportunity* 9 (January 1931): 14-15.

MacDowell, Deborah E. "The Neglected Dimension of Jessie Redmond Fauset." In Pryse and Spillers, *Conjuring*, 1985.

MacDowell, Margaret B. "The Narrows: A Fuller View of Ann Petry." *Black American Literature Forum* 14, no. 4 (Winter 1980): 135-41.

McFarlin, Annjennette Sophie. "Hallie Quinn Brown – Black Woman Elocutionist: 1845-1949." Ph.D. diss., Washington State University, 1975.

McIntosh, Peggy. "Interactive Phases of Curricular Re-Vision: A Feminist Perspective." Wellesley, Mass.: Wellesley College Center for Research on Women, 1983.

Mainiero, Lina, ed. *American Women Writers: A Critical Reference Guide from Colonial Times to the Present*. Vol. 1. New York: Frederick Ungar Publishing Co., 1979.

Mainiero, Lina, and Langdon Lynne Faust, eds. *American Women Writers: A Critical Reference Guide from Colonial Times to the Present*. Vols. 2-4. New York: Frederick Ungar Publishing Co., 2:1980; 3:1981; 4:1982.

Majors, Monroe A. *Noted Negro Women: Their Triumphs and Activities*. Chicago: Donohue and Henneberry Printers, Binders and Engravers. 1893. Reprint. Freeport, N.Y.: Books for Libraries Press, 1971.

Marcus, Samuel, ed. *An Anthology of Revolutionary Poetry*. New York: Active, 1929.

Marteena, Constance Hill. *The Lengthening Shadow of a Woman: A Biography of Charlotte Hawkins Brown*. Hicksville, N.Y.: Exposition Press, 1977.

Martin, Tony. *Literary Garveyism: Garvey, Black Arts, and the Harlem Renaissance*. Dover, Mass.: Majority Press, 1983.

Mather, Frank Lincoln, ed. *Who's Who of the Colored Race*. Vol. 1. 1915. Reprint. Detroit: Gale Research Co., 1976.

Matney, William. *Who's Who among Black Americans*. Northbrook, Ill.: Who's Who among Black Americans, 1978.

Matthews, Geraldine O. *Black American Writers, 1773-1949: A Bibliography and Union List*. Boston: G. K. Hall & Co., 1975.

Meese, Elizabeth A. "Archival Materials: The Problem of Literary Reputation." In Hartman and Messer-Davidow, *Women in Print*, 1982.

Meese, Elizabeth. *Crossing the Double-Cross: The Practice of Feminist Criticism*. Chapel Hill: University of North Carolina Press, 1986.

Miller, Jeanne Marie A. "Black Women Playwrights from Grimké to Shange: Selected Synopses of Their Works." In Hull, Bell-Scott, and Smith, *All the Women Are White*, 1982.

_____. "Images of Black Women in Plays by Black Playwrights." *CLA Journal* 20 (June 1977): 494-507.

Mitchell Loften. *Black Drama: The Story of the American Negro in the Theatre*. New York: Hawthorne, 1967.

_____, ed. *Voices of the Black Theatre*. Clifton, N.J.: J. T. White, 1975.

Mobley, Marilyn. "The Jewel Within: A Reconsideration of Myth and Folklore in the Novels of Zora Neale Hurston." *Barnard Occasional Papers on Women's Issues* 2, no. 1 (Fall 1986): 18-33.

Molette, Barbara. "Black Women Playwrights: They Speak. Who Listens?" *Black World* 25 (April 1976): 28-34.

Monroe, John Gilbert. "A Record of the Black Theatre in New York City: 1920-1929." Ph.D. diss., University of Texas, 1980.

"Mrs. Livingston Dies in Hawaii." *Harambee* (Lincoln University Bulletin) (March 1974): n.p. [photo].

Murphy, Beatrice. *Ebony Rhythm*. New York: Exposition Press, 1948. Reprint. Freeport, N.Y.: Books for Libraries, 1968.

_____. *Negro Voices: An Anthology of Contemporary Verse*. New York: Henry Harrison Poetry Publishers, 1938. Reprint. Ann Arbor, Mich.: University Microfilms, 1971.

_____. *Today's Negro Voices: An Anthology by Young Negro Poets*. New York: Messner, 1970.

Neely, Ruth. *Women of Ohio: A Record of Their Achievements in the History of the State*. 4 vols. Chicago: S. Clarke Publishing Co., 1939.

Nekola, Charlotte, and Paula Kabinowitz, eds. *Writing Red: An Anthology of American Women Writers, 1930-1940*. New York: Feminist Press, 1987.

Newsome, Effie Lee. "Miss Hallie Q. Brown, Lecturer and Reciter." Unpublished essay, 17 April 1942.

_____. Review of *Bronze*, by Georgia Douglas Johnson. *Opportunity* 1 (December 1923): 377.

_____. "The Significance of Hallie Q. Brown's Closing Days." Unpublished essay, September 1949.

Newson, Adele S. *Zora Neale Hurston: A Reference Guide*. Boston: G. K. Hall & Co., 1987.

Obituary of Eunice Hunton Carter. *New York Times* (26 January 1970.)

Obituary of Mercedes Gilbert. *New York Times* (6 March 1952).

Obituary of Shirley Graham. *New York Times* (16 December 1965).

O'Brien, Helen M., Lillian W. Voorhees, and Hugh M. Gloster, eds. *The Brown Thrush: An Anthology of Verse by Negro Students*. Vol. 2. Memphis, Tenn.: Malcolm-Roberts Publishing Co., 1932-.

O'Brien, John. *Interviews with Black Writers*. New York: Liveright, [1973].

Osofsky, Gilbert. *Harlem: The Making of a Ghetto*. New York: Harper & Row, 1966.

Ostriker, Alicia Suskin. *Stealing the Language: The Emergence of Women's Poetry in America*. Boston: Beacon Press, 1986.

Oxley, Lloyd G. *The Black Man in the World's Literature: Gladys May Hayford (1906-), Poet*. Starr Papers, Special Collections, Mugar Library, Boston University.

Page, James. *Selected Black American Authors: An Illustrated Bio-Bibliography*. Boston: G. K. Hall & Co., 1977.

Patterson, Lindsay, ed. *An Introduction to Black Literature in America from 1746 to the Present*. Cornwell Heights, Pa.: Publishers Agency, 1978.

_____, ed. *A Rock against the Wind: Black Love Poems; An Anthology*. New York: Dodd, Mead, 1973.

Patterson, Raymond R. "Helene Johnson." In Harris and Davis, *Dictionary of Literary Biography*, vol. 51, 1987.

Perkins, Kathy A. "The Unknown Career of Shirley Graham." *Freedomways* 25, no. 1 (1985): 6-17.

Perry, Margaret. *The Harlem Renaissance: An Annotated Bibliography and Commentary*. New York: Garland Publishing, 1982.

Perry, Margaret. *Silence to the Drums: A Survey of the Literature of the Harlem Renaissance*. Westport, Conn.: Greenwood, 1976.

Petry, Ann. [Autobiographical essay.] In *Contemporary Autobiography Series*. Detroit: Gale Research Co., 1987.

Pettis, Joyce. "Zora Neale Hurston." In Mainiero and Faust, *American Women Writers*, vol. 2, 1980.

Pinckney, Darryl. "In Sorrow's Kitchen." *New York Review of Books* 25, no. 20 (21 December 1978): 55-57.

Ploski, Harry, and Ernest Kaiser, eds. *The Negro Almanac*. 2d ed. New York: Bellwether, 1971. 4th ed., 1983.

Pool, Rosey E. *Beyond the Blues*. Kent, Eng.: International Publishers, 1964.

Porter, Dorothy. *North American Negro Poets: A Bibliographical Checklist of Their Writings, 1760 to 1940*. Hattiesburg, Miss.: Bookfarm, 1945.

Pryse, Marjorie. "Pattern against the Sky: Deism and Motherhood in Ann Petry's *The Street*." In Pryse and Spillers, *Conjuring*, 1985.

Pryse, Marjorie, and Hortense J. Spillers, eds., *Conjuring: Black Women, Fiction, and Literary Tradition*. Bloomington: Indiana University Press, 1985.

Randall, Dudley. "The Black Aesthetic in the Thirties, Forties, and Fifties." In Gayle, *The Black Aesthetic*, 1971.

Randolph, Ruth Elizabeth. "Another Day Will Find Me Brave: Clarissa Scott Delany, 1901-1927." *Sage: A Scholarly Journal on Black Women* 3 (Supplement, Summer 1988): 14-18.

Ransby, Barbara. "Eslanda Goode Robeson, Pan Africanist." *Sage: A Scholarly Journal on Black Women* 3 (Fall 1986) : 22-25.

Rayson, Ann. "The Novels of Zora Neale Hurston." *Studies in Black Literature* 5, no. 3 (Winter 1974): 1-10.

Reagon, Bernice Johnson. "Zora Neale Hurston." In Logan and Winston, *Dictionary of Negro Biography*, 1982.

Reardon, Joan, and Kristine A. Thorsen. *Poetry by American Women, 1900-1975: A Bibliography*. Metuchen, N.J.: Scarecrow Press, 1979.

Redding, J. Saunders. *To Make a Poet Black*. 1939. Ithaca: Cornell University Press, 1988.

Richardson, Marilyn. *Black Women and Religion*. Boston: G. K. Hall & Co., 1980.

Richardson, Willis, and May Miller, eds. *Negro History in Thirteen Plays*. Washington, D.C.: Associated Publishers, 1935.

Richardson, Willis, and May Miller, eds. *Plays and Pageants from the Life of the Negro*. Washington, D.C.: Associated Publishers, 1930.

Robeson, Susan. *The Whole World in His Hands: A Pictorial Biography of Paul Robeson*. Secaucus, N.J.: Citadel, 1981.

Rose Bibliography Project. *Analytical Guide and Indexes to "The Crisis," 1910-1960*. Westport, Conn.: Greenwood Press, 1975.

Rosenberger, Francis Coleman, ed. *Washington and the Post*. Charlottesville, Va.: University Press of Virginia, 1977.

Roses, Lorraine. "An Interview with Dorothy West." *Sage* (Spring 1985): 47-49.

Roses, Lorraine Elena, and Ruth Elizabeth Randolph. "Marita Bonner: In Search of Other Mothers' Gardens." *Black American Literature Forum* 21, no. 1-2 (Spring-Summer 1987): 165-83.

Row, Kenneth, ed. *University of Michigan Plays*. Ann Arbor: University of Michigan Press, 1932.

Rowell, Charles H. "Interview with Margaret Walker." *Black World* (December 1975): 4-17.

Ruether, Rosemary Radford, and Rosemary Skinner Keller, eds. *Women and Religion in America*. Vol. 3, *1900-1968*. San Francisco: Harper & Row, 1981.

Rush, Theresa Gunnels, Carol Fairbanks Myers, and Esther Spring Arata. *Black American Writers Past and Present: A Biogaphical and Bibliographical Dictionary*. 2 vols. Metuchen, N.J.: Scarecrow Press, 1975.

Salk, Erwin A., ed. *A Layman's Guide to Negro History*. Boston: McGraw-Hill Book Co., 1967.

Scally, Sister Mary Anthony. *Negro Catholic Writers, 1900-1943: A Bio-Bibliography*. Grosse Point, Mich.: Walter Romig, 1945.

Schomburg Center for Research on Black Culture. New York Public Library, New York City.

Schraufnagel, Noel. *From Apology to Protest: The Black American Novel*. Deland, Fla.: Everett/Edwards, 1973.

Scruggs, Charles. *The Sage in Harlem: H. L. Mencken and the Black Writers of the 1920s*. Baltimore: Johns Hopkins University Press, 1984.

Shay, Frank. *Fifty More Contemporary One-Act Plays*. New York: D. Appleton, 1928.

Sheffey, Ruthe T., ed. *Rainbow Round Her Shoulder: The Zora Neale Hurston Symposium Papers*. Baltimore: Morgan State University Press, 1982.

Sherman, Joan R. *Invisible Poets: Afro-Americans of the Nineteenth Century*. Urbana: University of Illinois Press, 1974.

_____, ed. *Collected Black Women's Poetry*, vols. 2, 4. The Schomburg Library of Nineteenth-Century Black Women Writers, edited by Henry Louis Gates, Jr. New York: Oxford University Press, 1988.

Shinn, Thelma. "Women in the Novels of Ann Petry." *Critique: Studies in Modern Fiction* 16, no. 1 (1974): 110-20.

Shockley, Ann Allen. *Afro-American Women Writers, 1746-1933: An Anthology and Critical Guide*. Boston: G. K. Hall, 1988.

_____. "A Biographical Excursion into Obscurity." *Phylon* (Spring 1972): 22-26.

Shockley, Ann Allen, and Sue P. Chandler, eds. *Living Black American Authors: A Biographical Dictionary*. London and New York: R. R. Bowker, 1973.

Sicherman, Barbara, Carol Hurd Green, Ilene Kantrov, and Harriet Walker, eds. *Notable American Women: The Modern Period: A Biographical Dictionary*. Cambridge: Harvard University Press, Belknap Press, 1980.

Simcox, Helene Earle, ed. *Dear Dark Faces*. Detroit: Lotus Press, 1980.

Sims-Wood, Janet L. *The Progress of Afro-American Women: A Selected Bibliography and Resource Guide*. Westport, Conn.: Greenwood Press, 1980.

Southgate, Robert L. *Black Plots and Black Characters*. Syracuse, N.Y.: Gaylord Professional Publications, 1979.

Spencer, Anne. Review of *An Autumn Love Cycle*, by Georgia Douglas Johnson. *Crisis* 36 (1929): 87.

Spradling, Mary Mace, ed. *In Black and White*. Detroit, Mich.: Gale Research Co., 1980.

Starke, Catherine Juanita. *Black Portraiture in American Fiction*. New York: Basic Books, 1971.

Stein, Karen F. "Alice Ruth Moore Nelson." In Mainiero and Faust, *American Women Writers*, vol. 3, 1981.

Sterling, Dorothy. *Black Foremothers: Three Lives*. Old Westbury, N.Y.: Feminist Press, 1979.

_____. "Mary Church Terrell." In Sicherman et al., *Notable American Women*, 1980.

_____. *We Are Your Sisters: Black Women in the 19th Century*. New York: W. W. Norton, 1984.

Stetson, Erlene. "Anne Spencer." *CLA Journal* 21 (March 1978): 400-9.

_____. "Black Women in and out of Print." In Hartman and Messer-Davidow, *Women in Print*, 1982.

_____. "Gwendolyn B. Bennett." In Mainiero, *American Women Writers*, 1979.

_____, ed. *Black Sister: Poetry by Black American Women, 1746-1980*. Bloomington: Indiana University Press, 1981.

Stevenson, Octave, ed. *City of Celebration*. Washington, D.C.: District of Columbia Public Library, 1977.

_____, ed. *The Poet Upstairs*. Washington: Washington Writers' Publishing House, 1979.

Stewart, Harry T. "The Poet-Actress: A Personal Interview with Miss Mercedes Gilbert." *Education: A Journal of Reputation* (September 1936): 7.

Stewart, Ruth Ann. "Charlotte Hawkins Brown." In Sicherman et al., *Notable American Women*, 1980.

Sullivan, Patricia A. "Eslanda Cardozo Goode." In Sicherman et al., *Notable American Women*, 1980.

Sylvander, Carolyn Wedin. "Jessie Redmon Fauset." In Harris and Davis, *Dictionary of Literary Biography*, vol. 51, 1987.

_____. "Jessie Redmon Fauset." In Mainiero and Faust, *American Women Writers*, vol. 2, 1980.

_____. *Jessie Redmon Fauset, Black American Writer*. Troy, N.Y.: Whitson Publishing Co., 1981.

Tate, Claudia. "Nella Larsen's *Passing*: A Problem of Interpretation." *Black American Literature Forum* 14 (Winter 1980): 142-46.

_____. "Pauline Hopkins, Our Literary Foremother." In Pryse and Spillers, *Conjuring*, 1985.

_____. "The Pondered Moment: May Miller's Meditative Poetry." *New Directions* (Howard University) 12 (January 1985): 30-33.

Taylor, Henry, ed. *Poetry: Points of Departure*. Cambridge, Mass.: Winthrop Publisher, 1974.

Thomas, Gwendolyn. "Pauli Murray." In Mainiero and Faust, *American Women Writers*, vol. 3, 1981.

Thompson, Mary Lou, ed. *Voices of the New Feminism*. Boston: Beacon Press, 1970.

Thornton, Hortense E. "Sexism as Quagmire: Nella Larsen's *Quicksand*." *CLA Journal* 16 (March 1973): 285-301.

"Three Professors to Retire." *Harambee* (Lincoln University Bulletin) (April 1972): n.p.

Trawick, A. M., ed. *The New Voice in Race Adjustment*. New York: Student Volunteer Movement, 1914, 215-19.

Tucker, Mae S. "Rose Leary Love (1898-1969)." In *Making a Difference: Women of Mecklenburg*. American Association of University Women, Charlotte Branch, n.d.

Turner, Darwin T. *Afro-American Writers*. Northbrook, Ill.: AHM Publishing Co., 1970.

_____. *In a Minor Chord: Three Afro-American Writers in Search of Identity*. Carbondale: Southern Illinois University Press, 1971.

Tuthill, Stacy, ed. *The Ear's Chamber*. College Park, Md.: Scop Publications, 1981.

Tuthill, Stacy, and Walter Kerr, eds. *Rye Bread*. College Park, Md.: Scop Publications, 1977.

Voorhees, Lillian W., and Robert W. O'Brien, eds. *The Brown Thrush: An Anthology of Verse by Negro Students*. Vol 1. Claremont, Calif.: Lawson Roberts Publishing Co, 1932-.

Walker, Alice. *In Search of Our Mothers' Gardens*. San Diego and New York: Harcourt Brace Jovanovich, 1983.

_____. "In Search of Zora Neale Hurston." *Ms.* (March 1975): 74-79, 85-87.

Wall, Cheryl A. "Anne Spencer." In Mainiero and Faust, *American Women Writers*, vol. 4, 1982.

_____. "Jessie Redmon Fauset." In Sicherman et al. *Notable American Women*, 1980.

_____. "Nella Larsen." In Mainiero and Faust, *American Women Writers*, vol. 2, 1980.

_____. "Three Novelists: Fauset, Larsen, and Hurston." Ph.D. diss., Harvard University, 1976.

_____. "Zora Neale Hurston." In Sicherman et al., *Notable American Women*, 1980.

Walrond, Eric D. Review of "Being Forty." *Opportunity* 2 (November 1924): 346.

Walrond, Eric, and Rosey Pool, eds. *Black and Unknown Bards: A Collection of Negro Poetry*. Aldington, Eng.: Hand and Flower Press, 1958.

Washington, Mary Helen. "Zora Neale Hurston: The Black Woman's Search for Identity." *Black World* 21 (August 1972): 68-75.

_____, ed. *Invented Lives: Narratives of Black Women, 1860-1960*. Garden City, N.Y.: Doubleday, 1987.

Weir, Sybil. "The Narrows: A Black New England Novel." *Studies in American Fiction* (English Department, Northeastern University) (Spring 1987): n.p.

Weisman, Leonard, and Elfreda S. Wright, eds. *Black Poetry for All Americans*. New York: Globe, 1971.

Werden, Frieda L. "Bernice Love Wiggins." In Mainiero and Faust, *American Women Writers*, vol. 4, 1982.

Wesley, Charles H. "Hallie Quinn Brown." In James, James, and Boyer, *Notable American Women*, 1971.

Weyant, N. Jill. "Dorothy West." In Mainiero and Faust, *American Women Writers*, vol. 4, 1982.

White, Newman Ivey, and Walter Jackson, eds. *An Anthology of Verse by American Negroes*. Durham, N.C.: Trinity College Press, 1924.

Whiteman, Maxwell. *A Century of Fiction by American Negroes, 1853-1952*. 1955. Reprint. [Philadelphia]: Albert Saifer, 1974.

Whitlow, Roger. *Black American Literature: A Critical History*. 1973. Reprint. Chicago: Nelson Hall, 1984.

Who's Who in America. Chicago: Marquis Who's Who, 1899-.

Who's Who in Colored America: A Biographical Dictionary of Notable Living Persons of Negro Descent in America. New York: Who's Who in Colored America Corp., 1927-50.

Who's Who in Library Service. New York: H. W. Wilson, 1933-[1955], 4 vols.

Who's Who of American Women: A Biographical Dictionary of Notable American Women. Chicago: Marquis Who's Who, 1958-.

Wilberforce University Archives, Wilberforce, Ohio.

Williams, Ora. "Alice Moore Dunbar-Nelson." In Harris and Davis, *Dictionary of Literary Biography*, vol. 50, 1986.

_____. *American Black Women in the Arts and Social Sciences: A Bibliographic Survey*. Metuchen, N.J: Scarecrow Press, 1978.

Wintz, Cary D. *Black Culture and the Harlem Renaissance*. Houston, Tex.: Rice University Press, 1988.

Wise, Claude Merton. *The Yearbook of Short Plays*. Evanston, Ill.: Row, Peterson & Co., 1931.

Woods, Katherine. "Juanita Harrison Has Known Twenty-Two Countries." *New York Times Magazine* (17 May 1936), 4.

_____. "Traveling for Adventure." *Saturday Review of Literature* 14, no. 11 (20 June 1936): 10-11.

Woodson, Carter G. "Review of *Negro Trailblazers of California*, by Delilah L. Beasley." *Journal of Negro History* (1920): 128-29.

Work, Monroe N. "California Freedom Papers" [essay]. *Journal of Negro History* (January 1918): 45-54.

Yarborough, Richard. "The Depiction of Blacks in the Early Afro-American Novel." Ph.D. diss., Stanford University, 1980.